A·N·N·U·A·L E·D·I·T·I·O·N·S

Marketing

Twenty-Fourth Edition

02/03

EDITOR

John E. Richardson

Pepperdine University

Dr. John E. Richardson is professor of marketing in The George L. Graziadio School of Business and Management at Pepperdine University. He is president of his own consulting firm and has consulted with organizations such as Bell and Howell, Dayton-Hudson, Epson, and the U.S. Navy as well as with various service, nonprofit, and franchise organizations. Dr. Richardson is a member of the American Marketing Association, the American Management Association, the Society for Business Ethics, and Beta Gamma Sigma honorary business fraternity.

McGraw-Hill/Dushkin

530 Old Whitfield Street, Guilford, Connecticut 06437

Visit us on the Internet
http://www.dushkin.com

Credits

1. **Marketing in the 2000s and Beyond**
   Unit photo—© 2002 by PhotoDisc, Inc.
2. **Research, Markets, and Consumer Behavior**
   Unit photo—© 2002 by Sweet By & By/Cindy Brown.
3. **Developing and Implementing Marketing Strategies**
   Unit photo—© 2002 by PhotoDisc, Inc.
4. **Global Marketing**
   Unit photo—© 2002 by PhotoDisc, Inc.

Copyright

Cataloging in Publication Data
Main entry under title: Annual Editions: Marketing. 2002/2003.
1. Marketing—Periodicals. 2. Marketing—Social aspects—Periodicals
3. Marketing management—Periodicals. I. Richardson, John, *comp.* II. Title: Marketing.
ISBN 0–07–250702–0   658'.05   ISSN 0730–2606

Twenty-Fourth Edition

Cover image © 2002 by PhotoDisc, Inc.
Printed in the United States of America   1234567890BAHBAH5432   Printed on Recycled Paper

Editors/Advisory Board

Members of the Advisory Board are instrumental in the final selection of articles for each edition of ANNUAL EDITIONS. Their review of articles for content, level, currentness, and appropriateness provides critical direction to the editor and staff. We think that you will find their careful consideration well reflected in this volume.

To the Reader

In publishing ANNUAL EDITIONS we recognize the enormous role played by the magazines, newspapers, and journals of the public press in providing current, first-rate educational information in a broad spectrum of interest areas. Many of these articles are appropriate for students, researchers, and professionals seeking accurate, current material to help bridge the gap between principles and theories and the real world. These articles, however, become more useful for study when those of lasting value are carefully collected, organized, indexed, and reproduced in a low-cost format, which provides easy and permanent access when the material is needed. That is the role played by ANNUAL EDITIONS.

The new millennium should prove to be an exciting and challenging time for the American business community. Recent dramatic social, economic, and technological changes have become an important part of the present marketplace. These changes—accompanied by increasing domestic and foreign competition—are leading a wide array of companies and industries toward the realization that better marketing must become a top priority now to assure their future success.

How does the marketing manager respond to this growing challenge? How does the marketing student apply marketing theory to the real world practice? Many reach for the *Wall Street Journal*, *Business Week*, *Fortune*, and other well-known sources of business information. There, specific industry and company strategies are discussed and analyzed, marketing principles are often reaffirmed by real occurrences, and textbook theories are supported or challenged by current events.

The articles reprinted in this edition of *Annual Editions: Marketing 02/03* have been carefully chosen from numerous different public press sources to provide current information on marketing in the world today. Within these pages you will find articles that address marketing theory and application in a wide range of industries. In addition, the selections reveal how several firms interpret and utilize marketing principles in their daily operations and corporate planning.

The volume contains a number of features designed to make it useful for marketing students, researchers, and professionals. These include the Industry/Company Guide, which is particularly helpful when seeking information about specific corporations; a *topic guide* to locate articles on specific marketing subjects; *World Wide Web* pages; the *table of contents* abstracts, which summarize each article and highlight key concepts; a *glossary* of key marketing terms; and a comprehensive *index*.

The articles are organized into four units. Selections that focus on similar issues are concentrated into subsections within the broader units. Each unit is preceded by a list of unit selections, as well as a list of key points to consider that focus on major themes running throughout the selections, Web links that provide extra support for the unit's data, and an overview that provides background for informed reading of the articles and emphasizes critical issues.

This is the twenty-fourth edition of *Annual Editions: Marketing.* Since its first edition in the mid-1970s, the efforts of many individuals have contributed toward its success. We think this is by far the most useful collection of material available for the marketing student. We are anxious to know what you think. What are your opinions? What are your recommendations? Please take a moment to complete and return the *article rating form* on the last page of this volume. Any book can be improved and this one will continue to be, annually.

John E. Richardson
Editor

iv

Contents

UNIT 1
Marketing in the 2000s and Beyond

Twelve selections examine the current and future status of marketing, the marketing concept, service marketing, and marketing ethics.

Unit Overview   xvi

The concepts in bold italics are developed in the article. For further expansion, please refer to the Topic Guide and the Index.

UNIT 2
Research, Markets, and Consumer Behavior

Nine selections provide an analysis of consumer demographics and lifestyles, the growth and maturation of markets, and the need for market research and planning.

The concepts in bold italics are developed in the article. For further expansion, please refer to the Topic Guide and the Index.

UNIT 3
Developing and Implementing Marketing Strategies

Fourteen selections analyze factors that affect the development and implementation of marketing strategies.

The concepts in bold italics are developed in the article. For further expansion, please refer to the Topic Guide and the Index.

The concepts in bold italics are developed in the article. For further expansion, please refer to the Topic Guide and the Index.

UNIT 4
Global Marketing

Six selections discuss the increasing globalization of markets, trends in world trade, and increasing foreign competition.

The concepts in bold italics are developed in the article. For further expansion, please refer to the Topic Guide and the Index.

Topic Guide

This topic guide suggests how the selections in this book relate to the subjects covered in your course. You may want to use the topics listed on these pages to search the Web more easily.

On the following pages a number of Web sites have been gathered specifically for this book. They are arranged to reflect the units of this *Annual Edition.* You can link to these sites by going to the DUSHKIN ONLINE support site at *http://www.dushkin.com/online/.*

ALL THE ARTICLES THAT RELATE TO EACH TOPIC ARE LISTED BELOW THE BOLD-FACED TERM.

Advertising
3. 10 Things to Know About Customers
9. A Primer on Quality Service: Quality Service Makes Happy Customers and Greater Profits
11. The Ethical Treatment of Customers
18. Asian-American Consumers as a Unique Market Segment: Fact or Fallacy?
19. Head Trips
25. Making Old Brands New
27. Color Me Popular: Marketers Shape Up Packaging
30. The Old Pillars of New Retailing
31. 10 Top Stores Put to the Test
33. More for Less
34. Choices, Choices
36. Global Marketing in the New Millennium
39. The Lure of Global Branding
40. The Nation as Brand

Brand recognition
25. Making Old Brands New

Brands and branding
2. Future Markets
7. What Drives Customer Equity
8. The Customer Experience
14. Product by Design
18. Asian-American Consumers as a Unique Market Segment: Fact or Fallacy?
19. Head Trips
20. How We Sell
24. Can Brand Management Help You Succeed?
25. Making Old Brands New
26. Can You Spot the Fake?
27. Color Me Popular: Marketers Shape Up Packaging
31. 10 Top Stores Put to the Test
34. Choices, Choices
37. Segmenting Global Markets: Look Before You Leap
39. The Lure of Global Branding
40. The Nation as Brand

Competition
2. Future Markets
3. 10 Things to Know About Customers
9. A Primer on Quality Service: Quality Service Makes Happy Customers and Greater Profits
11. The Ethical Treatment of Customers
22. The Very Model of a Modern Marketing Plan
23. Michael Porter's Big Ideas
24. Can Brand Management Help You Succeed?
26. Can You Spot the Fake?
29. Discovering Hidden Pricing Power
30. The Old Pillars of New Retailing
36. Global Marketing in the New Millennium
37. Segmenting Global Markets: Look Before You Leap
41. The Future of Japanese Marketing

Consumer behavior
1. Emerging and Burgeoning
2. Future Markets
3. 10 Things to Know About Customers

What Drives Customer Equity (cont.)
7. What Drives Customer Equity
10. Why Service Stinks
12. Too Close for Comfort
13. Taking an Expanded View of Customers' Needs: Qualitative Research for Aiding Innovation
14. Product by Design
15. A Beginner's Guide to Demographics
16. The Next Big Market
17. Generational Divide
18. Asian-American Consumers as a Unique Market Segment: Fact or Fallacy?
19. Head Trips
20. How We Sell
21. Defining Moments: Segmenting by Cohorts
30. The Old Pillars of New Retailing
31. 10 Top Stores Put to the Test
32. What's Ahead for … Retailing
37. Segmenting Global Markets: Look Before You Leap
40. The Nation as Brand
41. The Future of Japanese Marketing

Distribution planning
5. Marketing High Technology: Preparation, Targeting, Positioning, Execution
30. The Old Pillars of New Retailing
31. 10 Top Stores Put to the Test
32. What's Ahead for … Retailing

Economic environment
1. Emerging and Burgeoning
3. 10 Things to Know About Customers
4. The E-volving Salesman
9. A Primer on Quality Service: Quality Service Makes Happy Customers and Greater Profits
11. The Ethical Treatment of Customers
23. Michael Porter's Big Ideas
26. Can You Spot the Fake?
29. Discovering Hidden Pricing Power
35. Ice Cubes to Eskimos
36. Global Marketing in the New Millennium
37. Segmenting Global Markets: Look Before You Leap

Ethics
1. Emerging and Burgeoning
7. What Drives Customer Equity
11. The Ethical Treatment of Customers
12. Too Close for Comfort
30. The Old Pillars of New Retailing

Exportation
36. Global Marketing in the New Millennium
38. The Invisible Global Market
39. The Lure of Global Branding
40. The Nation as Brand
41. The Future of Japanese Marketing

Focus groups
9. A Primer on Quality Service: Quality Service Makes Happy Customers and Greater Profits

x

World Wide Web Sites

The following World Wide Web sites have been carefully researched and selected to support the articles found in this reader. The easiest way to access these selected sites is to go to our DUSHKIN ONLINE support site at *http://www.dushkin.com/online/*.

AE: Marketing 02/03

The following sites were available at the time of publication. Visit our Web site—we update DUSHKIN ONLINE regularly to reflect any changes.

General Sources

Krislyn's Favorite Advertising & Marketing Sites
http://www.krislyn.com/sites/adv.htm

This is a complete list of sites that include information on marketing research, marketing on the Internet, demographic sources, and organizations and associations. The site also features current books on the subject of marketing.

Retail Learning Initiative
http://www.retailsmarts.ryerson.ca

This series of small business and retail marketing links from Canada connects to many more business links in the United States and to workshops and dialogue forums.

STAT-USA/Internet Site Economic, Trade, Business Information
http://www.stat-usa.gov

This site, from the U.S. Department of Commerce, contains Daily Economic News, Frequently Requested Statistical Releases, Information on Export and International Trade, Domestic Economic News and Statistical Series, and Databases.

UNIT 1: Marketing in the 2000s and Beyond

American Marketing Association Code of Ethics
http://www.marketingpower.com/index

At this American Marketing Association's site, use the search mechanism to access the Code of Ethics for Marketing. itself.

"Envisioning Tomorrow's Business World Today"
http://www.cba.neu.edu/alumni/molloy/art-29.htm

In this article, the author takes advantage of the work of the World Future Society to discuss what the future will hold for business in the next century.

"Marketing in the Service Sector Key to Success"
http://www.cba.neu.edu/alumni/molloy/art-17.htm

Here is a professor's discussion of the major role that the service sector plays in the U.S. economy and the importance of marketing to the success of small business, often the provider of such services.

Center for Innovation in Product Development (CIPD)
http://web.mit.edu/cipd/research/prdctdevelop.htm

CIPD is one of the National Science Foundation's engineering research centers. It shares the goal of future product development with academia, industry, and government.

"New Century Will Bring With It New Challenges"
http://www.cba.neu.edu/alumni/molloy/art-20.htm

This discussion of the challenges that the new century will bring to business, especially small business, provides interesting reading about the importance of market research, among other factors, to success.

"Small Companies Face Off Against Ethical Dilemmas"
http://www.cba.neu.edu/alumni/molloy/art-13.htm

The importance of business ethics in the absence of any simple, universally applicable formula for solving ethical problems is discussed in this article. Unethical choices can lead to a company's quick demise.

UNIT 2: Research, Markets, and Consumer Behavior

CyberAtlas Demographics
http://cyberatlas.internet.com/big_picture/demographics/

The Baruch College–Harris poll commissioned by *Business Week* is used at this site to show interested businesses who is on the Net in the United States. Statistics for other countries can be found by clicking on Geographics.

General Social Survey
http://www.icpsr.umich.edu/GSS99/

The GSS (see DPLS Archive: *http://DPLS.DACC.WISC.EDU/SAF/*) is an almost annual personal interview survey of U.S. households that began in 1972. More than 35,000 respondents have answered 2,500 questions. It covers a broad range of variables, many of which relate to microeconomic issues.

"Identifying Your Appropriate Market Opportunity"
http://www.cba.neu.edu/alumni/molloy/art-21.htm

The importance of identifying a proper marketing opportunity or niche is the subject of this article, which also includes a few basic rules for small business entrepreneurs.

"Market Research Essential in Determining Firm's Viability"
http://www.cba.neu.edu/alumni/molloy/art-03.htm

This article outlines how to obtain market information from government, educational, financial, and other sources.

Marketing Tools Directory
http://www.maritzresearch.com

Maritz Marketing Research Inc. (MMRI) specializes in custom-designed research studies that link the consumer to the marketer through information. At this spot on their Web site they offer a Marketing Tools Directory, a comprehensive guide to resources for finding, reaching, and keeping customers. Sections include Demographics, Direct Marketing, Ethnic Marketing, Market Research, and more.

U.S. Census Bureau Home Page
http://www.census.gov

This is a major source of social, demographic, and economic information, such as income/employment data and the latest indicators, income distribution, and poverty data.

USADATA
http://www.usadata.com

This leading provider of marketing, company, advertising, and consumer behavior data offers national and local data covering the top 60 U.S. markets.

www.dushkin.com/online/

WWW Virtual Library: Demography & Population Studies
http://demography.anu.edu.au/VirtualLibrary/

Over 150 links can be found at this major resource to keep track of information of value to researchers in the fields of demography and population studies.

UNIT 3: Developing and Implementing Marketing Strategies

American Marketing Association Homepage
http://www.ama.org

This site of the American Marketing Association is geared to managers, educators, researchers, students, and global electronic members. It contains a search mechanism, definitions of marketing and market research, and links.

Consumer Buying Behavior
http://www.courses.psu.edu/mktg/mktg220_rso3/sls_cons.htm

The Center for Academic Computing at Penn State posts this course data that includes a review of consumer buying behaviors; group, environment, and internal influences; problem-solving; and post-purchasing behavior.

Product Branding, Packaging, and Pricing
http://www.fooddude.com/branding.html

Put forward by fooddude.com, the information at this site is presented in a lively manner. It discusses positioning, branding, pricing, and packaging in the specialty food market, but applies to many other retail products as well.

Welcome to CRUSH
http://www.rtks.com

This site presents an overview of Real Time Knowledge Systems and its product, CRUSH, a multimedia application for gathering, structuring, analyzing, and presenting competitive information that will help users to create winning strategies. Marketing case studies are included.

UNIT 4: Global Marketing

CIBERWeb
http://ciber.centers.purdue.edu

The Centers for International Business Education and Research were created by the U.S. Omnibus Trade and Competitiveness Act of 1988. Together, the 26 resulting CIBER sites in the United States are a powerful network focused on helping U.S. business succeed in global markets. Many marketing links can be found at this site.

Emerging Markets Resources
http://www.usatrade.gov/website/ccg.nsf

Information on the business and economic situation of foreign countries and the political climate as it affects U.S. business is presented by the U.S. Department of Commerce's International Trade Administration.

International Business Resources on the WWW
http://globaledge.msu.edu/ibrd/ibrd.asp

This Web site includes a large index of international business resources. Through *http://ciber.bus.msu.edu/ginlist/* you can also access the Global Interact Network Mailing LIST (GINLIST), which brings together, electronically, business educators and practitioners with international business interests.

International Trade Administration
http://www.ita.doc.gov

The U.S. Department of Commerce is dedicated to helping U.S. businesses compete in the global marketplace, and at this site it offers assistance through many Web links under such headings as Trade Statistics, Cross-Cutting Programs, Regions and Countries, and Import Administration.

World Chambers Network
http://www.worldchambers.net

International trade at work is viewable at this site. For example, click on Global Business eXchange (GBX) for a list of active business opportunities worldwide or to submit your new business opportunity for validation.

World Trade Center Association On Line
http://iserve.wtca.org

Data on world trade is available at this site that features information, services, a virtual trade fair, an exporter's encyclopedia, trade opportunities, and a resource center.

We highly recommend that you review our Web site for expanded information and our other product lines. We are continually updating and adding links to our Web site in order to offer you the most usable and useful information that will support and expand the value of your Annual Editions. You can reach us at: *http://www.dushkin.com/annualeditions/*.

UNIT 1

Marketing in the 2000s and Beyond

Unit Selections

Key Points to Consider

- Dramatic changes are occurring in the marketing of products and services. What social and economic trends do you believe are most significant today, and how do you think these will affect marketing in the future?

- Theodore Levitt suggests that as times change the marketing concept must be reinterpreted. Given the varied perspectives of the other articles in this unit, what do you think this reinterpretation will entail?

- In the present competitive business arena, is it possible for marketers to behave ethically in the environment and both survive and prosper? What suggestions can you give that could be incorporated into the marketing strategy for firms that want to be both ethical and successful?

 **Links: www.dushkin.com/online/**
These sites are annotated in the World Wide Web pages.

American Marketing Association Code of Ethics
http://www.marketingpower.com/index

"Envisioning Tomorrow's Business World Today"
http://www.cba.neu.edu/alumni/molloy/art-29.htm

"Marketing in the Service Sector Key to Success"
http://www.cba.neu.edu/alumni/molloy/art-17.htm

Center for Innovation in Product Development (CIPD)
http://web.mit.edu/cipd/research/prdctdevelop.htm

"New Century Will Bring With It New Challenges"
http://www.cba.neu.edu/alumni/molloy/art-20.htm

"Small Companies Face Off Against Ethical Dilemmas"
http://www.cba.neu.edu/alumni/molloy/art-13.htm

"If we want to know what a business is we must start with its purpose…. There is only one valid definition of business purpose: to create a customer. What business thinks it produces is not of first importance—especially not to the future of the business or to its success. What the customer thinks he is buying, what he considers 'value' is decisive—it determines what a business is, what it produces, and whether it will prosper."

—Peter Drucker, *The Practice of Management*

When Peter Drucker penned these words in 1954, American industry was just awakening to the realization that marketing would play an important role in the future success of businesses. The ensuing years have seen an increasing number of firms in highly competitive areas—particularly in the consumer goods industry—adopt a more sophisticated customer orientation and an integrated marketing focus.

The dramatic economic and social changes of the last decade have stirred companies in an even broader range of industries—from banking and air travel to communications—to the realization that marketing will provide them with their cutting edge. Demographic and lifestyle changes have splintered mass, homogeneous markets into many markets, each with different needs and interests. Deregulation has made once-protected industries vulnerable to the vagaries of competition. Vast and rapid technological changes are making an increasing number of products and services obsolete. Intense international competition, rapid expansion of the Internet-based economy, and the growth of truly global markets have many firms looking well beyond their national boundaries.

Indeed, it appears that during the new millennium marketing will take on a unique significance—and not just within the industrial sector. Social institutions of all kinds, which had thought themselves exempt from the pressures of the marketplace, are also beginning to recognize the need for marketing in the management of their affairs. Colleges and universities, charities, museums, symphony orchestras, and even hospitals are beginning to give attention the marketing concept—to provide what the consumer wants to buy.

The selections in this unit are grouped into four areas. Their purposes are to provide current perspectives on marketing, discuss differing views of the marketing concept, analyze the use of marketing by social institutions and nonprofit organizations, and examine the ethical and social responsibilities of marketing.

The five articles in the first subsection provide significant clues about salient approaches and issues that marketers need to address in the future in order to create, promote, and sell their products and services in ways that meet the expectation of consumers. Some of them reflect the positioning of the Internet as a significant part of their marketing focus.

The three selections that address the marketing concept include Levitt's now classic "Marketing Myopia," which first appeared in the *Harvard Business Review* in 1960. This version includes the author's retrospective commentary, written in 1975, in which he discusses how shortsightedness can make management unable to recognize that there is no such thing as a growth industry. "What Drives Customer Equity" discloses the importance of customer equity as a significant determinant of the long-term value of a company. The last article in this subsection describes how some Internet companies are reinventing the customer experience.

In the "Services and Social Marketing" subsection, the first article describes how quality products and appropriate and exemplary cyberservice may be critical benchmarks and determinants for future marketing success. The second article reveals how sometimes service is focused on elite consumers—while putting other consumers in a secondary position.

In the final subsection, a careful look is taken at the strategic process and practice of incorporating ethics and social responsibility into the marketplace. "The Ethical Treatment of Customers" points out the importance of marketers' spending genuine time to learn consumers' true needs and then to treat them with authentic respect. "Too Close for Comfort" reveals how the wrong use of a customer's personal and confidential information can possibly put the customer's privacy at risk.

Emerging and Burgeoning

Eight consumer markets that will flower in the 21st century.

By Allan J. Magrath

Consumer hot markets originate in both likely and unlikely places. This is what makes capitalism so frustratingly unpredictable and dynamic. It's also what makes millionaires of investors, venture capitalists, pundits, consultants, and other trendspotters.

The more predictable origins of emerging consumer-growth markets include technology, demographics, and economics:

- Technology invention has translated into consumer spending since the wheel begat the wagon, the printing press the popular King James Bible, and the lightbulb the Tiffany lamp. Today's technology is much more pervasive and diverse, so all branches of science and invention create new spending trails, from the pharmaceutical (Viagra) to the optical (smart credit cards) to the digital (Palm Pilot).

- Demographics has been a fast-growth driver of consumer dollars since the postwar rollout of new-household creation that drove new suburbs, appliances, cars, schools, roads, TV shows, and Popsicles. Today demographics remain key, as group dynamics have created MTV, daycare chains, planned investing for retirement, punk rock, and women entrepreneurs.

- And for evidence of the influence of economics—specifically, disposable-income levels—on hot markets, witness the broad participation in the stock market, specialty channels for investors of every stripe, and interest in the Martha Stewart/Ralph Lauren lifestyle. Another clear signpost has been the growth in casinos and lotteries: More than 260 casinos in 30 states were built in the 1990s alone.

A less predictable but nevertheless often crucial consumer hot-market catalyst is aspirational and value shifts, often derived from popular culture or newfound freedoms or beliefs. For instance, a more casual society has created a boom in casual dining and dress, while new beliefs about smokers or disruptive cell phones have led to all sorts of sanctioning in restaurants and theaters. The rapid rise and fall in the celebrity status of all manner of sports stars, media mavens, authors, and even fictional characters such as Austin Powers and Luke Skywalker have driven fashions, cosmetics, haircuts, bestseller choices, toys, and expressions.

Despite the difficulty of figuring out the more fleeting market blips, there appear to be eight emerging and burgeoning consumer markets as we enter the new millennium—leaving out the Internet explosion, which continues to blossom and diversify. Besides these eight, there are many other consumer hot markets out there, and it's worth a look to see how you can cash in on them—whether as a supplier, a customer, a channel player, or an investor.

Retailer Lineup Changes: One hot trend is the reconfiguration going on in retailing. For years, much of retailing was organized in one of two ways: by product (drugstores, food stores, hardware stores, bookstores) or by assortment (department stores, discounters, convenience stores, home-building assortments). Now three new models are emerging: "price-centric" retailers positioned around low-ball pricing ("dollar stores," off-price apparel retailers, secondhand-sporting-goods stores); retailers organized by lifestyle (Williams & Sonoma, Restoration Hardware, Pier 1 Imports, Linens N Things, the Museum Company, Crate & Barrel); and a third model that is just developing—"occasion-centric" retailers (gourmet-cooking-supply stores, party-supply stores, outdoor-entertaining and patio-supply retailers, "last-minute gifts" retailers). Watch how these new retailing models develop into the next decade.

Outdoor Living Markets: Whether for the garden, deck, patio, or pool, outdoor aesthetics are red-hot, reaching design heights and sales levels formerly attained only indoors. Witness the exploding market for garden architecture, landscaping products, bird feeders, gazebos—even sheds that have been upscaled to designer "English potting sheds." This may in part be driven by new stock-market wealth and the fact that the ranks of millionaires are growing 20 times faster than the general population. Garden "rooms" with plush upholstered furnishings, muslin throw cushions, ambient lighting from candles to lamps, and Mexican stoves as fireplaces are taking off. The standard-issue aluminum patio chairs and hardware-store-bought electric lights of old are being replaced by French metal bistro tables, Indonesian teak benches, tabletop water fountains in Japanese designs, and even Moorish hanging lanterns. The growth of lush garden-and-deck specialty magazines and syndicated TV shows will no doubt keep this market bubbling.

Consumer Electronics: This will continue to be a successful market as the wave of new digital conveniences rolls over us. HDTV, WebTV, digital photography, "smart" toys and dolls, virtual-reality games, and even personal karaoke machines are the hot items, to say nothing of the next generation of PCs, modems, and peripherals (scanners, printers, fax machines, wireless telephony) making their way into the home. This is a market that hasn't cooled off since the first transistor radio in the 1950s. Generation Xers will keep this one fueled for years, assuming they can find all the different remote controls for this multimedia mania.

Enhanced-Experience Businesses: While the '90s spurred new experiences in movie-going, home theaters, theme restaurants, and virtual videogaming, the millennium will extend and build on a variety of escapist fare. The stress of everyday living on time-strapped consumers guarantees that when they find time off, they will demand highly intense or diverting experiences. Spas, now beginning their growth ascent, will become an even broader and stronger market as more men patronize them. Cruise-ship traffic—already growing 40 percent in vacationer numbers per half decade—will continue its growth curve, driven by strong retiree incomes and boomers. Pleasure travel, already growing at double GDP rates of growth, will mature into a number of growing sub-segments. Three strata will emerge: the soft vacation-seekers wanting wine tours, gourmet-cooking holidays, or bird-watching; more ambitious activists going backpacking, mountain biking, or supervised whitewater rafting; and, lastly, the exotic thrill-seekers, who will go for adventure tours, dogsledding, hot-air ballooning, cattle driving, tall-ship sailing, rock climbing, heli-skiing, whale kissing, and cave exploring. These escape-oriented experience-seekers will spare no expense, including professional guides, GPS locators, digital video cameras, off-road transportation, and the best clothing designers can come up with.

Anti-Aging Products and Services: This market's already-high popularity will skyrocket as boomers approach retirement. A generation accustomed to the best of everything will not react well to the physical effects of aging. They'll be keen buyers of cosmetic surgery, sun-care remedies, anti-wrinkle "cosmeceuticals," laser-corrected eye surgery, baldness cures, sexual-potency drugs, and "active" vacation packages such as cruises with fitness programs. They intend to live well and look good far into their 80s, and they'll pay well for any service or product that helps achieve this goal, from calcium-fortified cereals to designer sun hats.

> # A generation accustomed to the best of everything will not react well to the physical effects of aging.

Health as a National Hobby: Hand in hand with looking good goes fitness, nutrition, dieting, and self-care-based wellness. No longer are doctors the authority figures they once were. More-educated consumers are driving fundamental changes in self-care. Home-diagnostic-kit markets are doubling every three to four years and moving far beyond pregnancy, blood-pressure, and diabetes-monitoring tests. Test kits now exist for checking body-fat levels and vision, and for checking for urinary-tract infections and hepatitis C. Home gyms are proliferating, as is use of the Internet to research personal-health issues. Alternative medicine, from homeopathy to chiropractic, is burgeoning. People are taking charge of their own allergy regimens, migraines, and bad backs with everything from herbal remedies to massage and vitamin therapy. Clearly, in large segments of the population, health as a hobby is a daily preoccupation. And as the "doctor knows best" notion becomes increasingly a thing of the past, hobby will become habit, creating a consistently escalating market opportunity.

High-End Sports Apparel and Equipment: This sector is growing fast, fed by golf's revival as well as by a revolution in materials. New fabrics, composites, ceramics, and metals are revolutionizing not just golf clubs but skis, snowboards, in-line skates, tennis rackets, hiking gear, bicycles, and even water skis (some of which use new piezoelectric materials to reduce vibration chatter). Sailing gear is more stretchable, wind-proof, water-resistant, breathable, and durable. Something as simple as a golf shirt can cost up to $200, depending upon how well it takes advantage of newer upscale cottons and silk combinations. Designers such as Tommy Hilfiger and Nautica have introduced new lines of golf sportswear to compete alongside the Ashworths and

Greg Normans. Bicycle frames now have highly engineered shocks and brakes. Snowboards have easy snap-on bindings, while in-line skates have boosted wheel durability. Some of the innovations in concept, design, and testing of athletic accoutrements have transferred from "extreme sports" such as high-mountain snowboarding or marathon cycling. For whatever reason, mainstream consumers (both men and women) just love these technology plays—whether they result in titanium-constructed golf balls or America's Cup-tested sailing jackets.

Safe Packaging, Pure Contents, and "Green" Concerns: This is another escalating market. Consumers want ingredient listings, product dating, and tamper-proof lids. Bottled and "spring" water sales attest to the desire for "purity" in beverages. More attention is being paid to whether or not containers are recyclable. Hotels are introducing customers to sensible water use and providing recycling bins for shampoo bottles and aluminum cans. Products containing recycled materials are gaining some sales momentum—products from pot and pan scrubbers (from 3M) to deck chairs (from L.L. Bean). Maytag's best-selling washing machine, "Neptune," has been successfully positioned as an "ecologically friendly" energy-saving appliance. It's true that these shifts are relatively subtle and selective. (Concern for the environment hasn't slowed the market for gas-guzzling SUVs.) But children and Generation-Y consumers are more aware of environmental issues than the "post-40" generation—a fact that will no doubt create positive forward momentum for "greener" products in the decades to come. The first recyclable home PC will likely do very well with Gen-Y buyers.

Consumer change has always driven market change. (Witness the new ethnic markets for Latin radio or the boom in Mexican food that has come out of America's changing diversity.) All of the opportunities profiled here have resulted from base-level consumer changes in demographics, wealth accumulation, values, and aspirations. The age wave is driving the self-health-care and anti-aging markets, while youth are driving consumer electronics. Wealth accumulation is driving upscale outdoor living and high-end sports accessories. And values and aspirations are creating markets for "greener" products and for different retailing models. As these trends mature, they'll no doubt be replaced by newer high-growth markets, representing the next round of demographic, income, and value-driven consumer behaviors.

ALLAN J. MAGRATH is director of corporate marketing services and new business ventures at 3M Canada Co., and has contributed writing on strategy to ATB for nearly a decade. His last article was a review of The Alchemy of Growth *in the September 1999 issue.*

Future Markets

***In the future, marketers will target niches. In niches there are riches.
By serving a niche well, we can earn a high margin.***

Philip Kotler

OUR ONLY CERTAINTY is that things will change. Back in the 1950s, who would have anticipated Internet home shopping, home banking, satisfaction guarantees on new automobiles, customized bicycles, and factory-outlet shopping malls? We will see the marketplace go through more radical changes. Specifically, we can anticipate the following eight developments.

1. Shifting demographics. More consumer marketing will focus on mature consumers—the 55-year-olds and older. The focus will shift toward health products, retirement homes, and forms of recreation and entertainment.

Mature consumers will want to be healthy forever. We'll see healthcare facilities where mature consumers pay to have regular diagnostic checks. Medical people will present a complete recommendation on exercise, nutrition, and stress management.

We will also witness a growing demand for light foods, low-calorie beverages, home exercise equipment, vitamins, beauty care and skin-care cosmetics—anything that will make you look and feel younger and healthier. Mature consumers will pay for luxuries like cosmetic surgery, personal exercise coaches, exotic travel, and continuing education.

They will have youthful attitudes and outlooks.

At the other end of the age spectrum, children and teenagers will be more grown-up. These "mini-adults" will master computers and have access to information over the Internet that was never before available. They will be smart consumers who shop electronically.

2. Entertainment explosion. I expect an explosion in entertainment. People will want to be entertained whatever they are doing, whether they're working, shopping, or consuming. Recently, I saw a cyclist on an expensive bike, peddling at a furious speed while listening to music on his Walkman. These multiprocessing consumers will do two or three things at the same time, primarily because their time is short and there is so much they still want to do. Smart retailers, restaurants, hotels, museums, and orchestras will build special atmospheres and surprises into their offerings.

3. High-income consumers. We'll see the buying market segmented into high-income consumers and low-income consumers, while the middle class will diminish in size. Many companies will still target the middle class. But more companies will clearly target their products and services at either the high-income or low-income class. High-income con-

sumers will demand high-quality products and personalized services. At the opposite end will be people who just want basic, no-frills products and services at the lowest possible price. Each class can be further segmented by education, occupation, and lifestyle variables. High-income consumers will be high-achieving people with technical knowledge. They will work to live, not live to work. They will want more quality time apart from work to enjoy other pursuits.

4. Convenience. Time-starved, high-income people want products and services made available to them in a hassle-free way. Their resistance to buying something may not be the price—it's the time, risk, and the psychic costs involved. There will be a great increase in home-based shopping and banking. More people will order clothes, appliances, and other products and services from catalogues.

5. New media. The key is response measurement. Direct marketing is about sending messages to specific addressable consumers and learning which ones placed an order. It started with direct mail and moved to telemarketing. Today, we have added infomercials, audio and videotape, CD-ROMs, computer disks, fax-mail, e-mail, and voice-mail. Companies are rapidly building customer databases from which they can draw the best prospects for an offer. Products, too, will increasingly be customized. Companies will work with you to design your own bicycle, bathing suit, computer, and car. The buying process will become far more interactive, with consumers co-designing the product.

6. *The importance of brands*. Brands will always be important, although the importance of national brands is diminishing. Consumers are comparing the brands on price, and if one is on sale they will buy that brand, regardless of preference. No wonder more money is pouring into sales promotion and price incentives, and less into advertising. And with less advertising, perceived brand differences are eroding. Also giant retailers are introducing private brands that cost less. If your brand is not No. 1 or 2, you may be kicked out of the market.

7. *Quality, pricing, and service*. If your company doesn't produce high quality, you must either sell to low-income groups or go out of business. High product quality will become a ticket into the marketplace. But to win, companies offer high quality for a lower price. The key to good pricing is to figure out to whom you want to sell the product and what they think the product is worth—and then to design the product and its service bundle so it can be priced that way. You will need to justify your prices, using arguments with substance rather than relying on image alone. Service will grow as a competitive tool, especially as products become more similar. Companies must enhance the use-value, or service-value, which goes beyond purchase-value.

8. *Cause-related marketing*. Many companies will differentiate themselves by seriously sponsoring high-consensus social causes, such as environmental protection, helping the homeless, and saving the whales. Building a civic character, not just a business character, can build interest, respect, and loyalty.

Philip Kotler is the SC Johnson & Son Distinguished Professor of Intl. Marketing at the Kellogg Graduate School of Management and author of Philip Kotler on Marketing *(Free Press). This article was adapted with permission from* Rethinking the Future *(Nicholas Brealey), edited by Rowan Gibson; 800-462-6420.*

Reprinted with permission from *Executive Excellence*, February 2000, p. 6. © 2000 by Executive Excellence Publishing. To order call (800) 304-9782; www.eep.com.

LOYALTY • *The rules have changed*

10 things to know about customers

By SHERRIE E. WEHNER

More and more, companies are realizing that their most precious asset is their existing customer base. As a result, the traditional marketing mix, which has focused heavily on gaining new customers through mass-marketing, is evolving. Marketers are moving funds from their advertising budgets and allocating them for customer loyalty and retention programs, which go by many names, including loyalty, frequency, retention and relationship marketing. But all define the same basic marketing approach: Identify, segment, grow and retain existing customers by communicating and rewarding desired behavior.

Here's a brief look at the 10 most important trends in loyalty marketing affecting almost every company selling almost every kind of product in almost every marketplace.

•**Consumers are smarter and expect more**. As the general population becomes better educated, consumers approach purchase decisions with greater scrutiny, and they have access to more data for comparison shopping. One example is the Nutrition Labeling Education Act established in 1990 by the Food and Drug Administration, which requires food companies to provide detailed nutritional information on every package. This allows consumers to compare the specific nutritional features of every food product within a specific category.

Also, the Internet and the growing popularity of consumer publications such as *Consumer Reports* and television news shows such as *Dateline* and *20/20* give consumers greater access to product information. With greater scrutiny comes stronger expectations and demand for product quality and customer service. To meet these demands and emphasize differentiation and added value, companies launch loyalty marketing programs.

•**The Internet has led to disloyalty**. The Internet as a distribution channel for product sales and information has caused many consumers to change buying habits and methods. Researchers report record-low consumer loyalty in the Internet environment.

•**Low unemployment is squeezing customer service**. As the labor pool shrinks, so does the quality and skill level of available labor for frontline customer service jobs. Additionally, retail organizations and service-based call centers face increased employee recruitment and retention challenges. As a result, customer service levels are eroding, particularly in fast food and mass merchandising retail. As consumers become frustrated with poor service, longer lines and other service-related problems, customer defection becomes a threat. The critical decline in customer service quality also damages and severs relationships with formerly loyal and profitable customers.

•**Price-based switching programs change expectations**. Most of us have gotten a tempting offer to switch telephone service: Switch your long distance service to the company that's calling, and it'll send you a check. Some were worth $20, some $50, and during extremely competitive periods, some companies offered as much as $100. These price- or cash-based offers have taught consumers to be on the lookout for the next best offer. But in many industries, loyalty marketing programs have helped companies establish value and create barriers to exit.

•**The global market introduces new competitors**. As the global economy opens, U.S. companies are seeing increased competition, and many are facing foreign competition for the first time. Many use loyalty marketing initiatives to establish stronger value propositions in the hopes of blocking foreign threats to market share.

•**Customer-focused marketing technology is developing rapidly**. The term "customer database" is outdated. Technical giants such as Microsoft and Oracle have developed, and continue to enhance, data warehousing systems that collect and mine valuable customer information in real time. And marketers are incorporating these systems with software innovations like E.piphany's E5 to use the data for smart and ROI-based loyalty marketing programs.

Loyalty programs meet many needs

•**Deregulation makes choice more complicated**. First, we had to choose long distance telephone service, and in the beginning, we had only price to differentiate among the big three. Eventually, large advertising budgets and price-based switching programs gave us more to consider. Now, deregulation gives us more choices to make. Soon, we'll be inundated with marketing campaigns for local telephone service, cable, electricity and even gas, as utility companies compete for customers for the first time.

Challenged with selling commodity-based service products offering little opportunity for brand differentiation, these companies look to establish increased value by developing loyalty marketing strategies. Pilot programs already are operating in early-adopting states. Legislation signed in 1999 by Texas Gov. George W. Bush provided the impetus for loyalty marketing programs like the Selections program, sponsored by Dallas-based TXU (Texas Utilities), which offers customers a variety of added benefits such as consolidated billing and home energy use evaluations. While this was the first program of its kind, other major Texas utilities are developing similar programs aimed at fostering loyalty.

•**Mergers and acquisitions can upset customers**. For many industries, acquire-or-be-acquired is the name of the game. Mergers and acquisitions can have a significant impact on brand and product loyalty, and may cause customers to look for alternatives. This trend has been especially pronounced in the financial service industry where customers struggle to keep up with the logo changes in their checkbooks.

•**Mass media costs are increasing**. Advertising is more expensive, and marketing budgets are getting tighter. The average cost of a 30-second spot during the 1986 Super Bowl was $500,000. That number reached $2.2 million in 2000, so marketers need to drive increased ROI on their marketing budgets. This trend fosters loyalty programs, because loyalty marketing focuses on existing customers whose behaviors and responses can be tracked, and marketers can pinpoint response and accurately attribute incremental revenues to marketing dollars spent.

•**Competitors are doing it**. Loyalty marketing has become a table-stake in many industries. Almost every hotel chain, airline and credit card company offer some type of frequent customer program; customers have come to expect them and compare benefits and rewards of competing companies. As a result, competitors are racing to introduce new perks, better benefits and some other element or twist that no other company offers.

These trends pervade every market situation, and companies are either jumping on board with loyalty marketing, or they're watching their customers go by on the competitor's train.

Sherrie E. Wehner is director of marketing for St. Louis-based Maritz Loyalty Marketing, which is part of Maritz Inc., also of St. Louis.

The *e*-volving salesman

If the profession, in the traditional sense, is dying, then e-commerce is writing the epitaph

By Marilyn Kennedy Melia

SPECIAL TO THE TRIBUNE

During the thousands of miles he logs on the road each year, Michael Shanley keeps a laptop computer by his side, using it, with the skill of a research librarian or a journalist, to constantly gather the latest information off the Internet.

Shanley, however, isn't in a profession that most people think involves much research or analytical skills. He's in sales.

"I would like to dispel that old stereotype of the slick, fast-talking salesman that kind of scared everyone," said Shanley, outside salesperson for Liebovich Bros. Inc., in Rockford. The company is a subsidiary of Los Angeles-based Reliance Steel&Aluminum Co.

Ed Harms, senior vice president of sales for CareerEngine.com, an on-line recruiting company, says amen to that. "The Willy Loman, whose stock in trade was a shoeshine and a smile, is the antithesis of the modern, solution-oriented salesperson," he said.

If the leaner, meaner business climate of the past decade wasn't enough to kill the three-martini-lunch, glib-talking salesman, the epitaph is now being written by the burgeoning world of e-commerce.

Indeed, one of the chief aims of the new dot-com world is to bring buyers and sellers of all types of goods and services together in cyberspace. The salesperson, traditional middleman between buyer and seller, is an endangered species, except for those who learn how to add real value to the transaction. Sales people who can do that are turning the job into a higher-paying, more-skilled profession. According to government statistics, 16 million people, or about 12 percent of the workforce, hold sales jobs in this country. Those most likely to be supplanted by e-commerce, said Jon Hawes, director of the Fisher Institute for Professional Selling at the University of Akron, hold low-paying, low-skill sales jobs. Actually, added Hawes, it's a misnomer to term many of these low-paying positions "sales" jobs in the first place. "Really, these are order-taking positions." It's the people answering phones to take customers' orders who are likely to go the way of the door-to-door salesman, who disappeared a decade or two ago when women left the homefront, asserts Hawes.

Michael Lavelle, an Evanston-based salesperson for Getinge-Castle Inc., a hospital equipment company headquartered in Rochester, N.Y., agrees.

"We are hearing a lot about how salespeople will go by the wayside (because of e-commerce). And that is true for commodity products, where customers are looking for the best price," said Lavelle. "But it's not true for the bigger-ticket items. In my business, hospitals might shop for commodities like rubber gloves and gowns on the Internet. Buying surgical equipment, though, is complex and requires lots of planning."

Like Shanley, Lavelle is rarely without his laptop and he's always hopping on the Web to check e-mail, track the progress of customers' orders and seek out news on the hospital industry, among other tasks.

In fact, the Internet is a two-edged sword for salespeople, said Allen Konopacki, president of Incomm International, a research and sales training company in Chicago. On the one hand, the Web is slicing some sales jobs, but at the same time salespeople are using the net to provide deeper and more comprehensive services to their customers.

The result, according to Konopacki and other experts, is that effective salespeople in these new complex roles are in demand, with the potential to earn more than ever. "We have a broader range of compensation levels for salespeople today," Konopacki said. "We have long been finding them in the $50,000 bracket, and more and more, I'm finding salespeople in the $250,000 bracket."

Salespeople who earn six-figure salaries are most likely to work in the business-to-business arena, said Konopacki. While consumer-oriented retail sites were the first wave on the Internet, B2B sites are now revolutionizing business purchasing, with sites emerging on which companies can buy everything from paper to steel.

A corollary trend is that companies are reducing the number of vendors they do business with. "Vendors are no longer just salespeople. They are now strategic partners with their business customers," said Konopacki.

Lavelle and Shanley can point to numerous examples of how their day-to-day worklife is now different than it was before the Internet explosion.

"I would go out on the street and sell a product and then let the in-house people handle the rest," said Lavelle. "Salespeople didn't use to have a lot of connection to the office. Now, with the Internet, we are connected and we can track shipping and delivery. We are more connected to the processes at the home office and we are also a partner with the customer. Sometimes, in fact, the customer may want us to tap into their computer system for tracking and follow-up."

And Shanley said the sales cycle is now shorter. "If you use the computer more effectively, you will be able to stretch yourself out more and call on more people," he said. "You can use the Internet, for example, to send clients product and market information by e-mail. If you know the price of stainless steel is going up in the next 60 days, for instance, that is something you send your customers."

Shanley adds that while his business customers use the Internet to purchase, he also uses it to determine prime sales prospects. "A salesman spends a lot of time qualifying customers, or figuring out whether a business manufactures products that would entail the use of our products. We used to have to look in manufacturers' directories. Now, you can easily pull this kind of information off the Internet, and you can do it quickly."

With sales increasingly involving research, analysis and problem-solving, many people who think they're not aggressive enough for sales may be missing opportunities. A librarian or an accountant could conceivably find a niche in sales, experts say.

"The demand for talented salespeople has never been keener," said Harms of CareerEngine.

A Chicago-based Internet company, BidBuyBuild.com, has certainly found that it requires a human sales force to get its e-commerce site, where builders can purchase supplies and equipment, up and running.

"The human touch is needed to explain to builders how to use the site, and to verify to manufacturers that they will be dealing with legitimate builders and contractors," said Bob Stockard, president of Salience Associates, an Andover, Mass., sales outsourcing firm. Indeed, Stockard says that in the world of e-commerce, he expects more companies to contract with firms like his, whereby a sales staff can temporarily boost Web sales via old-fashioned human skills.

To help their sales force become more effective in these changing times, Kono-packi says industry surveys show companies are spending more each year on sales training.

Although the B2B arena is where more of the higher-paying, complex sales positions are found, in many cases, selling to consumers is also evolving because of e-commerce. "I see e-mail in my sleep," said R. J. Serpico, Internet sales manager for Arlington Heights Ford. Customers often start shopping on the Web, he said, and e-mail him to inquire about options and prices.

Many of the same processes are still involved in selling cars, said Serpico, but they are now altered somewhat due to e-commerce.

For example, salesman and customer have long negotiated over the price of a vehicle. Now, customers can glean a clear idea of what the dealer has paid for the car on the Internet. Some people will take that figure and still haggle, even asking for a price below what they know the dealer has paid, said Serpico. Others will tag on a few hundred dollars, deeming that is a fair dealer profit. The salesman is still negotiating with the customer, only now the talks are probably more specific on dealer costs, he said.

"The speed and pace of the economy is quickening and there is a need to manage more and more information," said Harms. "It has all changed the role of the sales-person."

Marketing High Technology: Preparation, Targeting, Positioning, Execution

A range of strategies are available to the high-tech marketing manager taking a shot at launching the latest technology.

Chris Easingwood and Anthony Koustelos

Commercialization of new high-tech products is often the costliest stage of the entire product development process. Yet even when the process is well managed, the risk of failure remains high. New high-tech products usually have just one shot at the market. Get it wrong and the consequences are invariably fatal. And although the launch strategy is critical, this stage is largely neglected in the business press and academic literature on high-tech marketing, innovation, and new product development.

**Figure 1
Launching New Technology**

Market Preparation

↓

Targeting

↓

Positioning

↓

Execution

Persuading a market to adopt a new technology is generally comprised of four stages, shown in Figure 1. The first step, market preparation, involves readying customers and other companies for the change. Typically this stage takes place while the product is still in development, though not necessarily so. The second stage in planning the marketing of the product is targeting, followed by positioning based on the expected competitive situation. The final stage involves execution and consists of the strategies that are often the most visible part of the mix, used to achieve specific results. Each of the four stages will be described in turn.

MARKET PREPARATION

Market preparation is intended to get the market ready for the new technology by building awareness and, most important, forming relationships. Figure 2 shows some examples.

Cooperation/Licensing/Alliances

In many cases, the way a marketer chooses to set up the market is crucial. Some form of cooperation is increasingly seen not as an option but as a necessity. Few companies can go it alone, at least not when the launch of major technology is concerned.

Alliances and licensing arrangements encourage the adoption of technological standards for at least two good reasons.

One is because of the expected boost to sales. Customers are reluctant to adopt when faced with competing and incompatible technologies (recall the days of the VHS and Betamax videocassette formats). They realize that markets rarely allow two competing technologies to thrive, and eventually coalesce around the preferred one, condemning the other(s) to decline.

The other reason is that companies sometimes seek to establish their own technology as the standard, to preempt those of rivals and avoid having a competing standard imposed. This was very much the reason for Psion, Motorola, Ericsson, and Nokia forming a consortium called Symbian. The four agreed to adopt Psion's computer operating system, called EPOC, in the hope that this would become the industry standard for the next generation of wireless communication devices, such as mobile phones and palm-top computers. The mobile phone is expected to become "smart," sending and receiving data, downloading from the Internet, and storing large amounts of information. The alliance is also an attempt to prevent Microsoft's Windows CE operating system in consumer electronics from becoming the standard. Ericsson, Motorola, and Nokia each had to abandon its own operating system in adopting Psion's—a sacrifice that may prove worthwhile, given *Fortune's* claim that David Potter, Psion's CEO, is the man Microsoft's Bill Gates fears the most (Wallace 1998).

Figure 2
Market Preparation: Some Examples

Form alliances	Psion, Motorola, Ericsson, and Nokia adopting Psion's computer operating system to thwart Microsoft's Windows CE operating system
Supply to OEMs	IBM licensing its hard disk drives
Provide pre-launch information	Apple providing information on the Macintosh NC

Sometimes the alliances formed can be informal or "loose," arising through mutual advantage. This is because, more and more, technological products rarely stand alone. They depend on the existence of other products and technologies. A good example is the World Wide Web, with its groupings of businesses that include browsers, on-line news, e-mail, network retailing, and financial services. Arthur (1996) calls these networks of products and services that support and enhance each other "mini-ecologies." They are increasingly the basic frameworks of knowledge-based industries, and companies have to secure themselves a place in these loose alliances built around a mini-ecology.

Supply to OEMs

Market preparation can also be tackled by sharing the new technology with original equipment manufacturers (OEMs). This increases the awareness of the product and the technology, and boosts sales via expansion to new markets. IBM developed two powerful hard disk drives, Travel-Star 8GS and 3GN, for its own ThinkPad notebooks, but decided to license them to Acer, Gateway 2000, Dell, and other OEMs as well, which plan to use the drives in their portable PCs. This market preparation tactic enables the producer to retain full ownership of its technology while at the same time expanding market potential beyond its own marketing capacity, albeit at a lower margin.

Provide Pre-Launch Information

The type of information released before launch, and the manner in which it is delivered, can be a key tactical decision in the product launch. The publicly visible demonstration of this strategy is the article in the press, detailing the time the product will reach the market, the basis of the technology, and other information. Intel has been releasing details of its new MMX technology-based Pentium-II chip. Articles have also appeared on the Macintosh NC, Apple's forthcoming network computer, based on the company's powerful new chip, PowerPC 750. Those who typically need to be informed before the launch are the distribution network, service suppliers (such as software houses), and the media, who in turn inform potential customers.

The information to be released has to be planned carefully so as to arouse sufficient interest in the new product without losing a competitive edge in a market where imitation can materialize with lightning speed. A careful balance must be drawn that allows for the need to have influential components of the market's infrastructure informed without giving a technological lead away to competitors.

Educate the Market

A special form of providing pre-release information is an education program. This is very ambitious and more long-term than merely releasing information, and thus it is less common. It is exactly what Intel did in the early days of the microchip. Rather than marketing the product directly—there were just too many markets with too many applications for that—it set about educating the various markets on the potential of the technology, leaving them with much greater in-depth knowledge to work out how the product might be used in their particular markets.

However, education has to be managed and timed carefully. Otherwise, the company sells the vision before it has the product to deliver that vision. Not surprisingly, smaller companies shy away from trying to educate markets, leaving it to larger corporations with their greater resources and longer planning horizons.

Create Special Distribution Arrangements

Finally, technology may be launched into new markets as well as currently served markets, which would entail establishing new channels of distribution. Distribution rights may be given to competitors in these new markets. New distribution can also be gained through joint ventures, possibly involving collaborative development of the technology.

TARGETING

Adoption of a new technology is likely to be faster if the marketing strategy is compatible with the segment targeted. Easingwood and Lunn (1992) examined the diffusion of telecommunications products and found that clearly targeted products diffused more rapidly than non-targeted ones (see Figure 3 for examples).

Target Innovative Adopters

Targeting innovative adopters can take two main forms: (a) targeting both companies and innovative individuals within those companies, or (b) targeting sectors.

Innovative Companies and Individuals. Based on the familiar model, the technology adoption life cycle, this strategy identifies innovative adopters because they are prepared to buy without seeing the product up and running elsewhere. They do not insist that the technology have a "track record." Moore (1991) divides these early buyers—only a small percentage of the total potential market, but hugely influential—into technological enthusiasts, or "techies," and visionaries. Techies are intrigued by technology and will explore a

Figure 3
Targeting: Some Examples

Target innovative adopters	NTT taking its global photo transmission system to sectors, such as the insurance industry, that are likely to be early adopters
Target pragmatists	Amgen using a large sales force to promote its hepatitis C drug to *all* hospital specialists
Target conservatives	Microsoft aiming its integrated software product Works at the PC conservative market
Target current customers	IBM Software Group working with many of the Global 5000
Target competitors' customers	Xerox targeting its digital copiers at Hewlett-Packard customers

product's potential for themselves. Their endorsement is vital because it means the product does, in fact, work. Visionaries are the managers with clout, often very senior, who can see a product's potential for overturning existing ways of operating, delivering significant value and competitive advantage to those organizations prepared to grasp the new technology.

Technological enthusiasts and visionaries, although placed together in this innovative group, are very different in some regards. Techies are excited by the technology itself, whereas the visionaries try to find its greater worth—some single, compelling application that uses the full range of the new technology. A visionary is motivated by a potentially significant leap forward, not by the newness of the technology.

Visionaries are a rare breed. They not only have the ability to see the potential when no one else can, they also have the management drive and charisma to persuade the rest of an organization to back the vision. They anticipate a radical discontinuity between the old ways and the new, realizing that this rarely happens smoothly, and so they will tolerate the glitches and setbacks that inevitably occur before this is achieved.

The only way to work with visionaries, says Moore, is to use a small, high-level sales force. Constantly looking to leverage technology, visionaries typically maintain good relationships with techies, so this segment should not be neglected. And techies can be reached fairly easily through the technical and business press. It is their job to stay alert to all developments, wher-

ever their sources, not just to focus on their own industry.

Early Adopting Sectors. Innovators can sometimes be hard to identify, but they are worth searching out. They start the ball rolling. However, an alternative to identifying individuals with these special attractive characteristics is to target whole sectors that are likely to be early buyers.

USDC developed an active-matrix flat panel display screen—in effect, the first "paper-quality" screen, with each pixel linked to its own transistor—and targeted the product at some of the world's leading air forces, a sector with a pressing need for the latest technology.

In the telecommunications sector, NTT has developed Digital Photo System, a means of transmitting a photo by a digital camera over the airways via cellular phones to a laptop computer and from there to a printer. The whole process takes about 10 seconds and can be done globally. The service was aimed initially at the newspaper and insurance sectors, both of which would particularly benefit from an acceleration in the speed of the internal processing of photographs.

Target the Pragmatists

Sometimes called the "early majority," pragmatists (as Moore calls them) are the large group of adopters following behind the techies and visionaries, though Moore argues that the gap between the two groups is so large it deserves to be called a chasm. Pragmatists typically comprise large organizations with a clear need to adopt new technologies to retain or improve competi-

tiveness, but with a reluctance to do so. The dislocation would be so extensive and the size of the investment required to switch the whole firm over to the new technology so large that they are risk-averse. People in this group are reasonably comfortable about taking on new technology, but only when some well-established references exist. Their preference is for evolution, not revolution. They are looking for something that can be slotted into existing ways of doing things. "If the goal of visionaries is to take a quantum leap forward," explains Moore, "the goal of pragmatists is to make a percentage improvement—incremental, measurable, predictable progress."

Marketing to pragmatists is a matter of:

- attending the industry conferences and trade shows;
- getting frequent mentions in the industry magazines;
- being installed in other companies in the same industry;
- developing industry-specific applications;
- having alliances with other key suppliers to the industry.

As Moore observes, pragmatists like to hear companies talk about their new products as "industry standards." What they hate to hear is products described as "state-of-the-art." This makes them extremely edgy. Pharmaceutical companies are well known for targeting their new drugs at hospital specialists working in the leading teaching hospitals. However, they do not neglect the pragmatists either. Amgen has assembled a sales team of about 50 people to promote its new hepatitis C drug to all the hematologists and gastroenterologists working in hospitals who may have to treat patients with the ailment.

Target Conservatives

The "conservatives," or "late adopters," really are not that keen on new technology. By and large, they would really rather not adopt any if they could get away with it, but competitive pressures may force them to do so. They are not that confident in their ability to adapt to new technology, so they like to see evidence of support. By the time the technology gets to them, there will probably be an established standard. Conservatives like to buy pre-assembled packages, with everything bundled. "They want high-tech products to be like refrigerators," says Moore. "You open the door, the light comes on automatically, your food stays cold, and you don't have to think about it."

However, it can he a big mistake to neglect this section of the market. For one thing, it is large—probably around a third of the whole market. It is often not developed as systematically as it should be, possibly because high-tech companies do not generally find it easy to empathize with this group. The product development costs are apt to be fully amortized at this stage, so extending the product's life should be highly profitable.

Because of conservatives' reluctance to come to grips with a new technology and its implications, a product has to be made increasingly easy to adopt if a high-tech company is to succeed with this group. The DOS PC operating system stalled when it reached the late adopter segment—the home market, the home office, the small business. This segment does not have the support offered in large companies and was disinclined to teach itself DOS. It took the greater simplicity of Windows 3.0 to bring it into the market. Microsoft has aimed its product Works, an integrated, all-in-one word processor, spreadsheet, and database (none of which are state-of-the-art), at the PC conservative market.

Target Current Customers

Existing customers can be an obvious target group for well-established companies. So it makes sense for IBM Software Group, the world's second largest software firm—which has very strong customer relationships with the Global 5000, the world's largest companies—to think first

of its current customers. Although current customers ought to be the most secure market, this is not necessarily the case. They can he hard to satisfy and quite costly to retain. Such is Intel's experience. It is having to cut the prices of some of its computer chips in an attempt to retain big corporate customers such as Compaq and Packard Bell. The latter are threatening to switch to Cyrix, the rival microprocessor producer, as they do everything possible to reduce the costs of their lowest-priced PCs.

Targeting existing customers is a strategy particularly appropriate to rapidly changing, advanced technologies. It can be particularly relevant for complex technologies when the decision to adopt often relies on a high degree of technical expertise and mutual trust between buyer and supplier.

Target Competitors' Customers

Finally, competitors' customers can present a prime opportunity, especially when the company's own product is competitive and the competitor has a large market share. Xerox would claim that this is the case for the new digital copiers designed by its Office Document Product Group. The copiers, which have faxing, scanning, and printing capabilities when connected to the personal computers of Hewlett-Packard's customers, are targeted toward HP and its dominance in the printer market.

Such a practice is commonplace in the pharmaceutical industry. Amgen has pitched its new hepatitis C treatment drug, Infeger, at those customers for whom the existing treatments, such as Schering-Plough's Intron A or Roche Holdings' Roferon A, have not been successful.

Of course, this strategy is very aggressive. For brand new technologies, it may be counterproductive. Aggressive competitive tactics may be seen as undermining the credibility of the entire technology, rather than just the competitor's product, as may have been intended.

POSITIONING

Some new technologies are so specialized that targeting and positioning strategies are too unambiguous and virtually redundant. Other new technologies are so wide-ranging in their potential applications that the market needs some strong clues as to targeting and positioning before it will respond. Many products fall between these two extremes.

Positioning can be based on tangible (technological) or intangible characteris-

tics (such as image), with technologically intensive industrial markets favoring the former. Where the market is not so technologically informed, or the benefits of the new technology are not so easily differentiated from competitors, positioning characteristics are likely to be more intangible. Positioning possibilities can be numerous, but some of those used most often are described here (see Figure 4 for examples).

Emphasize Exclusivity

A way to differentiate the product offer is by emphasizing how exclusive it is. In other words, can the product be placed in the upper segment of the market, where the margins are usually higher? For example, by focusing on quality, engineering, and adjustability, Recaro is offering a top-of-the-range child's safety seat—the Recaro-Start—that appeals to wealthier parents who place high priority on their children's safety. The company is playing heavily on its reputation for producing high-tech safety seats for Porsche and Aston-Martin.

Emphasize a Low Price

It used to be that low prices were considered an inappropriate lever for high-tech products and services. The market's reluctance to purchase was due to the misgivings it held about the new product's performance, which was largely unproven. The best strategy, marketers believed, was to address this reluctance directly by lowering the perceived risk that the product would not come up to expectations, or by reducing the perceived likelihood that it might be made redundant by a superior technology. In any case, high margins were needed to recoup the high costs of development.

Well, not necessarily anymore. Low price is used more and more in high-tech markets. For instance, phone companies will have to pay just $5 per device to use EPOC from Symbian, versus a reported $25 for Microsoft's Windows CE.

Emphasize Technological Superiority

Focusing on the technological superiority of a new high-tech product is common. When technology is changing rapidly and perhaps radically, it would seem that positioning a product on the basis of the latest technology built into it should reflect the product's true *raison d'etre*.

Figure 4
Positioning: Some Examples

Emphasize exclusivity	Recaro (supplier to Porsche and Aston Martin) with its top-of-the-range child's safety seat
Emphasize a low price	Just $5 per mobile phone for the operating system from Symbian ($25 quoted for the alternative)
Emphasize technological superiority	Xerox focusing on the superiority of digital copiers over the old technology
Emphasize a "safe bet"	Lucent Technologies designing its digital phones to be compatible with international standards

Xerox's new digital copiers are priced about 10 percent higher than old-style copiers because of the greater quality and reliability they offer compared to the old "light lens" technology copiers. This practice is also observed in the computer component manufacturing industry, where such new products as "bonded modems," storing units, and processor chips justify their premium pricing through their advanced technological features.

However, emphasizing such superiority does have its drawbacks. First, by stressing technological features, the marketer is assuming a certain level of knowledge that may not be present in at least part of the target market. Second, the preoccupation with technological specifications may obscure the genuine benefits customers could realize from the technology. Given the buying center nature of many high-tech adoption decisions involving technical specialists and nonspecialists, not all of whom are capable of translating technical specifications into everyday benefits, it may be more successful to come up with a more benefit-specific positioning tactic.

Emphasize a 'Safe Bet'

Stressing customer protection in the product is important because it enhances the product's credibility element and reduces the associated risk of moving to a new technology. Lucent Technologies focused on the fact that the specifications of both of its two newly introduced digital phones fall under established standards. One of the phones operates on the Code Division Multiple Access (CDMA) technology standard of the United States. The other, which is a "dual mode/dual band" handset, operates on the Time Division Multiple Access (TDMA) standard introduced by

AT&T to serve the entire European market, where the existence of different networks can otherwise hinder compatibility.

EXECUTION

As the final stage and therefore the one that completes the product's projection into the marketplace, execution is designed to trigger a positive purchase decision. The strategies used depend on the objectives of the launch itself, which in turn depend on the state of technology and the awareness the market has of it. For a very new technology, of which the market is unaware, execution tends to focus on conveying the generic benefits. At the other extreme, where the technology is well known to the market, the launch objectives focus more on establishing a brand name and competitive advantage. Figure 5 provides examples.

Use Opinion Leaders

It makes good sense to obtain the support of opinion leaders. As Moore states, "No company can afford to pay for every marketing contact made. Every programme must rely on some on-going chain-reaction effects, what is usually called 'word of mouth.'" Word-of-mouth is invaluable, of course, but the support of opinion leaders, who are industrial rather than public celebrities, can also be taken on board more formally, such as in advertising or through appearances at company seminars.

Compaq and NEC Technologies have managed to secure the endorsement of a number of well-known technical journalists for their FPDS screen. Pharmaceutical companies try to communicate the views of prominent doctors on their new drugs to influence the views of general practitioners and other doctors.

Reduce the Risk of Adoption

It is sometimes possible to reduce adoption risks. Can the product be offered on an introductory trial? Can it be leased? Luz Engineering, a producer of industrial solar heaters costing between $2–4 million, came up with a novel variation on this approach. Now Luz is prepared to sell its systems. However, it is also prepared to install and operate the solar heaters itself, in which case the client merely contracts to buy steam at 350°F for 20 years at a discount from the prevailing local power company rate. This is a "no-lose deal" from the client's perspective. The client pays for none of the installation and operating costs, but enjoys most of the expected benefits of the technology, without the associated risks.

Cultivate a Winner Image

Individuals and organizations can easily be confused by too much choice. Their first reaction, when faced with a confusing purchasing decision, is to postpone it. But when this is no longer possible, they vote for the safe choice: the market leader. There is safety in numbers. And this position can be reinforcing in technology markets. Other companies will recognize the leadership position and design supporting products and services around the market leader, which will thus become even more the preferred choice. The number one product becomes easier to use, cheaper to use, and better supported. There is a "winner take most" tendency, as Arthur states—the phenomenon of increasing returns. The bigger you get, the more apt you are to get bigger still. Conversely, the smaller you get, the more apt you are to shrink even more. Success breeds success, failure breeds failure. You have to become

15

Figure 5
Execution: Some Examples

Use opinion leaders	Compaq and NEC Technologies securing endorsements from technical journalists
Reduce the risk of adoption	Luz Engineering installing and running its industrial solar heaters that supply clients with energy at guaranteed prices
Cultivate a winner image	IBM advertising its position as recipient of the most U.S. patents for the fifth year running
Concentrate on a particular application	Lotus Notes focusing on worldwide accounting and consulting firms

a "gorilla," because if you do not, you'll be a "chimpanzee" or, more likely, a "monkey."

Thus, companies should try to cultivate a winner image for themselves and their products. However, this often involves allocating considerable resources to a big media splash aimed at communicating the (preordained) success of the new product. So this strategy is most popular with large companies. When Microsoft launched Windows 95, it did not pull its punches or spare its expenses. In the U.S., the Empire State Building was bathed in Windows colors. In the U.K., the *Times*, sponsored by Microsoft, doubled its print run and was given away free. In Australia, the Sydney Opera House was commandeered. The worldwide event, accompanied by the Rolling Stones' hit "Start Me Up," was said to have cost $200 million, but was hugely successful: one million copies sold in the U.S. in the first four days, compared to the 60 days it took the upgrade to MS-DOS to reach that level.

Of course, the approach to this position can be more subtle. In the last year, IBM received more U.S. patents than any other company, taking the top spot for the fifth consecutive year in a list that used to be dominated primarily by Japanese firms. This achievement has been stressed by IBM through articles in the technology sections of top-rated journals. It has also been the theme of an advertising campaign that aims to build a leader image for the company.

Sometimes the leadership position cannot be established across the entire market, in which case it should be established in a market segment. It is important to be the biggest fish in the pond, even if it means searching out a very small pond.

A market leader position is particularly important for pragmatists. These are the people who are contemplating committing their organizations to the new product—a much less risky gamble if the new product is the market leader.

A company that can establish a lead in a segment is in a very strong position. All the major customers have committed themselves to the product and so want it to remain the standard. The company can only lose such a position by shooting itself in the foot. Moore believes that segments conspire, unconsciously, "to install some company or product as the market leader and then do everything in their power to keep [it] there." This, of course, puts up huge barriers to entry for other competitors. If the leader plays its cards right, it can end up "owning" the segment.

Concentrate on a Particular Application

Concentrating on a particular application is all about crossing the chasm, the huge gulf that separates the techies and visionaries, few in number, from the much larger mainstream market dominated by pragmatists. The way across the chasm is to target the company's resources to one or two very specific niche markets where it can dominate rapidly and force out competitors. It can then use the dominance of the first niche to attack the surrounding niches.

Moore uses the analogy of the Allies' D-Day invasion strategy in World War II: assembling a huge invasion force and focusing it on one narrowly defined target, the beaches of Normandy, routing the enemy, then moving out to dominate surrounding areas of Normandy. In other

words, establish a beachhead, then broaden the basis of operations.

Serving the needs of a particular segment is all about focusing the company's resources on customizing the product to the needs of that segment. The segment wants a customized solution. It wants the "whole product" with all relevant services, not 80 percent of the whole product with the responsibility of supplying the missing 20 percent itself. Sales in several segments would soon stretch the company's development resources to the breaking point as it tried to customize the product to each segment's needs. Lotus Notes managed to escape the chasm when it focused on the global account management sector; particularly on worldwide accounting and consulting firms.

In addition, niche sales are driven by references and word-of-mouth within that niche. Failure to build up a core level of business in a particular segment means that momentum in any one single segment is never established. Pragmatists and conservatives talk to people in their own industry and look for solutions that have been proven to work there.

Tactical Alliances. Companies sometimes have the opportunity to form tactical alliances with smaller firms to help put a "complete product" in place. Market niches will coalesce behind a product much more readily—elevating it effectively to the position of a standard—if that product is supported by a number of products that fill in the gaps the market values but that the main product could not possibly supply. Producers of software packages often welcome the entry of smaller firms with their add-on programs to help provide the fully rounded complete product. It is a matter of gathering the appropriate partners and allies to jointly deliver a more complete product.

This is, however, very different from the cooperation/licensing/alliance approach discussed earlier, which is more formal and strategic. Tactical alliances tend to occur spontaneously at a later stage in a technology's development as smaller companies, realizing that a product has the potential to become a standard, desire to become associated with that standard.

Introducing a new technology offers a marketplace the first opportunity to experience the brand new product. So the manner in which the introduction is handled is critical. Everything has to come together in what is usually a narrow window of opportunity. Get it wrong, and there may be little time to put things right. By this stage, the investment in the new technology may be considerable, yet the chances of rejection or indifference are quite high.

The strategies proposed here are all designed to reduce the risks of failure. Of course, a complete and consistent strategy will assemble one or more components from each of the preparation, targeting, positioning, and execution stages.

Technology-intensive products and companies are at the leading edge of many Western countries' economies. By examining the range of illustrations included here, it is hoped that managers can help the new technology take its intended role in these economies.

References

W. Brian Arthur, "Increasing Returns and the New World of Business," *Harvard Business Review*, July–August 1996, pp. 100–109.

Christopher Easingwood and Simon O. Lunn, "Diffusion Paths in a High-Tech Environment: Clusters and Commonalities," *R&D Management, 22,* 1 (1992): 69–80.

Geoffrey A. Moore, *Crossing the Chasm: Marketing and Selling High-Technology Products to Mainstream Customers* (New York: HarperBusiness, 1991).

Geoffrey A. Moore, *Inside the Tornado: Marketing Strategies from Silicon Valley's Cutting Edge* (New York: HarperBusiness, 1995).

Charles P. Wallace, "The Man Bill Gates Fears Most," *Fortune*, November 23, 1998, pp. 257–260.

Chris Easingwood is the Caudwell Professor of Marketing and Head of Marketing and Strategy at Manchester Business School, Manchester, England, where **Anthony Koustelos** was an MBA student before becoming a market analyst with the Competitive Intelligence Unit, Business Development Group, DHL Worldwide Network NV/SA Brussels, Belgium.

Marketing myopia
(With Retrospective Commentary)

Shortsighted managements often fail to recognize that in fact there is no such thing as a growth industry

Theodore Levitt

How can a company ensure its continued growth? In 1960 "Marketing Myopia" answered that question in a new and challenging way by urging organizations to define their industries broadly to take advantage of growth opportunities. Using the archetype of the railroads, Mr. Levitt showed how they declined inevitably as technology advanced because they defined themselves too narrowly. To continue growing, companies must ascertain and act on their customers' needs and desires, not bank on the presumptive longevity of their products. The success of the article testifies to the validity of its message. It has been widely quoted and anthologized, and HBR has sold more than 265,000 reprints of it. The author of 14 subsequent articles in HBR, Mr. Levitt is one of the magazine's most prolific contributors. In a retrospective commentary, he considers the use and misuse that have been made of "Marketing Myopia," describing its many interpretations and hypothesizing about its success.

Every major industry was once a growth industry. But some that are now riding a wave of growth enthusiasm are very much in the shadow of decline. Others which are thought of as seasoned growth industries have actually stopped growing. In every case the reason growth is threatened, slowed, or stopped is *not* be-

cause the market is saturated. It is because there has been a failure of management.

Fateful purposes: The failure is at the top. The executives responsible for it, in the last analysis, are those who deal with broad aims and policies. Thus:

• The railroads did not stop growing because the need for passenger and freight transportation declined. That grew. The railroads are in trouble today not because the need was filled by others (cars, trucks, airplanes, even telephones), but because it was *not* filled by the railroads themselves. They let others take customers away from them because they assumed themselves to be in the railroad business rather than in the transportation business. The reason they defined their industry wrong was because they were railroad-oriented instead of transportation-oriented; they were product-oriented instead of customer-oriented.

• Hollywood barely escaped being totally ravished by television. Actually, all the established film companies went through drastic reorganizations. Some simply disappeared. All of them got into trouble not because of TV's inroads but because of their own myopia. As with the railroads, Hollywood defined its business incorrectly. It thought it was in the movie business when it was actually in the entertainment business. "Movies" implied a specific, limited product. This produced a

fatuous contentment which from the beginning led producers to view TV as a threat. Hollywood scorned and rejected TV when it should have welcomed it as an opportunity—an opportunity to expand the entertainment business.

Today TV is a bigger business than the old narrowly defined movie business ever was. Had Hollywood been customer-oriented (providing entertainment), rather then product-oriented (making movies), would it have gone through the fiscal purgatory that it did? I doubt it. What ultimately saved Hollywood and accounted for its recent resurgence was the wave of new young writers, producers, and directors whose previous successes in television had decimated the old movie companies and toppled the big movie moguls.

There are other less obvious examples of industries that have been and are now endangering their futures by improperly defining their purposes. I shall discuss some in detail later and analyze the kind of policies that lead to trouble. Right now it may help to show what a thoroughly customer-oriented management can do to keep a growth industry growing, even after the obvious opportunities have been exhausted; and here there are two examples that have been around for a long time. They are nylon and glass—specifically,

E. I. duPont de Nemours & Company and Corning Glass Works.

Both companies have great technical competence. Their product orientation is unquestioned. But this alone does not explain their success. After all, who was more pridefully product-oriented and product-conscious than the erstwhile New England textile companies that have been so thoroughly massacred? The DuPonts and the Cornings have succeded not primarily because of their product or research orientation but because they have been thoroughly customer-oriented also. It is constant watchfulness for opportunities to apply their technical knowhow to the creation of customer-satisfying uses which accounts for their prodigious output of successful new products. Without a very sophisticated eye on the customer, most of their new products might have been wrong, their sales methods useless.

Aluminum has also continued to be a growth industry, thanks to the efforts of two wartime-created companies which deliberately set about creating new customer-satisfying uses. Without Kaiser Aluminum & Chemical Corporation and Reynolds Metals Company, the total demand for aluminum today would be vastly less.

Error of analysis: Some may argue that it is foolish to set the railroads off against aluminum or the movies off against glass. Are not aluminum and glass naturally so versatile that the industries are bound to have more growth opportunities than the railroads and movies? This view commits precisely the error I have been talking about. It defines an industry, or a product, or a cluster of know-how so narrowly as to guarantee its premature senescence. When we mention "railroads," we should make sure we mean "transportation." As transporters, the railroads still have a good chance for very considerable growth. They are not limited to the railroad business as such (though in my opinion rail transportation is potentially a much stronger transportation medium than is generally believed).

What the railroads lack is not opportunity, but some of the same managerial imaginativeness and audacity that made them great. Even an amateur like Jacques Barzun can see what is lacking when he says:

"I grieve to see the most advanced physical and social organization of the last century go down in shabby disgrace for lack of the same comprehensive imagination that built it up. [What is lacking is] the will of the companies to survive and to satisfy the public by inventiveness and skill."[1]

Shadow of obsolescence

It is impossible to mention a single major industry that did not at one time qualify for the magic appellation of "growth industry." In each case its assumed strength lay in the apparently unchallenged superiority of its product. There appeared to be no effective substitute for it. It was itself a runaway substitute for the product it so triumphantly replaced. Yet one after another of these celebrated industries has come under a shadow. Let us look briefly at a few more of them, this time taking examples that have so far received a little less attention:

• *Dry cleaning*—This was once a growth industry with lavish prospects. In an age of wool garments, imagine being finally able to get them safely and easily clean. The boom was on.

Yet here we are 30 years after the boom started and the industry is in trouble. Where has the competition come from? From a better way of cleaning? No. It has come from synthetic fibers and chemical additives that have cut the need for dry cleaning. But this is only the beginning. Lurking in the wings and ready to make chemical dry cleaning totally obsolescent is that powerful magician, ultrasonics.

• *Electric utilities*—This is another one of those supposedly "no-substitute" products that has been enthroned on a pedestal of invincible growth. When the incandescent lamp came along, kerosene lights were finished. Later the water wheel and the steam engine were cut to ribbons by the flexibility, reliability, simplicity, and just plain easy availability of electric motors. The prosperity of electric utilities continues to wax extravagant as the home is converted into a museum of electric gadgetry. How can anybody miss by investing in utilities, with no competition, nothing but growth ahead?

But a second look is not quite so comforting. A score of nonutility companies are well advanced toward developing a powerful chemical fuel cell which could sit in some hidden closet of every home silently ticking off electric power. The electric lines that vulgarize so many neighborhoods will be eliminated. So will the endless demolition of streets and service interruptions during storms. Also on the horizon is solar energy, again pioneered by nonutility companies.

Who says that the utilities have no competition? They may be natural monopolies now, but tomorrow they may be natural deaths. To avoid this prospect, they too will have to develop fuel cells, solar energy, and other power sources. To survive, they themselves will have to plot the obsolescence of what now produces their livelihood.

• *Grocery stores*—Many people find it hard to realize that there ever was a thriving establishment known as the "corner grocery store." The supermarket has taken over with a powerful effectiveness. Yet the big food chains of the 1930s narrowly escaped being completely wiped out by the aggressive expansion of independent supermarkets. The first genuine supermarket was opened in 1930, in Jamaica, Long Island. By 1933 supermarkets were thriving in California, Ohio, Pennsylvania, and elsewhere. Yet the established chains pompously ignored them. When they chose to notice them, it was with such derisive descriptions as "cheapy," "horse-and-buggy," "cracker-barrel storekeeping," and "unethical opportunists."

The executive of one big chain announced at the time that he found it "hard to believe that people will drive for miles to shop for foods and sacrifice the personal service chains have perfected and to which Mrs. Consumer is accustomed."[2] As late as 1936, the National Wholesale Grocers convention and the New Jersey Retail Grocers Association said there was nothing to fear. They said that the supers' narrow appeal to the price buyer limited the size of their market. They had to draw from miles around. When imitators came, there would be wholesale liquidations as volume fell. The current high sales of the supers was said to be partly due to their novelty. Basically people wanted convenient neighborhood grocers. If the neighborhood stores "cooperate with their suppliers, pay attention to their costs, and improve their service," they would be able to weather the competition until it blew over.[3]

It never blew over. The chains discovered that survival required going into the supermarket business. This meant the wholesale destruction of their huge investments in corner store sites and in established distribution and merchandising methods. The companies with "the courage of their convictions" resolutely stuck to the corner store philosophy. They kept their pride but lost their shirts.

Self-deceiving cycle: But memories are short. For example, it is hard for people who today confidently hail the twin messiahs of electronics and chemicals to see how things could possibly go wrong with these galloping industries. They probably also cannot see how a reasonably sensible businessman could have been as myopic as the famous Boston millionaire who 50 years ago unintentionally sentenced his heirs to poverty by stipulating that his entire estate be forever invested exclusively in electric streetcar securities. His posthumous declaration, "There will always be a big demand for efficient urban transportation," is no consolation to his heirs who sustain life by pumping gasoline at automobile filling stations.

Yet, in a casual survey I recently took among a group of intelligent business executives, nearly half agreed that it would be hard to hurt their heirs by tying their estates forever to the electronics industry. When I then confronted them with the Boston streetcar example, they chorused unanimously, "That's different!" But is it? Is not the basic situation identical?

In truth, *there is no such thing* as a growth industry, I believe. There are only companies organized and operated to create and capitalize on growth opportunities. Industries that assume themselves to be riding some automatic growth escalator invariably descend into stagnation. The history of every dead and dying "growth" industry shows a self-deceiving cycle of bountiful expansion and undetected decay. There are four conditions which usually guarantee this cycle:

1. The belief that growth is assured by an expanding and more affluent population.
2. The belief that there is no competitive substitute for the industry's major product.
3. Too much faith in mass production and in the advantages of rapidly declining unit costs as output rises.
4. Preoccupation with a product that lends itself to carefully controlled scientific experimentation, improvement, and manufacturing cost reduction.

I should like now to begin examining each of these conditions in some detail. To build my case as boldly as possible, I shall illustrate the points with reference to three industries—petroleum, automobiles, and electronics—particularly petroleum, because it spans more years and more vicissitudes. Not only do these three have

excellent reputations with the general public and also enjoy the confidence of sophisticated investors, but their managements have become known for progressive thinking in areas like financial control, product research, and management training. If obsolescence can cripple even these industries, it can happen anywhere.

Population myth

The belief that profits are assured by an expanding and more affluent population is dear to the heart of every industry. It takes the edge off the apprehensions everybody understandably feels about the future. If consumers are multiplying and also buying more of your product or service, you can face the future with considerably more comfort than if the market is shrinking. An expanding market keeps the manufacturer from having to think very hard or imaginatively. If thinking is an intellectual response to a problem, then the absence of a problem leads to the absence of thinking. If your product has an automatically expanding market, then you will not give much thought to how to expand it.

One of the most interesting examples of this is provided by the petroleum industry. Probably our oldest growth industry, it has an enviable record. While there are some current apprehensions about its growth rate, the industry itself tends to be optimistic.

But I believe it can be demonstrated that it is undergoing a fundamental yet typical change. It is not only ceasing to be a growth industry, but may actually be a declining one, relative to other business. Although there is widespread unawareness of it, I believe that within 25 years the oil industry may find itself in much the same position of retrospective glory that the railroads are now in. Despite its pioneering work in developing and applying the present-value method of investment evaluation, in employee relations, and in working with backward countries, the petroleum business is a distressing example of how complacency and wrongheadedness can stubbornly convert opportunity into near disaster.

One of the characteristics of this and other industries that have believed very strongly in the beneficial consequences of an expanding population, while at the same time being industries with a generic product for which there has appeared to be no competitive substitute, is that the individual companies have sought to outdo their competitors by improving on what they are already doing. This makes sense, of

course, if one assumes that sales are tied to the country's population strings, because the customer can compare products only on a feature-by-feature basis. I believe it is significant, for example, that not since John D. Rockefeller sent free kerosene lamps to China has the oil industry done anything really outstanding to create a demand for its product. Not even in product improvement has it showered itself with eminence. The greatest single improvement—namely, the development of tetraethyl lead—came from outside the industry, specifically from General Motors and DuPont. The big contributions made by the industry itself are confined to the technology of oil exploration, production, and refining.

Asking for trouble: In other words, the industry's efforts have focused on improving the *efficiency* of getting and making its product, not really on improving the generic product or its marketing. Moreover, its chief product has continuously been defined in the narrowest possible terms, namely, gasoline, not energy, fuel, or transportation. This attitude has helped assure that:

• Major improvements in gasoline quality tend not to originate in the oil industry. Also, the development of superior alternative fuels comes from outside the oil industry, as will be shown later.

• Major innovations in automobile fuel marketing are originated by small new oil companies that are not primarily preoccupied with production or refining. These are the companies that have been responsible for the rapidly expanding multipump gasoline stations, with their successful emphasis on large and clean layouts, rapid and efficient driveway service, and quality gasoline at low prices.

Thus, the oil industry is asking for trouble from outsiders. Sooner or later, in this land of hungry inventors and entrepreneurs, a threat is sure to come. The possibilities of this will become more apparent when we turn to the next dangerous belief of many managements. For the sake of continuity, because this second belief is tied closely to the first, I shall continue with the same example.

Idea of indispensability: The petroleum industry is pretty much persuaded that there is no competitive substitute for its major product, gasoline—or if there is, that it will continue to be a derivative of crude oil, such as diesel fuel or kerosene jet fuel.

There is a lot of automatic wishful thinking in this assumption. The trouble is that most refining companies own huge amounts of crude oil reserves. These have value only if there is a market for products into which oil can be converted—hence the tenacious belief in the continuing competitive superiority of automobile fuels made from crude oil.

This idea persists despite all historic evidence against it. The evidence not only shows that oil has never been a superior product for any purpose for very long, but it also shows that the oil industry has never really been a growth industry. It has been a succession of different businesses that have gone through the usual historic cycles of growth, maturity, and decay. Its overall survival is owed to a series of miraculous escapes from total obsolescence, of last-minute and unexpected reprieves from total disaster reminiscent of the Perils of Pauline.

Perils of petroleum: I shall sketch in only the main episodes.

First, crude oil was largely a patent medicine. But even before that fad ran out, demand was greatly expanded by the use of oil in kerosene lamps. The prospect of lighting the world's lamps gave rise to an extravagant promise of growth. The prospects were similar to those the industry now holds for gasoline in other parts of the world. It can hardly wait for the underdeveloped nations to get a car in every garage.

In the days of the kerosene lamp, the oil companies competed with each other and against gaslight by trying to improve the illuminating characteristics of kerosene. Then suddenly the impossible happened. Edison invented a light which was totally nondependent on crude oil. Had it not been for the growing use of kerosene in space heaters, the incandescent lamp would have completely finished oil as a growth industry at that time. Oil would have been good for little else than axle grease.

Then disaster and reprieve struck again. Two great innovations occurred, neither originating in the oil industry. The successful development of coal-burning domestic central-heating systems made the space heater obsolescent. While the industry reeled, along came its most magnificent boost yet—the internal combustion engine, also invented by outsiders. Then when the prodigious expansion for gasoline finally began to level off in the 1920s, along came the miraculous escape of a central oil heater. Once again, the escape was

provided by an outsider's invention and development. And when that market weakened, wartime demand for aviation fuel came to the rescue. After the war the expansion of civilian aviation, the dieselization of railroads, and the explosive demand for cars and trucks kept the industry's growth in high gear.

Meanwhile, centralized oil heating—whose boom potential had only recently been proclaimed—ran into severe competition from natural gas. While the oil companies themselves owned the gas that now competed with their oil, the industry did not originate the natural gas revolution, nor has it to this day greatly profited from its gas ownership. The gas revolution was made by newly formed transmission companies that marketed the product with an aggressive ardor. They started a magnificent new industry, first against the advice and then against the resistance of the oil companies.

By all the logic of the situation, the oil companies themselves should have made the gas revolution. They not only owned the gas; they also were the only people experienced in handling, scrubbing, and using it, the only people experienced in pipeline technology and transmission, and they understood heating problems. But, partly because they knew that natural gas would compete with their own sale of heating oil, the oil companies pooh-poohed the potentials of gas.

The revolution was finally started by oil pipeline executives who, unable to persuade their own companies to go into gas, quit and organized the spectacularly successful gas transmission companies. Even after their success became painfully evident to the oil companies, the latter did not go into gas transmission. The multibillion dollar business which should have been theirs went to others. As in the past, the industry was blinded by its narrow preoccupation with a specific product and the value of its reserves. It paid little or no attention to its customers' basic needs and preferences.

The postwar years have not witnessed any change. Immediately after World War II the oil industry was greatly encouraged about its future by the rapid expansion of demand for its traditional line of products. In 1950 most companies projected annual rates of domestic expansion of around 6% through at least 1975. Though the ratio of crude oil reserves to demand in the Free World was about 20 to 1, with 10 to 1 being usually considered a reasonable work-

ing ratio in the United States, booming demand sent oil men searching for more without sufficient regard to what the future really promised. In 1952 they "hit" in the Middle East; the ratio skyrocketed to 42 to 1. If gross additions to reserves continue at the average rate of the past five years (37 billion barrels annually), then by 1970 the reserve ratio will be up to 45 to 1. This abundance of oil has weakened crude and product prices all over the world.

Uncertain future: Management cannot find much consolation today in the rapidly expanding petrochemical industry, another oil-using idea that did not originate in the leading firms. The total United States production of petrochemicals is equivalent to about 2% (by volume) of the demand for all petroleum products. Although the petrochemical industry is now expected to grow by about 10% per year, this will not offset other drains on the growth of crude oil consumption. Furthermore, while petrochemical products are many and growing, it is well to remember that there are nonpetroleum sources of the basic raw material, such as coal. Besides, a lot of plastics can be produced with relatively little oil. A 5,000-barrel-per-day oil refinery is now considered the absolute minimum size for efficiency. But a 5,000-barrel-per-day chemical plant is a giant operation.

Oil has never been a continuously strong growth industry. It has grown by fits and starts, always miraculously saved by innovations and developments not of its own making. The reason it has not grown in a smooth progression is that each time it thought it had a superior product safe from the possibility of competitive substitutes, the product turned out to be inferior and notoriously subject to obsolescence. Until now, gasoline (for motor fuel, anyhow) has escaped this fate. But, as we shall see later, it too may be on its last legs.

The point of all this is that there is no guarantee against product obsolescence. If a company's own research does not make it obsolete, another's will. Unless an industry is especially lucky, as oil has been until now, it can easily go down in a sea of red figures—just as the railroads have, as the buggy whip manufacturers have, as the corner grocery chains have, as most of the big movie companies have, and indeed as many other industries have.

The best way for a firm to be lucky is to make its own luck. That requires knowing what makes a business successful. One of the greatest enemies of this knowledge is mass production.

Production pressures

Mass-production industries are impelled by a great drive to produce all they can. The prospect of steeply declining unit costs as output rises is more than most companies can usually resist. The profit possibilities look spectacular. All effort focuses on production. The result is that marketing gets neglected.

John Kenneth Galbraith contends that just the opposite occurs.[4] Output is so prodigious that all effort concentrates on trying to get rid of it. He says this accounts for singing commercials, desecration of the countryside with advertising signs, and other wasteful and vulgar practices. Galbraith has a finger on something real, but he misses the strategic point. Mass production does indeed generate great pressure to "move" the product. But what usually gets emphasized is selling, not marketing. Marketing, being a more sophisticated and complex process, gets ignored.

The difference between marketing and selling is more than semantic. Selling focuses on the needs of the seller, marketing on the needs of the buyer. Selling is preoccupied with the seller's need to convert his product into cash, marketing with the idea of satisfying the needs of the customer by means of the product and the whole cluster of things associated with creating, delivering, and finally consuming it.

In some industries the enticements of full mass production have been so powerful that for many years top management in effect has told the sales departments, "You get rid of it; we'll worry about profits." By contrast, a truly marketing-minded firm tries to create value-satisfying goods and services that consumers will want to buy. What it offers for sale includes not only the generic product or service, but also how it is made available to the customer, in what form, when, under what conditions, and at what terms of trade. Most important, what it offers for sale is determined not by the seller but by the buyer. The seller takes his cues from the buyer in such a way that the product becomes a consequence of the marketing effort, not vice versa.

Lag in Detroit: This may sound like an elementary rule of business, but that does not keep it from being violated wholesale. It is certainly more violated than honored. Take the automobile industry.

Here mass production is most famous, most honored, and has the greatest impact on the entire society. The industry has hitched its fortune to the relentless requirements of the annual model change, a policy that makes customer orientation an especially urgent necessity. Consequently the auto companies annually spend millions of dollars on consumer research. But the fact that the new compact cars are selling so well in their first year indicates that Detroit's vast researches have for a long time failed to reveal what the customer really wanted. Detroit was not persuaded that he wanted anything different from what he had been getting until it lost millions of customers to other small car manufacturers.

How could this unbelievable lag behind consumer wants have been perpetuated so long? Why did not research reveal consumer preferences before consumers' buying decisions themselves revealed the facts? Is that not what consumer research is for—to find out before the fact what is going to happen? The answer is that Detroit never really researched the customer's wants. It only researched his preferences between the kinds of things which it had already decided to offer him. For Detroit is mainly product-oriented, not customer-oriented. To the extent that the customer is recognized as having needs that the manufacturer should try to satisfy, Detroit usually acts as if the job can be done entirely by product changes. Occasionally attention gets paid to financing, too, but that is done more in order to sell than to enable the customer to buy.

As for taking care of other customer needs, there is not enough being done to write about. The areas of the greatest unsatisfied needs are ignored, or at best get stepchild attention. These are at the point of sale and on the matter of automotive repair and maintenance. Detroit views these problem areas as being of secondary importance. That is underscored by the fact that the retailing and servicing ends of this industry are neither owned and operated nor controlled by the manufacturers. Once the car is produced, things are pretty much in the dealer's inadequate hands. Illustrative of Detroit's arm's-length attitude is the fact that, while servicing holds enormous sales-stimulating, profit-building opportunities, only 57 of Chevrolet's 7,000 dealers provide night maintenance service.

Motorists repeatedly express their dissatisfaction with servicing and their apprehensions about buying cars under the present selling setup. The anxieties and problems they encounter during the auto buying and maintenance processes are probably more intense and widespread today than 30 years ago. Yet the automobile companies do not *seem* to listen to or take their cues from the anguished consumer. If they do listen, it must be through the filter of their own preoccupation with production. The marketing effort is still viewed as a necessary consequence of the product, not vice versa, as it should be. That is the legacy of mass production, with its parochial view that profit resides essentially in low-cost full production.

What Ford put first: The profit lure of mass production obviously has a place in the plans and strategy of business management, but it must always *follow* hard thinking about the customer. This is one of the most important lessons that we can learn from the contradictory behavior of Henry Ford. In a sense Ford was both the most brilliant and the most senseless marketer in American history. He was senseless because he refused to give the customer anything but a black car. He was brilliant because he fashioned a production system designed to fit market needs. We habitually celebrate him for the wrong reason, his production genius. His real genius was marketing. We think he was able to cut his selling price and therefore sell millions of $500 cars because his invention of the assembly line had reduced the costs. Actually he invented the assembly line because he had concluded that at $500 he could sell millions of cars. Mass production was the *result* not the cause of his low prices.

Ford repeatedly emphasized this point, but a nation of production-oriented business managers refuses to hear the great lesson he taught. Here is his operating philosophy as he expressed it succinctly:

"Our policy is to reduce the price, extend the operations, and improve the article. You will notice that the reduction of price comes first. We have never considered any costs as fixed. Therefore we first reduce the price to the point where we believe more sales will result. Then we go ahead and try to make the prices. We do not bother about the costs. The new price forces the costs down. The more usual way is to take the costs and then determine the price; and although that method may be scientific in the narrow sense, it is not scientific in the broad sense, because what earthly use is it to know the cost if it tells you that you cannot manufacture at a price at which the article can be sold? But more to the point is the fact that, although one may calculate what a cost is, and of course all of our costs are carefully calculated, no one knows what a cost ought to be. One of the ways of discovering … is to name a price so low as to force everybody in the place to the highest point of efficiency.

The low price makes everybody dig for profits. We make more discoveries concerning manufacturing and selling under this forced method than by any method of leisurely investigation."[5]

Product provincialism: The tantalizing profit possibilities of low unit production costs may be the most seriously self-deceiving attitude that can afflict a company, particularly a "growth" company where an apparently assured expansion of demand already tends to undermine a proper concern for the importance of marketing and the customer.

The usual result of this narrow preoccupation with so-called concrete matters is that instead of growing, the industry declines. It usually means that the product fails to adapt to the constantly changing patterns of consumer needs and tastes, to new and modified marketing institutions and practices, or to product developments in competing or complementary industries. The industry has its eyes so firmly on its own specific product that it does not see how it is being made obsolete.

The classical example of this is the buggy whip industry. No amount of product improvement could stave off its death sentence. But had the industry defined itself as being in the transportation business rather than the buggy whip business, it might have survived. It would have done what survival always entails, that is, changing. Even if it had only defined its business as providing a stimulant or catalyst to an energy source, it might have survived by becoming a manufacturer of, say, fanbelts or air cleaners.

What may some day be a still more classical example is, again, the oil industry. Having let others steal marvelous opportunities from it (e.g., natural gas, as already mentioned, missile fuels, and jet engine lubricants), one would expect it to have taken steps never to let that happen again. But this is not the case. We are now getting extraordinary new developments in fuel systems specifically designed to power automobiles. Not only are these developments concentrated in firms outside the petroleum industry, but petroleum is almost systematically ignoring them, securely content in its wedded bliss to oil. It is the story of the kerosene lamp versus the incandescent lamp all over again. Oil is trying to improve hydrocarbon fuels rather than develop *any* fuels best suited to the needs of their users, whether or not made in different ways and with different raw materials from oil.

Here are some things which nonpetroleum companies are working on:

• Over a dozen such firms now have advanced working models of energy systems which, when perfected, will replace the internal combustion engine and eliminate the demand for gasoline. The superior merit of each of these systems is their elimination of frequent, time-consuming, and irritating refueling stops. Most of these systems are fuel cells designed to create electrical energy directly from chemicals without combustion. Most of them use chemicals that are not derived from oil, generally hydrogen and oxygen.

• Several other companies have advanced models of electric storage batteries designed to power automobiles. One of these is an aircraft producer that is working jointly with several electric utility companies. The latter hope to use off-peak generating capacity to supply overnight plug-in battery regeneration. Another company, also using the battery approach, is a medium-size electronics firm with extensive small-battery experience that it developed in connection with its work on hearing aids. It is collaborating with an automobile manufacturer. Recent improvements arising from the need for high-powered miniature power storage plants in rockets have put us within reach of a relatively small battery capable of withstanding great overloads or surges of power. Germanium diode applications and batteries using sintered-plate and nickel-cadmium techniques promise to make a revolution in our energy sources.

• Solar energy conversion systems are also getting increasing attention. One usually cautious Detroit auto executive recently ventured that solar-powered cars might be common by 1980.

As for the oil companies, they are more or less "watching developments," as one research director put it to me. A few are doing a bit of research on fuel cells, but almost always confined to developing cells powered by hydrocarbon chemicals. None of them are enthusiastically researching fuel cells, batteries, or solar power plants. None of them are spending a fraction as much on research in these profoundly important areas as they are on the usual run-of-the-mill things like reducing combustion chamber deposit in gasoline engines. One major integrated petroleum company recently took a tentative look at the fuel cell and concluded that although "the companies actively working on it indicate a belief in ultimate success ... the

timing and magnitude of its impact are too remote to warrant recognition in our forecasts."

One might, of course, ask: Why should the oil companies do anything different? Would not chemical fuel cells, batteries, or solar energy kill the present product lines? The answer is that they would indeed, and that is precisely the reason for the oil firms having to develop these power units before their competitors, so they will not be companies without an industry.

Management might be more likely to do what is needed for its own preservation if it thought of itself as being in the energy business. But even that would not be enough if it persists in imprisoning itself in the narrow grip of its tight product orientation. It has to think of itself as taking care of customer needs, not finding, refining, or even selling oil. Once it genuinely thinks of its business as taking care of people's transportation needs, nothing can stop it from creating its own extravagantly profitable growth.

'Creative destruction': Since words are cheap and deeds are dear, it may be appropriate to indicate what this kind of thinking involves and leads to. Let us start at the beginning—the customer. It can be shown that motorists strongly dislike the bother, delay, and experience of buying gasoline. People actually do not buy gasoline. They cannot see it, taste it, feel it, appreciate it, or really test it. What they buy is the right to continue driving their cars. The gas station is like a tax collector to whom people are compelled to pay a periodic toll as the price of using their cars. This makes the gas station a basically unpopular institution. It can never be made popular or pleasant, only less unpopular, less unpleasant.

To reduce its unpopularity completely means eliminating it. Nobody likes a tax collector, not even a pleasantly cheerful one. Nobody likes to interrupt a trip to buy a phantom product, not even from a handsome Adonis or a seductive Venus. Hence, companies that are working on exotic fuel substitutes which will eliminate the need for frequent refueling are heading directly into the outstretched arms of the irritated motorist. They are riding a wave of inevitability, not because they are creating something which is technologically superior or more sophisticated, but because they are satisfying a powerful customer need. They are also eliminating noxious odors and air pollution.

Once the petroleum companies recognize the customer-satisfying logic of what another power system can do they will see that they have no more choice about working on an efficient, long-lasting fuel (or some way of delivering present fuels without bothering the motorist) than the big food chains had a choice about going into the supermarket business, or the vacuum tube companies had a choice about making semiconductors. For their own good the oil firms will have to destroy their own highly profitable assets. No amount of wishful thinking can save them from the necessity of engaging in this form of "creative destruction."

I phrase the need as strongly as this because I think management must make quite an effort to break itself loose from conventional ways. It is all too easy in this day and age for a company or industry to let its sense of purpose become dominated by the economies of full production and to develop a dangerously lopsided product orientation. In short, if management lets itself drift, it invariably drifts in the direction of thinking of itself as producing goods and services, not customer satisfactions. While it probably will not descend to the depths of telling its salesmen, "You get rid of it; we'll worry about profits," it can, without knowing it, be practicing precisely that formula for withering decay. The historic fate of one growth industry after another has been its suicidal product provincialism.

Dangers of R&D

Another big danger to a firm's continued growth arises when top management is wholly transfixed by the profit possibilities of technical research and development. To illustrate I shall turn first to a new industry—electronics—and then return once more to the oil companies. By comparing a fresh example with a familiar one, I hope to emphasize the prevalence and insidiousness of a hazardous way of thinking.

Marketing shortchanged: In the case of electronics, the greatest danger which faces the glamorous new companies in this field is not that they do not pay enough attention to research and development, but that they pay *too much* attention to it. And the fact that the fastest growing electronics firms owe their eminence to their heavy emphasis on technical research is completely beside the point. They have vaulted to affluence on a sudden crest of unusually strong general receptiveness to new technical ideas. Also, their success has been shaped in the virtually guaranteed market of military subsidies and by military orders that in many cases actually preceded the existence of facilities to make the products.

Their expansion has, in other words, been almost totally devoid of marketing effort.

Thus, they are growing up under conditions that come dangerously close to creating the illusion that a superior product will sell itself. Having created a successful company by making a superior product, it is not surprising that management continues to be oriented toward the product rather than the people who consume it. It develops the philosophy that continued growth is a matter of continued product innovation and improvement.

A number of other factors tend to strengthen and sustain this belief:

1. Because electronic products are highly complex and sophisticated, managements become top-heavy with engineers and scientists. This creates a selective bias in favor of research and production at the expense of marketing. The organization tends to view itself as making things rather than satisfying customer needs. Marketing gets treated as a residual activity, "something else" that must be done once the vital job of product creation and production is completed.

2. To this bias in favor of product research, development, and production is added the bias in favor of dealing with controllable variables. Engineers and scientists are at home in the world of concrete things like machines, test tubes, production lines, and even balance sheets. The abstractions to which they feel kindly are those which are testable or manipulatable in the laboratory, or, if not testable, then functional, such as Euclid's axioms. In short, the managements of the new glamour-growth companies tend to favor those business activities which lend themselves to careful study, experimentation, and control—the hard, practical realities of the lab, the shop, the books.

What gets shortchanged are the realities of the *market*. Consumers are unpredictable, varied, fickle, stupid, shortsighted, stubborn, and generally bothersome. This is not what the engineer-managers say, but deep down in their consciousness it is what they believe. And this accounts for their concentrating on what they know and what they can control, namely, product research, engineering, and production. The emphasis on production becomes particularly attractive when the product can be made at declining unit costs. There is no more in-

viting way of making money than by running the plant full blast.

Today the top-heavy science-engineering-production orientation of so many electronics companies works reasonably well because they are pushing into new frontiers in which the armed services have pioneered virtually assured markets. The companies are in the felicitous position of having to fill, not find markets; of not having to discover what the customer needs and wants, but of having the customer voluntarily come forward with specific new product demands. If a team of consultants had been assigned specifically to design a business situation calculated to prevent the emergence and development of a customer-oriented marketing viewpoint, it could not have produced anything better than the conditions just described.

Stepchild treatment: The oil industry is a stunning example of how science, technology, and mass production can divert an entire group of companies from their main task. To the extent the consumer is studied at all (which is not much), the focus is forever on getting information which is designed to help the oil companies improve what they are now doing. They try to discover more convincing advertising themes, more effective sales promotional drives, what the market shares of the various companies are, what people like or dislike about service station dealers and oil companies, and so forth. Nobody seems as interested in probing deeply into the basic human needs that the industry might be trying to satisfy as in probing into the basic properties of the raw material that the companies work with in trying to deliver customer satisfactions.

Basic questions about customers and markets seldom get asked. The latter occupy a stepchild status. They are recognized as existing, as having to be taken care of, but not worth very much real thought or dedicated attention. Nobody gets as excited about the customers in his own backyard as about the oil in the Sahara Desert. Nothing illustrates better the neglect of marketing than its treatment in the industry press.

The centennial issue of the *American Petroleum Institute Quarterly*, published in 1959 to celebrate the discovery of oil in Titusville, Pennsylvania, contained 21 feature articles proclaiming the industry's greatness. Only one of these talked about its achievements in marketing, and that was only a pictorial record of how service station architecture has changed. The issue also contained a special section on "New

Horizons," which was devoted to showing the magnificent role oil would play in America's future. Every reference was ebulliently optimistic, never implying once that oil might have some hard competition. Even the reference to atomic energy was a cheerful catalogue of how oil would help make atomic energy a success. There was not a single apprehension that the oil industry's affluence might be threatened or a suggestion that one "new horizon" might include new and better ways of serving oil's present customers.

But the most revealing example of the stepchild treatment that marketing gets was still another special series of short articles on "The Revolutionary Potential of Electronics." Under that heading this list of articles appeared in the table of contents:

- "In the Search for Oil"
- "In Production Operations"
- "In Refinery Processes"
- "In Pipeline Operations"

Significantly, every one of the industry's major functional areas is listed, *except* marketing. Why? Either it is believed that electronics holds no revolutionary potential for petroleum marketing (which is palpably wrong), or the editors forgot to discuss marketing (which is more likely, and illustrates its stepchild status).

The order in which the four functional areas are listed also betrays the alienation of the oil industry from the consumer. The industry is implicitly defined as beginning with the search for oil and ending with its distribution from the refinery. But the truth is, it seems to me, that the industry begins with the needs of the customer for its products. From that primal position its definition moves steadily back-stream to areas of progressively lesser importance, until it finally comes to rest at the "search for oil."

Beginning & end: The view that an industry is a customer-satisfying process, not a goods-producing process, is vital for all businessmen to understand. An industry begins with the customer and his needs, not with a patent, a raw material, or a selling skill. Given the customer's needs, the industry develops backwards, first concerning itself with the physical *delivery* of customer satisfactions. Then it moves back further to *creating* the things by which these satisfactions are in part achieved. How these materials are created is a matter of indifference to the customer, hence the particular form of manufacturing, processing, or what-have-you cannot be considered as a vital aspect of the industry.

Finally, the industry moves back still further to *finding* the raw materials necessary for making its products.

The irony of some industries oriented toward technical research and development is that the scientists who occupy the high executive positions are totally unscientific when it comes to defining their companies' overall needs and purposes. They violate the first two rules of the scientific method—being aware of and defining their companies' problems, and then developing testable hypotheses about solving them. They are scientific only about the convenient things, such as laboratory and product experiments.

The reason that the customer (and the satisfaction of his deepest needs) is not considered as being "the problem" is not because there is any certain belief that no such problem exists, but because an organizational lifetime has conditioned management to look in the opposite direction. Marketing is a stepchild.

I do not mean that selling is ignored. Far from it. But selling, again, is not marketing. As already pointed out, selling concerns itself with the tricks and techniques of getting people to exchange their cash for your product. It is not concerned with the values that the exchange is all about. And it does not, as marketing invariably does, view the entire business process as consisting of a tightly integrated effort to discover, create, arouse, and satisfy customer needs. The customer is somebody "out there" who, with proper cunning, can be separated from his loose change.

Actually, not even selling gets much attention in some technologically minded firms. Because there is a virtually guaranteed market for the abundant flow of their new products, they do not actually know what a real market is. It is as if they lived in a planned economy, moving their products routinely from factory to retail outlet. Their successful concentration on products tends to convince them of the soundness of what they have been doing, and they fail to see the gathering clouds over the market.

Conclusion

Less than 75 years ago American railroads enjoyed a fierce loyalty among astute Wall Streeters. European monarchs invested in them heavily. Eternal wealth was thought to be the benediction for anybody who could scrape a few thousand dollars together to put into rail stocks. No other form of transportation could compete with the railroads in speed, flexibility, durability, economy, and growth potentials.

As Jacques Barzun put it, "By the turn of the century it was an institution, an image of man, a tradition, a code of honor, a source of poetry, a nursery of boyhood desires, a sublimest of toys, and the most solemn machine—next to the funeral hearse—that marks the epochs in man's life."[6]

Even after the advent of automobiles, trucks, and airplanes, the railroad tycoons remained imperturbably self-confident. If you had told them 30 years ago that in 30 years they would be flat on their backs, broke, and pleading for government subsidies, they would have thought you totally demented. Such a future was simply not considered possible. It was not even a discussable subject, or an askable question, or a matter which any sane person would consider worth speculating about. The very thought was insane. Yet a lot of insane notions now have matter-of-fact acceptance—for example, the idea of 100-ton tubes of metal moving smoothly through the air 20,000 feet above the earth, loaded with 100 sane and solid citizens casually drinking martinis—and they have dealt cruel blows to the railroads.

What specifically must other companies do to avoid this fate? What does customer orientation involve? These questions have in part been answered by the preceding examples and analysis. It would take another article to show in detail what is required for specific industries. In any case, it should be obvious that building an effective customer-oriented company involves far more than good intentions or promotional tricks; it involves profound matters of human organization and leadership. For the present, let me merely suggest what appear to be some general requirements.

Visceral feel of greatness: Obviously the company has to do what survival demands. It has to adapt to the requirements of the market, and it has to do it sooner rather than later. But mere survival is a so-so aspiration. Anybody can survive in some way or other, even the skid-row bum. The trick is to survive gallantly, to feel the surging impulse of commercial mastery; not just to experience the sweet smell of success, but to have the visceral feel of entrepreneurial greatness.

No organization can achieve greatness without a vigorous leader who is driven onward by his own pulsating *will to succeed*. He has to have a vision of grandeur, a vision that can produce eager followers

25

in vast numbers. In business, the followers are the customers.

In order to produce these customers, the entire corporation must be viewed as a customer-creating and customer-satisfying organism. Management must think of itself not as producing products but as providing customer-creating value satisfactions. It must push this idea (and everything it means and requires) into every nook and cranny of the organization. It has to do this continuously and with the kind of flair that excites and stimulates the people in it. Otherwise, the company will be merely a series of pigeonholed parts, with no consolidating sense of purpose or direction.

In short, the organization must learn to think of itself not as producing goods or services but as *buying customers*, as doing the things that will make people *want* to do business with it. And the chief executive himself has the inescapable responsibility for creating this environment, this viewpoint, this attitude, this aspiration. He himself must set the company's style, its direction, and its goals. This means he has to know precisely where he himself wants to go, and to make sure the whole organization is enthusiastically aware of where that is. This is a first requisite of leadership, for *unless he knows where he is going, any road will take him there.*

If any road is okay, the chief executive might as well pack his attaché case and go fishing. If an organization does not know or care where it is going, it does not need to advertise that fact with a ceremonial figurehead. Everybody will notice it soon enough.

Retrospective commentary

Amazed, finally, by his literary success, Isaac Bashevis Singer reconciled an attendant problem: "I think the moment you have published a book, it's not any more your private property.... If it has value, everybody can find in it what he finds, and I cannot tell the man I did not intend it to be so." Over the past 15 years, "Marketing Myopia" has become a case in point. Remarkably, the article spawned a legion of loyal partisans—not to mention a host of unlikely bedfellows.

Its most common and, I believe, most influential consequence is the way certain companies for the first time gave serious thought to the question of what businesses they really are in.

The strategic consequences of this have in many cases been dramatic. The best-known case, of course, is the shift in thinking of oneself as being in the "oil business" to being in the "energy business." In some instances the payoff has been spectacular (getting into coal, for example) and in others dreadful (in terms of the time and money spent so far on fuel cell research). Another successful example is a company with a large chain of retail shoe stores that redefined itself as a retailer of moderately priced, frequently purchased, widely assorted consumer specialty products. The result was a dramatic growth in volume, earnings, and return on assets.

Some companies, again for the first time, asked themselves whether they wished to be masters of certain technologies for which they would seek markets, or be masters of markets for which they would seek customer-satisfying products and services.

Choosing the former, one company has declared, in effect, "We are experts in glass technology. We intend to improve and expand that expertise with the object of creating products that will attract customers." This decision has forced the company into a much more systematic and customer-sensitive look at possible markets and users, even though its stated strategic object has been to capitalize on glass technology.

Deciding to concentrate on markets, another company has determined that "we want to help people (primarily women) enhance their beauty and sense of youthfulness." This company has expanded its line of cosmetic products, but has also entered the fields of proprietary drugs and vitamin supplements.

All these examples illustrate the "policy" results of "Marketing Myopia." On the operating level, there has been, I think, an extraordinary heightening of sensitivity to customers and consumers. R&D departments have cultivated a greater "external" orientation toward uses, users, and markets—balancing thereby the previously one-sided "internal" focus on materials and methods; upper management has realized that marketing and sales departments should be somewhat more willingly accommodated than before, finance departments have become more receptive to the legitimacy of budgets for market research and experimentation in marketing, and salesmen have been better trained to listen to and understand customer needs and problems, rather than merely to "push" the product.

A mirror, not a window

My impression is that the article has had more impact in industrial-products compa-nies than in consumer-products companies—perhaps because the former had lagged most in customer orientation. There are at least two reasons for this lag: (1) industrial-products companies tend to be more capital intensive, and (2) in the past, at least, they have had to rely heavily on communicating face-to-face the technical character of what they made and sold. These points are worth explaining.

Capital-intensive businesses are understandably preoccupied with magnitudes, especially where the capital, once invested, cannot be easily moved, manipulated, or modified for the production of a variety of products—e.g., chemical plants, steel mills, airlines, and railroads. Understandably, they seek big volumes and operating efficiencies to pay off the equipment and meet the carrying costs.

At least one problem results: corporate power becomes disproportionately lodged with operating or financial executives. If you read the charter of one of the nation's largest companies, you will see that the chairman of the finance committee, not the chief executive officer, is the "chief." Executives with such backgrounds have an almost trained incapacity to see that getting "volume" may require understanding and serving many discrete and sometimes small market segments, rather than going after a perhaps mythical batch of big or homogeneous customers.

These executives also often fail to appreciate the competitive changes going on around them. They observe the changes, all right, but devalue their significance or underestimate their ability to nibble away at the company's markets.

Once dramatically alerted to the concept of segments, sectors, and customers, though, managers of capital-intensive businesses have become more responsive to the necessity of balancing their inescapable preoccupation with "paying the bills" or breaking even with the fact that the best way to accomplish this may be to pay more attention to segments, sectors, and customers.

The second reason industrial products companies have probably been more influenced by the article is that, in the case of the more technical industrial products or services, the necessity of clearly communicating product and service characteristics to prospects results in a lot of face-to-face "selling" effort. But precisely because the product is so complex, the situation produces salesmen who know the product more than they know the customer, who are more adept at explaining what they have and what it can do than learning what the customer's needs and problems are. The result has been a narrow product orientation rather than a liberating customer orientation, and "service" often suffered. To be sure, sellers said, "We have to provide service," but they tended to define service by looking into the mirror rather than out the window. They *thought* they were looking out the window at the customer, but it was actually a mirror—a reflection of their own product-oriented biases rather than a reflection of their customers' situations.

A manifesto, not a prescription

Not everything has been rosy. A lot of bizarre things have happened as a result of the article:

• Some companies have developed what I call "marketing mania"—they've become obsessively responsive to every fleeting whim of the customer. Mass production operations have been converted to approximations of job shops, with cost and price consequences far exceeding the willingness of customers to buy the product.

• Management has expanded product lines and added new lines of business without first establishing adequate control systems to run more complex operations.

• Marketing staffs have suddenly and rapidly expanded themselves and their research budgets without either getting sufficient prior organizational support or, thereafter, producing sufficient results.

• Companies that are functionally organized have converted to product, brand, or market-based organizations with the expectation of instant and miraculous results. The outcome has been ambiguity, frustration, confusion, corporate infighting, losses, and finally a reversion to functional arrangements that only worsened the situation.

• Companies have attempted to "serve" customers by creating complex and beautifully efficient products or services that buyers are either too risk-averse to adopt or incapable of learning how to employ—in effect, there are now steam shovels for people who haven't yet learned to use spades. This problem has happened repeatedly in the so-called service industries (financial services, insurance, computer-based services) and with American companies selling in less-developed economies.

"Marketing Myopia" was not intended as analysis or even prescription; it was intended as manifesto. It did not pretend to take a balanced position. Nor was it a new idea—Peter F. Drucker, J. B. McKitterick, Wroe Alderson, John Howard, and Neil Borden had each done more original and balanced work on "the marketing concept." My scheme, however, tied marketing more closely to the inner orbit of business policy. Drucker—especially in *The Concept of the Corporation* and *The Practice of Management*—originally provided me with a great deal of insight.

My contribution, therefore, appears merely to have been a simple, brief, and useful way of communicating an existing way of thinking. I tried to do it in a very direct, but responsible fashion, knowing that few readers (customers), especially managers and leaders, could stand much equivocation or hesitation. I also knew that the colorful and lightly documented affirmation works better than the tortuously reasoned explanation.

But why the enormous popularity of what was actually such a simple preexisting idea? Why its appeal throughout the world to resolutely restrained scholars, implacably temperate managers, and high government officials, all accustomed to balanced and thoughtful calculation? Is it that concrete examples, joined to illustrate a simple idea and presented with some attention to literacy, communicate better

than massive analytical reasoning that reads as though it were translated from the German? Is it that provocative assertions are more memorable and persuasive than restrained and balanced explanations, no matter who the audience? Is it that the character of the message is as much the message as its content? Or was mine not simply a different tune, but a new symphony? I don't know.

Of course, I'd do it again and in the same way, given my purposes, even with what more I now know—the good and the bad, the power of facts and the limits of rhetoric. If your mission is the moon, you don't use a car. Don Marquis's cockroach, Archy, provides some final consolation: "an idea is not responsible for who believes in it."

Notes

1. Jacques Barzun, "Trains and the Mind of Man," *Holiday*, February 1960, p. 21.

2. For more details see M. M. Zimmerman, *The Super Market: A Revolution in Distribution* (New York, McGraw-Hill Book Company, Inc., 1955), p. 48.

3. Ibid., pp. 45–47.

4. *The Affluent Society* (Boston, Houghton Mifflin Company, 1958), pp. 152–160.

5. Henry Ford, *My Life and* Work (New York, Doubleday, Page & Company, 1923), pp. 146–147.

6. Jacques Barzun, "Trains and the Mind of Man," *Holiday*, February 1960, p. 20.

At the time of the article's publication, Theodore Levitt was lecturer in business administration at the Harvard Business School. He is the author of several books, including The Third Sector: New Tactics for a Responsive Society *(1973) and* Marketing for Business Growth *(1974).*

What **Drives** Customer **Equity**

A company's current customers provide the most
reliable source of future revenues and profits.

By Katherine N. Lemon, Roland T. Rust, and Valarie A. Zeithaml

Consider the **issues** facing a typical brand
manager, product manager, or marketing-oriented CEO:
How do I manage the brand? How will my customers
react to changes in the product or service offering?
Should I raise price? What is the best way to enhance the
relationships with my current customers? Where should
I focus my efforts?

Business executives can answer such questions by
focusing on customer equity—the total of the discounted
lifetime values of all the firm's customers. A strategy
based on customer equity allows firms to trade off
between customer value, brand equity, and customer
relationship management. We have developed a new
strategic framework, the Customer Equity Diagnostic,
that reveals the key drivers increasing the firm's customer
equity. This new framework will enable managers to
determine what is most important to the customer and to
begin to identify the firm's critical strengths and hidden
vulnerabilities. Customer equity is a new approach to
marketing and corporate strategy that finally puts the
customer and, more important, strategies that grow the
value of the customer, at the heart of the organization.

For most firms, customer equity is certain to be the
most important determinant of the long-term value of the
firm. While customer equity will not be responsible for
the entire value of the firm (eg., physical assets, intellectual property, and research and development competencies), its current customers provide the most reliable
source of future revenues and profits. This then should be
a focal point for marketing strategy.

Although it may seem obvious that customer equity
is key to long-term success, understanding how to grow
and manage customer equity is more complex. How to
grow it is of utmost importance, and doing it well can
create a significant competitive advantage. There are
three drivers of customer equity—value equity, brand
equity, and relationship equity (also known as retention
equity). These drivers work independently and together.
Within each of these drivers are specific, incisive actions,

or levers, the firm can take to enhance its overall customer
equity.

Value Equity

Value is the keystone of the customer's relationship
with the firm. If the firm's products and services do not
meet the customer's needs and expectations, the best
brand strategy and the strongest retention and
relationship marketing strategies will be insufficient.
Value equity is defined as the customer's objective
assessment of the utility of a brand, based on perceptions
of what is given up for what is received. Three key levers
influence value equity: quality, price, and convenience.

EXECUTIVE
briefing

Customer equity is critical to a firm's long-term success. We developed a strategic marketing framework
that puts the customer and growth in the value of the
customer at the heart of the organization. Using a
new approach based on customer equity—the total of
the discounted lifetime values of all the firm's customers—we describe the key drivers of firm growth:
value equity, brand equity, and relationship equity.
Understanding these drivers will help increase customer equity and, ultimately, the value of the firm.

Quality can be thought of as encompassing the
objective physical and nonphysical aspects of the product
and service offering under the firm's control. Think of the
power FedEx holds in the marketplace, thanks, in no
small part, to its maintenance of high quality standards.
Price represents the aspects of "what is given up by the
customer" that the firm can influence. New e-world
entrants that enable customers to find the best price (e.g.,
www.mysimon.com) have revolutionized the power of

price as a marketing tool. Convenience relates to actions that help reduce the customer's time costs, search costs, and efforts to do business with the firm. Consider Fidelity Investments' new strategy of providing Palm devices to its best customers to enable anytime, anywhere trading and updates—clearly capitalizing on the importance of convenience to busy consumers.

Brand Equity

Where value equity is driven by perceptions of objective aspects of a firm's offerings, brand equity is built through image and meaning. The brand serves three vital roles. First, it acts as a magnet to attract new customers to the firm. Second, it can serve as a reminder to customers about the firm's products and services. Finally, it can become the customer's emotional tie to the firm. Brand equity has often been defined very broadly to include an extensive set of attributes that influence consumer choice. However, in our effort to separate the specific drivers of customer equity, we define brand equity more narrowly as the customer's subjective and intangible assessment of the brand, above and beyond its objectively perceived value.

The key actionable levers of brand equity are brand awareness, attitude toward the brand, and corporate ethics. The first, brand awareness, encompasses the tools under the firm's control that can influence and enhance brand awareness, particularly marketing communications. The new focus on media advertising by pharmaceutical companies (e.g., Zyban, Viagra, Claritin) is designed to build brand awareness and encourage patients to ask for these drugs by name.

Second, attitude toward the brand encompasses the extent to which the firm is able to create close connections or emotional ties with the consumer. This is most often influenced through the specific nature of the media campaigns and may be more directly influenced by direct marketing. Kraft's strength in consumer food products exemplifies the importance of brand attitude—developing strong consumer attitudes toward key brands such as Kraft Macaroni and Cheese or Philadelphia Cream Cheese. The third lever, corporate ethics, includes specific actions that can influence customer perceptions of the organization (e.g., community sponsorships or donations, firm privacy policy, and employee relations). Home Depot enhanced its brand equity by becoming a strong supporter of community events and by encouraging its employees to get involved.

Relationship Equity

Consider a firm with a great brand and a great product. The company may be able to attract new customers to its product with its strong brand and keep customers by meeting their expectations consistently. But is this enough? Given the significant shifts in the new economy—from goods to services, from transactions to relationships—the answer is no. Great brand equity and value equity may not be enough to hold the customer. What's needed is a way to glue the customers to the firm, enhancing the stickiness of the relationship. Relationship equity represents this glue. Specifically, relationship equity is defined as the tendency of the customer to stick with the brand, above and beyond the customer's objective and subjective assessments of the brand.

The key levers, under the firm's control, that may enhance relationship equity are loyalty programs, special recognition and treatment, affinity programs, community-building programs, and knowledge-building programs. Loyalty programs include actions that reward customers for specific behaviors with tangible benefits. From airlines to liquor stores, from Citigroup to Diet Coke, the loyalty program has become a staple of many firms' marketing strategy. Special recognition and treatment refers to actions that recognize customers for specific behavior with intangible benefits. For example, US Airways' "Chairman Preferred" status customers receive complimentary membership in the US Airways' Club.

Affinity programs seek to create strong emotional connections with customers, linking the customer's relationship with the firm to other important aspects of the customer's life. Consider the wide array of affinity Visa and MasterCard choices offered by First USA to encourage increased use and higher retention. Community-building programs seek to cement the customer-firm relationship by linking the customer to a larger community of like customers. In the United Kingdom, for example, soft drink manufacturer Tango has created a Web site that has built a virtual community with its key segment, the nation's youth.

Finally, knowledge-building programs increase relationship equity by creating structural bonds between the customer and the firm, making the customer less willing to recreate a relationship with an alternative provider. The most often cited example of this is amazon.com, but learning relationships are not limited to cyberspace. Firms such as British Airways have developed programs to track customer food and drink preferences, thereby creating bonds with the customer while simultaneously reducing costs.

Determining the Key Drivers

Think back to the set of questions posed earlier. How should a marketing executive decide where to focus his or her efforts: Building the brand? Improving the product or service? Deepening the relationships with current customers? Determining what is the most important driver of customer equity will often depend on characteristics of the industry and the market, such as market maturity or consumer decision processes. But determining the critical driver for your firm is the first step in building the truly customer-focused marketing organization.

When Value Equity Matters Most

Value equity matters to most customers most of the time, but it will be most important under specific circumstances. First, value equity will be most critical when discernible differences exist between competing products. In commodity markets, where products and competitors are often fungible, value equity is difficult to build. However, when there are differences between competing products, a firm can grow value equity by influencing customer perceptions of value. Consider IBM's ThinkPad brand of notebook computers. Long recognized for innovation and advanced design, IBM has been able to build an advantage in the area of value equity by building faster, thinner, lighter computers with advanced capabilities.

Second, value equity will be central for purchases with complex decision processes. Here customers carefully weigh their decisions and often examine the trade-offs of costs and benefits associated with various alternatives. Therefore, any company that either increases the customer benefits or reduces costs for its customers will be able to increase its value equity. Consider consumers contemplating the conversion to DSL technology for Internet access. This is often a complex, time-consuming decision. DSL companies that can reduce the time and effort involved in this conversion will have the value equity advantage.

Third, value equity will be important for most business-to-business purchases. In addition to being complex decisions, B2B purchases often involve a long-term commitment or partnership between the two parties (and large sums of money). Therefore, customers in these purchase situations often consider their decisions more carefully than individual consumers do.

Fourth, a firm has the opportunity to grow value equity when it offers innovative products and services. When considering the purchase of a "really new" product or service, customers must carefully examine the components of the product because the key attributes often may be difficult to discern. In many cases, consumers make one-to-one comparisons across products, trying to decide whether the new product offers sufficient benefits to risk the purchase. New MP3-type devices that provide consumers with online access to music are examples of such innovative products and services. Consumers will seek out substantial information (e.g., from the Web, friends, and advertisements) to determine the costs and benefits of new products. Firms that can signal quality and low risk can grow value equity in such new markets.

Finally, value equity will be key for firms attempting to revitalize mature products. In the maturity stage of the product life cycle, most customers observe product parity, sales level off, and, to avoid commoditization, firms often focus on the role of the brand. But value equity also may grow customer equity. By introducing new benefits for a current product or service, or by adding new features to the current offering, firms can recycle their products and services and grow value equity in the process. Consider the new Colgate "bendable" toothbrush. It seeks to revitalize the mature toothbrush market with a new answer to an age-old problem. The success of this new innovation increases Colgate's value equity.

Clearly then, the importance of value equity will depend on the industry, the maturity of the firm, and the customer decisionmaking process. To understand the role of value equity within your organization, ask several key customers and key executives to assess your company using the set of questions provided in the Customer Equity Diagnostic on the following page.

When Brand Equity Matters Most

While brand equity is generally a concern, it is critical in certain situations. First, brand equity will be most important for low-involvement purchases with simple decision processes. For many products, including frequently purchased consumer packaged goods, purchase decisions are often routinized and require little customer attention or involvement. In this case, the role of the brand and the customer's emotional connection to the brand will be crucial. In contrast, when product and service purchase decisions require high levels of customer involvement, brand equity may be less critical than value or relationship equity. Coca-Cola, for example, has been extremely successful making purchases a routine aspect of consumer's shopping trips by developing extremely strong connections between the consumer and the brand.

Second, brand equity is essential when the customer's use of the product is highly visible to others. Consider Abercrombie & Fitch, the home of in-style gear for the "Net Generation." For A&F aficionados, the brand becomes an extension of the individual, a "badge" or statement the individual can make to the world about himself or herself. These high-visibility brands have a special opportunity to build brand equity by strengthening the brand image and brand meanings that consumers associate with the brand.

Third, brand equity will be vital when experiences associated with the product can be passed from one individual or generation to another. To the extent that a firm's products or services lend themselves to communal or joint experiences (e.g., a father teaching his son to shave, shared experiences of a special wine), the firm can build brand equity. The Vail ski resort knows the value of this intergenerational brand value well. The resort encourages family experiences by promoting multigenerational visits.

Fourth, the role of the brand will be critical for credence goods, when it is difficult to evaluate quality prior to consumption. For many products and services, it is possible to "try before you buy" or to easily evaluate the quality of specific attributes prior to purchase. However, for others, consumers must use different cues for quality. This aspect of brand equity is especially key for law firms, investment banking firms, and advertising agencies, which are beginning to recognize the value of strong brand identities as a key tool for attracting new clients.

Customer Equity Diagnostic

How much do your customers care about value equity?

- ❏ Do customers perceive discernible differences between brands? Do they focus on the objective aspects of the brand?
- ❏ Do you primarily market in a B2B environment?
- ❏ Is the purchase decision process complex in your industry?
- ❏ Is innovation a key to continued success in your industry?
- ❏ Do you revitalize mature products with new features and benefits?

How are you doing?

- ❏ Are you the industry leader in overall quality? Do you have initiatives in place to continuously improve quality?
- ❏ Do your customers perceive that the quality they receive is worth the price they paid?
- ❏ Do you consistently have the lowest prices in your industry?
- ❏ Do you lead the industry in distribution of your products and services?
- ❏ Do you make it most convenient for your customers to do business with you?

How important is brand equity?

- ❏ Are the emotional and experiential aspects of the purchase important? Is consumption of your product highly visible to others?
- ❏ Are most of your products frequently purchased consumer goods?
- ❏ Is the purchase decision process relatively simple?
- ❏ Is it difficult to evaluate the quality of your products or services prior to consumption or use?
- ❏ Is advertising the primary form of communication to your customers?

How are you doing?

- ❏ Are you the industry leader in brand awareness?
- ❏ Do customers pay attention to and remember your advertising and the information you send them?
- ❏ Are you known as a good corporate citizen? Active in community events?
- ❏ Do you lead your industry in the development and maintenance of ethical standards?
- ❏ Do customers feel a strong emotional connection to the brand?

How does relationship equity weigh in?

- ❏ Are loyalty programs a necessity in your industry?
- ❏ Do customers feel like "members" in your community?
- ❏ Do your customers talk about their commitment to your brand?
- ❏ Is it possible to learn about your customers over time and customize your interactions with them? Do your customers perceive high switching costs?
- ❏ Are continuing relationships with customers important?

How are you doing?

- ❏ Do customers perceive that you have the best loyalty program in your industry?
- ❏ Do you lead the industry in programs to provide special benefits and services for your best customers?
- ❏ To what extent do your customers know and understand how to do business with you?
- ❏ Do customers perceive you as the leader in providing a sense of community?
- ❏ Do you encourage dialogue with your customers?

Therefore, brand equity will be more important in some industries and companies than others. The role of brand equity will depend on the level of customer involvement, the nature of the customer experience, and the ease with which customers can evaluate the quality of the product or service before buying it. Answering the questions in the Customer Equity Diagnostic will help determine how important brand equity is for your organization.

When Relationship Equity Matters Most

In certain situations, relationship equity will be the most important influence on customer equity. First, relationship equity will be critical when the benefits the customer associates with the firm's loyalty program are significantly greater than the actual "cash value" of the benefits received. This "aspirational value" of a loyalty program presents a solid opportunity for firms to strengthen relationship equity by creating a strong incentive for the customer to return to the firm for future purchases. The success of the world's frequent flyer programs lies, to some extent, in the difference between the "true" value of a frequent flyer mile (about three cents) and the aspirational value—the customer's perception of the value of a frequent flyer mile ("I'm that much closer to my free trip to Hawaii!").

Second, relationship equity will be key when the community associated with the product or service is as important as the product or service itself. Certain products and services have the added benefit of building a strong community of enthusiasts. Customers will often continue to purchase from the firm to maintain "membership" in the community. Just ask an active member of a HOG (Harley-Davidson Owners Group) to switch to a Honda Gold Wing; or ask a committed health club member to switch to an alternate health club. Individuals who have become committed to brand communities tend to be fiercely loyal.

Third, relationship equity will be vital when firms have the opportunity to create learning relationships with customers. Often, the relationship created between the firm and the customer, in which the firm comes to appreciate the customer's preferences and buying habits, can become as important to the customer as the provision of the product or service. Database technology has made such "learning" possible for any company or organization willing to invest the time and resources in collecting, tracking, and utilizing the information customers reveal. For example, Dell has created learning relationships with its key business customers through Dell's Premier Pages—customized Web sites that allow customers to manage their firm's purchases of Dell computers. The benefit: It becomes more difficult for customers to receive the same personal attention from an alternative provider without "training" that new provider.

Finally, relationship equity becomes crucial in situations where customer action is required to discontinue the service. For many services (and some product continuity programs), customers must actively decide to stop consuming or receiving the product or service (e.g., book clubs, insurance, Internet service providers, negative-option services). For such products and services, inertia helps solidify the relationship. Firms providing these types of products and services have a unique opportunity to grow relationship equity by strengthening the bond with the customer.

As with value and brand equity, the importance of relationship equity will vary across industries. The extent to which relationship equity will drive your business will depend on the importance of loyalty programs to your customers, the role of the customer community, the ability of your organization to establish learning relationships with your customers, and your customer's perceived switching costs. Answer the questions in the Customer Equity Diagnostic framework to see how important relationship equity is to your customers.

A New Strategic Approach

We have now seen how it is possible to gain insight into the key drivers of customer equity for an individual industry or for an individual firm within an industry. Once a firm understands the critical drivers of customer equity for its industry and for its key customers, the firm can respond to its customers and the marketplace with strategies that maximize its performance on elements that matter.

Taken down to its most fundamental level, customers choose to do business with a firm because (a) it offers better value, (b) it has a stronger brand, or (c) switching away from it is too costly. Customer equity provides the diagnostic tools to enable the marketing executive to understand which of these three motivators is most critical to the firm's customers and will be most

effective in getting the customer to stay with the firm, and to buy more. Based on this understanding, the firm can identify key opportunities for growth and illuminate unforeseen vulnerabilities. In short, customer equity offers a powerful new approach to marketing strategy, replacing product-based strategy with a competitive strategy approach based on growing the long-term value of the firm.

Additional Reading

Aaker, David A. (1995), *Managing Brand Equity*. NY: The Free Press.

Dowling, Grahame R. and Mark Uncles (1997), "Do Customer Loyalty Programs Really Work?" *Sloan Management Review*, 38 (Summer), 71–82.

Keller, Kevin L. (1998), *Strategic Brand Management: Building, Measuring and Managing Brand Equity*. NJ: Prentice-Hall.

Newell, Frederick (2000), *Loyalty.com: Customer Relationship Management in the New Era of Internet Marketing*. NY: McGraw-Hill.

Rust, Roland T., Katherine N. Lemon, and Valarie A. Zeithaml (2000), *Driving Customer Equity: How Customer Lifetime Value Is Reshaping Corporate Strategy*. NY: The Free Press.

Zeithaml, Valarie A. (1988), "Consumer Perceptions of Price, Quality and Value: A Means-End Model and Synthesis of Evidence," *Journal of Marketing*, 52 (July), 2-22.

About the Authors

Katherine N. Lemon is an assistant professor at Wallace E. Carroll School of Business, Boston College. She may be reached at katherine.lemon@bc.edu.

Roland T. Rust holds the David Bruce Smith Chair in Marketing at the Robert H. Smith School of Business at the University of Maryland, where he is director of the Center for E-Service. He may be reached at rrust@rhsmith.umd.edu.

Valarie A. Zeithaml is professor and area chair at the Kenan-Flagler Business School of the University of North Carolina, Chapel Hill. She may be reached at valariez@unc.edu.

From *Marketing Management*, Spring 2001, Vol. 10, No. 1, pp. 20-25. © 2001 by the American Marketing Association. Reprinted by permission.

Forget faster or cheaper. The Web challenges you to rethink the most basic relationship in business: the one between you and your customers. How well do you meet their needs and solve their problems? The Web requires you to make bold promises—and to deliver. Here's how four cutting-edge Net companies are reinventing

the customer experience

BY SCOTT KIRSNER

It began selling products online in July 1996. It now gets 2 million Web visits per week and does 30% of its business via the Web. That's $18 million worth of hardware, software, and accessories *per day*. Dell's Premier Pages—customized sites for thousands of business accounts—are reinventing how Dell sells products to corporate customers. So when Michael Dell and his colleagues declare that three words hold the key to their company's future, and that these words will determine who wins and who loses in the next round of Web competition, it pays to ask a simple question: What are those three words?

Visit Dell's headquarters in Round Rock, Texas, outside of Austin, and you can't miss them. Nearly every bulletin board in every office has a sign that reads "The Customer Experience: Own It." Hanging above a set of cubicles—home to employees who sell computers to government accounts—is a gift-wrapped box labeled "the 'Customer Experience.'" That label serves as a reminder that at Dell, bonuses and profit sharing are tied to what those three words signify. Thousands of employees wear a laminated photo ID around their neck that spells out the Dell mission. "To be the most successful computer company in the world at delivering the best customer experience in markets we serve."

The customer experience. Building a great company on the Web isn't about "aggregating eyeballs," "increasing stickiness," or embracing any of the other slogans that masquerade as strategy. It's about rethinking the most basic relationship in business: the one between you and your customers. How well do you meet their needs? How smoothly do you solve their problems? How quickly do you

anticipate what they'll want next? The real promise of the Web is a once-and-for-all transfer of power: Consumers and business customers will get what they want—when and how they want it, and even at the price they want. Jerry Gregoire, 47, chief information officer at Dell, puts it this way: "The customer experience is the next competitive battleground."

"Every public company tells shareholders how it's doing every quarter. But few companies have a set of metrics that measure the customer experience month to month, quarter to quarter."

paul bell, senior vp, dell computer

What is the customer experience? "It's the sum total of the interactions that a customer has with a company's products, people, and processes," says Richard Owen, 34, vice president of Dell Online worldwide. "It goes from the moment when customers see an ad to the moment when they accept delivery of a product—and beyond. Sure, we want people to think that our computers are great. But what matters is the totality of customers' experiences with us: talking with our call-center representatives, visiting our Web site, buying a PC, owning a PC. The customer experience reflects all of those interactions."

Dell doesn't claim to have discovered all of the elements that create a definitive customer experience. Indeed, 16 months ago, the company formed the Customer Experience Council, a group that is scrutinizing every aspect of how Dell interacts with customers. A handful of other Net companies are operating on the cutting edge. At Furniture.com Inc., a Web retailer based in Framingham, Massachusetts, delivering a great customer experience means addressing the limitations that come with buying furniture at a store. At Biztravel.com Inc., a great customer experience means offering only those features that are of value to frequent business travelers. At Gap Inc. Direct, the Web arm of the popular clothing retailer, delivering a great experience means translating the value of the Gap brand from the physical world to the virtual world. (See box "Brand Matters.")

Few companies understand the power of the Web better than Dell Computer.

What follows is a summary of the best practices developed by these four customer-experience innovators. Together, they form a lesson plan for the next stage of Web-based competition. "Online, you don't differentiate yourself by what you sell," argues Jeffrey F. Rayport, a professor at Harvard Business School and the executive director of Marketspace Center, the e-commerce division of Monitor Co., based in Cambridge, Massachusetts. "You have to differentiate yourself by *how* you well—by the experiences that you create around finding, trying, and purchasing. In the actual world, providing a bad experience is damaging. But people will keep going to the same supermarket, because it's on the way home. On the Web, a bad customer experience can be fatal."

FURNITURE.COM EVEN BETTER THAN THE REAL THING

It's awfully convenient to buy books from Amazon.com. But surfing the Web still can't compare with spending a lazy Sunday afternoon browsing in a bookstore. It's often cheaper to buy music at CDNow. But if you want to see the new hip-hop styles, or the latest developments in body piercing, nothing beats a late-night trip to Tower Records. There is still something satisfying about shopping for products that you want in retail environments that you enjoy.

Then there's buying furniture. Is there any big-ticket consumer item that is less fun to buy? The $178 billion furniture industry is infamous for its disregard of customers and for its slow-as-molasses cycle times. "This has been a manufacturing-driven industry rather than a customer-driven industry," says Andrew Brooks, 36, a McKinsey alum who recently left a position as chief operating officer of Channel One Network. "It's strange, really. You almost never buy furniture for an 'unhappy' reason. You buy furniture because you have a new child, or you've bought a house, or you've landed a new job. And yet customers almost never have anything but horror stories about the experience."

"Putting the customer at the center isn't something that this industry usually does," adds Carl Prindle, 31, executive producer at Furniture.com. "There are so many frustrations: the length of time that you have to wait, the fact that you may have to go to five or six stores to find the style you want."

Brooks and Prindle mean to change all that—by reinventing the customer experience as furniture retailing moves from the physical world to the Web. Today, Brooks is leading a tour through an empty showroom in downtown Worcester, Massachusetts. On January 31, the business that had been housed in this facility vanished as a brick-and-mortar operation. Empire Furniture Showroom, a family-owned company that had occupied the same building since 1947, finished up its clearance sale. In its place, another company emerged: Furniture.com. Along with Empire's old inventory—dressers, sofas, beds—went all of the old rules that had governed the furniture business.

Like online merchants in many industries, Furniture.com can offer greater variety than its storefront counterparts. It features more than 50,000 items, compared with the roughly 30,000 items that you'll find at the biggest of the "big box" retailers. But breadth of selection isn't the primary driver of a great furniture-buying experience. Personalization is what counts. A twentysomething looking for the perfect nightstand doesn't much care if a store carries 150 different sofas. A middle-aged couple whose home is decorated with country styles won't spend time evaluating the latest dining-room tables from Scandinavia.

Customers "don't want a football field of furniture," says Brooks, who is now CEO of Furniture.com. "They want a boutique filled exclusively with the stuff they love."

"It's strange, really. You almost never buy furniture for an 'unhappy' reason. And yet customers almost never have anything but horror stories about the experience."

andrew brooks

That's why Furniture.com is deploying a range of technologies that can zero in on a shopper's tastes and then offer products that fit those tastes. The most important of these technologies is a throwback: human interaction. Furniture.com employs 20 "design consultants"—many of them certified interior designers—who offer advice by phone, email, and live chat. These consultants are not traditional salespeople. Customers can't see them, and they don't get paid by commission (although they are eligible for a bonus that is tied to team sales goals). But like traditional salespeo-Diane McGowan, 49, is a case in point. She's a design consultant who has been trained to use Furniture.com's live-chat software. She monitors the site, sending out "feelers" to ask users if she can be of assistance. Here's a typical exchange:

"Yes, thanks, I'm looking for a rectangular dining-room table with chairs—possibly Windsor chairs—and maybe a hutch."

"Can you tell me what type of wood, and what style, you are looking for?" McGowan types.

"Hmmm. I know I don't like oak very much. I know I like cherry and maybe maple. I prefer dark- to medium-colored woods. But harvest tables are sometimes made of pine, aren't they? I wonder if they can be stained to a more medium color."

"Yes, they can be," McGowan types. "And every manufacturer uses its own stains. On the site, we usually have a thumbnail for a color, which you can click on to get a better idea of how it looks."

"People would look at a price tag. Then they'd turn over cushions, looking for the fire-retardant tags that say how a product was made. But that's all manufacturer-oriented information; it doesn't help at all."

peter halunen, vp of merchandising,

furniture.com

Design consultants can send out swatches of fabric, along with handwritten notecards. They can also look at what a customer has placed in the site's shopping cart (with the customer's permission, of course). That way, they can suggest compatible pieces. "Selling furniture online is more challenging than selling books," says Rose Mauriello, 42, vice president of sales and customer care. "But it's easier for us to provide a great experience than it is for a traditional retailer."

How did Furniture.com learn so much about selling furniture online? By analyzing the frustrations associated with buying furniture in physical settings. Brooks and his colleagues spent long hours watching customers shop. One of their conclusions was that consumers were hungry for more information about products. "People don't really know the difference between a $499 sofa and $699 sofa," says Peter Halunen, 32, vice president of merchandising. "People would look at a price tag. Then they'd turn over cushions, looking for the fire-retardant tags that say how a product was made. But that's all manufacturer-oriented information; it doesn't help at all."

So Furniture.com decided to create a "Fact Tag" for every product that it features. "It tells people about the dimensions," says Brooks. "Is the product oversized? Do you need to measure your doorways? What's the surface material or finish? How do you need to care for the fabric? What are the construction methods?" Brooks is so determined to make the furniture-buying experience more transparent that he has begun talking about posting manufacturer's on-time delivery records. In an industry famous for delays, that's heresy. "We want to reward companies that take the customer experience as seriously as we do," he says.

Furniture.com treats the delivery process as another major aspect of the customer experience. Once an order is placed, the design consultants hand it off to the customer-care department, which works with the manufacturer to make sure that it stays on track. Furniture.com sends out regular emails to customers about the status of their order. If there is a shipping delay, a customer-care staffer contacts the buyer in question immediately. "We don't want customers to have to call *us* to find out what's going on with their order," says Mauriello.

For Furniture.com the shipping process doesn't end until the furniture is safely situated in the customer's home. The company outsources delivery to a high-end common carrier, such as North American Van Lines. But according to Brooks, customers hold his company, rather than the carrier, responsible for the quality of the delivery experience. "If the delivery guys don't wipe their shoes before they go in, or if they leave a scuff mark on the wall—well, Furniture.com might as well have done that." That's why the company pays for each carrier's highest level of service. Specially trained staffers from the trucking company deliver, unwrap, assemble, and inspect the furniture, place it where the customer wants it to go, and take away any packaging. On delivery day, the buyer gets a call from the customer-care department—"just to make sure that everything's okay," says Brooks.

"Our customers are road warriors. They're smart, they're resourceful, and they are pressed for time. And they have high expectations."

mimi bloom

Furniture.com also offers a "Satisfaction Guarantee." Customers who aren't happy with what they've ordered can exchange it—without paying any restocking or handling charges. "That's a big departure from the old approach," Brooks boasts. "But the customer's goodwill is more important to us than anything else."

Brooks's ultimate goal is to challenge the underlying logic of the furniture-retailing business—a business that views delivery times of 6 to 12 weeks as normal. Working with sev-

FOUR RULES FOR GREAT EXPERIENCES

MARK HURST IS A MAN ON A MISSION: TO ERADICATE agonizing customer experiences from the Web. After leaving Yoyodyne Entertainment, a pioneering Internet marketing company, Hurst began writing a series of cranky (but dead-on) critiques of popular commercial Web sites, including Amazon.com, CDNow, Dell Online, and Microsoft Expedia. To his amazement, many of these sites began taking his advice.

Today, Hurst, 26, is president of Creative Good Inc., an e-commerce consulting firm based in New York City that works with clients such as Gateway 2000, Time Inc. New Media, Travelocity, and American Express. Last February, Phil Terry, 33, formerly the manager of new media at McKinsey & Co., signed on as Creative Good's CEO.

In an interview with NET COMPANY, Hurst and Terry offered advice on how to deliver compelling online experiences—and on how to avoid what they call "showstopper problems."

YOU ARE NOT THE CUSTOMER. "The people who shop on the Web are different from the people who create Web sites," says Terry. "Web developers know the difference between Java and JavaScript, and they like downloading plug-ins. Customers come to a site and say, 'When do I get my plane ticket?'"

SEEK AND YE SHALL (RARELY) FIND. Too many sites operate with search engines that just don't do the job. Either they can't handle long queries (like "blue ralph lauren blazer"), or they generate page after page of irrelevant results. "When you go to drugstore.com and you type in 'Tylenol,'" says Hurst, "the search engine comes back with *six pages* of search results." That's a great way to give your customer a headache.

That's why it's crucial to offer tips on performing more-precise searchers, says Hurst. Web sites should also make common searchers—"How can I find Tylenol?"—easier to do. Hurst recommends a process called "keyword mapping": Each week, identify the items that your customers search for most frequently, and then program your search engine to send users directly to the pages devoted to those products—instead of forcing them to sort through reams of data.

ORGANIZE WITH THE CUSTOMER IN MIND. Many companies use their internal org chart as a template for designing their Web site. Each product line gets its own area. That's a mistake, says Terry: "You need to organize based on the way customers buy. What are they looking for? They don't want to hopscotch from one part of your site to another, gathering all of the components of a stereo—speakers, speaker wire, tape deck, CD player—just because that's how your company is set up."

THINK SMALL—AND THINK SIMPLE. The customer experience often gets spoiled by overzealous designers and overambitious developers. "We all have T1 lines and big monitors," says Hurst, "but most of our customers have old computers, slow modems, and small monitors. The Web is still a highly constrained medium." So it's important to distill the online experience into the most essential visual and textual elements. Excessive use of graphics, marketing copy, sound files, or Java applets can destroy a customer's will to buy.

And don't forget to say what you mean. Too many Web sites ask users to navigate using buttons that are so clever as to be cryptic. Hurst mentions a button on the Starbucks Web site that's labeled "Beyond the Bean." "I have better things to do with my life than click on 'Beyond the Bean,'" he says. "You need to be clear about what the payoff is: Why should I go there?" Which leads to a Creative Good cardinal rule: "To succeed in e-commerce, make it easy for the customer to buy."

COORDINATES Creative Good Inc., www.creativegood.com; Mark Hurst, mark@creativegood.com; Phil Terry, pterry@creativegood.com

---

eral North Carolina-based manufacturers, Furniture.com is gathering data about its customers' preferences—whether people prefer sleigh beds to canopy beds, for example, or whether they tend to choose cherry over oak. Furniture.com and the manufacturers use this data to make a limited set of products that satisfy a broad range of customer demand. For each of those products, Furniture.com and its partner commit to a delivery time of as little as 3 weeks.

"In the world of e-commerce, 3 weeks is an eternity," says Brooks. "But in the world of furniture, it's a snap of the fingers. Our vision is to collaborate with customers and manufacturers to make this a better experience. This is an industry that has lots of room for improvement."

BIZTRAVEL.COM
WHICH FEATURES SHOULD WE FEATURE?

Members of the development team at Biztravel.com are arguing *again*—about Web design. Which new features, among the many options under consideration, should they include in the next version of their site? The argument is friendly—it sounds like the kids on *The Brady Bunch* debating who gets to ride in the front seat—but the stakes are high. The company, launched three years ago with blue-chip venture-capital backing (and with such corporate investors as Comcast, Intel, and Rupert Murdoch's News Corp.), has been working to persuade frequent business travelers to leave their human travel agents behind and to rely on the Web. That means offering an online service that streamlines the booking process for airline tickets, hotel reservations, and rental cars. It also means rolling out innovations that traditional travel agents can't match—and that people in Biztravel.com's target market won't be able to resist.

Biztravel.com unveils a new edition of its site every six weeks. Such upgrades have introduced visitors to a slew of killer apps. One feature, called bizAlert, sends a message to your pager an hour before your flight, complete with gate information and updates on any delays or cancellations. Another feature, called CalendarDirect, downloads an itinerary to your desktop-calendar program or to your PalmPilot. Perhaps most impressive, there's an automated upgrade feature that works with lightning speed to bump you from coach to business class—and all you have to do is sign up

BRAND MATTERS

MICHAEL MCCADDEN DOESN'T SEE THE WEB AS A NEW frontier of digital commerce. He sees it as another playground for his company's powerful brand. McCadden joined the Gap Inc. three years ago as head of marketing. One of his first objectives was to launch a Web site for the giant retailer (1998 revenues: $9 billion). He didn't much care about installing cool technology or devising a break-the-rules retailing model. "The site grew out of the brand," says McCadden, 41, now executive vice president of Gap Inc. Direct. "That's how we came into the online world—as another way to let customers experience the brand."

More seamlessly than almost any other retailer, the Gap has figured out how to integrate its brand—and the way customers experience the brand—across three channels: physical stores, 800-numbers, and the Web. One example: A customer who buys a pair of jeans over the phone or via the Web can return the item to any of the Gap's 1,700 stores.

What does the Gap brand represent?
Ease. We hope that our advertising is easy to understand, and we hope that our web site is easy to use. Our basic goal is to be simple. That's why we've kept the site clean and straightforward. Our big challenge is to offer a full product line on the site while also making the site easy to navigate—keeping to a minimum the number of clicks that it takes to get to a given product. That's something that we measure: How quickly can you find the shirt that you're looking for?

What role does an online story play?
It's primarily about convenience. Insomnamics can shop there.

People who love our retail stores can use the Web to buy gifts, or to find styles that they can't find at their local store. It's hard to replicate the energy of a Gap store: the music, the physical environment, the human element. But we are trying to replicate as much of that energy online as we can. The ultimate goal is for people to say, "This really feels like the Gap."

How do the various channels complement one another?
We look at everything that the Gap does as the expression of one brand—not as a separate channel or distribution system. So do our customers. From the moment we launched our site, customers have been walking into our stores with printouts of Web pages. They'll point to a page and say, "This is the product that I want." Or, if they're in a store, trying to buy a pair of jeans, and they can't find their size, an associate will tell them to log onto the Gap Online. On our Web site, we carry almost every size and style. Meanwhile, in our flagship stores, we're installing Web Lounges. You can explore Gap Online in the store and order from there.

Is there a trick to all of this?
First, think the way the customer thinks, not the way technical people think. Second, don't force the Web on people. We're not trying to change behavior. We're just trying to give people more options. However they want to experience our brand, the Gap will be there.

COORDINATES Michael McCadden, michael_mccadden@gap.com

---

for the service. (According to Biztravel.com, this feature snares upgrades for 85% to 95% of eligible travelers, compared with a 25% to 30% success rate for traditional travel agents.)

"Most travelers don't feel like they're in control," says George Roukas, 43, vice president of product management and customer service. "The rental-car companies and the airlines are always asserting control. We're trying to give some control back to the traveler. We not only listen to what customers ask for; we think about features that they wouldn't know to ask for."

The feature under consideration today addresses a problem that has become increasingly common in a world of crowded skies and delayed flights. It would automatically notify your hotel if your flight was delayed, increasing your chances of holding on to a room reservation— even if you were going to arrive much later than you had planned. Some members of the development team are unconvinced. "We have to figure out when it makes sense for us to fax the hotel," worries Julian Winter, 41, director of member services. "Do we tell the hotel when your flight is delayed from 11 AM to 3 PM? Or do we send a fax only when you'll be delayed past 6 PM?" It's an important question. How well this feature meets the needs of harried hotel staffers

will help determine how well it meets the needs of Biztravel.com's customers. Says Winter: "We want to be sure that if a hotel is oversold, and if it's going to 'walk' some folks, it doesn't walk ours."

Lots of Web sites offer lots of whiz-bang features simply because they can. At Biztravel.com, the essence of creating a great customer experience is offering only those features that its customers truly value. "Our customers are road warriors," says Mimi Bloom, 34, director of customer acquisition and retention. "They're smart, they're resourceful, and they're pressed for time. And they have high expectations: If there's one remaining first-class seat and they've got an upgrade credit, they want to be in that seat. So we're forever asking the same question: What kind of service do people like and need when they travel?"

Bloom and her colleagues gather answers to that question directly from their customers, via telephone contact and email. Programmers make it a point to spend a few minutes each day reading submissions to the site's customer-feedback inbox. Some recent additions to the site, such as a feature that prints out expense-account documents, are a direct outgrowth of those suggestions. Other enhancements—such as a tool that filters out spelling errors when a user types in the name of a destination—come from watching people use (and misuse) the site. A final group of features—what Roukas calls "the sizzlers"—get created mainly because they're cool, and because they set Biztravel.com even further apart from traditional travel agents.

Once the development team has approved and prioritized a new feature, the coding process begins. Here, too, the customer experience figures into how the company operates. Biztravel.com breaks down big ideas into small chunks defined by functionality. That way, the company can roll out new features more quickly, and its programmers can discover problems and gauge customer reaction—before they spend months developing a feature that doesn't quite work or that people don't really want.

"We like incremental enhancements," says Winter, "because that way, we can tweak things and change direction much more easily in response to customer feedback. Lots of times, when you take big steps, you wind up telling customers that they had better like what you've done for them—because you've spent so much time and so much money on developing it."

There have been lots of "incremental enhancements" since Biztravel.com was launched, in November 1996. Roukas says that he can't imagine a time when the six-week upgrade cycle would cease. "Our list [of new features] never shrinks," he says. "When we page someone who's scrambling to get to the airport, and we let him know that his flight has been canceled, and then he's able to book another flight because he was the first to know about the cancellation—well, that's the experience that we're going for. That creates a customer for life."

DELL COMPUTER MEASURE WHAT MATTERS

When it comes to delivering a great customer experience, lots of companies talk a good game. A few companies even play a good game. Dell Computer wants to reinvent the rules of the game—so it's fanatical about keeping score. "We're a numbers-driven organization," says Jerry Gregoire, the company's CIO. "We're in our comfort zone when we can measure something."

Dell's eight-person Customer Experience Council was formed two years ago in order to focus all 26,000 pairs of eyes in the organization on a single priority. By Dell's reckoning, the company has more than 16 million "customer contacts" per week, whether in the form of emails, phone calls, deliveries, or returns. The challenge: How to monitor and measure the quality of those contacts?

"Every public company tells shareholders how it's doing every quarter," says Paul Bell, 39, senior vice president for Dell's home and small-business group, who is a member of the Customer Experience Council. "But few companies have a set of metrics that measure the customer experience month to month, quarter to quarter." So the company decided to track three major elements of the customer experience: order fulfillment, performance, and service-and-support. Then it picked one metric to represent each ele-

ment. For order fulfillment, Dell tracks "ship to target": How often does a completely accurate order get to the customer on time? For performance, Dell follows the "initial field-incident rate": How often does something go wrong with a system once it has been delivered? For service-and-support, Dell measures something called "on-time, first-time fix": How often do service people arrive on time, and how often do they fix a problem on the first visit? There are dozens of other metrics that Dell follows—such as the "initial soft-incident rate," which reflects how often customers merely think that they have a problem—but when it comes to capturing the customer experience, those three metrics are the ones that count. Dell aimed to improve each metric by at least 15% last year, and it succeeded.

Where does the Web fit in? During 1999, there has been a major emphasis on moving more of the company's tech support to the Web. Shifting to online support not only saves Dell money; it also helps the company generate more revenue. Web-based service frees up phone reps to deliver in-depth consultations. "We used to measure how many calls we could take per hour," says Manish Mehta, 30, senior manager of service-and-support online. "Now we focus on first-time resolves—solving the problem once and for all—even if that means talking longer with a customer."

> ## "We used to measure how many calls we could take per hour. Now we focus on first-time resolves— solving the problem once and for all—even if that means talking longer with a customer."
>
> manish mehta

Mehta explains the role of his group by declaring, "We own the customer experience once the machine leaves the factory." Lately, the group has been designing online innovations that enable consumers to solve their own problems. One of the most compelling forms of service is self-service, Mehta argues. That's why Dell hosts a bulletin board where die-hard customers answer questions for other customers at the rate of 400 to 500 per day. The Dell site also features a massive database of FAQs and other documentation, along with a natural-language search engine (called "Ask Dudley") that handles 50,000 inquires per week. Mehta is now testing an automated-response system to analyze incoming support requests. The system attempts to answer about 30% of those requests on its own, passing along the rest to support technicians (who almost always respond within four hours). So far, the system has had an 86% success rate with questions that it attempts to answer.

If numbers matter at Dell, one number may matter more in the future than any other: each computer's "service-tag number." It's a five-digit alphanumeric code that describes the model, the amount of memory, and the configuration of each machine that Dell sells. Today, customers can visit Dell's Web site, type in their service-tag number, and find out whether their PC is ready for the year 2000—or learn how they can upgrade their machine to the latest version of Windows. Eventually, Dell envisions using the service-tag number to track the software that customers have running on their machines (with their permission, of course). That way, if a customer wanted to purchase a flight simulator, for example, Dell could specify how much additional memory would be needed.

"That sort of thing—helping customers add accessories or software when they're between PC purchases—is what separates the people who understand the customer experience from the people who don't," explains Gregoire. "That shows the difference between offering a great experience and selling a commodity, and that difference turns into real dollars."

"Our challenge is to instill a companywide commitment to the customer experience," he continues. "It's like the way Disney teaches its people to be aggressively friendly: 'Can I help you find something?' Our metrics give us a read on the experience that we're delivering and on the loyalty that we're creating. We're doing pretty well, but we still feel like the tallest midgets in the forest. We know we can do much better."

SCOTT KIRSNER (KIRSNER@WORLDNET.ATT.NET), A *NET COMPANY* CONTRIBUTING EDITOR, IS BASED IN BOSTON.

A Primer on Quality Service

Quality Service Makes Happy Customers and Greater Profits

Gene Milbourn, Jr.
G. Timothy Haight

"Pul-eeze! Will Someone Help Me?" screamed a headline in *Time* magazine in the late 1980s. The cover story focused on the deterioration of customer service and blamed it on general economic upheavals such as high inflation, labor shortage, and low-cost business strategies.[1] Prices for consumer goods had increased 87 percent during the 1970s and, to keep prices from further skyrocketing, customer-service training was slashed and computers and self-service schemes were introduced in wholesale fashion. Businesses developed the same habits and inattention to quality service that had plagued American manufacturers in previous years.

In the new millennium, a new force is pressuring the bricks-and-mortar businesses to upgrade their customer focus to be competitive—e-commerce. A recent article about a customer service survey in *Marketing Week* asserted, "… in a competitive world driven by new technology and the Internet, what was an acceptable level of service five or ten years ago may no longer be good enough today."[2]

There is ample evidence that the economic success of companies fluctuates with the quality of service that is offered. Among the most recent scholarship is a study published in the *Journal of Business Research*

that validated an earlier much-discussed work that linked market orientation with business performance.[3]

The Strategic Planning Institute studied confidential data provided by thousands of business units—the PIMS database—and found that quality service leads to financial and strategic success.[4] Grouping businesses into those offering low and those offering high quality service revealed that, in addition to maintaining a price differential of 11 percent, return on sales was 11 percent higher, and annual sales growth was 9 percent higher in the group providing high quality service. In addition, the high service quality group experienced a 4 percent increase in market share while the low quality service group registered a –2 percent change.

An earlier report concluded that many companies "overinvest in cost reduction and capacity-expansion projects because they believe they can 'run the numbers' to 'justify' a project. They underinvest in quality service improvement because they have not learned how to calibrate its strategic or financial payoff."[5]

Research Is Consistent

Research on the behavior of dissatisfied customers is consistent and expected.[6] Typically, a dissatisfied

customer does not complain and simply purchases from another store. Research across eight industries revealed that 25 percent of dissatisfied customers do not return to the offending store; 41 percent of customers experience a problem in shopping; 94 percent of customers do not complain about a problem; 63 percent of customers are not pleased with a business' responses to their complaints; and, customers are five times more likely to switch stores because of service problems than for price or product quality issues. However, when customers *do* complain and when their problems are *quickly* resolved, an impressive 82 percent would buy again from the business.[7]

> *"There is ample evidence that the economic success of companies fluctuates with the quality of service that is offered."*

Research contained in a *Harvard Business Review* article found that high quality service is a dominant cause of repeat customers across industries.[8] More noteworthy, however, is that a customer generates an increasing amount of profit each year that the "customer is a customer." A business becomes skilled in dealing with the customer and the customer buys more and refers others to the business.

Quality Service Model

A 22-item survey tool called the ServQual is used to collect information from customers on five factors of quality service:

- **reliability**—the ability to provide what was promised, dependably and accurately
- **assurance**—the knowledge and courtesy of employees, and their ability to convey trust and confidence
- **tangibles**—the physical facilities, equipment, and the appearance of personnel
- **empathy**—the degree of caring and individual attention provided to customers
- **responsiveness**—the willingness to help customers and provide prompt service.

These five factors account for much of the variation of customer's perception of quality service across industries (see the *Journal of Retailing*, Spring, 1990, Volume 66, No. 1 for a copy of the ServQual or Report No. 86–108, Marketing Science Institute, Cambridge, Mass.).

The Quality Service Model is shown in Figure One. The model shows that five general factors of quality service influences three customer behaviors that are desired by businesses—repurchasing, providing positive word-of-mouth advertising, and cross buying.

> *"We have found that disenchanted rank- and-file employees are an excellent source for ideas to improve service."*

The model also identified ten specific factors such as the guarantee, repair and maintenance, and technical support that are components of the general factors. For instance, a business can be *reliable* in repair and maintenance but *unreliable* in technical support and ordering and billing. A below average restaurant may serve unevenly prepared food (poor reliability), on oily trays (poor tangibles), slowly (poor responsiveness), to customers in an impersonal manner (low empathy). Customers would likely not return to this business or provide positive word-of-mouth advertising. Conversely, customers would likely return and tell others about the experience if they rated the business highly according to the five dimensions of service quality.

Improvement Strategies

The Forum Corporation, a research company that specializes in this topic, says the reliability dimension is the most important followed by responsiveness, assurance, empathy, and the tangible elements. However, some research shows that companies do best in dealing with the dimensions in almost the reverse order. In other words, they do very well in taking care of what customers view as relatively unimportant.[9]

The organizational themes that differentiate the best customer-focused companies include these actions:

- Setting customer-focused performance goals and standards
- Taking personal action to help solve customers' problems
- Seeking innovative ways to serve customers better
- Helping employees learn how to serve customers better

Some of the improvement strategies underlying this customer-focus that the Forum Corporation has found helpful include:

- Companies must address all dimensions of service quality

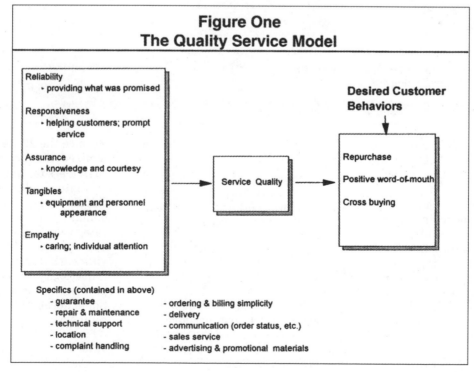

**Figure One
The Quality Service Model**

Reliability
- providing what was promised

Responsiveness
- helping customers; prompt service

Assurance
- knowledge and courtesy

Tangibles
- equipment and personnel appearance

Empathy
- caring; individual attention

Service Quality

Desired Customer Behaviors

Repurchase

Positive word-of-mouth

Cross buying

Specifics (contained in above)
- guarantee
- repair & maintenance
- technical support
- location
- complaint handling
- ordering & billing simplicity
- delivery
- communication (order status, etc.)
- sales service
- advertising & promotional materials

Figure Two
The Quality Service Questionnaire

DIRECTIONS: This survey asks you about how well a business serves customers. Show your opinion by circling one of the five (5) numbers next to each statement. If you think the company does **much worse** than expected **select 1**. If the company does **much better** than expected **select 5**. If your feelings are not strong, circle one of the numbers in the **middle**.

1 Much worse than expected	2 Somewhat worse than expected	3 About what I expected	4 Better than expected	5 Much better than expected

	1	2	3	4	5
1. The quality of our equipment	1	2	3	4	5
2. The appearance of our physical facilities	1	2	3	4	5
3. The appearance of our employees	1	2	3	4	5
4. The appearance of our materials (pamphlets, statements, etc.)	1	2	3	4	5
5. Delivering on promises to do something by a certain time	1	2	3	4	5
6. The sincerity of our interest in solving your problems	1	2	3	4	5
7. Performing service right the first time	1	2	3	4	5
8. Providing services at the time we promise to do so	1	2	3	4	5
9. The accuracy of records	1	2	3	4	5
10. Telling you exactly when services will be performed	1	2	3	4	5
11. Receiving prompt service from our employees	1	2	3	4	5
12. The willingness of our employees to help you	1	2	3	4	5
13. Never being too busy to respond to your requests	1	2	3	4	5
14. Employee actions that instill confidence in you	1	2	3	4	5
15. The safety you feel in transactions with our employees	1	2	3	4	5
16. The courteousness of our employees	1	2	3	4	5
17. The ability of our employees to answer your questions	1	2	3	4	5
18. The individual attention you received from us	1	2	3	4	5
19. The convenience of our operating hours	1	2	3	4	5
20. The personal attention you received from our employees	1	2	3	4	5
21. Having your best interests at heart	1	2	3	4	5
22. The ability of our employees to understand your specific needs	1	2	3	4	5

Overall Quality

	1	2	3	4	5
23. How would you rate the overall service you received?	1	2	3	4	5
24. Considering the time, effort and money you spent with us, how would you rate the overall value provided?	1	2	3	4	5

Source: Parasuraman, A., et al., "Servqual: A Multiple-item Scale for Measuring Customer Perceptions of Service Quality," Report No. 86-108, Marketing Science Institute, Cambridge, Mass.

- Companies must be accurate and specific about what employees must do to improve service quality
- Companies seeking a simple way to look at how their customers judge service should evaluate the general viewpoint of employees, because employees are good estimators of service
- Companies must seek ways to reduce, avoid, and speedily solve problems with customers
- Companies should work to retain customers who report that they are satisfied, but rate the company as having only fair or poor service
- Companies must examine and correct anything that impedes employee performance to maximize customer focus

The Survey Questionnaire

A popular research tool that was developed to collect attitudes about quality service is called the ServQual scale.[10] A copy of the most recent version is shown in Figure Two.

Once the 22-item survey is customized, it is given to a sample of customers to complete. Scores are tabulated and average scores are calculated for each of the five factors of quality service. Some of the 22 categories in the survey may not be appropriate. A task force should review each item, re-write statements if necessary, and construct a final professional-looking instrument. Some norms that can be used for comparison are: overall average 3.89; overall service 4.05; overall value 4.13; and each service quality factor 3.50.

While the survey process is underway, other types of measurement can also be employed (see a good organizational development book on the topic of survey feedback). Some forms include focus groups of 'sophisticated' customers and a group of internal managers who brainstorm the factors that are rated below average by customers. We have found that disenchanted rank-and-file employees are an excellent source for ideas to improve service.

"Quality service need not be your businesses Achilles' heel."

What are needed are specific statements such as: "We need to improve the *reliability* of our repair and maintenance process," "We need to improve our *responsiveness* in deliveries and complaint handling," and "We need to improve our *empathy* in addressing complaints." An improvement plan can then be developed that places the ideas for change into "fix first," "fix second," and "fix last" categories. The task force leader must identify the cost, time frame, labor intensity, and review process needed for each recommendation.

Quality service need not be your businesses Achilles' heel. Employing a quality service model such as that which we've presented in this article will decidedly result in greater business—and profits.

References

1. *Time*, "Pul-eeze! Will Someone Help Me?" *Economics and Business,* cover story, February 2, 1987.
2. Hemsley, Steve, "Keeping Customers," *Marketing Week*, March 16, 2000, 39.
3. Slater, Stanley F., John C. Narver, "The Positive Effect of a Market Orientation on Business Profitability; A Balanced Replication, *Journal of Business Research*, Vol. 48, No. 1, April, 2000.
4. Gale, B. T., *Managing Customer Value*, The Free Press, NY, 1994, Chapter 6.
5. Strategic Planning Institute, "Strategic Management of Service Quality," No. 33, 1985, Cambridge, MA.
6. TARP: Technical Assistance Research Program, *"Tarp's Approach to Customer Driven Quality: Moving From Measuring to Managing Customer Satisfaction*, TARP Corporation, Arlington, VA, 1995.
7. Gale, B. T., op. cit., 17.
8. Reichheld, F. F. and W. Earl Sasser, "Zero Defections: Quality Comes to Service," *Harvard Business Review*, 69, September–October, 1990, 7.
9. Forum Corporation, *"Customer Focus Research: Executive Briefing,"* Boston, MA, 1988.
10. Parasuraman, A., V. A. Zeithaml and L. L. Berry, *"Servqual: A Multiple-item Scale for Measuring Customer Perceptions of Service Quality,"* Report No. 86–108, August, 1986, Marketing Science Institute, Cambridge, MA.

GENE MILBOURN, JR., Ph.D., is a professor of management at the University of Baltimore. He teaches undergraduate and graduate business policy and strategy as well as organizational behavior. He is a noted consultant to business and industry on issues that include quality service, leadership, and motivation. He is the author of the organizational behavior textbook, Human Behavior in the Work Environment: A Managerial Perspective.

G. TIMOTHY HAIGHT, D.B.A. is dean of the School of Business and Economics at California State University, Los Angeles. He is an expert in the field of financial management, investment and securities analysis. He is the general editor of Insurer's Guide to Enterprise-Wide Management *and* Derivatives Risk Management Service. *In addition to many articles published in magazines and journals, he is the author of* The Analysis of Portfolio Management Performance: An Institute Guide to Assessing and Analyzing Pension Fund, Endowment, Foundation, and Trust Investment Performance *(McGraw-Hill, 1998).*

From *Business Forum*, Vol. 23, Nos. 3-4, pp. 15-18. © 1998 by Business Forum. Reprinted by permission.

WHY SERVICE STINKS

Companies know just how good a customer you are—and unless you're a high roller, they would rather lose you than take the time to fix your problem

By Diane Brady

When Tom Unger of New Haven started banking at First Union Corp. several years ago, he knew he wasn't top of the heap. But Unger didn't realize just how dispensable he was until mysterious service charges started showing up on his account. He called the bank's toll-free number, only to reach a bored service representative who brushed him off. Then he wrote two letters, neither of which received a response. A First Union spokeswoman, Mary Eshet, says the bank doesn't discuss individual accounts but notes that customer service has been steadily improving. Not for Unger. He left. "They wouldn't even give me the courtesy of listening to my complaint," he says.

And Unger ought to know bad service when he sees it. He works as a customer-service representative at an electric utility where the top 350 business clients are served by six people. The next tier of 700 are handled by six more, and 30,000 others get Unger and one other rep to serve their needs. Meanwhile, the 300,000 residential customers at the lowest end are left with an 800 number. As Unger explains: "We don't ignore anyone, but our biggest customers certainly get more attention than the rest."

As time goes on, that service gap is only growing wider. Studies by groups ranging from the Council of Better Business Bureaus Inc. to the University of Michigan vividly detail what consumers already know: Good service is increasingly rare (charts). From passengers languishing in airport queues to bank clients caught in voice-mail hell, most consumers feel they're getting squeezed by Corporate America's push for profits and productivity. The result is more efficiencies for companies—and more frustration for their less valuable customers. "Time saved for them is not time saved for us," says Claes Fornell, a University of Michigan professor who created the school's consumer satisfaction index, which shows broad declines across an array of industries. Fornell points to slight improvements in areas like autos and computers.

FLYING
Canceled flight? No problem. With top status, you're whisked past the queue, handed a ticket for the next flight, and driven to the first-class lounge. The rest can cross their fingers and come back tomorrow

Andrew Chan's experience with Ikea is typical. The Manhattan artist recently hauled a table home from an Ikea store in New Jersey only to discover that all the screws and brackets were missing. When he called to complain, the giant furniture retailer refused to send out the missing items and insisted he come back to pick them up himself, even though he doesn't own a car. Maybe he just reached the wrong guy, says Tom Cox, customer-service manager for Ikea North America, noting that the usual procedure is to mail small items out within a couple of days.

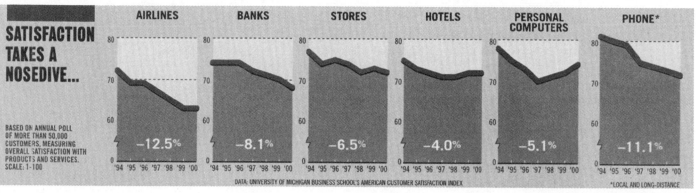

SATISFACTION TAKES A NOSEDIVE...

BASED ON ANNUAL POLL OF MORE THAN 50,000 CUSTOMERS, MEASURING OVERALL SATISFACTION WITH PRODUCTS AND SERVICES. SCALE: 1-100

AIRLINES −12.5%
BANKS −8.1%
STORES −6.5%
HOTELS −4.0%
PERSONAL COMPUTERS −5.1%
PHONE* −11.1%

DATA: UNIVERSITY OF MICHIGAN BUSINESS SCHOOL'S AMERICAN CUSTOMER SATISFACTION INDEX

*LOCAL AND LONG-DISTANCE

CHARTS BY RAY VELLA/BW

NO ELEPHANT? Life isn't so tough for everyone, though. Roy Sharda, a Chicago Internet executive and road warrior is a "platinum" customer of Starwood Hotels & Resorts Worldwide. When he wanted to propose to his girlfriend, Starwood's Sheraton Agra in India arranged entry to the Taj Mahal after hours so he could pop the question in private. Starwood also threw in a horse-drawn carriage, flowers, a personalized meal, upgrades to the presidential suite, and a cheering reception line led by the general manager. It's no wonder Sharda feels he was "treated like true royalty."

Welcome to the new consumer apartheid. Those long lines and frustrating telephone trees aren't always the result of companies simply not caring about pleasing the customer anymore. Increasingly, companies have made a deliberate decision to give some people skimpy service because that's all their business is worth. Call it the dark side of the technology boom, where marketers can amass a mountain of data that gives them an almost Orwellian view of each buyer. Consumers have become commodities to pamper, squeeze, or toss away, according to Leonard L. Berry, marketing professor at Texas A&M University. He sees "a decline in the level of respect given to customers and their experiences."

More important, technology is creating a radical new business model that alters the whole dynamic of customer service. For the first time, companies can truly measure exactly what such service costs on an individual level and assess the return on each dollar. They can know exactly how much business someone generates, what he is likely to buy, and how much it costs to answer the phone. That allows them to deliver a level of service based on each person's potential to produce a profit—and not a single phone call more.

BILLING

Big spenders can expect special discounts, promotional offers, and other goodies when they open their bills. The rest might get higher fees, stripped-down service, and a machine to answer their questions

The result could be a whole new stratification of consumer society. The top tier may enjoy an unprecedented level of personal attention. But those who fall below a certain level of profitability for too long may find themselves bounced from the customer rolls altogether or facing fees that all but usher them out the door. A few years ago, GE Capital decided to charge $25 a year to GE Rewards MasterCard holders who didn't rack up at least that much in annual interest charges. The message was clear: Those who pay their bills in full each month don't boost the bottom line. GE has since sold its credit-card business to First USA. Others are charging extra for things like deliveries and repairs or reducing service staff in stores and call centers.

Instead of providing premium service across the board, companies may offer to move people to the front of the line for a fee. "There has been a fundamental shift in how companies assess customer value and apply their resources," says Cincinnati marketing consultant Richard G. Barlow. He argues that managers increasingly treat top clients with kid gloves and cast the masses "into a labyrinth of low-cost customer service where, if they complain, you just live with it."

Companies have always known that some people don't pay their way. Ravi Dhar, an associate professor at Yale University, cites the old rule that 80% of profits come from 20% of customers. "The rest nag you, call you, and don't add much revenue," he says. But technology changed everything. To start, it has become much easier to track and measure individual transactions across businesses. Second, the Web has also opened up options. People can now serve themselves at their convenience at a negligible cost, but they have to accept little or no human contact in return. Such huge savings in service costs have proven irresistible to marketers, who are doing everything possible to push their customers—especially low-margin ones—toward self-service.

FRONT-LOADING ELITE. That's a far cry from the days when the customer was king. In the data-rich new millennium, sales staff no longer let you return goods without question while rushing to shake your hand. And they don't particularly want to hear from you again unless you're worth the effort. How they define that top tier can vary a lot by industry. Airlines and hotels love those who buy premier offerings again and again. Financial institutions, on the other hand, salivate over day traders and the

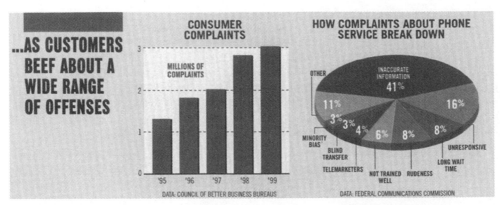

...AS CUSTOMERS BEEF ABOUT A WIDE RANGE OF OFFENSES

CONSUMER COMPLAINTS

MILLIONS OF COMPLAINTS

'95 '96 '97 '98 '99

DATA: COUNCIL OF BETTER BUSINESS BUREAUS

HOW COMPLAINTS ABOUT PHONE SERVICE BREAK DOWN

INACCURATE INFORMATION 41%

OTHER 11%

3% 3% 4% 6% 8% 8% 16%

MINORITY BIAS
BLIND TRANSFER
TELEMARKETERS
NOT TRAINED WELL
RUDENESS
LONG WAIT TIME
UNRESPONSIVE

DATA: FEDERAL COMMUNICATIONS COMMISSION

plastic-addicted who pay heavy interest charges because they cover only the minimum on their monthly credit-card bills.

Almost everyone is doing it. Charles Schwab Corp.'s top-rated Signature clients—who start with at least $100,000 in assets or trade 12 times a year—never wait longer than 15 seconds to get a call answered, while other customers can wait 10 minutes or more. At Sears, Roebuck & Co., big spenders on the company's credit card get to choose a preferred two-hour time slot for repair calls while regular patrons are given a four-hour slot. Maytag Corp. provides premium service to people who buy pricey products such as its front-loading Neptune washing machines, which sell for about $1,000, twice the cost of a top-loading washer. This group gets a dedicated staff of "product experts," an exclusive toll-free number, and speedy service on repairs. When people are paying this much, "they not only want more service; they deserve it," says Dale Reeder, Maytag's general manager of customer service.

BANKING

There's nothing like a big bank account to get those complaints answered and service charges waived every time. Get pegged as a money-loser, and your negotiating clout vanishes

Of course, while some companies gloat about the growing attention to their top tier, most hate to admit that the bottom rungs are getting less. GE Capital would not talk. Sprint Corp. and WorldCom Inc. declined repeated requests to speak about service divisions. Off the record, one company official explains that customers don't like to know they're being treated differently.

Obviously, taking service away from the low spenders doesn't generate much positive press for companies. Look at AT&T, which recently agreed to remove its minimum usage charges on the 28 million residential customers in its lowest-level basic plan, many of whom don't make enough calls to turn a profit. "To a lot of people, it's not important that a company make money," says AT&T Senior Vice-President Howard E. McNally, who argues that AT&T is still treated by regulators and the public as a carrier of last resort. Now, it's trying to push up profits by giving top callers everything from better rates to free premium cable channels.

SERIAL CALLERS. Is this service divide fair? That depends on your perspective. In an era when labor costs are rising while prices have come under pressure, U.S. companies insist they simply can't afford to spend big bucks giving every customer the hands-on service of yesteryear. Adrian J. Slywotzky, a partner with Mercer Management Consulting Inc., estimates that gross margins in many industries have shrunk an average of 5 to 10 percentage points over the past decade because of competition. "Customers used to be more profitable 10 years ago, and they're becoming more different than similar" in how they want to be served, he says.

The new ability to segment customers into ever finer categories doesn't have to be bad news for consumers. In many cases, the trade-off in service means lower prices. Susanne D. Lyons, chief marketing officer at Charles Schwab, points out that the commission charged on Schwab stock trades has dropped by two-thirds over the past five years. Costs to Schwab, meanwhile, vary from a few cents for Web deals to several dollars per live interaction. And companies note that they're delivering a much wider range of products and services than ever before—as well as more ways to handle transactions. Thanks to the Internet, for example, consumers have far better tools to conveniently serve themselves.

Look at a company like Fidelity Investments, which not only has a mind-boggling menu of fund options but now lets people do research and manipulate their accounts without an intermediary. Ten years ago, the company got 97,000 calls a day, of which half were automated. It now gets about 550,000 Web site visits a day and more than 700,000 daily calls, about three-quarters of which go to automated systems that cost the company less than a buck each, including development and research costs. The rest are handled by human beings, which costs about $13 per call. No wonder Fidelity last year contacted 25,000 high-cost "serial" callers and told them they must use the Web or automated calls for simple account and price information. Each name was flagged and routed to a special representative who would direct callers back to automated services—and tell them how to use it. "If all our customers chose to go through live reps, it would be cost-prohibitive," says a Fidelity spokeswoman.

ENTITLED? Segmenting is one way to manage those costs efficiently. Bass Hotels & Resorts, owners of such brands as Holiday Inn and Inter-Continental Hotels, know so much about individual response rates to its promotions that it no longer bothers sending deals to those who did not bite in the past. The

'WE'RE SORRY, ALL OF OUR AGENTS ARE BUSY WITH MORE VALUABLE CUSTOMERS'

Companies have become sophisticated about figuring out if you're worth pampering—or whether to just let the phone keep ringing. Here are some of their techniques:

CODING

Some companies grade customers based on how profitable their business is. They give each account a code with instructions to service staff on how to handle each category.

ROUTING

Based on the customer's code, call centers route customers to different queues. Big spenders are whisked to high-level problem solvers. Others may never speak to a live person at all.

TARGETING

Choice customers have fees waived and get other hidden discounts based on the value of their business. Less valuable customers may never even know the promotions exist.

SHARING

Companies sell data about your transaction history to outsiders. You can be slotted before you even walk in the door, since your buying potential has already been measured.

---

result: 50% slashed off mailing costs but a 20% jump in response rates. "As information becomes more sophisticated, the whole area of customer service is becoming much more complex," says Chief Marketing Officer Ravi Saligram.

Consumers themselves have cast a vote against high-quality service by increasingly choosing price, choice, and convenience over all else. Not that convenience always takes the sting out of rotten service—witness priceline.com Inc., the ultimate self-service site that lets customers name their own price for plane tickets, hotels, and other goods. Many consumers didn't fully understand the trade-offs, such as being forced to stop over on flights, take whatever brand was handed to them, and forgo the right to any refund. And when things went wrong, critics say, no one was around to help. The results: a slew of complaints that has prompted at least one state investigation. Priceline.com responds that its revamping the Web site and intensifying efforts to improve customer service. While many consumers refuse to pay more for service, they're clearly dismayed when service is taken away. "People have higher expectations now than two or three years ago because we have all this information at our fingertips," says Jupiter Communications Inc. analyst David Daniels.

Indeed, marketers point to what they call a growing culture of entitlement, where consumers are much more demanding about getting what they want. One reason is the explosion of choices, with everything from hundreds of cable channels to new players emerging from deregulated industries like airlines and telecom companies. Meanwhile, years of rewards programs such as frequent-flier miles have contributed to the new mindset. Those who know their worth expect special privileges that reflect it. Says Bonnie S. Reitz, senior vice-president for marketing, sales, and distribution at Continental Airlines Inc.: "We've got a hugely educated, informed, and more experienced consumer out there now."

For top-dollar clients, all this technology allows corporations to feign an almost small-town intimacy. Marketers can know your name, your spending habits, and even details of your personal life. Centura Banks Inc. of Raleigh, N.C., now rates its 2 million customers on a profitability scale from 1 to 5. The real moneymakers get calls from service reps several times a year for what Controller Terry Earley calls "a friendly chat" and even an annual call from the CEO to wish them happy holidays. No wonder attrition in this group is down by 50% since 1996, while the percentage of unprofitable customers has slipped to 21% from 27%.

LODGING

Another day, another upgrade for frequent guests. Sip champagne before the chef prepares your meal. First-time guest? So sorry. Your room is up three flights and to the left

Even for the lower tier, companies insist that this intense focus on data is leading to service that's better than ever. To start with, it's more customized. And while executives admit to pushing self-help instead of staff, they contend that such service is often preferable. After all, many banking customers prefer using automated teller machines to standing in line at their local branch. American Airlines Inc., the pioneer of customer segmentation with its two-decade-old loyalty program, says it's not ignoring those in the cheap seats, pointing to the airline's recent move to add more legroom in economy class. Says Elizabeth S. Crandall, managing director of personalized marketing: "We're just putting more of our energies into rewarding our best customers."

MARKED MAN. This segmentation of sales, marketing, and service, based on a wealth of personal information, raises some troubling questions about privacy. It threatens to become an intensely personal form of "redlining"—the controversial practice of identifying and avoiding unprofitable neighborhoods or types of people. Unlike traditional loyalty programs, the new tiers are not only highly individualized but they are often invisible. You don't know when you're being directed to a different

HOW TO IMPROVE YOUR PROFILE

Even if you're not a big spender, there are ways to improve your standing with companies in order to command better service. The key is to recognize that your spending habits, payment history, and any information you volunteer can be used for or against you. What's more, if you do think you're being pegged at a low tier, there are ways to get the recognition you feel you deserve.

The first step in fighting segmentation is to be stingy with the information you give out—especially if it's unlikely to help your status. Don't fill our surveys, sweepstakes forms, or applications if you're not comfortable with how the information might be used. Be wary when a company asks if it can alert you to other products and services. A yes may permit them to sell data that you don't want distributed.

PIGEONHOLING. The Consumers Union points out that it's unnecessary to fill out surveys with warranty cards. Just send in a proof of purchase with your name and address. "Protecting your privacy is a significant tool to prevent yourself from being pigeonholed as undesirable," says Gene Kimmelman, Washington co-director for the CU. It's equally important to recognize what kind of information companies are looking for. If you don't live in an upmarket Zip Code, consider using your work address for correspondence. Be optimistic when estimating your income or spending: The better the numbers look, the better you'll be treated.

Still, it's tough to keep personal information to yourself, especially when companies are compiling data on the business they do with you. A critical concern for all consumers is their actual payment record. Donna Fluss, a vice-president at the technology consultants Gartner Group Inc., advises pulling your credit history at least once a year to check if there are any liens or mistakes. "You may discover that you're listed as having missed a payment that you thought you made on time," she says. The three main reporting bureaus—Experian, Trans Union, and Equifax—charge a small fee for a copy of your credit history. If, however you have recently been denied credit, employment, or insurance, such a report is free from all three companies. The largest bureau is Equifax, which has data on 190 million Americans, but all three may have slightly different records based on who reports to them.

Multiple credit cards can be a mistake, especially if they're the no-frills variety that are frequently offered to less desir-

MAKING THE GRADE

How to get better service

CONSOLIDATE YOUR ACTIVITIES Few things elevate status and trim costs like spending big in one place. Be on the lookout for packages or programs that reward loyal behavior.

PROTECT YOUR PRIVACY Avoid surveys and be frugal with releasing credit-card or Social Security information. The less companies know, the less they can slot you.

JUMP THE PHONE QUEUE If you want to reach a live human, don't admit to having a touch-tone phone at the prompt. Or listen for options that are less likely to be handled automatically.

FIGHT BACK If you feel badly treated, complain. Make sure management knows just how much business you represent and that you're willing to take it elsewhere.

able candidates. Not only can they drain the credit you might need for other activities, but they're also unlikely to propel you into a higher category. Using a spouse's card or account is also to be avoided, because it robs you of a chance to build your own credit history. If a mistake is made on your account, fight it.

Pros disagree on tactics for bypassing the service maze. One customer representative argues that when calling a service center it's better to punch in no account number if you're a low-value customer. The reason? Without proper identification, he says, a live person has to get on the line. "Pretend you're calling from a rotary phone," he advises. But another tactic may be to punch zero or choose an option that's likely to get immediate attention.

In the end, resistance may be futile, and the best strategy for beating the system may be to join it. Shop around for the best company, and try to consolidate your business there. These days, the best way to ensure good service is to make yourself look like a high-value, free-spending customer.

By Diane Brady in New York

telephone queue or sales promotion. You don't hear about the benefits you're missing. You don't realize your power to negotiate with everyone from gate agents to bank employees is predetermined by the code that pops up next to your name on a computer screen.

When the curtain is pulled back on such sophisticated tiering, it can reveal some uses of customer information that are downright disturbing. Steve Reed, a West Coast sales executive, was shocked when a United Airlines Inc. ticketing agent told him: "Wow, somebody doesn't like you." Not only did she have access to his Premier Executive account information but there was a nasty note about an argument he had had with a gate agent in San Francisco several months earlier. In retrospect, he feels that

explained why staff seemed less accommodating following the incident. Now, Reed refuses to give more than his name for fear "of being coded and marked for repercussions." United spokesman Joe Hopkins says such notes give agents a more complete picture of passengers. "It's not always negative information," says Hopkins, adding that the practice is common throughout the industry.

Those who don't make the top tier have no idea how good things can be for the free-spending few. American Express Co. has a new Centurion concierge service that promises to get members almost anything from anywhere in the world. The program, with an annual fee of $1,000, is open by invitation only. "We're seeing a lot of people who value service more than price," says Alfred F. Kelly Jr., AmEx group president for consumer and small-business services. Dean Burri, a Rock Hill (S.C.) insurance executive, found out how the other half lives when he joined their ranks. Once he became a platinum customer of Starwood Hotels, it seemed there was nothing the hotel operator wouldn't do for him. When the Four Points Hotel in Lubbock, Tex., was completely booked for Texas Tech freshman orientation in August, it bumped a lower-status guest to get Burri a last-minute room. Starwood says that's part of the platinum policy, noting that ejected customers are put elsewhere and compensated for inconvenience. With the right status, says Burri, "you get completely different treatment."

RETAILING

Welcome to an after-hours preview
for key customers where great sales abound
and staff await your every need.
Out in the aisles, it's back to self-service

The distinctions in customer status are getting sliced ever finer. Continental Airlines Inc. has started rolling out a Customer Information System where every one of its 43,000 gate, reservation, and service agents will immediately know the history and value of each customer. A so-called intelligent engine not only mines data on status but also suggests remedies and perks, from automatic coupons for service delays to priority for upgrades, giving the carrier more consistency in staff behavior and service delivery. The technology will even allow Continental staff to note details about the preferences of top customers so the airline can offer them extra services. As Vice-President Reitz puts it: "We even know if they put their eyeshades on and go to sleep." Such tiering pays off. Thanks to its heavy emphasis on top-tier clients, about 47% of Continental's customers now pay higher-cost, unrestricted fares, up from 38% in 1995.

Elsewhere, the selectivity is more subtle. At All First Bank in Baltimore, only those slotted as top customers get the option to click on a Web icon that directs them to a live service agent for a phone conversation. The rest never see it. First Union, meanwhile, codes its credit-card customers with tiny colored squares that flash when service reps call up an account on their computer screens. Green means the person is a profitable customer and should be granted waivers or otherwise given white-glove treatment. Reds are the money losers who have almost no negotiating power, and yellow is a more discretionary category in between. "The information helps our people make decisions on fees and rates," explains First Union spokeswoman Mary Eshet.

Banks are especially motivated to take such steps because they have one of the widest gaps in profitability. Market Line Associates, an Atlanta financial consultancy, estimates that the top 20% of customers at a typical commercial bank generate up to six times as much revenue as they cost, while the bottom fifth cost three to four times more than they make for the company. Gartner Group Inc. recently found that, among banks with deposits of more than $4 billion, 68% are segmenting customers into profitability tranches while many more have plans to do so.

Tiering, however, poses some drawbacks for marketers. For one thing, most programs fail to measure the potential value of a customer. Most companies can still measure only past transactions—and some find it tough to combine information from different business units. The problem, of course, is that what someone spends today is not always a good predictor of what they'll spend tomorrow. Life situations and spending habits can change. In some cases, low activity may be a direct result of the consumer's dissatisfaction with current offerings. "We have to be careful not to make judgments based on a person's interaction with us," cautions Steven P. Young, vice-president for worldwide customer care at Compaq Computer Corp.s' consumer-products group. "It may not reflect their intentions or future behavior."

PAY NOT TO WAIT? Already, innovative players are striving to use their treasure trove of information to move customers up the value chain instead of letting them walk out the door. Capital One Financial Corp. of Falls Church, Va., is an acknowledged master of tiering, offering more than 6,000 credit cards and up to 20,000 permutations of other products, from phone cards to insurance. That range lets the company match clients with someone who has appropriate expertise. "We look at every single customer contact as an opportunity to make an unprofitable customer profitable or make a profitable customer more profitable," says Marge Connelly, senior vice-president for domestic card operations.

In the future, therefore, the service divide may become much more transparent. The trade-off between price and service could be explicit, and customers will be able to choose where they want to fall on that continuum. In essence, customer service will become just another product for sale. Walker Digital, the research lab run by priceline.com founder Jay S. Walker, has patented a "value-based queuing" of phone calls that allows companies to prioritize calls according to what each person will pay. As Walker Digital CEO Vikas Kapoor argues, customers can say: "I don't want to wait in line—I'll pay to reduce my wait time."

For consumers, though, the reality is that service as we've known it has changed forever. As Roger S. Siboni, chief executive of customer-service software provider E.piphany Inc., points out, not all customers are the same. "Some you want to absolutely retain and throw rose petals at their feet," Siboni says. "Others will never be profitable." Armed with detailed data on who's who, companies are learning that it makes financial sense to serve people based on what they're worth. The rest can serve themselves or simply go away.

With bureau reports

THE ETHICAL TREATMENT OF CUSTOMERS

© John E. Richardson and David L. Ralph

Marketing has been labeled one of the most corrupt and unethical areas of business. Sadly, these claims are often well-founded. The opportunities for fraud, deception, and the use of other misleading and unethical marketing techniques are endless. In the area of personal interaction between the salespeople and consumer, the salesperson often feels enormous pressure to make the sale—even if it means not being entirely "straight" with the consumer.

As consumers, our treatment by some marketers may unfortunately be neither exemplary nor laudable.

- When having a problem with a mail-order or online transaction, how onerous is the process to arrive at a satisfactory resolution or outcome? How long does it take to go through the bureaucratic hurdles until we are able to connect with a "live" person to assist us with our problem?
- When we visit a retail establishment to buy a product, how long does it take to get a salesperson to help us? Does the salesperson take the necessary time to carefully consider our product requirements and price parameters to optimally find a product that will best meet our needs?
- When we return a product purchased from an online marketer or a retail establishment, are we treated in a courteous, caring, and expeditious manner?

For the marketer who desires to act both responsibly and ethically, an understanding of the congruence between the Marketing Concept and the Golden Rule may provide some help.

The Marketing Concept—Its Three Integral Parts:

1. Intentional focus on customer needs: This involves a conscious and deliberate focus on listening to, understanding, and meeting the customer's needs (cf., difference between "marketing" approach and "selling approach."

2. Integrated management orientation: The organization should not be structured in a way such that its financial, personnel, production, and marketing areas are viewed as isolated entities— these should be orchestrated and coordinated together as integral parts of a synergistic whole. This necessitates management communicating a clear picture of the organizational purpose and mission to all levels of the company.

3. Long-term profitability: While there is no guarantee of achieving profitability, there is a tendency to believe that a well-conceived and executed marketing strategy should increase a product's probability for success.

The Golden Rule: "Do unto others as you would have them do unto you."

The Golden Rule is an injunction that represents one of humankind's highest moral ideals. Its essential connotation can be found in most of the great religions of the world (Shaw and Berry, pp. 9–10):

Good people proceed while considering that what is best for others is best for themselves. (*Hitopadesa*, Hinduism)

Thou shalt love they neighbor as thyself. (*Leviticus 19:18*, Judaism)

Therefore all things whatsoever ye would that men should do to you, do ye even so to them. (*Matthew 7:12*, Christianity)

Hurt not others with that which pains yourself. (*Udanavarga 5:18*, Buddhism)

What do you not want done to yourself, do not do to others. (*Analects 15:23*, Confucianism)

No one of you is a believer until he loves for his brother what he loves for himself. (*Traditions*, Islam)

It would be misleading to leave the impression that all ethicists feel that the Golden Rule is tenable in all business situations. Some criticize the Golden Rule because it seems presumptuous to predetermine what is best for another person, as individuals differ in their preference for personal treatment. Others feel that the application of the Golden Rule is situational since our interpretation of it seems to vary with personal circumstances (Hosmer, p. 108).

… Even the Golden Rule, that simple, elegant, sensible guide to life, can't somehow be applied universally. If you were a wealthy person, you would expect to be treated in the same way. If I were a poor person, I would wish others to share their income and benefits, just as I would be willing to share the title I had. Religious rules of conduct tend to be situation dependent; that is, our interpretation of them seems to vary with our personal circumstances.

While it is important to be cognizant of its limitations, the Golden Rule still is a worthy ingredient of our ethnical battery in the marketplace. As Richard Chewning says: "A genuine consideration of others is essential to an ethical life" (Chewning, pp. 175–176).

… Ethics, as an expression of reality, is predicated upon the assumption that there are right and wrong motives, attitudes, traits of character, and actions that are exhibited in interpersonal relationships. Respectful social interaction is considered a norm by almost everyone.

… the overwhelming majority of people perceive others to be ethical when they observe what is considered to be their genuine kindness, consideration, politeness, empathy, and fairness in their interpersonal relationships. When these are absent, and unkindness, inconsideration, rudeness, hardness, and injustice are present, the people exhibiting such conduct are considered unethical. A genuine consideration of others is essential to an ethical life.

The following are some principles and organizational examples which point to the importance of applying the salient ingredients of the Marketing Concept and the Golden Rule.

E-Commerce:

It is important for marketers to build mutually valuable relationships with customers through a trust-based collaboration process. Recent research with 50 e-businesses reflect that companies that create and nurture trust find customers return to find their sites repeatedly (Dayal…, p. 64).

Six components of trust critical to developing trusting, satisfied customers are: (1) state-of-art reliable security measures on your site; (2) merchant legitimacy (e.g., ally your product or service with an established brand); (3) order fulfillment (i.e., placing orders and getting merchandise efficiently and with minimal hassles); (4) tone and ambiance—handling consumers' personal information with sensitivity and

iron-clad confidentiality; (5) customers feeling that they are in control of the buying process; and (6) consumer collaboration—e.g., having chat groups to let consumers query each other about their purchases and experiences (Dayal…, pp. 64–67).

> Let customers reveal themselves at their own pace—so they can learn to trust you and so that you can serve them one at a time. Don't force them to follow a one-size-fits-all, information-gathering approach. Instead, provide shortcuts to experiences that are free of roadblocks and detours. Make it easy for customers to browse or to find assistance, and give first-time shoppers readily accessible information and gift giving, shipping, and returns. (Muoio, p. 27)

An excellent article in *Net Company* (Muoio, pp. 025ff.) makes some thoughtful observations about successful online retailing:

- A customer is in a self-service environment. Therefore, retailers must know what the customer wants *before* he/she tells them.
- A primary responsibility of an online retailer is to make its site easy, intuitive and accessible—to get a customer to click because she is engaged, not because she is confused.
- Hire a vice president of customer experience who will be a champion for the customer.

Some sites that have been listed as those which "clicked" with customers include:

- The Lands' End site (www.landsend.com) providing a service for customers to order free swatches—which are mailed out so you can actually see and feel the fabrics before you buy
- Garden.com (www.garden.com) offers a one-year 110%-satisfaction guarantee which is unrivaled in the world of e-commerce
- Amazon.com (www.amazon.com) posts a customer's Bill of Rights which is fair, honest, and to the point
- Gap online (www.gap.com) has a section called "gapstyle" providing photographs of actual clothes to help you put together your own outfit. As you add new items to your outfit, the site keeps a running tally of your purchases (Muoio, p. 26).

Southwest Airlines:

In the present economically treacherous times, Southwest Airlines has boosted its profits by championing the customer. Executive vice president Colleen Barrett's primary objective is to oversee every aspect of Southwest's business that touches the public and making that contact more pleasant. Says Barrett: "We will never jump on employees for leaning too far toward the customer, but we come down on them hard for not using common sense" (Teitelbaum, p. 115).

Through a travel agent, a businessman purchased a "non-refundable" and "non-changeable" round-trip ticket on Southwest from LA-Las Vegas-LA. When purchasing the ticket, he did not realize that he would be able to catch an earlier return flight than the one scheduled with this particular ticket. When he arrived at the Las Vegas airport four hours before his scheduled departure, the Southwest attendant informed him that his ticket technically could be used only for the later departure time. But, understanding his wish to leave earlier than scheduled (i.e., need orientation of Marketing Concept) and not wanting him to sit idly at the airport for four more hours (i.e., Golden Rule), she graciously—at no additional cost to him—changed his ticket to the earlier flight.

Nordstrom:

Southwest Airlines has the goal of dignifying the customer (Teitelbaum, pp. 115–116); Nordstrom has goal of delighting their customers (Sheuing, pp. 1, 3). Nordstrom employees receive excellent training and empowerment. During their training, the importance of Nordstrom's service culture is instilled in their employees. They are shown the importance of having an unrelenting pursuit of customer service excellence. They are encouraged to use sound business judgment, are empowered to give refunds with no questions asked, and to go out of their way to please customers. They are also given instant desktop access to an up-to-date data base containing customer characteristics and account history. This knowledge helps create familiarity with customer needs and requirements and conveys to customers that their expectations are understood and respected.

Hertz:

Asking customers what they want, and listening and responding to those requests, is one of the things that has enabled Hertz to maintain its lead in the highly competitive car-rental industry (Harris, pp. 233ff.).

Every time a customer returns a rental car to one of its 5,000 locations worldwide, the Hertz Corp. asks its customers a simple question: "What can we do to improve our level of service to you?" The response: "We want a clean, safe car that's easy to return at a price we can afford (no hidden costs, please)—and we want it fast!"

Conclusion

Some of the characteristics that seem to be prevalent in organizations that treat customers ethically by practicing the Marketing Concept and the Golden Rule in their day-to-day dealings with customers are as follows:

1. There is a strong commitment to corporate culture and a clearly defined mission which is frequently and unambiguously voiced by upper-management.
2. Employees—not only managers—have significant decision-making discretion or autonomy.
3. These organizations are fervently dedicated to empowering organizational members to accomplish their sharply focused goals, while playing down hierarchy, bureaucracy, and internal politicking.
4. Thinking is creative—and at times is perceived as revolutionary—in the marketplace.
5. These organizations are both value-oriented and market-driven (Peters and Levering, Moskowitz, and Katz).

a. They take time to ask customers what qualities of their products and services are most important to them, or what concerns typically dictate their purchasing habits. They then use the information to create a position which meets these needs (Kaydo, p. 106).
b. They make products or dispense services with the right benefits because they take time to gain an understanding of what their customers are trying to achieve and how they want to achieve it. Peapod, an online food grocer based in Skokie, Illinois, for example, has found the significance of constantly improving the user-friendliness of its Web site so that novice computer users have a first-use experience that will encourage ongoing use (Berggren and Nacher, pp. 32–33).

c. They practice genuine relationship marketing with the customers—*before, during*, and *after* the initial purchase (Strout, p. 69).

6. These organizations neither take their own employees nor their customers for granted.
a. They encourage teamwork while at the same time promoting the individual responsibility and enterprise, rewarding performance by merit bonuses, and other incentives (e.g., Herman-Miller, Nordstrom, and Southwest Airlines).
b. They like to say they are in partnership with their customers. They stress the importance of service to the customer—both during the sale as well as many years later.

7. Companies which exemplify treating customers ethically are founded on a covenant of trust. There is a shared belief, confidence, and faith that the company and its people will be fair, reliable, competent, and ethical in all dealings. *Total trust is the belief that a company and its people will never take opportunistic advantage of customer vulnerabilities* (Hart and Johnson, pp. 11–13).

References

Berggren, Erin, and Thomas Nacher, "Why Good Ideals Go Bust," *Management Review*, February 2000, pp. 32–36.

Chewning, Richard C., *Business Ethics in a Changing Culture* (Reston, Virginia: Reston Publishing, 1984).

Dayal, Sandeep, Landesberg, Helen, and Michael Zeissner, "How to Build Trust Online," *Marketing Management*, Fall 1999, pp. 64–69.

Harris, Adrienne S., "The Customer's Always Right," *Black Enterprise*, June 1991, pp. 233–242.

Hart, Christopher W. and Michael D. Johnson, "Growing the Trust Relationship," *Marketing Management*, Spring 1999, pp. 9–19.

Kaydo, Chad, "A Position of Power," *Sales & Marketing Management*, June 2000, pp. 104–106, 108ff.)

Hosmer, La Rue Tone, *The Ethics of Management*, second edition (Homewood, Illinois: Irwin, 1991).

Lantos, Geoffrey P., "An Ethical Base for Marketing Decision Making," *The Journal of Business and Industrial Marketing*, Spring 1987, pp. 11–16.

Levering, Robert, Moskowitz, Milton, and Michael Katz, *The 100 Best Companies to Work for in America* (Reading, Mass.: Addison-Wesly, 1984).

Magnet, Myron, "Meet the New Revolutionaries," *Fortune*, February 24, 1992, pp. 94–101.

McGarvey, Robert, "Ice Cubes to Eskimos," *Entrepreneur*, August 2000, pp. 68–69, 71ff.

Muoio, Anna, "The Experienced Customer," *Net Company*, Fall 1999, pp. 025–027.

Nelson-Horchler, Joani, "The Magic of Herman Miller," *Industry Week*, February 18, 1991, pp. 11–12, 14, 17.

Palmeri, Christopher, "Filling Big Shoes," *Forbes*, November 15, 1999, pp. 170, 172.

Peters, Tom, "20 Ideas on Service," *Executive Excellence*, July 1991, pp. 3–5.

Peters, Thomas J., and Robert H. Waterman Jr., *In Search of Excellence* (New York: Harper & Row, 1982).

Power, Christopher, Driscoll, Lisa, and Earl Bohn, "Smart Selling," *Business Week*, August 3, 1992, pp. 46–48.

Richardson, John (ed.), *Annual Editions: Business Ethics 00/01* (Guilford, CT: Dushkin/McGraw-Hill, 2000).

_____, *Annual Editions: Marketing 00/01* (Guilford, CT: Dushkin/McGraw-Hill, 2000).

Scheuing, Eberhard, "Going Beyond Customer Satisfaction," *Marketing Forum*, September 1991, pp. 1.3.

Shaw, William H., and Vincent Barry, *Moral Issues in Business*, fourth edition (Belmont, CA: Wadsworth Publishing Company, 1989).

Strout, Erin, "Tough Customers," *Sales Marketing Management*, January 2000, pp. 63–69.

Teitelbaum, Richard S., "Where Service Flies Right," *Fortune*, August 24, 1992, pp. 115–116.

Dr. John E. Richardson *is Professor of Marketing in the Graziadio School of Business and Management at Pepperdine University, Malibu, California.*

Dr. David L. Ralph *is Associate Professor of Marketing in the Graziadio School of Business and Management at Pepperdine University, Malibu, California*

Too Close for Comfort

WHAT YOU KNOW ABOUT YOUR CUSTOMERS MAY BE DANGEROUS. NO MARKETING TEAM OR SALES FORCE CAN AFFORD TO IGNORE TODAY'S GROUNDSWELL OF CONCERN OVER CUSTOMER PRIVACY

By Mark McMaster

Can you keep a secret?

FOR EVERY MORSEL of information you collect about your clients, the answer had better be yes. That applies to the scribbles in your salespeoples' notebooks just as much as the databases of online browsing habits, credit card numbers, and purchasing histories stored on the company network. The looming debate on consumer privacy challenges assumptions about what client information may be collected, shared, and sold, and it will soon touch every business. Large or small, online or off, companies face new responsibilities in explaining and justifying their use of personal data.

"If you lack a privacy policy and haven't educated your sales force about the ramifications of privacy law, you may be putting your company at risk legally and financially."

If you think privacy is a matter for the legal department to take care of, think again. Sales and marketing teams deal more closely with customer data than any other company unit, so if you lack a privacy policy and haven't educated your sales force about the ramifications of privacy law, you may be putting your company at risk legally and financially. "If you have personally identifiable information about customers and you misuse it, you'll find yourself on the unfriendly end of a lot of attention," says attorney Ray Everett-Church, the manager of PrivacyClue, a consulting firm in San Jose, California. "Customers do not forgive companies that misuse information."

Need proof? Look at Internet advertising powerhouse Double-Click. Its Big Brother approach earned it an FTC inquiry, a class action suit, and a 75 percent tumble in its stock price. Likewise, GeoCities, the CVS drug store chain, and Chase Manhattan Bank have all taken legal heat and weeks of bad public relations for the release of unsuspecting consumers' identifying info. And the issue is just starting to unravel. "Anyone who thinks the privacy issue has peaked is greatly mistaken," says Jay Stanley, an e-commerce analyst at Forrester Research in Cambridge, Massachusetts. "We are in the early years of a sweeping change in attitudes that will fuel years of political battles and put once routine business practices under the microscope."

NEW TECHNOLOGIES, NEW FEARS

TODAY'S SHIFTING ATTITUDES about privacy are largely a reaction to the unprecedented opportunity for gathering consumer data on the Internet. "When you visit a Web site about baby care, and suddenly for three weeks every banner ad you see is for baby items, you start to feel like you're being watched," says Larry Ponemon, the former head of privacy practice at PricewaterhouseCoopers and the president of Guardent, a privacy management and data security firm in Waltham, Massachusetts. "Customers have learned to assume the worst," he says. Threats to privacy with innocent names like cookies and spam have entered the consumer lexicon, making Web surfers reluctant to give up information about individual preferences or identity.

As businesses track customers ever more closely with sophisticated personalization techniques and data mining technology, these fears have spread to the offline world, and consumer anxiety has produced a political response. No less than six privacy protection bills await debate in Congress, all of which would limit the ability of businesses to collect personal information about their customers. Meanwhile, the Federal Trade Commission (FTC) is using existing law to aggressively punish companies that violate consumers' rights, says Simon Lazarus, an attorney at Powell, Goldstein, Frazer & Murphy in, Washington, D.C.

A key piece of privacy legislation, the Gramm-Leach-Bliley Act, went into effect in July and requires financial institutions to provide written notice of its privacy policies and practices, and prohibits any disclosure of nonpublic personal information—such as purchase histories, birth dates, or even phone numbers—to third parties unless the consumer has the opportunity to opt out of the disclosure. Its ramifications may extend far beyond the industry it was intended to regulate, Lazarus says, extending to any company that offers credit to its customers.

B-TO-B COMPANIES AT RISK

IT'S NOT JUST business-to-consumer companies that are vulnerable. "The damages [of privacy invasion] can be more pronounced in the business-to-business world, because you're dealing with situations where information that is shared can be of serious strategic and financial significance to the victim. The damages become much greater," says Jack Vonder Heide, the president of the Technology Briefing Center, a training organization in Oakbrook Terrace, Illinois, that offers privacy training.

Vonder Heide cites the most visible example of a company strained by privacy concerns, New York-based DoubleClick, which sells its services to businesses, not consumers. DoubleClick's name has been synonymous with privacy fears since January 2000, when news broke that DoubleClick was soon to offer about 100,000 unique user profiles lifted from a dozen Web sites, complete with real-world identities and contact information gleaned from the company's recent purchase of offline consumer data seller Abacus Direct. Tracking the online behavior of these profiles would have produced a treasure trove of information for online marketers, but consumer advocates weren't pleased that advertisers would be aware of their real-world identities each time they logged onto a site affiliated with DoubleClick. Denouncing the company in the national media and threatening legal action, the words of DoubleClick's critics would scar the company for months to come.

Even more damaging, DoubleClick had unceremoniously abridged the privacy statement contained on its Web site just days before these news reports, a move that hinted at its intention to begin merging online and offline data, but offered little warning for Web users who might wish to remove their names from its lists. The popular backlash against DoubleClick shocked the company, which had a sales force focused on businesses and never saw itself as accountable to consumers themselves. "At that point, DoubleClick viewed itself as a business-to-business company—we didn't interact with consumers directly, and we didn't really have a good means of explaining how DoubleClick interacted with customers," says Jules Polonetsky, who in March 2000 was appointed DoubleClick's chief privacy officer.

Another blow was yet to come. In February 2000 the FTC opened an investigation into DoubleClick's potentially deceptive data handling practices. The company kept news of the investigation under wraps, not issuing a press release until the story was uncovered by reporters just two days before the company was to open a major stock offering. It was a mar-

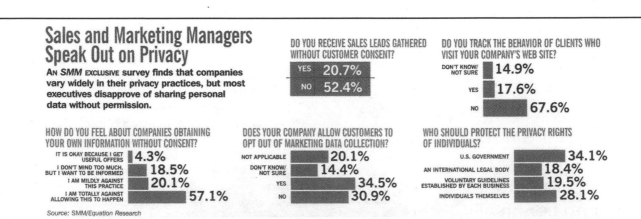

Sales and Marketing Managers Speak Out on Privacy

AN *SMM* EXCLUSIVE survey finds that companies vary widely in their privacy practices, but most executives disapprove of sharing personal data without permission.

DO YOU RECEIVE SALES LEADS GATHERED WITHOUT CUSTOMER CONSENT?
- YES 20.7%
- NO 52.4%

DO YOU TRACK THE BEHAVIOR OF CLIENTS WHO VISIT YOUR COMPANY'S WEB SITE?
- DON'T KNOW/NOT SURE 14.9%
- YES 17.6%
- NO 67.6%

HOW DO YOU FEEL ABOUT COMPANIES OBTAINING YOUR OWN INFORMATION WITHOUT CONSENT?
- IT IS OKAY BECAUSE I GET USEFUL OFFERS 4.3%
- I DON'T MIND TOO MUCH, BUT I WANT TO BE INFORMED 18.5%
- I AM MILDLY AGAINST THIS PRACTICE 20.1%
- I AM TOTALLY AGAINST ALLOWING THIS TO HAPPEN 57.1%

DOES YOUR COMPANY ALLOW CUSTOMERS TO OPT OUT OF MARKETING DATA COLLECTION?
- NOT APPLICABLE 20.1%
- DON'T KNOW/NOT SURE 14.4%
- YES 34.5%
- NO 30.9%

WHO SHOULD PROTECT THE PRIVACY RIGHTS OF INDIVIDUALS?
- U.S. GOVERNMENT 34.1%
- AN INTERNATIONAL LEGAL BODY 18.4%
- VOLUNTARY GUIDELINES ESTABLISHED BY EACH BUSINESS 19.5%
- INDIVIDUALS THEMSELVES 28.1%

Source: SMM/Equation Research

keting blunder, and over the next week, the stock fell nearly 25 percent. Unable to squeeze a return out of its sizable investment in Abacus Direct, it plunged to less than $15 a share by December 2000, after a high of $135.25 in January of that year. "It was a learning moment for the entire industry," says Nuala O'Connor, the vice president of data protection at DoubleClick. "I think DoubleClick crystallized concerns about data collection online and off. We found ourselves in the middle of a huge issue."

SALES FORCES—THE WEAKEST LINK?

SURPRISINGLY, SALESPEOPLE MAY be companies' most vulnerable point-of-contact when it comes to privacy liability. "The problem you have in a sales organization is that individual sales reps tend to be the masters of their own data," Vonder Heide says. "Salespeople have systems that range anywhere from day planners and traditional filing cabinets with paper notes, all the way up to sophisticated programs like Outlook, ACT!, and GoldMine that share data and upload it to a centralized database." Savvy salespeople slip in personal information useful in keeping up relationships with clients—perhaps the ages of a customer's children, or that a particular client is prone to overdrinking, or that Mr. Thompson's wife is battling cancer—knowledge that, in the wrong hands, could embarrass clients and encourage lawsuits. "Most companies that sell exclusively through sales organizations don't have privacy policies," Vonder Heide says. "But every sales rep should understand which customer information should be maintained, and which is appropriate to share with other parties."

Nationwide Insurance, based in Columbus, Ohio, has been grappling with the challenge of educating its salespeople about privacy for two years, says Kirk Herath, the company's chief privacy officer. "It took us half a year to determine our information practices for all of our companies and affiliates, but before we published our policies we had to educate the people on the front lines about what our privacy practices were and what their individual responsibilities were," he says.

It's not just b-to-c companies that are vulnerable. Privacy violation can be even more damaging in the business-to-business world, where leaked information can be of serious strategic significance to the victim.

Herath was particularly concerned about the company's sales force. Decades-old prospecting techniques used by insurance agents would soon become illegal under the Gramm-Leach-Bliley Act and violate Nationwide's new policies. For example, insurance agents often form partnerships with other local salespeople, such as real estate agents, car dealers, and bank representatives, passing on leads about clients new to the area and referring valuable customers. If personal information about Nationwide customers were to be shared in these exchanges, both the agents and the company itself could be sued.

"We knew our sales force would be a big source of liability," Herath says, so he developed a comprehensive training program on privacy that includes dozens of pages of practices to follow, a guide for managers on how to train agents, and a certification test for agents. The curriculum is in the early stages of implementation, and with more than 8,000 agents, including many who work at independent agencies not managed by Nationwide, achieving full compliance will take months of work.

PRACTICE MUST FOLLOW POLICY

GEOCITIES LEARNED A universal lesson in privacy law back in 1998: After you state what your policy is, you have to live up to it. The Web hosting site's registration page then contained the statement, "We will not share this information without your permission." The company nonetheless released the responses—including customers' age, education, occupation, income, and personal interests—to business partners and advertisers. In response the FTC, in its first Internet privacy enforcement action, charged GeoCities with engaging in deceptive practices. After three months of investigation, GeoCities emerged with a lucky settlement. There was no admission of wrongdoing, fine, or penalty; instead the site simply changed its privacy policy to reflect its behavior. (Federal law allows penalties of up to $11,000 per violation in such cases, Everett-Church says, and GeoCities had 2 million subscribers at the time of the FTC inquiry.) Despite emerging clean from the inquiry, GeoCities' stock fell 15 percent the day the charges were announced.

In short, any violation of a privacy policy is fraud, says Everett-Church. And this not only holds true to a company's own behavior, but its business partners' actions as well. John Blaber learned this firsthand when his company was slapped with a lawsuit for work it had done for the now-defunct Toysrus.com Web site. Blaber is the vice president of marketing for Coremetrics, a San Francisco data analysis firm that processes consumer information on Web sites. In its privacy policy, Toys "R" Us had never informed its customers that a third party was involved in collecting data, but because Coremetrics was acting as a contractor, Blaber never saw this as his concern. "The lawsuit surprised us," he says, because Coremetrics never owned the data or distributed it to an outside party. It simply recorded consumer behavior on Toysrus.com, repackaged it, and gave reports back to the company. At press time the suit was still in litigation, but Coremetrics has taken steps to avoid such problems in the future.

"As we work with clients, we step through a process of educating them," Blaber says, and the company now insists that each client notify its customers of Coremetrics' service. After his experience, Blaber suggests that in any business partnership, if any consumer data is shared, the partner must live up to the same standards set in your own company's privacy policy.

FOLLOWING THE TRAIL OF CUSTOMER DATA

WHEN BUSINESSES ARE bought or sold, or salespeople change jobs, difficult questions arise about who owns customer data and how it can be used. Sales organizations are famous for high turnover, and when reps move from company to company, they often carry along their stash of customer information. This knowledge of purchasing habits and personal facts, along with contact names and numbers, could land the rep and her former company in a lawsuit, Vonder Heide says. "The stimulus for [current and pending privacy legislation] was the growth of electronic data exchange, largely through the Internet. But the rules aren't limited to electronic methods. They cover the sharing of data in and of itself, and that sharing could be done in a word-of-mouth manner," he says.

> Salespeople, who trade daily in clients' personal information, may be the weakest link in privacy protection. Few reps are kept up-to-date on corporate privacy policies.

When entire businesses are bought and sold, similar privacy quandaries emerge. CVS, a Rhode Island-based pharmacy chain, was hit with a class action lawsuit earlier this year as a result of its acquisition of 250,000 customer records from the purchase of 300 independent pharmacies. The suit was launched by an AIDS patient who felt violated by the sharing of information that clearly identified him as having the disease. Although there is no legal precedent regarding the sale of pharmacy records, Vonder Heide says there is no reason to believe that courts will not find companies liable in groundbreaking cases. "There's a certain danger now because of the litigious society we live in," he says. "You have all kinds of parties looking for test cases. If individuals feel they were wronged because their information was shared, they'll have no trouble finding a lawyer to take the case on a pro bono basis."

COMMUNICATING PRIVACY TO CUSTOMERS

WHEN IT COMES time to confront the privacy issue, many companies turn to experts like PricewaterhouseCoopers or Ernst & Young to create policies and ensure enterprisewide compliance. In 2000 PricewaterhouseCoopers completed 200 privacy audits

compared with only 20 in 1999. (Among companies that already had a privacy policy in place, only 80 percent complied with their policies, Ponemon estimated while at PricewaterhouseCoopers.)

Everett-Church suggests that companies also need an internal expert who can manage privacy issues throughout the company. "Respect for customer data has to permeate a company's contacts with its customers, continually reassuring them that they are protected," he says. "That's more than just someone in the legal department slapping a privacy policy on the company Web site. Sales and marketing people must be in on the privacy story." Communication must go both ways, he adds, with salespeople and marketers receiving training on privacy policies and procedures while helping privacy officers develop rules that meet their clients' expectations.

"[Sales executives] are learning that they have to take a proactive step to explain their practices and policies so they won't be misrepresented by those who are critical of marketing and advertising," DoubleClick's Polonetsky adds. "Instead of focusing on the specifics of technologies, we need to explain simply what's taking place. As everyone understands the reality of how the technology is used, it increases consumers' comfort level."

Successful communication also benefits a brand's image. "When you've got other companies out there that aren't clued in on these issues, you can differentiate yourself by giving customers more control over their privacy," Everett-Church says. "Trust is something that is very hard to build and easy to lose, but if you incorporate it into your message, it can be a huge advantage."

That's why it's crucial that sales and marketing teams focus on matters of privacy. "They've absolutely not yet paid enough attention," Ponemon says. "The mindset of sales and marketing executives has been that privacy is the nemesis of marketing. Yes, respecting privacy creates some roadblocks and barriers. But ultimately, it's about knowing your customers and what they want and expect. It's not necessarily antagonistic."

THE MARKETING CHALLENGE

MICHAEL MIORA, a consultant with the ePrivacy Group, in Playa del Rey, California, summarizes the situation marketers face when dealing with personal information as "the privacy paradox." He says, "on the one hand, people want more privacy. They want the sites they visit to know less about them, but on the other hand, they only want information that's relevant to them to come into their mailbox."

The solution is effective marketing communication—understanding customers' concerns, addressing them in policy, and sending the right message about why your company can be trusted. Violate customers' perceptions of privacy once, and they may never come back, says Ponemon, so the time to look at your company's privacy practices is now. In the meantime, salespeople and marketers maintaining stockpiles of customer data had best keep their mouths shut.

ASSOCIATE EDITOR MARK McMASTER CAN BE REACHED AT MMCMASTER@SALESANDMARKETING.COM

Are You Putting Your Customers' Privacy at Risk?

WITHOUT A CLEAR privacy policy, your customers may be wary of offering personal information and your sales force won't have a code of contact to adhere to. Here are what industry experts say are the four components to an airtight privacy policy:

NOTICE A clearly written and easily accessible privacy statement allows people to understand what information is being collected about them.

CHOICE Customers should be able to decline the sharing or collection of information if they so desire. A simple e-mail form or check box should be presented at the time information is gathered so that clients can decline to participate. Opt-in policies require a customer to explicitly give approval before data is shared, while less restrictive opt-out policies assume customer consent unless they otherwise give notice.

ACCESS The ability for consumers to review the data that has been collected, then correct any errors that could result in misrepresentation or shoddy marketing, is another must for companies that collect large amounts of data.

SECURITY Companies must ensure that the systems and procedures used for collecting and storing customer information are protected enough that employee error, technology problems, or data theft won't jeopardize clients' privacy. "Even if you've developed the best policy, if suddenly your Web server goes berserk and shoots out personal information all over the Internet like a garden sprinkler, then you've got bigger problems," attorney Ray Everett-Church says.

—M.M.

From *Sales & Marketing Management,* July 2001, pp. 42-48. © 2001 by Sales & Marketing Management. Reprinted by permission.

UNIT 2

Research, Markets, and Consumer Behavior

Unit Selections

Key Points to Consider

- As marketing research techniques become more advanced, and as psychographic analysis leads to more sophisticated models of consumer behavior, do you believe marketing will become more capable of predicting consumer behavior? Explain.

- Where the target population lives, its age, and its ethnicity are demographic factors of importance to marketers. What other demographic factors must be taken into account in long-range market planning?

- In what areas or ways do you feel that the millennial generation significantly differs from prior generations?

- Psychographic segmentation is the process whereby consumer markets are divided up into segments based upon similarities in lifestyles, attitudes, personality type, social class, and buying behavior. In what specific ways do you envision psychographic research and findings helping marketing planning and strategy in the next decade?

 **Links: www.dushkin.com/online/**
These sites are annotated in the World Wide Web pages.

CyberAtlas Demographics
http://cyberatlas.internet.com/big_picture/demographics/

General Social Survey
http://www.icpsr.umich.edu/GSS99/

"Identifying Your Appropriate Market Opportunity"
http://www.cba.neu.edu/alumni/molloy/art-21.htm

"Market Research Essential in Determining Firm's Viability"
http://www.cba.neu.edu/alumni/molloy/art-03.htm

Marketing Tools Directory
http://www.maritzresearch.com

U.S. Census Bureau Home Page
http://www.census.gov

USADATA
http://www.usadata.com

WWW Virtual Library: Demography & Population Studies
http://demography.anu.edu.au/VirtualLibrary/

If marketing activities were all we knew about an individual, we would know a great deal. By tracing these daily activities over only a short period of time, we could probably guess rather accurately that person's tastes, understand much of his or her system of personal values, and learn quite a bit about how he or she deals with the world.

In a sense, this is a key to successful marketing management: tracing a market's activities and understanding its behavior. However, in spite of the increasing sophistication of market research techniques, this task is not easy. Today a new society is evolving out of the changing lifestyles of Americans, and these divergent lifestyles have put great pressure on the marketer who hopes to identify and profitably reach a target market. At the same time, however, each change in consumer behavior leads to new marketing opportunities.

The writings in this unit were selected to provide information and insight into the effect that lifestyle changes and demographic trends are having on American industry.

The first unit article in the "Marketing Research" subsection provides an enlightening look at ways that social value-focused interviews can uncover customer's real desire for new products. The next article describes how a popular research technique helps marketers and consumers get what they really want.

The three articles in the "Markets and Demographics" subsection examine the importance of demographic data, geographic settings, economic forces, and age considerations in making marketing decisions. In the first article, "A Beginner's Guide to Demographics," Berna Miller provides a helpful background for understanding demographics. The remaining three articles scrutinize some unique demographic and psychographic considerations to be reckoned with for Hispanics, Asian Americans, and various "generational" groupings.

The three articles in the final subsection examine how consumer behavior, social attitudes, cues, and quality considerations will have an impact on the evaluation and purchase of various products and services for different consumers.

Taking an
E X P A N D E D View of Customers'
Needs: Qualitative Research for Aiding Innovation

Social value-focused interviews can uncover customers' real desires for new products and help yield critical insights for innovations.

By Maria F. Flores Letelier, Charles Spinosa, and Bobby J. Calder

Marketing practitioners and theorists have recognized the limited ability of marketing research to generate innovative product concepts. A common complaint of managers is that marketing research does not allow them to decide whether a radical innovation will succeed in the marketplace or not. Consumers can discuss potential innovations in focus groups and respond to surveys, and the results will be repeatable. But managers still feel as though the results are insufficient to understand what consumers will do. In many cases, a product has failed even though extensive research showed customers had the need and favorable quantitative concept tests showed the product met the need. Other times, competitors have been able to innovate in so-called saturated markets where management believed that no need existed for a new product. Therefore, most managers end up believing that managerial intuition is better than customer research for the case of innovative concepts.

Most market researchers and strategic theorists would allow that the limit has to do with the capability of consumers to say what they really want or to predict how they will really behave. According to Gary Hamel and C.K. Prahalad, "[M]arket research carried out around a new product or service concept is notoriously inaccurate ... and is of little use in helping a company better target its development efforts around emerging markets." (See Additional Reading) With new ideas, technologies, and innovations of any kind—with anything unfamiliar to a particular market—research cannot determine how people will act. Leonard, Wyner, and others have led innovative thinking around research for unknown customer categories. They have shown us the importance of understanding customers' "unarticulated needs" through customer observation and by using more than one conventional technique to investigate issues that customers will have a difficult time expressing.

In observing market research directed toward new-product generation in more than 100 high-performance companies over the past five years, we have learned that most companies receive weak results because they attempt to listen for one, single consistent voice from customers, one that clearly expresses a need for a particular product. The problem with this approach is that it completely misses a key resource that qualitative customer interviews can provide. Namely, research can identify those areas in customers' lives related to a product category where customers express conflict or ambivalence. Such ambivalence covers not only what they need from the product category, but also their goals and the meaning they receive from the category in the context of the rest of their lives. These ignored expressions present opportunities for producing market-creating innovations that most companies today overlook.

In this article, we first present an expanded view of customers' needs that will allow researchers to explore the conflicts among certain kinds of values since these conflicts lie behind the ambivalences and inconsistent expressions. We then present techniques, which we call "Articulative Interviewing Techniques," that can be used along with customer observation and other market research techniques to uncover value conflicts. Finally, we show how findings from articulative interviews can be used to design innovative product concepts. Managers do not need to rely on intuition alone; customers can in fact reveal quite a bit about the directions in which they are changing and, consequently, about new products they will bring into their lives.

EXECUTIVE SUMMARY

Market research is limited in generating innovative product concepts because of the consumers' inability to say what they really want or how they will really behave. Our work shows that research can generate successful product concepts by focusing on consumers' ambivalent and confused expressions. "Articulative Interviewing Techniques" reveal the conflicts among "orienting evaluations" that lie behind ambivalent and inconsistent expressions. Market researchers and managers can, in turn, use conflict analysis to produce successful, new product concepts.

SOCIALLY DRIVEN ORIENTING VALUES AND CONFLICTS AMONG ORIENTING VALUES

A different approach to primary customer research, particularly interviews with customers, can help managers design strategic, market-creating innovations with which customers have no experience. This approach enables researchers to gain insights about the conflict among what we call "orienting values" that emerge through social change.

Orienting values, a term based on the work of philosopher Charles Taylor, are a class of values that people hold. We draw the term "orientating value" from his term "strong evaluation." The term value here is not being used in an economic sense, but rather in the philosophical sense. An orienting value is one that orients our general sense of a worthwhile life, one that is socially estimable or not estimable. A person might value the pleasure of owning and wearing a certain skirt, but is unlikely to orient a life around that. Being a serious professional, however, might be one value that orients a person's life. Other values such as the pleasure of a hot red, satin skirt would be evaluated and acted on in relation to the orienting value. Unlike other values, orienting values are bipolar. The opposite of an orienting value is inestimable or unworthy and experienced as contemptible or disgusting. A professional person is disgusted by her lapses into unprofessional behavior. A person who seeks to be cutting edge rejects all that is not cutting edge. We will not discuss these philosophical views here in detail; our point is that market researchers can learn a lot from exploring orienting values and how they change for understanding consumer behavior.

The orienting values that customers hold change with history. Let us look at the changes in orienting values that affected how people esteemed cars in the last two decades. Few would doubt that the BMW was the upper-middle-class car of the 1980s, meaning not that BMWs brought in the most revenue but rather that BMWs represented the standard against which other cars were judged. The BMW was the high-performance, optimizing car. Desiring a BMW was worthwhile because it showed that a person cared about the orienting value of high performance. In the 1990s, however, sport-utility vehicles such as the Range Rover and Jeep Cherokee became the ideal cars. These cars

bring out the orienting evaluation of flexible optimization. They are still high-performance cars, as high performance still matters in many domains of our lives (such as work). But these cars also reflect today's more flexible lifestyles; they reveal multiple personal roles such as relaxed family member, adventurous hiker, and high-performance career person.

Customers will often hold conflicting orienting values. Such conflicts reveal how customers are changing and hence offer insights into innovative offer concepts. We can easily see how being responsible can come into conflict with being free. Desiring a Honda Accord is good because it allows a person to feel responsible, but a Ferrari is good because it lets the driver feel free. The Mazda Miata was one response to this conflict. It was responsible enough in price, quality, and gas consumption and yet allowed the freedom of taking off in a roadster. Successful breakthrough products resolve these conflicts.

ARTICULATIVE INTERVIEWING

The best method market researchers can employ to listen for and to identify key conflicts in orienting values is a practice of qualitative group interviewing called articulative interviewing. We call this interviewing articulative because it draws interviewees to articulate orienting values and their inherent conflicts, which might otherwise seem inexpressible.

Articulative interviewing, unlike standard consumer research, is structured so as to elicit narratives as opposed to the factual truth. Standard focus-group interviewers attempt to design interviews to generate "objective" results, which, for investigating consumers' relationship to products with which they have experience, are crucial. However, in articulative interviewing the point is to uncover what consumers find worthy and unworthy in their lives, and the best source of this material is the narrative matter that participants provide about how they live in particular roles and in certain domains of activity. Whether these narratives are accurate or populated with small infelicities, narratives reveal the values that participants esteem or dislike. As interviewees tell their narratives, they also get themselves and others in touch with the important roles that they play. So their conversations become increasingly molded by the values relevant to the product category.

EXHIBIT 1 Expanded view of customers' needs

EXHIBIT 2 Listening for value conflicts:
Articulative interviewing

Identifying Orienting Values	Identifying Value Conflicts
1. Question the obvious	1. Listen for confusions, resignations, contradictions
2. Study the present	2. Listen for individual distinctions
3. Know the past	3. Identify product category life roles
4. Learn the descriptive vocabulary	4. Elicit defining narratives of life role changes

Narratives enable articulative interviewers to raise questions about the parts of the story that were left out and tend to bring out expressions of conflict. The past-present-future structure of a narrative allows the researcher to identify which values are changing. By asking the participants about the context of a story, the interviewer brings the participants to describe how the different roles they hold are in conflict and produce seemingly insoluble dilemmas.

Most conflicts among orienting values can be identified by exercising four basic listening and analytical techniques for identifying orienting values and four other techniques for articulating conflicts among orienting values. As a practical matter, identification of orienting values takes place best in one-to-one interviews. In practice, it is best to begin such interviewing by finding an informant like the kind anthropologists use. An informant knows the product category well, has a wide range of friends in the segment to whom he or she gives advice, likes talking frankly about the product category, and is sensitive to the differences in understanding between him or herself and the researcher. Once one-to-one interviews have uncovered orienting values, group interviewing is best for getting at shared social conflicts in orienting values. Groups assembled by the informant work best. The informant serves as the investigator's connection to the group of customers being interviewed and draws together acquaintances who already share similar orienting values. With such a group, trust is quickly built, and, consequently, authentic life narratives are revealed. Ideally, the group should be small (three-five people); the interview should last one and a half to two hours; and the researcher should take steps to ensure that [the] group shares a trust-building level of similarity.

By understanding these techniques, strategists, managers, and market researchers can take lead roles to produce market-changing innovations in products and services. Ultimately, listening to value conflicts is a visionary skill that should be developed in the strategic and marketing areas of an organization.

FOUR TECHNIQUES FOR IDENTIFYING ORIENTING VALUES

Technique 1: Question the obvious and listen for difference. Standard market research is meant to be objective, investigators are supposed to keep any preconceived assumptions they may have regarding their interviewees from interfering with the interview process. However, researchers cannot identify their interviewees' orienting values in a value-free or value-neutral way. So they learn rather to identify which of their own values they will use to identify their interviewees' values. The interviewer's recognition of his or her own cultural or subculturally distinctive values makes the differing values of others intelligible in the first place. For instance, in interviewing parents from different cultures and economic classes, we have learned that all parents will claim something seemingly universal: "I want what is best for my children. And that is that they do well in life." What this means, however, varies greatly. By listening for difference from our own orienting values and thereby questioning the obvious, we were able to learn that, in middle-class Mexican culture, "doing well" means visibly achieving the next economic class status without regard to calling. In low-income Mexican culture, "doing well" means that the children will have their own home without regard to whether it came by good fortune or hard work.

We have been able to identify the significantly different shadings of "doing well" among different economic groups in Mexico by simply questioning the obvious American meaning of "doing well," that is, achieving one's dreams or being fully independent. An interviewer who assumed that individualism was part of human constitution would miss the point of what "doing well" meant to Mexicans. Another example from newly arrived Mexicans is their response when asked what they miss most about Mexico: "One feels free in Mexico." Taken as a straight response, a U.S. interviewer might understand freedom to mean spontaneous independence or the desire to do what one wishes. However, upon listening for difference, a listener would understand that dedication to family and friends, not independence, is precisely the Mexican way of experiencing freedom. They might say, "There is a lot of time left over in Mexico. There is no routine. One finishes work, and walks over to a friend's house in the evening."

By acknowledging peoples' tendency to listen according to their own dominant values (such as a love of individualism), researchers can learn to listen to people from other cultures and subcultures. To uncover a key orienting value (e.g., freedom means dedication to family), an articulative interviewer has to attend to his or her own weaker or marginal values such as family dependence. Listening with these orienting values in mind directs a line of questioning that elicits what is meant by "doing well in life" or by "being free." Thus, a listener can begin to explore how seemingly obvious statements can have meanings that are quite different from the ones the interviewer assumes. Whenever something sounds obvious and right, the articulative interviewer has to question it and begin looking for the difference.

Technique 2: Study the present. Most conflicts among orienting values arise as social change occurs. Researchers have to determine the nature of the present changes, and the best way to do this is to conduct research on the currently popular exemplars or figures in the culture of interest. Some of this research can be conducted before conducting interviews as preparation. A market researcher could start by looking at the basic cultural domains—politics, education, economics, art, fashion, and entertainment—and ask about the nature of the figures in each. How are they similar? How have they changed from the figures of the previous decade? When interviewing women in their late twenties for new fashion concepts, we learned that the superwoman of the eighties, represented by such figures as Maddie on the TV show *Moonlighting* or a host of career executives, are no longer exemplars for these women. Suddenly, creative, entrepreneurial types became more interesting. But this entrepreneurial creativity is important only in contrast to high-performing intensity. Without the correct contrasting orienting values, the current ones and their stresses are not genuinely understood.

Answers to other questions can be used to build a context for these questions about popular cultural figures. What are the popular college majors or areas of study? What are the hit movies, plays, and TV shows? What ways of doing things do students, entertainment figures, and performances promote? The point is not to see these domains as separate, but to ask what threads unify them. A researcher will also want to distinguish the dominant cultural figures from the marginal subcultural ones. It is important to determine which currently marginal figures are possible indicators of the direction in which the culture is moving.

Technique 3: Know the past. Adequate identification of conflicts among orienting values requires knowledge of the cultural or subcultural background of the participants. In exploring new market possibilities with a producer of building materials in Mexico, we interviewed do-it-yourself, low-income homebuilders to help explore new-product offers that the company could make.

It was evident that these customers had highly inefficient habits for purchasing and using materials, but attempts to sell efficiency-improving products such as bulk-purchase discounts, materials sized according to the average job, and more convenient locations had failed.

In investigating and articulating the historical context, we discovered that do-it-yourself homebuilders gave an extremely high value to dignity and status within the local community. The historical context for this characteristic dated back to medieval Spain when fixed status was preserved by inalienable landholding. In Mexico, status is commonly maintained by participating and contributing to the local town's annual celebrations and festivities. Low-income do-it-yourselfers would typically spend two month's income on a daughter's Quinceañera, essentially a coming-out party. We also learned that the historical creditors' shame practice of having someone remarkably dressed follow a defaulter around all day was still effective. Maintaining social position was everything, and that made sense of the expensive festivities. It followed that, for these do-it-yourself homebuilders, focusing resources on building one's own family home could count as antisocial behavior while at the same time having a home marked one's status. To see this bind and recognize its power, our researchers had to become familiar with the slow Spanish historical transformation from a status-oriented culture to a transactions-oriented culture.

Technique 4: Learn the descriptive vocabulary. Prior to jumping to any conclusions about a particular customer group, it is necessary to become familiar with the local modes of characterization. In particular, careful listening needs to identify a subculture's "descriptive distinctions," which are the terms that people use to talk about what is important.

In our investigation of new fashion concepts for women in their late twenties, we elicited the distinctions of "hip," "cool," "comfortable," "sexy," "funky," and "sleek." To do this, we could not simply ask consumers why they liked or disliked a fashion product whose nature we thought we understood. Similar verbal expressions across segments or generations are false friends. "Comfortable clothing" can, for instance, ambiguously mean clothes that allow consumers to move easily or clothes that allow consumers to feel comfortable about their bodies. At different times, people value different aspects of comfort. Knowing this, we began our interviews by inquiring about how these women dressed for different occasions. These conversations gave us the basic vocabulary of descriptive distinctions for successful and failed dressing attempts.

It is important to distinguish ordinary descriptive distinctions that highlight orienting values in particular. Since orienting values are bipolar—meaning the orienting value is admired and its opposite is loathed—an orienting value can be identified by asking for examples of a description's opposite. Again, when customers express contempt or disgust at examples of a description's opposite, the description contains an orienting value. So, to return to the fashion example, when we learned that "powerful" is an important term today, we asked for examples of weakness. Weakness was bad, but not disgusting. When we asked about the opposite of being independent or being true to oneself, we found that cases of giving in, selling out, caring only for money, or families were repulsive. Independence, then, was an orienting value.

FOUR TECHNIQUES FOR IDENTIFYING AND ARTICULATING VALUE CONFLICTS

Technique 1: Listen for resignations, confusions, awkwardness, and contradictions. Researchers often aim to elicit clearly voiced expressions from customers when interviewing them with respect to new products. As Leonard points out, "customers' ability to guide the development of new products and services is limited by their experience and their ability to imagine and describe possible innovations." (See Additional Reading.) Clearly voiced assessments are obviously unavailable when attempting to move beyond consumers' current experience.

An expanded view of customers' needs leads researchers to pay attention to resignations, awkwardness, and confusions. Customers show these by declaring, "That is just the way life is" or "It is impossible for me to ever reach that goal in life" or simply by exhibiting an awkward moment and a difficulty in expressing themselves. For instance, while interviewing mid- and late-twenties women to generate magazine topics on career issues, we learned that women in their twenties do not have clearly voiced assessments about careers. When asked about their career choices, they quickly discredited money as a primary issue and instead stressed job and life fulfillment. However, at other moments, when perhaps more in touch with their roles as potentially successful women, they said they would never work for less than $50,000 a year. A big house, a nice car, and the ability to travel were very important. These later comments, however, slipped out with embarrassment; they were noticeably in tension with the participants' earlier comments. The embarrassment was mixed with such awkward and resigned comments as "It is just impossible to have it all" or "There just are no fulfilling jobs out there. That is the problem." Yet, it would be a mistake to conclude simply that both job fulfillment and compensation are primary drivers of career choice. Rather, to resolve this conflict, these women were developing a new way of working. They were becoming job and career shifters. So, articles speaking directly about how to manage such shifts could effectively replace those about ideal careers or fast tracks to financial success.

> # Conflicts among orienting values also are often expressed in contradictions.

Customers' awkward feelings conceal not only conflicts among orienting values, but also the emergence of new orienting values. In the Latino market, for example, Mexican immigrant women do not usually express their admiration of "independence." Instead, they feel awkward when discussing how they have changed in the United States and insist they are still dedicated family caretakers. They insisted they had not changed; yet they admit that old friends see them as liberal when they go back to Mexico. Also, they view Mexican women who have recently immigrated as "very conservative." When asked about their accomplishments in the United States, they would invariably say, "Just

a year ago I learned to drive on the freeway. Now I can go anywhere." Other comments could then come in passing such as "The difference is that here, if you don't want to put up with your husband, you don't have to. You get a divorce. You don't depend on a husband because you work. Men are a luxury here." A bank that listened to the clearest claims spoken with the greatest confidence would promote joint accounts. Another bank that listened to the vexed statements would promote products for financial independence. Both, however, would heighten the conflict. Financial offers that resolved the conflict between dedication to family and independence would create new possibilities for living, new drivers, and new markets.

Conflicts among orienting values also are often expressed in contradictions that occur at various moments of discussion. To return to the fashion example, women contradicted themselves over how they feel about wearing suits. When "the suit" first appeared in the conversation, the participants described the suit as something they "had to wear" but would not wear otherwise. Instead, they would choose to be "hip" or "funky." The suit—and in particular the eighties power suit—projected an image of a woman who is "power-driven," "predictable," and "uptight" (characteristics these women had identified as contemptible). Later in the conversation, when discussing how they wished to feel at work, these women described how suits enabled them to feel as if they were being taken seriously. As individuals in the group put it, "When I'm wearing a suit, others focused on me and not what I'm wearing," or "I felt together once in a meeting with a suit on." Although the respondents clearly contradicted themselves, the contradiction provided an important insight: being a coordinated, together person mattered as a value as much as being cutting edge or "hip." Wanting to be hip and wanting to be taken seriously turned out to be the primary orienting values that come into conflict in this segment's professional life.

Technique 2: Listen for invidious distinctions and self-righteous expressions. We use the term "invidious distinctions" to describe terms people use to distinguish others in a way that implies a slight. "Self-righteous expressions" are expressions customers use to designate customers' descriptions that characterize the group in which they identify themselves by reference to the seeming inferiority of another group. Invidious distinctions and self-righteous expressions usually indicate conflicts among orienting values. A participant who uses an invidious distinction usually either feels drawn to the inferior value or is unable to maintain the superior one. This failure of confidence does not grow out of ethical incompetence so much as by the pull of the inferior value. In the U.S. Latino market, the women wanted to claim they were just like any other traditional, family-oriented woman in Mexico, and that they had not adopted the "loose" practices of American women. However, they later repeatedly stated that they were not like those "conservative, shy, newly arrived immigrant women who allow their husbands to dominate them." These distinctions allowed us to see that being independent from one's husband was a new orienting value that conflicted with the traditional orienting value of being a family-oriented woman. The women were trying to live by both.

Another conflict among orienting values in the U.S. Latino community came out through invidious distinctions. Latinos who cared about festive magnanimity would say such things as "those Latinos that think they can just take care of themselves. That is not right. Sure they go to college and have their fancy cars, but I bought a home for my mom in Mexico." On the other side, those who cared for promoting the nuclear family would say, "My husband and I have had big disagreements. When he wants to send money to his brothers in Mexico, I say 'What about the girls? We have to leave something for the girls.'" The former righteously suggests that Latinos who go to college and have nice cars leave their mothers homeless. On the other side, those who take care of their Mexican relatives do not even take care of their daughters. Frequently, the same people were on both sides. A financial institution that could resolve this conflict with regular and automatic savings and money-transfer plans would appeal to and develop the financial capacities of such customers. This offering would be more effective than ethnic advertising about family values or treating immigrants as though they simply want U.S. independence.

> # Describing the life roles in which conflicts are experienced is critical when designing new offerings.

Technique 3: Identify the roles the consumer plays in relation to the product category. Qualitative customer interview research often treats group discussions of issues related to their personal lives as distractions not obviously related to the product category. An approach that investigates conflicts in orienting values, however, uncovers the particular social roles that customers play in their lives. Take, for instance, the conflict between being responsible and loving carefree excitement. This conflict is directed at such roles such as being a particularly responsible family man or woman and being an adventurous individual. How can being a free, adventurous individual not violate being responsible in the domain of family? One way, as we already suggested, is to purchase a sporty-looking car that does not guzzle a lot of gas or require costly insurance and is not outrageously priced.

Although conflicts among orienting values can sometimes be uncovered without noting the roles in which they occur, describing the life roles in which conflicts are experienced is critical when designing new offerings. In the fashion interviews, we learned women in their late twenties

were conflicted between the values of being taken seriously on the one hand and of "risk taking" and "working for themselves" (being hip) on the other. The disintegration of career life was so complete that their new productive role could be characterized as project work (moving serially from interesting project to interesting project) or portfolio work (having a portfolio of projects all at once).

If a designer only heard the conflict between the orienting values of seriousness and hipness, he or she might well focus on developing evening-like clothes that display distinctly feminine seriousness and hipness. But learning about the new nomadic work role, the designer would see the conflict as regarding the desire to dress with the casualness, autonomy, and independence of a female Steve Jobs without appearing girlish.

Finally, roles change. For instance, most consumer-goods companies in Mexico categorize their customers as middle-class "housewives" who buy such food as cold cuts for the family. In our interviews, we learned that, in describing their activities, women did not see themselves simply as housewives. Instead, they saw themselves as family improvers or class climbers who did everything from taking classes to improve themselves to having coffee in the evening with the "right" people. They were particularly interested in ways to reduce the time spent cooking, and they did not want to live as their mothers had. Feeding their children ham and hot dogs, rather than tacos, was part of the class-climbing activity that required less time in the kitchen and gave their children food that seemed more international. Most cold-cuts producers, however, believed that price, followed by freshness, was the main purchasing driver for hot dogs. Identifying the class-climbing activity allowed us to see the greater context in which serving hot dogs to the family made sense and led us to direct our line of exploration toward the conflicts among orienting values produced within the new class-climbing social role.

Technique 4: Eliciting defining narratives of life changes. Listening for conflicts among orienting values requires leading the discussion away from a product focus to a conversation about defining life changes in general. A narrative that reveals the values that have oriented customers' lives can be elicited by asking how a certain orienting value may have guided a person in the past and how it does so now. From here, the researcher can elicit the way in which values are changing.

In the fashion case, we learned at some point that "being taken seriously" oriented many of the activities and roles that customers described. When asked how this value appeared to these women as undergraduates, they reported that, back then, they thought their careers would mean everything to them. Being taken seriously meant being the kind of person who would do anything to get ahead in a career. But, as they began working, a new orienting value arose, living a balanced, "quality" life. Living in accord with this orienting value required having a family, engaging in healthy physical activity, taking vacations, and being a serious person. Having elicited such an account, an investigator would need to listen for how much "being taken seriously" has really changed for participants and how they dealt with the stress of needing both to be "taken seriously" and to have balance. Again, the most useful questions would be crafted so as to extract supplemental narratives of change. Important questions would be "Where do you see your professional lives moving in the future? What do you wish you could keep from the old way of being serious? How does having a family fit in? How do you view yourself in comparison to your mother?"

Similarly, in the case of the middle-income Mexican women, we heard they cared enormously about education, even if they didn't necessarily pursue the careers they had trained for. When we asked them whether their mothers had cared about education, they told stories of how their mothers had worked hard and how they had imitated that hard work. When we asked what their mothers thought of their daughters' education as opposed to the hard work in the home, we found that these middle-class women were often on the defensive. They still cared about the hard work of their mothers and were not sure that they were living up to this orienting value with their "educated" lives. Ultimately, we saw that, although they wanted to simplify cooking so that they could pursue "educated" class-climbing activities, they could not turn their backs on the orienting value of hard work in the kitchen. Meals that at least looked and tasted as if they had worked all day to prepare them would appease the conflict.

GENERATING INNOVATIVE CONCEPTS: BRIDGE PRACTICES

Once conflicts in orienting values are uncovered, a researcher can begin to aid in innovation directly. This process works best with the help of an interdepartmental team that includes a senior manager responsible for strategy, a manager responsible for execution, and designers or product developers. Business modelers and marketers responsible for customer experiences also play key roles in such teams.

The research begins by finding those ad hoc, unsystematic practices that customers have adopted to cope with the conflict. Innovation comes from improving these practices to make them more effective and turning them into recurrent processes to produce a solid business offering.

For instance, in researching the conflicts of Mexican immigrants in the U.S. with household incomes between $28,000 and $50,000, we found a series that grew out of the basic conflict between the Mexican festive life and the independent, planned, vocational life of the United States. Typical conflicts among orienting values included festive freedom vs. planned disciplines, fate vs. vocation, seeking patronage vs. learning new skills, dedication to family vs. independence, and so forth.

Three bridging techniques could serve as the basis of the innovation. First, many Mexican immigrants bridged love of family with love of independence by setting up two bank accounts, one they shared with their spouse and a second private one. In particular, this technique enabled secret gifts to relatives in Mexico. However, it left its practitioners feeling guilty. Second, Mexican immigrants loved career ladders. These bridged a number of conflicts, for instance, between festive freedom and planning a life, respecting fate and dedicating oneself to a vocation, getting ahead through a patron and learning new skills. The career ladders enabled Mexican immigrants to discipline themselves and plan for only the next step and then take time off to enjoy festive freedom upon achieving it. The ladder prevented them from having to acknowledge that they were dedicating their lives to a certain path, while it enabled them to treat the ladder as a gift of fate. They could also always treat the most recent teacher or boss as a patron who encouraged them to learn the skills for the next step. Third, we found these recent Mexican immigrants to rely heavily on word of mouth and to enjoy discussing in festive groups the relative merits of certain actions. Some people, who lacked the distinctions for speaking about the stock market, for example, had given all their money to a friend to invest in a particular company because they were told "it's the right thing to do."

We can see how the first bridge technique could be regularized into a family money-market checking account that was shared by the heads of the household. This account could also include "independent," satellite checking/savings accounts for each joint-account holder and for other members of the family (both in Mexico and the United States). Such a system of accounts would help resolve the conflict between independence and festive family unity. The account also could be designed so those consumers could feel they were climbing a ladder. After holding the account for a certain amount of time, it would graduate to a next step, at which certain low-interest loans become available. The next step would offer another benefit, say, a set of investment tools such as blended mutual funds that promise a base return with market exposure with some upside potential, REITs, and so on. Finally, the last value conflict could be addressed with a new channel such as a Mexican-American advocacy organization or credit union with newsletter in which members could report on the right things to do with their money. Financial products such as the family accounts would be sold through this channel.

This innovation aims at developing the financial capacities of Mexican immigrants. Innovations deriving from resolving conflicts among orienting evaluations open new possibilities for customers to act on and consequently help them develop new habits that make them better customers. This penetrate-and-develop strategy that derives from these innovations differs markedly from the skim-and-wait Latino strategies of most financial institutions who seek to gain profitable market share of higher-end Latinos by exalting family values, offering literature in Spanish, and offering no-fee products.

RESEARCHER AS PARTNER TO INNOVATOR AND STRATEGIST

Customer-oriented innovators and designers have long been sensitive to the power of insights that come from talking to customers. Without their full awareness, many widely diverse kinds of entrepreneurs have engaged in the techniques described above to produce innovations. The founders of the company ROLM invented call forwarding and other innovative voice-distribution technologies by bridging the pre-high-tech conflict between managing the business from the office and going out to spend time with customers. Anita Roddick's Body Shop arose from bridging the '60s and '70s conflict between appearing attractive and feminine dignity. This article shows that entrepreneurial intuition can be usefully coupled with customer research. Listening to value conflicts and finding bridge practices leads to the consistent production of innovations. By identifying conflicts in orienting values, managers can note how customers change. Developing offerings that resolve these conflicts opens new possibilities for action for customers and thereby helps companies deploy strategically superior business models that focus on penetrating old markets and developing customers. Since this kind of research also leads to innovations that transform product categories, it enables senior managers to focus designers and product developers on innovations that will penetrate seemingly unprofitable or saturated markets.

ADDITIONAL READING

Hamel, Gary and C. K. Prahalad (1994), *Competing for the Future.* Harvard Business School Press.

Lautman, Martin R. (1996), "Listen and Win," *Marketing Research,* 3 (Fall), 21–25.

Leonard, Dorothy and Jeffrey F. Rayport (1997), "Spark Innovation Through Emphatic Design," *Harvard Business Review,* 6 (November–December), 102–113.

Spinosa, Charles, Fernando Flores, and Dreyfus Hubert (1997), *Disclosing New Worlds: Entrepreneurship, Democratic Action, and the Cultivation of Solidarity.* Cambridge: MIT Press.

Taylor, Charles (1985), *"What Is Human Agency?"* Human Agency and Language, Philosophical Papers 1, Cambridge University Press.

Wyner, Gordon A. (1999), "Anticipating Customer Priorities," *Marketing Research,* 1 (Spring), 36–38.

——(1998), "Rethinking Product Development," *Marketing Research,* 4 (Winter), 49–51.

Maria F. Flores Letelier is co-leader of the Strategic Innovation Practice at Business Design Associates Inc.

Charles Spinosa is co-leader of the Strategic Innovation Practice at Business Design Associates Inc.

Bobby J. Calder is the Charles H. Kellstadt Distinguished Professor of Marketing and Professor of Psychology at the J.L. Kellogg Graduate School of Management, Northwestern University.

Product by Design

*An increasingly popular research technique helps
marketers and consumers get what they really want.*

BY DAVID J. LIPKE

This past November, the Lands' End Web site launched "My Personal Shopper," a recommendation engine for customers who want help sorting through the retailer's vast selection of sweaters, skirts, and button-downs. Big whoop, you say—Amazon's been doing this for years. But unlike companies that use past purchases to proffer suggestions to cyber-browsers, Lands' End is the first apparel retailer to use a technique called conjoint analysis. In a brief survey, six pairs of outfits are shown to the shopper, who chooses a preferred outfit among each pair. Through analysis of these six simple choices, and the answers to a few other questions, the site sorts through 80,000 apparel options and presents the most suitable ones to the busy shopper.

While the use of conjoint analysis by Lands' End is unique, the methodology itself is not. It's a research technique that has been around for three decades, but which is increasing in popularity as software developments and the Internet make it easier to use, as well as more powerful and flexible. Understanding how conjoint analysis works, and the innovative ways it's now being used, provides a good opportunity

for any company to increase its chances of giving consumers more of what they want, and less of what they don't. "Use of this method will increase as more marketers realize what it can do, and how well it can work," says John Seal, senior analytical consultant at Burke, Inc., a Cincinnati-based research firm.

So what is conjoint analysis? The rationale underlying the technique is that consumers weigh all the many elements of a product or service—such as price, ingredients, packaging, technical specifications, and on and on—when choosing, say, a sweater, airline ticket, or stereo system. While this may seem obvious to anyone who's faced a wall of DVD players at Circuit City, figuring out how to leverage this concept in the marketing arena can be difficult. Conjoint analysis does this by breaking products down into their many elements, uncovering which ones drive consumer decisions and which combination will be most successful. But rather than directly asking survey respondents to state the importance of a certain component *à la* traditional surveys, participants judge hypothetical product profiles, consisting of a range of defining characteristics called "el-

ements." Their responses are run through an analytical process that indirectly identifies the importance and appeal of each element, based upon their pattern of preferences for the element groups.

If this process sounds more complicated than a traditional survey, it is. And it tends to be more expensive as well. But, as the saying goes, you get what you pay for. While traditional surveys can gauge interest in product features, the results can be misleading. This is because it can be difficult for respondents to directly relate how valuable a particular product feature will be to them. "If you ask respondents how much they are willing to pay for a certain feature, they often can't or won't answer truthfully," says Tom Pilon, a Carrollton, Texas-based consultant who specializes in conjoint research projects. "They'll tend to say they're interested in all the new features." They wouldn't be lying, but they might not actually pay for those features when the product comes to the market. Similarly, focus groups are a good way to draw out consumer opinion on new products, but it's difficult to accurately quantify how a product will perform in the marketplace from this data.

A BRIEF HISTORY OF CONJOINT

1964
The fundamental theories for conjoint analysis are laid out in a paper by R. D. Luce and J. W. Tukey, "Simultaneous Conjoint Measurement: A New Type of Fundamental Measurement," in the *Journal of Mathematical Psychology*.

1971
Conjoint is introduced to market research firm by Professors Paul Green and V. R. Rao, in the guide "Conjoint Measurement for Quantifying Judgemental Data," in the *Journal of Marketing Research*. First commercial use of conjoint analysis is conducted.

1980
Approximately 160 conjoint research projects are completed by market research firms, according to a survey of 17 firms known to conduct this type of research by Professors Philippe Cattin and Richard Wit-

tink. In total, 700 projects are completed from 1971 through 1980.

1983
Choice-based conjoint is introduced to the market research industry by J. J. Louviere and G. G. Woodworth, in an article in the *Journal of Marketing Research*.

1985
Bretton-Clark introduces the first commercial, full-profile conjoint system, called Conjoint Designer.
Sawtooth Software introduces ACA, a software package for adaptive conjoint analysis. It is now the most widely used software for this type of research.

1989
Professors Cattin and Wittink find that 1,062 conjoint research projects have been completed since 1984, and estimate that

close to 2,000 conjoint research projects will be conducted that year.

1990
SPSS introduces a full-profile conjoint analysis software package for the computer.

1993
Sawtooth Software introduces the first commercial choice-based conjoint software for the computer.

Source: Sawtooth Software: The Journal of Marketing, Summer 1982: The Journal of Marketing, July 1989; The Journal of Marketing Research, Fall 1995.

"Conjoint mimics the way that consumers actually think," says Joel Greene, director of database marketing at Akron, Ohio-based Sterling Jewelers. Greene first used conjoint research last spring, and is impressed with the results. Fed up with consumers tossing his mailings into the trash, Greene hired White Plains, New York-based market research firm Moscowitz Jacobs Inc. (MJI) to figure out a way to make them more appealing. Using a proprietary research tool called IdeaMap, MJI worked with Greene to systematically break down the brand image and communication efforts of Shaw's (a division of Sterling Jewelers) into bite-size elements. These factors were culled through focus groups and brainstorming sessions that examined previous marketing efforts and possible new approaches. Well over a hundred elements were part of the tested pool, which included different ways to convey messages about Shaw's stores, merchandise, brand differentiation, and emotional appeals. "We wanted to cast a wide net, because we didn't know what would work," says Greene.

MJI recruited a group of more than a hundred survey respondents to its testing facilities in Chicago and White Plains. Seated at computers, they were systematically exposed to the different elements, grouped as words, phrases, and pictures. For each random grouping of elements, the respondent would rate the appeal of the

group as a whole. From an analysis of the pattern of ratings, MJI was able to give a utility score to each element. Using these scores, Shaw's could then create marketing messages from this universe of elements appealing to the widest group of customers, or to specific segments. The words, phrases, and pictures (i.e. elements) that scored highest for each segment were then used to create new mailings. And the glittering result? The creative geared toward each segment resulted in significantly higher rates of response, as well as increased dollar sales per response.

Understanding how conjoint analysis works **is a good way for any company** to increase its chances of **giving consumers more of what they want,** and less of what they don't.

The effectiveness with which conjoint can be used to understand precisely which aspects and features of a product are driving sales is especially crucial in an industry

such as consumer electronics. With an increase in digital convergence, and with hybrid electronic products coming to the market—think refrigerators connected to the Internet, and cameras as MP3 players—the question arises: Will consumers actually pay for these products, and how much? "We really have to avoid the 'if you build it, they will come' pitfall," says Maria Townsend-Metz, a marketing manager at Motorola.

Heeding this warning, Townsend-Metz used conjoint analysis while working on enhancing Motorola's popular TalkAbout two-way radios. "We couldn't put all the different options we were thinking about on the radio, so we needed to know which ones were going to be of most value to the consumer, and help sell the most radios," says Townsend-Metz. Because of the complexity of creating and modeling well-run conjoint studies, she brought in Boise, Idaho-based research firm POPULUS, Inc. In six markets across the U.S., the company conducted conjoint surveys of consumers who participated in activities, such as camping and biking, where a two-way radio would be a natural accessory. POPULUS tested 18 attributes, covering technical specifications, price points, and the appearance of the devices.

Using a conjoint methodology was especially appropriate because all the at-

CONJOINT ANALYSIS IN A NUTSHELL

Conjoint analysis presents a way for researchers to understand which specific elements (i.e. parts or features) of a product, package design, or marketing message are most valued by consumers when making a decision to purchase. It involves placing a series of product concepts, composed of different elements, in front of survey respondents. The respondents express their preferences for the different concepts, and the importance of each element is determined by analyzing the pattern of the respondents' choices. The elements tested are "attributes" (such as color, brand, and price) and "levels" within those attributes (such as blue or red, Ford or Honda, $100 or $150). After the survey, "utility scores" are calculated for each level showing which ones were most preferred, and which were most important in the hypothetical purchase decision. Many researchers have created their own unique methodology for conducting this type of research, but there are three main types of conjoint analysis:

TYPE	DESCRIPTION	PROS & CONS
TRADITIONAL (a.k.a.: full-profile; preference-based; ratings-based; card-sort)	Respondents are given a series of product profiles to rate. Each profile is composed of one level for each attribute being tested (e.g. How likely are you to buy a blue Ford that costs $150?)	• Easy, straightforward design process • Can be administered on paper or by computer • Encourages respondents to evaluate the product individually, rather than in comparison to others • Because full profiles are used (a level for each attribute is included in every profile), large numbers of attributes can confuse respondents. Respondents can begin to ignore some attributes to simplify the process. This limits the number of attributes that can be successfully tested.
CHOICE-BASED (a.k.a.: discrete choice)	Respondents are given two or more profiles at once and asked to choose the one they prefer, or none (e.g., Which would you purchase: a blue Ford that costs $100 or a red Honda that costs $150, or neither?).	• Allows for measurement of "special effects" (complex interactions between utility scores across attributes and levels in certain types of analysis). • Some researchers believe this method better re-creates the real-life shopping experience, in which consumers choose among products. • Other researchers don't believe consumers always make these side-by-side comparisons and prefer the traditional conjoint rating system. • Comparisons of side-by-side full profiles, with large numbers of attributes, can lead respondents to ignore some attributes, as in traditional conjoint methods.
ADAPTIVE (a.k.a.: Sawtooth Software's ACA)	This technique is divided into three main phases. Respondents first rate or rank the levels within an attribute (e.g., Rank these brands in order of preference: Sony, Toshiba, Compaq). Second, they rate how important a certain attribute is to them (e.g., How important is brand in considering this purchase?). Respondents then rate partial profiles (two to three attributes at a time) that are chosen to test those attributes that mattered most to them.	• Because only "partial profiles" are tested, it can be easier for respondents to make accurate preference choices between the different profiles. • More attributes can be tested in the first phase, and then the questions can hone in on the most important attributes. • Software, such as ACA, makes the design and administration of these surveys easier. • Can only be administered on a computer. • Some researchers dislike the adaptive methodology, as it depends largely on the first questions being answered accurately. If they are not, subsequent questions can focus on the wrong product attributes. • Cannot directly measure certain "special effects."

Source: Information compiled from reports by Maritz Marketing Research; Sawtooth Software, POPULUS, Moscowitz Jacobs, and DSS Research.

tributes were interdependent—different features, for example, would affect the look of the radio, as well as the price. "The goal was to find the combination of features that would maximize interest at the lowest production cost," says John Fiedler of POPULUS. The resulting product was right on consumers' wavelength, and the TalkAbout now leads the market for recreational and industrial two-way radios.

The popularity of conjoint research was greatly increased by the development of software in the 1980s that made it easier to design and run these types of studies. The leader in this field is Sequim, Washington-based Sawtooth Software, whose ACA brand of conjoint is the most widely used

in the world. Other software suppliers include SPSS Inc. and SAS Systems. Prior to computer-assisted research, conjoint surveys were conducted using cards that had groups of attributes printed on them, and which were sorted by preference. The number of attributes that could be tested in this manner was severely limited, as was the concluding analysis.

The trend toward conducting survey research on the Web will further increase the use of conjoint, according to experts in the field. The Web provides an easy way to present respondents with groups of attributes, something that was much more difficult to do over the phone (people can only remember so many features at once).

Fuji Film, for one, has used conjoint Web surveys to uncover the effects of price, brand, and package configurations (i.e. the number of rolls in a package) on sales. "Film is a low-involvement category, the product is standardized, and the effects of price and packaging are significant," says Doug Rose, president of Austin, Texas-based DRC Group, who worked on conjoint projects last year for Fuji.

By showing respondents side-by-side attribute profiles of different brand, price, and packaging configurations, Fuji was able to analyze their patterns of preference, and deduce what was driving their choices. The film manufacturer was further able to estimate exactly what effect a certain price point on a particular package of film would have on market share. This conjoint study was so accurate that its estimates perfectly matched ACNielsen data on price elasticity in the film sector, which appeared after the Fuji study.

One research firm taking conjoint analysis a step further on the Web is Burlingame, California-based Active Research. Its proprietary "Active Buyer's Guide" is a powerful research tool for marketers, disguised as a shopping search engine for consumers. Licensed to over 70 popular sites, such as Lycos and MySimon, it helps Web shoppers find the computers, appliances, and financial services (135 categories in all) that most closely match their needs, both online and offline. By filling out a conjoint survey that hones in on what features, price points, and attributes they are looking for, the Guide delivers a list of products that are most likely to interest the shopper.

But Active Research doesn't do this just to help out consumers. By answering the questions required by the search engine, shoppers are providing the company with a gold mine of continuous information on what kind of products they want, and at what price. In effect, Active Research is compiling 1.5 million surveys a month. What's more, these surveys are from people who are providing the most accurate information possible and are in the market, at that moment, to buy a particular product. By compiling and analyzing this data, Active Research provides up-to-the-minute information for clients such as Ford, GE, and Sony on which aspects of a product are driving consumer decisions, which demographic segments are driving sales, and who's interested in different features.

In addition, clients of Active Research can create hypothetical products and measure what their likely market share would be. Using the conjoint-produced utility scores of different product features, marketers can preview how a new product will sell in the marketplace, without the time and cost of a test launch. Because of the size of its sample, Active Research can slice-and-dice hypothetical products in an array of categories, demographics, and configurations. "It's not an exaggeration to say that what they are doing is an absolutely unique way to do primary research," says client Suzanne Snygg, futures product manager at Palm, Inc. The dual nature of their service is highlighted by the fact that Snygg herself has used Active Research data not only to shape product concepts for Palm but also to find the best mini-stereo system for her home. As the Web makes conjoint analysis more popular, it's important to note that conjoint research is still more complicated to conduct than straightforward survey research. To produce worthwhile results, it is crucial to create a pool of attributes that actually influences consumer choice. This requires careful and creative brainstorming. Researchers have to choose the correct conjoint method (there are several types, with many researchers creating their own unique variants). They have to show groupings of elements to respondents that cover many possible combinations, in a balanced and useful way. The final results are only as good as the design and analysis of the research, which can be complicated. Keith Chrzan, director of marketing sciences at Maritz Marketing Research, goes so far as to say that "a lot of people are using conjoint who shouldn't be," due to the easy-to-use software.

That said, the effectiveness and accuracy of conjoint techniques make them powerful tools for marketers who use them properly. Says Tom Pilon, the Texas-based consultant, "once a company has done it once, they always come back for more."

A BEGINNER'S GUIDE TO
Demographics

Who are your customers?
Where do they live?
How many are there?

Answering these and similar questions can help you sharpen your marketing strategy.

BERNA MILLER
WITH AN INTRODUCTION BY PETER FRANCESE

Whatever you sell, customer demographics are important to your business. Demographics can tell you who your current and potential customers are, where they are, and how many are likely to buy what you are selling. Demographic analysis helps you serve your customers better by adjusting to their changing needs. This article provides a review of the basic concepts used in such analysis.

The most successful use of demographic analysis identifies those population or household characteristics that most accurately differentiate potential customers from those not likely to buy. The second part of using demographics is finding those geographic areas with the highest concentrations of potential customers. Once potential customers are described and located, and their purchase behavior analyzed, the next step is to determine their media preferences in order to find the most efficient way to reach them with an advertising message.

It wasn't always this complicated. Until fairly recently everyone practiced mass marketing, dispersing one message via media—newspapers, radio, broadcast television—that presumably reached everyone. No special effort was made to ensure that the message would appeal to (or even reach) the most likely customers.

The result: A great deal of money was spent pitching products and services to sections of the audience who didn't want or need them. In buying a prime-time spot for its television ads, a motorcycle company would be paying to
(continued)

The most important marketing question a business faces is: "Who are my customers?" And the first **demographic*** question a business must ask about its product or service is whether it is to be sold to an individual or a **household**. Refrigerators, for example, are household products; and most households have only one or two refrigerators. On the other hand, everyone within the household has their own toothbrush and dozens of other personal-care products.

There are more than 261 million individuals in the United States and nearly 100 million households. Those classified as "**family** households" include married couples with **children** (26 percent), married couples without children (29 percent), single parents living with their children (9 percent), and brothers and sisters or other related family members who live together (7 percent). "**Nonfamily** households" include people who live alone (24 percent) and cohabiting couples and other unrelated roommates (5 percent).

Different types of households are more prevalent among certain age groups. For instance, the majority of women who live alone are over age 65, while the majority of men who live alone are under age 45. Household types differ between **generations** as well. Younger people today are much more likely to live in the other type of nonfamily household because they are moving out of their parents' *reach the housebound elderly as well as the young adults for whom their product was designed. A swimsuit manufacturer that ran an ad in a national magazine would pay a premium to reach the inhabitants of Nome, Alaska, as well as Floridians. Gradually it was recognized that the "shotgun" approach is not an efficient use of marketing dollars.*

Mass marketing has since given way to target marketing, whose guiding principle is Know Thy Customers. How old are they? Where do they live? What are their interests, concerns, and aspirations? Knowing the answers to questions like these gives you insight into the marketing approaches most likely to appeal to your customers—and whether you're even shooting for the right customers in the first place! (Sometimes there is more than one set of customers: for example, research shows that low-fat frozen dinners are purchased by young women wishing to stay slim and by much older retired people who just want a light meal.)

Let's say that you find out that your customers are predominantly college graduates, and that you know in which zip codes your existing customers reside. How do you use this information?

The first step is to obtain a tabulation of the number of college graduates by zip code, which is available through an information provider (see the American Demographics Directory of Marketing Information Companies for names and numbers) or the Census Bureau. Then, for any metropolitan area that you serve, establish the percent of all college graduates in the metropolitan area who reside in each zip code. Calculate the percent of existing customers who reside in each zip code. By dividing the percent of college graduates in zip 12345 by percent of customers (and multiplying by 100), we get an index of penetration for each zip code. If the index of penetration is 100 or above, the market is being adequately served. If it is below 100, there is more potential, which can be realized through direct mail to those specific zip codes.

This analysis can be done using any group of geographic areas that sum to a total market area, such as counties within a state or metropolitan areas within a region. The object is to compare the percent of customers who should be coming from each sub-market area against the percent who are actually coming from there. The resulting indexes essentially measure marketing performance zip by zip or county by county.

Not so long ago, demographic information came printed on reams of paper or rolls of computer tape. With the tremendous advances in technology in recent years, it is now readily available on your personal computer. Demographic statistics can be obtained on CD-ROM or via the Internet, complete with software for accessing the data.

Information providers can analyze these data for you, as well as provide customized data, such as how many pairs of shoes people own and how often they shop for new ones. Census demographics can't tell you how many times a week people use floor cleaners, but it does have basic demographic characteristics that will help determine who your market is, how many of them there are, and where they live. Information providers can help you take these data and merge them with customer data to form a clearer picture of your market and its potential.

—Peter Francese

Peter Francese is founding president of American Demographics Inc., and publisher of American Demographics *and* Marketing Tools *magazines.*

homes before marriage and living with friends or lovers; such living arrangements being more acceptable today, younger people are much more likely than earlier generations to do so.

The U.S. can no longer be effectively treated as a mass market, because Americans and their lifestyles have changed dramatically.

Everyone in the United States except for the homeless lives in either a household or **group quarters**. Many businesses ignore group-quarter populations, reasoning that nursing-home patients and prison inmates probably are not doing much shopping. However, if your market is computers, beer, pizza, or any number of products that appeal to young adults or military personnel, you cannot afford to overlook these populations. This is especially important when marketing a product in a smaller area where a college or military base is present. People who live in these situations may have different wants and needs from those who live in households; in addition, the area may have a much higher rate of population turnover than other **places** do.

Refining Your Customer's Profile

Once you have determined whether you want to market to households or people, the next step is to find out which segment of households or of the population would be most likely to want your product or service. Demographics allow you to refine your conception of who your market is, who it can or should be, and how it is likely to change over time. People have different needs at different ages and lifestages, and you need to factor that into your customer profile. In addition, there are both primary and secondary markets. For instance, if you were marketing baby food, you would first target married couples with young children and single parents, and then possibly grandparents.

This level of refinement was made necessary by the massive social, economic, and technological changes of the past three decades. The United States can no longer be effectively treated as a mass market, because the people who live here and their lifestyles have changed dramatically. Due to increasing divorce rates, increasing cohabitation, rising number of nonmarital births, and increased female participation in the labor force, married couples with one earner make up only 15 percent of all households. Dual-earner households have become much more common—the additional income is often necessary for the family to pay their bills. Thus, the stereotypical family of the 1950s has been replaced by two harried, working parents with much less time available.

At the same time, there has been an explosion in the number of products available to the American public, each of which, either by design or default, tends to appeal to the very different segments of the population.

Another important trend is the increasing diversity of that population. The United States has always been an immigrant nation. However, large numbers of immigrants from Latin America and Asia have increased the proportion of minorities in the country to one in four, up from one in five in 1980.

This increasing diversity is particularly noticeable in the children's market. Minorities are overrepresented in the younger age brackets due to the higher fertility and the younger population structure of these recent immigrants. The result: one in three children in the United States is black, **Hispanic**, or Asian. Nearly all of today's children grow up in a world of divorce and working mothers. Many are doing the family shopping and have tremendous influence over household purchases. In addition, they may simply know more than their elders about products involving new technology, such as computers.

The recent influx of Hispanics, who may be of any **race**, has important implications for understanding the demographic data you have on your customers. "Hispanic" is an ethnicity, not a race; a person who describes himself as Hispanic must also choose a racial designation: white, black, Asian/Pacific Islander, American Indian/Eskimo/Aleut, or "other." Confusion on this score… can result in accidentally counting Hispanics twice, in which case the numbers won't add up.

Income and education are two other important demographic factors to consider when refining your customer profile. As a general rule, income increases with age, as people get promoted and reach their peak earning years. Married couples today often have the higher incomes because they may have two earners. Married couples may also have greater need for products and services, because they are most likely to have children and be homeowners.

Income is reported in several different ways, and each method means something very different in terms of consumer behavior. Earnings, interest, dividends, royalties, social security payments, and public assistance dollars received before taxes and union dues are subtracted are defined in the **census** as money income. **Personal** income, as reported by the Bureau of Economic Analysis, is money income plus certain noncash benefits (such as food stamps and subsidized housing). **Disposable** income is the money available after taxes, while **discretionary** income is the money available after taxes and necessities (food, shelter, clothing) have been paid for.

All of these are useful measures as long as their differences are fully understood. For example, discretionary income of $30,000 has much more potential for businesses than does a personal income of $30,000. But none of these statistics measures wealth, which includes property owned. Ignoring wealth may provide a skewed picture: a 70-year-old woman with a personal income of $15,000 who must pay rent is much less able to afford additional items than a woman of the same age and income who owns a fully paid-for house, which she could sell if she needed to.

Income can be reported for people or households; household income is the most commonly used measure in business demographics since it provides the best picture of the overall situation of everyone in the household. Income is often reported as **mean income**. But mean income can be distorted by very large or small incomes, called "outliers," which are very different from most of the other values. Thus multimillionaires skew the mean income upward, overestimating the income of the population in question. Using a measure called **median** income can avoid this bias and is more widely used as a measure of income in demographics. The mean income of all United States households is $41,000. The median income is $31,200—almost $10,000 lower than the mean.

It is important to not only identify today's customers, but to predict how their wants and needs will change tomorrow.

Education is another very important and commonly used demographic characteristic—in today's increasingly technological and highly skilled economy, education makes a big difference in occupation and thus in earning power. Education is most often measured as number of years of schooling or in terms of level of education completed. Today's adults are better educated than ever before; however, only one in four adults older than age 24 has a college degree or higher. Another 23 percent have attended college. Eight in ten American adults have a high school diploma. One reason for the low percentages of college graduates is that many older people did not attend college. Therefore, we should expect to see the percentage of college graduates and attendees increase substantially in the future.

College-educated people are one of the most lucrative markets, but you may have to work extra hard to get and keep them as customers. They are more open to technology and innovation, but they are also less brand loyal, since they are more able financially to take risks. They are more likely to read and less likely to watch television than those without any college education. They like to make informed decisions about purchases; hence, they are the most likely group to request product information.

Segmenting the Market

All of these demographic data are available in easy-to-understand packages called **cluster systems** (also known as **geodemographic** segmentation systems), which are available from information providers. Cluster systems take many demographic variables and create profiles of different individual or household characteristics, purchase behaviors, and media preferences. Most cluster systems have catchy, descriptive names, such as "Town and Gown" or "Blue Blood Estates," making it easier to identify the groups most likely to be interested in what you have to sell.

Cluster systems are especially powerful when used in conjunction with business mapping. Sophisticated mapping software programs easily link demographics to any level of geography (a process called geocoding). Some software can pinpoint specific households within neighborhoods from your customer data and then create schematic maps of neighborhoods by cluster concentrations. Geocoding can be done for **block group,** counties, zip codes, or any other market area. Businesses can integrate knowledge of customer addresses and purchase decisions with basic demographic data based on geography and come up with a clearer, more informative picture of customers—and where they can be found.

Cluster analysis is sometimes confused with **psychographics,** but the two are very different. Cluster systems are based on purchase decisions and demographics that cover physical characteristics like age, sex, income, and education. Psychographics measure motivations, attitudes, **lifestyles,** and feelings, such as openness to technology or reluctance to try new products. Both demographics and psychographics need to be taken into account.

Looking to the Future

It is not only important to identify who your customers are and how many of them there are today, but how many of them there will be in five or ten years, and whether their wants and needs will change.

Projections of population or households by **marital status,** age, or income can be very useful in determining the potential of a market a few years down the road. All projections start with the assumption that the projected population will equal the current population plus births minus deaths and plus net **migration.** For example, let's take projections at the household level. New household configurations occur through in-migration of residents or through the formation of a household due to the separation of an already existing household (such as when a child moves out of a parent's home or a divorce occurs). Household losses occur when existing households are combined due to marriage, when a child moves back home, etc., or when the residents in a household move away from the area (out-migration).

Projections can vary greatly, so it is important to ask about the methodology and assumptions behind them and make sure you fully understand why these assumptions were made. Accurate demographic data can be very valuable, but data that are flawed or biased can be seriously misleading.

In general, the future population of a larger area of geography, such as the United States or a particular state, is much easier to **estimate** accurately than populations for small areas, such as neighborhoods, which often experience greater population fluctuations. In addition, the shorter the time period involved, the more accurate the projections are likely to be, because there's less time for dramatic changes to take place. There will be factors in 15 years that we cannot begin to include in our assumptions, because they do not exist yet.

You can have more confidence in your educated guesses about the future if you know a little about past population trends in the United States, especially the **baby boom** and **baby bust** cycle. It is also important to understand the difference between a generation and a **cohort.**

The events for which generations are named occur when their members are too young to remember much about them (i.e., the Depression generation includes people born during the 1930s). That's why cohort is often the more useful classification for marketers; it provides insight into events that occurred during the entire lifetimes of the people in question.

To illustrate, let's look at the baby boomers, who were born between 1946 and 1965. In their youth, they experienced a growing economy, but they also dealt with competition and crowding in schools and jobs due to the sheer number of cohort members. Their lives were shaped by events like the civil rights movement, the Vietnam conflict, the women's movement, and Watergate. Baby boomers have seen increasing diversity and technology. They're living longer, healthier lives than the cohorts that came before them.

All these factors make baby boomers very different from 32-to-51-year-olds of 20 years ago. Traditional ideas concerning the preferences of 50-year-olds versus 30-year-olds are no longer accurate; age-old adages such as "coffee consumption increases with age, and young people drink cola" are no longer as valid as they once were—people who grew up on cola often continue to drink it. The same is true for ethnic foods and a host of other products.

The received wisdom will have to change constantly to reflect new sets of preferences and life experiences. For example, baby boomers remember when the idea of careers for women was considered pretty radical. Not so for younger Generation X women; most of them work as a matter of course, just like their own mothers. As a result, ideas about marriage, family, and jobs are changing and will continue to do so.

If you are marketing a product to a certain age range, be aware that the people who will be in that range in five or ten years will not be the same as the ones who are there now. A strategy that has worked for years may need to be rethought as one cohort leaves an age range and another takes its place.

Therein lies the challenge in contemporary marketing: the fact that it is no longer advisable to treat a market as an undifferentiated mass of people with similar fixed tastes, in-

Define Your Terms

A GLOSSARY OF DEMOGRAPHIC WORDS AND PHRASES

Demographic terms consist of fairly common words and phrases, but each one has a highly specific meaning. Study them carefully to ensure that when you discuss demographics with someone, you're both talking about the same thing.

demography: derived from two Greek words meaning "description of" and "people," coined by the French political economist Achille Guillard in 1855. Sometimes a distinction is drawn between "pure" demography (the study of vital statistics and population change) and "social" demography, which gets into socioeconomic characteristics. Business demography is also often understood to include consumer attitudes and behavior.

POPULATION COMPONENTS

The three things that add to or subtract from population are:
- **fertility:** having to do with births. There are several measures of fertility, mostly different kinds of annual rates using different base populations.
- **mortality:** otherwise known as death. There are different death rates, as there are for births.
- **migration:** the movement of people into or out of a defined region, like a state. It typically refers only to moves that cross county lines.

A related term is **mobility**, meaning change of residence. This usually refers to how many people move any distance in a given period of time, even if they just move across town.

HOUSEHOLDS/FAMILIES/ MARITAL STATUS

household: one or more people who occupy a housing unit, as opposed to group quarters (dorms, hospitals, prisons, military barracks, etc.). The vast majority of Americans live in households.

householder: formerly called "head of household," the householder is the one adult per household designated as the reference person for a variety of characteristics. An important thing to check when looking at demographics of households (such as age or income) is to see whether the information pertains to the householder or to the entire household.
Household composition is determined by the relationship of the other people in the household to the householder.

family: a household consisting of two or more people in which at least one person is related to the householder by blood, marriage, or adoption. The major types of families are **married** couples (these may be male- or female-headed and with or without children), and **families without a spouse present**, which may also be headed by a man or a woman. The latter category includes single parents as well as other combinations of relatives, such as siblings living together or grandparents and grandchildren. Note that seemingly single parents may live with a partner or other adult outside of marriage.

nonfamily: households consisting of persons living alone, or multiple-person households in which no one is related to the householder, although they may be related to each other. This includes unmarried and gay couples, as well as roommates, boarders, etc.

children: The United States Census Bureau makes a distinction between the householder's own children under age 18 (including adopted and stepchildren), and other related children, such as grandchildren or children aged 18 and older. Other surveys may define children differently.

marital status: this is an individual characteristic, usually measured for people aged 15 and older. The four main categories are never married; married; divorced; and widowed. The term "single" usually refers to a person who has never married, but may include others not currently married. Likewise, the term "evermarried" also includes widowed and divorced people. "Married" includes spouse present and spouse absent. "Spouse absent" includes couples who are separated or not living together because of military service.

RACE/ETHNICITY
race: white, black, Asian and Pacific Islander, and native American (includes American Indians, Eskimos, and Aleutian Islanders). That's it. The government does not use the term African American, but many others do.

Hispanics: the only ethnic origin category in current use. NOT A RACE. Most Hispanics are actually white. Used to be called Spanish Origin. The term Latino is becoming popular, but is currently not used by the government. It is becoming more common to separate out Hispanics from race categories and talk about non-Hispanic whites, blacks, etc. This way, the numbers add up to 100 percent.
Note: The Office of Management and Budget is considering revamping the racial categories used in federal data collection, including the addition of a mixed-race group. This may happen in time for use in the 2000 census.

GENERATIONS/COHORTS

cohort: a group of people who share an event, such as being born in the same year, and therefore share a common culture and history. The most commonly used cohorts are birth cohorts, although there are also marriage cohorts, etc.

generations: more loosely defined than cohorts, typically refers to people born during a certain period of time. These examples are not definitive:

- **GI Generation:** born in the 1910s and 1920s, served in WWII. Today's elderly.
- **Depression:** born in the 1930s. Boomers' parents. Now aged 56 to 65.
- **War Babies:** born during WWII, now aged 50 to 55. Sometimes lumped with the Depression group as the "silent generation."
- **Baby Boom:** born between 1946 and 1964, now aged 31 to 49. Further introductions are probably unnecessary.
- **Baby Bust:** born 1965 to 1976. Today's twentysomethings, although

(continued)

the oldest turned 30 this year. Also called **Generation X**.

- **Baby Boomlet:** or Echo Boom. Born 1977 to 1994. Today's children and teens.

EDUCATION

attainment: completed education level, typically measured for adults aged 25 and older because it used to be the case that virtually everyone was finished with school by then. This is less true today, with one-third of all college students over age 25. Until 1990, attainment was measured by years completed rather than actual degrees earned. The new categories include no high school, some high school but no diploma, high school graduate, some college but no degree, associate's degree, and other types of college degrees.

INCOME

Income can be measured for households, persons, or even geographic areas. When you look at income figures, make sure you know which kind is being referred to!

disposable: after-tax (net) income. In other words, all the money people have at their disposal to spend, even if most of it goes for things we have little choice about, like food, electric bills, and kids' braces.

discretionary: income left over after necessities are covered. This is extremely tough to measure: Who's to say what's necessary for someone else? It's generally accepted that very few of the poorest households have any discretionary income at all, but also that the level of necessary expenses rises with income.

personal and **per capita:** aggregate measures for geographic areas such as states and counties. Personal income is total income for all people in an area, and per capita divides it equally by total population, regardless of age or labor force status.

mean income: the average of all income in the population being studied.

median income: the midway point, at which half of the people being studied have higher incomes and half have lower incomes.

ESTIMATES/PROJECTIONS

census: complete count of a population.

survey: the process of collecting data from a sample, hopefully representative of the general population or the population of interest.

estimate: calculation of current or historic number for which no census or survey data are available. Usually based on what's known to have happened.

projection: calculation of future population or characteristic, based on assumptions of what might happen—a "what if" scenario. Two related terms are **prediction** and **forecast**. Both refer to a "most likely" projection—what the forecaster feels may actually happen.

MEDIA/MARKETING TERMS

The following are not defined by the government, so there are no real standards.

mature: an age segment, usually defined as those 50- or 55-plus, although some go so far as to include those in their late 40s. This is often seen as an affluent and active group, but it actually consists of several age segments with vastly diverse economic and health status. Related terms include:

- **elderly:** usually 65 and older, although sometimes narrowed down to very old (85 and older).
- **retired:** not necessarily defined by age; although most retirees are older people, not all older people are retired.
-

middle class: This is one of the most widely used demographic terms. it is also perhaps one of the most statistically elusive: If you ask the general public, the vast majority will claim to be middle class. It might be most sensible to start with the midpoint—that is, median income ($31,200 for households in 1993)—and create a range surrounding it (e.g., within $10,000 of the median) until you come up with a group of households that says "middle class" to you.

affluent: most researchers used to consider households with annual incomes

of $50,000 or more as affluent, although $60,000 and $75,000 thresholds are becoming more popular. Upper-income households are sometimes defined more broadly as those with incomes of $35,000 or more. As of the mid-1990s, this merely means they are not lower income, suggesting that there is no middle class.

lifestyles/psychographics: these terms are somewhat interchangeable, but **psychographics** usually refers to a formal classification system such as SRI's VALS (Values and Lifestyles) that categorizes people into specific types (Achievers, Belongers, etc.). **Lifestyle** is a vaguer term, and many 'lifestyle' types or segments have been defined in various market studies. Generally speaking, these systems organize people according to their attitudes or consumer behavior, such as their involvement with and spending on golf. These data may seem soft, but they often use statistical measures such as factor analysis to derive the segments.

cluster systems/geodemographic segmentation: developed by data companies to create meaningful segments based on residence, and the assumption that people will live in areas where there are a lot of other people just like them. This geographic element is one thing that distinguishes clusters from psychographic segments. Another difference is that cluster categories are virtually always based on socioeconomic and consumer data rather than attitudinal information. Each system has at least several dozen clusters. The four major cluster systems are: Claritas's PRIZM, National Decision Systems' MicroVision, CACI's ACORN, and Strategic Mapping's ClusterPlus 2000.

GEOGRAPHIC TERMS

Census geography: areas defined by the government.

- **regions:** Northeast, Midwest, South, and West.
- **divisions:** there are nine Census Statistical Areas: Pacific, Mountain, West North Central, East North Central, West South Central, East South Central, New England, Middle Atlantic, and South Atlantic.
- **states:** note: data about states often include the District of Columbia for a total of 51.

(continued)

- **Congressional district:** subdivision of a state created solely for Congressional representation; not considered a governmental area by the Census Bureau.
- **enumeration district:** census area with an average of 500 inhabitants, used in nonmetropolitan areas.
- **counties:** the U.S. had over 3,000 counties as of 1990.
- **places:** these include cities, towns, villages, and other municipal areas.
- **tracts:** these are subcounty areas designed to contain a roughly homogeneous population ranging from 2,500 to 8,000.
- **blocks** and **block groups:** blocks are what they sound like: an administrative area generally equivalent to a city block and the smallest unit of geography for which census data are published. Block groups are groups of blocks with average populations of 1,000 to 1,200 people; they are approximately equal to a neighborhood.
- **metropolitan areas:** these are defined by the Office of Management and Budget, and are built at the county level. Each consists of at least one central city of the appropriate size (usually at least 50,000), its surrounding "suburban" territory within the same county, and any adjacent counties with strong economic ties to the city. Metros may have one or more central cities and/or counties. Stand-alone metros are called **MSAs** (Metropolitan Statisical Areas). Metros that are right next to each other are called **PMSAs** (Primary MSAs), and the larger areas that they make up are called **CMSAs** (Consolidated MSAs). The U.S. currently has over 300 metros (depending on how you count PMSAs and CMSAs) that include about three-fourths of the nation's population.
- **NECMAs** are New England Metropolitan Areas and are similar to MSAs.
- **central city:** largest city in the MSA and other cities of central character to an MSA.

zip code: subdivision of an area for purposes of delivering mail; not a census area.

Two related terms are **urban** and **rural** The essential difference between "metropolitan" and "urban" is that metros are defined at the county level, while urbanized areas are more narrowly defined by density. An **urban area** has 25,000 or more inhabitants, with urbanized zones around the central city comprising 50,000 or more inhabitants. This means that the outlying portions of counties in many metropolitan areas are considered rural. Oddly enough, suburbs are commonly defined as the portions of metro areas outside of central cities and have nothing to do with the urban/rural classification system.

—Diane Crispell

Diane Crispell is executive editor of American Demographics *magazine, and author of* The Insider's Guide to Demographic Know-How.

---

terest, and needs. In the age of target marketing, it is imperative to know who the customers are and how to reach them. When the customer's needs change, it's essential to know that, too, so you can adjust your marketing efforts accordingly. A working knowledge of demographics will keep you on top of the situation. It's a piece of marketing know-how that no one can afford to ignore.

---

*For definitions for this and other terms in **bold-faced type**, see the [article] glossary.

Berna Miller is a contributor to American Demographics *magazine.*

The Next Big Market

*America's fastest-growing consumer segment
rewards thoughtful marketing.*

by **FRANK SOLIS**

The Hispanic population is booming. Note these facts:

At 33 million and counting, there are more Hispanics in the United States than there are Canadians in Canada.

One year from now, whether by birth or migration, there will be 1.4 million new Hispanics in the country—enough to fill a city the size of Miami.

Within five years, Hispanics will be America's largest ethnic group.

And as the size of the population grows, so does the size of its collective pocketbook.

According to the Census Bureau, Hispanics make up the nation's fastest-growing consumer segment, spending some $380 billion on products and services annually.

If this weren't enough to compel any company to reach out to Hispanics, consider this: they are very open to all forms of advertising—particularly when it's culturally relevant.

Studies show that minority consumers, particularly Hispanics, are more loyal to the services, products, and companies that show a direct interest in them through electronic or print advertising or in community activities.

Astoundingly, many businesses choose to ignore the Hispanic population despite the fact that it is a potentially lucrative—and largely untapped—consumer group.

TRANSLATION TRAVAILS

But before a company can be awash in a sea of dinero, it must develop an understanding of the mercado, or market.

As someone who has been in the business of marketing for the past two decades, I've seen firsthand what can happen when a company lacks such understanding.

Take for instance the story of a former client who wanted to reach the Hispanic market in the worst way—literally.

A local retailer wanted to throw itself a birthday party as a promotion. Anxious to publicize the event in a neighboring, predominantly Hispanic community, the store's marketing department translated an English flier into a Spanish-language piece they believed would promote their anniversary.

But instead of promoting its birthday, the store invited neighbors to celebrate the nethermost region of a birthday suit.

In Spanish, the word "año" (year) minus the "~" (tilde) refers to the area of the body where the sun doesn't shine.

Not exactly the image you want to convey.

So unless you can find a copywriter who is fluent and aware of the grammatical rules, I generally discourage translations.

Need another reason to avoid translating word-for-word? Some words, phrases, and ideas aren't easily translated from English into Spanish—and vice-versa. Other words and phrases are lengthier in Spanish than they are in English (such as "nosotros," the Spanish word for "us") and will on average add 30 percent more text to your piece.

Regardless of the language used, text-laden and laborious collaterals don't move a product.

Yet for a long time, companies have gotten away with the technique.

Often, companies simply take their English advertising, translate it directly into Spanish, and run it in Hispanic newspapers. This serves as their ethnic marketing campaign.

ADAPTATION VERSUS TRANSLATION

To reach any audience, marketers must tap into the segment's culture, experiences, preferences, and vernacular. The same rule applies to ethnic groups. In fact, marketing to ethnic populations is no different than marketing to any niche of the general market audience—based, of course, on their preferences and experiences.

When going after this huge Hispanic buying power, you must adapt your advertising so that it is relevant and meaningful to your audience.

For Hispanics, that means tapping into and focusing on the following ideals: respect, good behavior, and a strong sense of family unity.

Nowhere is the latter theme more prevalent than in Spanish television.

Top Tips for Ethno-Marketing

1. uno

Do your homework, and know your audience.

2. dos

Adaptations, not translations, work most effectively.

3. tres

Cross-promotions maximize visibility and stretch resources.

4. cuatro

Sponsorships go a long way.

5. cinco

Think strategically, not tactically.

While on American shows like *Friends* or *Seinfeld* you might see the characters gently jest and quip about their mothers and families, you will never see that kind of content on Spanish television—where the concept of "mama" and "familia" are nearly sacred.

A LITTLE RESPECT GOES A LONG WAY

One way to align your company with Hispanic cultural values is to support special events.

According to the *Yankelovic Monitor*, 78 percent of Hispanics say they prefer products made by companies that sponsor community activities. Sponsoring Hispanic cultural activities, health fairs, job fairs, parades, and music festivals can help distinguish your company among Hispanics.

Cross-promotions are another good way to generate top-of-mind awareness among Hispanic audiences. My advertising agency has enjoyed great success pairing like-minded clients for cross-promotional purposes.

Recently, we paired two disparate clients trying to reach Hispanics—a major airline and a ski resort—in a cross promotional campaign to generate traffic and awareness for both.

These techniques are effective for companies of any size—and are a good way to build a solid consumer base.

GOOD MARKETING TRANSCENDS AUDIENCES

And while the differences in marketing to Hispanics are numerous, there are a handful of marketing techniques that cross over.

For example, the duration and frequency of a Hispanic-targeted marketing campaign should mirror that of a general market campaign.

If you were the CEO of a department store, you wouldn't advertise your biggest sale of the year for only one day and expect to see the traffic you need. So why would you expect good results with an abbreviated ethnic-marketing campaign?

Too often, companies devote only minimal resources to attracting this growing audience.

When the results fail to materialize, they give up. Diminutive efforts will lead to diminutive results—short-circuiting your campaigns and shortchanging your company in the long run.

Someone in your industry is realizing new revenue by reaching out to this growing audience.

Why aren't you?

Frank Solis is president and CEO of Solis Advertising and Public Relations, a Denver-based advertising and public relations agency with niche-marketing expertise.

GENERATIONAL
DIVIDE

ARE TRADITIONAL METHODS OF CLASSIFYING A GENERATION STILL MEANINGFUL IN A DIVERSE AND CHANGING NATION?

BY ALISON STEIN WELLNER

As a decade, the 1970s stand out in Americans' minds for many reasons: Nixon's resignation, disco, the big blackout, bell-bottoms. But for Jonathan Pontell—then a teenager—the defining moment of the decade came in the classroom. His high school teacher, a full 15 years older than him, broke the news: She was from the same generation as all of the students dutifully sitting at their desks.

"The whole class just burst out laughing," recalls Pontell, now a sociologist and author. "It was just so obvious that we were not Baby Boomers. We were not the same as people of her age." (Baby Boomers, according to the U.S. Census Bureau, were born between 1946 and 1964, years when the number of births was substantially higher than in years before or immediately after.)

The memory lingered, and when the media began covering a new generation in the 1980s—a post-Baby Boom generation—Pontell's ears perked up. But by then the spotlight was now firmly fixed on Generation X—younger, more cynical than Pontell and his age mates. History had skipped "his" generation, he says. So he decided to write a book highlighting this forgotten group: Those too young to be Baby Boomers, yet too old to be Gen Xers. Says Pontell: "It's not too late for this generation to be found."

This month, Pontell's book, devoted to this "lost" generation hits bookstores. His conclusion: Baby Boomers should be defined as those born between 1942 and 1953. Those born between 1954 and 1965 should fall into a new group, which he calls Generation Jones. (Gen X, by his calculations, falls between 1966 and 1978.) The author has spent the last four years researching Generation Jones, poring over data from the Census Bureau and other sources, and analyzing hundreds of movies, television shows, and other cultural artifacts from his formative years. He's even lined up a list of celebrity testimonials. Talk show host Rosie O'Donnell, comedian Drew Carey, and actress Maureen McCormick are among the celebs who represent the face of Generation Jones.

Certainly, Pontell is not the first to point out that the traditional definition of the Baby Boom is too wide. Many researchers have noted that early Boomers—people born during the first half of the Baby Boom's 18-year span—and later Boomers, are different in many ways. But where Pontell breaks with conventional demographic thinking is in his belief that the differences that exist among Boomers are enough to warrant the declaration of a whole new generation.

More importantly, there's the issue of how Pontell groups Boomers and Xers; his reasoning has nothing to do with birth data previously used to define these generations. In fact, Pontell says that defining generations around the number of births in a given year is "a widely discredited theory"—nevermind that it's a widely-used method within leading demography circles. More than just a question of semantics, the discussion of Generation Jones opens up a wider debate: What defines a generation? Are traditional ways of looking at generation still meaningful in a diverse and ever-changing world? And what does it all mean for marketers who seek a deeper understanding of consumers?

A GENERATION DEFINED

Among Webster's definitions of generation is the following: "a category of people born and living contemporaneously." Marketers have often defined "generation" as a group of people who share the same formative experiences. These experiences bind people that are born in continuous years into "cohorts"—a group of individuals that have a demographic statistic in common. Most frequently, demographers use birth year as that common statistic, explains Mark Mather, an analyst at the Population Research Group, a demographic think tank in Washington D.C. "Demographers like to package things in a way that's easy to measure, and date of birth is the easiest way to define generations," he says. Birth dates don't change as income, geographic region, or marital status do, and relying on birth dates makes it easier to track a group of people over time.

During the 20th century, the number of babies born in a given year has fluctuated dramatically, explains Louis Pol, demographer and associate dean at the College of Business Administration at the University of Nebraska at Omaha. In the early 1900s, the number of babies born each year was relatively stable. The number of births fell during the Great Depression, and the major wars of the century also pushed the number of births down, as would-be fathers were out of the country. But when the GIs returned, birthrates rebounded. With these dips and surges, the shape of the World War II generation (born 1909 to 1932) and the Swing Generation (born 1933 to 1945) was formed.

After World War II, America was in the mood to procreate. Between 1946 and 1964, roughly 76 million babies were born, and each year there were more babies born than in the year before. After 1964, this trend reversed—hence the Baby Bust, or Generation X. In 1977, many Boomer women decided to have children, and the birthrate began to climb steadily—creating an "Echo-Boom," or Generation Y.

Adherents of "generational marketing" take this pure statistical analysis a step further, and overlay major world events that occurred during a generation's formative years, to construct a picture of a generational personality. Historians Neil Howe and William Strauss are well-known for linking cohorts with historical and cultural events to define generations as far back as 1584. But to do this involves a subjective assessment of history and its impact. This moves the concept of "generation" out of the cold reality of numbers and into the murky depths of a social science. It is what opens the door for Jonathan Pontell and the idea of Generation Jones.

MERITS TO THE GEN JONES ARGUMENT

The 18-year span of the Baby Boom, as defined by the number of babies born each year, encompassed a period of rapid change in American history. An early Boomer, born in 1946, came of age and entered the workplace during the 1960s, whereas the latest Boomers, born in 1964, came of age and entered the workplace in the mid-1980s—as different as two eras separated by just two decades could possibly be, points out David Stewart, deputy dean at the University of Southern California's Marshall School of Marketing. Here's a simpler comparison: Early Boomers had Vietnam and Woodstock, later Boomers had AIDS and personal computers. "Generation Jones is an accurate realization that the Baby Boomers are really not a homogeneous group. There are some big differences, and indeed, huge differences between the leading edge and trailing end of the Baby Boom," says Stewart.

These differences are at the heart of Pontell's argument for Generation Jones. "Generation has everything to do with cultural mood and shared experiences, what impacted you, and your feelings of trust," he says. Yankelovich Monitor teased out some of these distinctions in its 2000 study "Dissecting Boomers." The company found three distinct Boomer segments: 23 percent of Boomers fall into the "Leading Boomers" category, born 1946 to 1950; 49 percent are "Core Boomers," born 1951 to 1959; and 28 percent are "Trailing Boomers," born 1960 to 1964.

Yankelovich found different attitudes and priorities among these different Boomer segments. Trailing Boomers were the most likely to say they like to plan 5 to 10 years ahead (66 percent) compared with 49 percent of Leading Boomers. And, while 75 percent of Leading Boomers say they're better off than their parents were at their age, just 54 percent of Trailing Boomers believe that's true. Yet, Trailing Boomers aren't exactly lagging in the quality of life department: 46 percent say they plan to take a special vacation this year, compared with just 33 percent of Leading Boomers.

If the attitudes of the youngest Boomers seem familiar to marketers, that's because many of the attitudes that younger Boomers hold are similar to those typically associated with Generation X,

observes Cheryl Russell, demographer and Baby Boom expert, based in Ithaca, New York. "It was once predicted that times would be good for Generation X because they were a small generation replacing a large generation," she says. But older Boomers got the best education, housing, and jobs, and "their shadow fell far down into the age structure, making things difficult for those even 10 years younger than the youngest Boomer," she says.

The long shadow of the older Boomers, and the differences in attitude between leading and Trailing Boomers are the core reasons why Pontell believes that the traditional definition of Baby Boom from 1946 to 1964 should be scrapped. "The fact that the Baby Boom generation was pegged to the rise in birthrates was 'just a historical accident,'" he says. "It's just a blatantly inaccurate way to determine who a generation is, to base it on something as random as birthrate. Why not base it on how many rainy days there were in a year?"

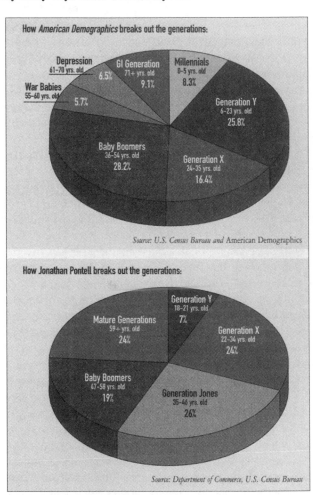

How *American Demographics* breaks out the generations:

Depression 61–70 yrs. old 6.5%
GI Generation 71+ yrs. old 9.1%
Millennials 0–5 yrs. old 8.3%
War Babies 55–60 yrs. old 5.7%
Generation Y 6–23 yrs. old 25.8%
Baby Boomers 36–54 yrs. old 28.2%
Generation X 24–35 yrs. old 16.4%

Source: U.S. Census Bureau and American Demographics

How Jonathan Pontell breaks out the generations:

Generation Y 18–21 yrs. old 7%
Mature Generations 59+ yrs. old 24%
Generation X 22–34 yrs. old 24%
Baby Boomers 47–58 yrs. old 19%
Generation Jones 35–46 yrs. old 26%

Source: Department of Commerce, U.S. Census Bureau

SIZE MATTERS

To marketers, the number of births in a given year does make a world of difference, especially those interested in projecting market size. "Imagine if you were in the diaper business in 1945, how your business would change by the size of the cohort born from 1946 to 1964, and how it would change again in the mid-60s and the mid-70s," says Pol of the University of Nebraska. In fact, the number of births in a given time period is one of the best indicators of what the economy is going to look like 10, 20, even 30 years from now, says David K. Foot, an economist at the University of Toronto, and the author of *Boom, Bust, Echo*. If you marry knowledge of fluctuations in the birthrate, with an understanding of how consumers tend to act at different stages of their lives (buying a first car in their 20s, traveling in their 50s), you can get a rough picture of the market challenges and opportunities that lie in your future.

But how can the number of births impact a generation's personality? "Simply put, the Baby Boom generation experiences crowds wherever it goes, whatever it does. That is what defines the Baby Boom—sheer numbers," says Russell. "Early and late Boomers share a common child-centric time of upbringing," observes USC's Stewart. "That was not the case for Xers."

Besides size, there are other similarities among Boomers that transcend the differences, points out Stephen Kraus, a partner at Yankelovich Partners in San Francisco. For Boomers of all ages, the classic elements of the Boomer mindset are all present: "Individuality; emphasis on youth; emphasis on, for lack of a better word, self-absorption, are all there," he says.

Ken Dychtwald, president of Age Wave LLC, in Emeryville, California, and one of the nation's leading authorities on the Baby Boom, likens the similarities and differences among Boomers to a group of individual trees that share the same root system. "Boomers are an extremely diverse generation, extraordinarily complex yet individualistic collection of men and women," he says. "But under the surface, we're a generation with many, many common values and experiences. We're bound together by deeply rooted values." Among the values Dychtwald lists are a belief in a meritocracy, respect for knowledge, and a lack of respect for authority.

In fact, Ann A. Fishman, demographer and president of Generational-Targeted Marketing Corporation in New Orleans, believes that when Pontell carves a new generation out of the Baby Boom, he's acting like a true Baby Boomer. "Baby Boomers tend to be a self-absorbed generation—these were the most parented children in our history," she explains. "When you get that kind of parenting, and you have to compete with a great number of people, you tend to get self-absorbed." Their "me generation" nickname reflects that, she says.

"Within this self-absorption is a need to be treated special, an expectation of being treated special," Fishman says. "What to Generation Jones seems like an extreme difference, is actually just a transition to Generation X. It's Boomer hubris, and I hate to say that, but I don't know what else to call it. They've made a special generation just for them. The other characteristic is the focus on youth, and by becoming a Gen Joneser, they're identifying themselves as younger than the other Boomers. These characteristics are very Boomer-like."

AGE-DEFYING DEMOGRAPHICS

Should Americans born between 1954 and 1965 be classified as their own generation, or is Generation Jones nothing more than just a snazzy way of saying "Trailing Boomer?" For marketers, it depends on whether you're trying to understand demographics or psychographics. If you're trying to understand the attitudes of people born in the latter years of the Baby Boom, then Pontell's analysis of Generation Jones is an excellent supplementary guide to the culture and events that formed the perspectives of those consumers. But if, on the other hand, you're trying to forecast market size, stick to demographic estimations of generations.

For Age Wave's Dychtwald, the bottom line is that Jonathan Pontell has asked the right question, but has come up with the wrong answer. "If we're going to agree that we can't over-generalize about Boomers, and that Boomers are not one big monolithic group, then we need to scratch our heads and do some deep thinking about what the ideal segmentation should be," he says. Rather than relying on birth year at all, Dychtwald believes that the most valuable re-segmentation would be based on psychographics—and that the segments would not need to be pegged to birth years.

In fact, given the sophistication of market-segmentation tools today, and the rapid pace of change, marketers will find themselves turning away from generational identity as a marketing guide, says Dychtwald. "Modern men and women are exposed to such depth and breadth of ideas that they aren't quite as intellectually landlocked as the other generations were," he says. "Beginning with the Baby Boom, defining people by their birth date is going to become increasingly useless. That measuring stick is no longer potent. People will be marketed to by their lifestyle, life stage, and health stage more than their generation," he adds.

As social researchers start to make sense of that change, marketers should get ready to hear about "niche generations"—increasingly smaller groups of people that share common experiences. "It's going to get harder to talk to people who are shaped by the same experience, because our society is becoming so much more diverse, people aren't really sharing the same experiences even when they're born in the same year," says Bruce Tulgan, principal of Rainmaker Thinking, a consultancy that studies post-Boomer generations.

And while major global events and trends will continue to shape cohorts, "Generation will be only one of many, many factors influencing consumer behavior, whereas in prior generations, it would have been the defining factor," concludes Stewart. To some demographers, Pontell's argument for a "new" generation may be flawed, but his timing is impeccable. The author's reasoning for Generation Jones may not be "demographically sound," but it comes at a time when marketers are seeking deeper answers into what drives consumer behavior—and how they can tap into psychographic reasons to sell products. By placing a sliver of the Baby Boom under a psychographic microscope, Pontell has made some noteworthy observations. And he's taken the important step of giving the first "niche" generation a name. As the pace of change continues to accelerate, and as America becomes more diverse, one thing's for certain: Generation Jones will not be the last niche generation to generate a buzz.

Asian-American consumers as a unique market segment: **fact or fallacy?**

Keywords *Consumer behavior, Market segmentation, Consumer marketing, Ethnic groups*

Abstract *The Asian-American consumer group is thought to be the fastest-growing market in the USA. Asian-Americans are thought to be well-educated, generally affluent, and geographically concentrated. However, significant cultural and language differences among Asian subgroups are often overlooked. These include patterns of information gathering, use of promotional media, and methods of household decision making. This article presents a comparative marketing examination of the similarities and differences among five of the largest Asian-American groups and develops implications for marketing strategies.*

Carol Kaufman-Scarborough
Associate Professor of Marketing, School of Business,
Rutgers University—Camden, New Jersey, USA

Introduction

Fastest growing population

Marketers today are attracted by the Asian-American consumer market as growing numbers of Asians emigrate to the USA. In fact, Asian-Americans are the fastest growing population in the USA, with a 99 percent increase since the 1980 census (Paisano, 1993). Currently, they account for 9.8 million of the US population. By the year 2050, they are expected to account for 10 percent of the total US population. If the Asian-American population in the USA were viewed as a separate country, it would be ranked the 85th largest country out of 220 nations (*Marketing Review*, 1994). With spending power estimates of over $200 billion, and tendencies toward brand loyalty, Asian-American consumers form a desirable market (Edmondson, 1997).

Some analysts, particularly in the popular press, have suggested that this group of consumers can be treated as one large segment, without analyzing the key acculturation issues that may be particular to each specific subgroup. Others have focused on each specific market without identifying the similarities among them that are useful to marketers. Still others have argued that Asian-Americans are over-stereotyped in ads, overemphasizing business settings, while downplaying home settings and family relationships (Taylor and Stern, 1997). Industry's eagerness to capitalize on their substantial spending power may compromise the need to identify and examine areas in which the Asian-American "market" is really composed of numerous submarkets, with neglected similarities and critical differences to take into account (Campanelli, 1995).

Similarities and differences

The present paper will present an examination of the similarities and differences among five of the largest Asian-American segments with a focus on key consumer behaviors. These groups are Chinese, Filipino, Asian Indian, Japanese, and Korean-Americans. Numerous background sources on each group's homeland consumer behaviors and immigration consumer behaviors are examined to present a summary of areas which likely to require specific subgroup attention. In addition, key similarities will also be derived, and recommendations for marketing to Asian-Americans as a unified group will be discussed.

Method of investigation

The goals of the present article are:

1. to compare and contrast existing "definitions" of Asian-Americans;
2. to summarize prevalent misconceptions in marketing regarding Asian-Americans;
3. to investigate and present some of the under-represented household aspects of consumer behavior; and
4. to describe key areas of consumer behavior and media use which are thought to differentiate one Asian subcultural group from another.

Factors which impact cultural influence

Key concepts: socialization, consumer acculturation and traditional assimilation

Many Asian-Americans have lived in the USA for numerous years and have blended their households with persons from the USA and from other cultures. Over time, second- and third-generation families have emerged, with their own particular blends of traditional and "new" consumer habits. Asian-Americans are thought to learn and use US culture in relation to the length of time they have been in the USA and their level of involvement in the workforce. Motivation for moving to the new culture or reason for being influenced by the new culture (e.g. fleeing the takeover of one's home country, searching for the "good life" in another country, traveling to acquire education or as part of one's employment) are also thought to impact cultural influence (Wallendorf and Reilly, 1983).

Less need to assimilate

Assimilation. Assimilation is generally known as the process of transforming aspects of a nondominant (in this case, immigrant Asian) culture into a status of relative adjustment to the form of the dominant culture. Changes in behavior may be deliberately undertaken, as each new generation of immigrant attempts to better fit into the dominant host culture. A critical point when considering Asian-Americans is that, given their familiarity with US life from travel, education, and global communications, they may not feel the need to assimilate in the same ways that prior generations of European immigrants did. Moreover, their ability to live in ethnically dominant Asian communities makes it possible to retain one's home country behaviors, habits, and preferences.

Socialization. Socialization occurs when people learn socially relevant behaviors from their surrounding environment. This initial "view of the world" is called primary socialization. However, as new environments are encountered, individuals learn new ways through "secondary" socialization (Penaloza, 1989). Immigrants gradually learn a new culture as they increase their contact with it; this is called the "traditional assimilation model" (Wallendorf and Reilly, 1983).

Acculturation. Acculturation can be defined as the process of learning and adopting cultural traits, different from the ones with which the person was originally reared (Berelson and Steiner, 1967; Ownbey and Horridge, 1997; Sturdivant, 1973; Valencia, 1985). New symbols and new customs are experienced, new foods are consumed, and new ways of thinking are learned. Social and cultural changes occur when people from different cultures come in direct contact with each other. That is, they learn each other's behaviors and customs.

Shaping consumer behavior

Consumer acculturation. As part of these processes, people acquire skills, knowledge, and attitudes relevant to their functioning as consumers in the marketplace. This is called consumer acculturation (Penaloza, 1989). New ways of shopping are tried, and new products are encountered. Several possibilities are thought to occur in shaping the consumer behavior that emerges. Consumers can learn and adopt all new consumer behaviors, they can maintain their consumer practices from their homeland or heritage, or they can form completely new patterns of behavior that are hybrids of both homeland and the new culture (Wallendorf and Reilly, 1983).

Contradictory themes

Misconceptions regarding the Asian-American consumer segment

Several misconceptions and contradictory themes are sometimes found in the popular press in their discussions of marketing to Asian-Americans. These misconceptions appear to overgeneralize on certain similarities among Asian-Americans, while apparently overlooking the differences which occur because of national origin, language habits, level of acculturation, reason for immigration, and so forth. While this list is not exhaustive, it is thought to be representative of some of the overly simplistic approaches which can create problems, rather than efficiencies, in marketing to Asian-American consumers. Eight misconceptions are identified as follows:

Misconception 1: Asian-Americans can be grouped together into a single segment. In this review, I argue that such an overall grouping can be useful for some aspects of consumer behavior, but may cause the manager to overlook other key differences.

Misconception 2: Since English is a common language across Asian-American subgroups, translating an English message into an Asian language will communicate the intended message. While English may be relatively common as a second language, its use, idioms, and meanings are not likely to be conceptually equivalent nor appropriate for all Asian-American groups.

Misconception 3: Since English is a common language across Asian-American subgroups, it is efficient and effective to advertise to them in English, with adjustments and inclusion of specific Asian themes. Such an approach is likely to miss the significant numbers of Asian-Americans who are not fluent in "consumer English."

Misconception 4: Asian-Americans constitute too small a percentage of the US population to target for specific messages. The overall Asian-American group is growing rapidly and will continue to do so.

Significant media differences

Misconception 5: Targeting the Asian-American market is not necessary because they can be reached through the mass media. Significant media differences are found across Asian-American subgroups.

Misconception 6: There are too many Asian-American cultures and languages to create different marketing strategies for each. Different strategies may not be necessary in all product areas; many common needs can be found. Moreover, while over 800 Asian languages are thought to exist, dominant tongues do occur within each subgroup.

Misconception 7: There are numerous similarities among Asian-American cultures; common advertising themes are always desirable. Researchers have identified both

similarities and differences among preferred and acceptable themes across Asian groups.

Misconception 8: There are numerous differences among Asian-American cultures; common advertising themes aimed at Asian-Americans will not be possible. Researchers have identified both similarities and differences among preferred and acceptable themes across Asian groups.

Classification of Asian groups

Just who is an Asian-American?

There are numereous similarities that characterize persons of Asian descent. These include a strong emphasis on family and education, ties to the homeland, geographic concentration in the USA, and relative affluence in relation to the general population. However, it is often unclear just which Asian groups are included in the term "Asian-American." Several studies were consulted in identifying commonly-used methods of classification.

Problems with definitions

Depending on which study is consulted, Asian-Americans include over 30 ethnic groups who trace their roots to Asia and the islands located in the Pacific Ocean. Some definitions include a different combination of countries than others. The inconsistency in definitions creates a research nightmare, since it is essential to create a consistent understanding across researchers about which national groups are actually under consideration. Table I summarizes five different definitions that are found in the literature.

Growth of population

General characteristics

The Asian-American population has grown from 3.8 million in 1980, to 7.3 million, which is an increase of 95 percent, comprising 3 percent of the US population. The US Census Bureau statistics as of August 1, 1997, estimate that the Asian-American population is over 10 million, which constitutes 3.8 percent of the total US population. By the years 2010 and 2050, it is estimated that Asian-Americans will number over 12 million and 40 million respectively, equal to 6 percent and 10 percent of the total projected population (Natividad and Gall, 1996).

According to Ho (1997), Asians may actually be underrepresented in the annual US census. Reasons cited for this problem include:

Table I. Selected definitions used in Asian-American classification schemata

1. Persons whose ancestors came from one of over 20 Asian nations: Bangladesh, Bhutan, Cambodia (including Hmong), China (including Hong Kong or Taiwan), India, Indonesia, Japan, Korea, Laos, Malaysia, Mongolia, Myanmar (Burma), Nepal, Pakistan, the Philippines, Singapore, Sri Lanka, Thailand, and Vietnam (Baron and Gall, 1996).

2. A member of one of over 30 ethnic groups from different parts of Asia: Cambodia, China, India, Indonesia, Japan, Korea, Malaysia, Pakistan, the Philippines, Singapore, Vietnam, American Samoa, Northern Mariana Islands, Micronesia, Guam, Marshall Islands, Palau, and Hawaii (Natividad and Gall, 1996).

3. The Census Bureau's category Asian and Pacific Islander covers more than 17 countries. The Immigration and Naturalization Service counts people from more than 29 countries, ranging from the Middle East to Taiwan (Edmondson, 1997).

4. Asian-Americans are defined as persons whose ancestry is rooted in any Asian country, other than of the Indian Subcontinent (Cohen, 1992).

5. Asian-American is a term that is used to describe people who were born in the USA such as American-born Chinese, and those people who emigrated from Asian countries long ago (Ho, 1997).

1. Asian groups may distrust information collected by the government;
2. Asian persons may be unwilling to divulge personal information on black and white official forms (even if they are in their native language); and
3. illegal immigrants tend to avoid census-takers, but are still part of the consumer market.

Geographical concentration

Asian-Americans also tend to be concentrated geographically. The ten states that have the largest Asian-American population are: California, New York, Hawaii, Texas, Illinois, New Jersey, Washington, Florida, and Massachusetts. In addition, Asian-Americans tend to locate in or near major metropolitan centers. The ten cities with the largest Asian-American population are Los Angeles, New York, Honolulu, San Francisco, Oakland, San Jose, Orange County, Chicago, San Diego, and Washington D.C.

Household characteristics

Asian-Americans are recognized and often stereotyped as being technically competent, hardworking, serious, well assimilated, with a high value on education and family (Taylor and Lee, 1994; Taylor and Stern, 1997; Natividad and Gall, 1996). They have a higher average income, education, and occupational status than the average American. Of Asian-Americans 38 percent have achieved

a bachelor's degree or higher by 1990, versus 20 percent of the total population.

Of Asian households 53 percent have at least two earners, which is a higher proportion than other racial groups. The median household income of Asian-Americans is higher than that of the overall market: $38,540 versus $29,943. In contrast, their poverty rate is also higher than the national average, given at 14 percent versus 13 percent.

Strong cultural ties

Asian-Americans have strong ties to their native cultures and continue to keep their identities within the host culture of the USA. One force, which appears to link all of the Asian cultures, is Confucian ethics, which can be represented by two terms: filial piety and loyalty to authority. These are manifested in the family structure that is strong throughout each group (Larson and Kleiner, 1992). For instance, Asian-American marriages are less than half as likely to end in divorce compared to the national average (Braun, 1991).

Asian-Americans hold their families in high regard, which is a value strongly held in the homelands. Family is a source of individual identity, and a strong sense of connectedness to heritage and tradition is maintained. Asian Americans value achievement, since achievements will reflect well on one's family and group. Traditional household decision making attempts to consider the relative roles of husband and wife in understanding how purchase decisions are made, or not made. Since children and teenagers may be the dominant English-speakers in Asian-American households, their roles may be more influential than those of children/teens in US households.

Significant language differences

Language

Language is possibly one of the most significant areas of difference. Experts report that there are 800 or more different languages used in Southeast Asia. While many Asian-Americans do share the English language in common, their own native tongues are often used in a variety of situations. Because of improvements in technology, worldwide educational programs, and the ease and frequency of international travel, recent immigrants are not finding the need to assimilate into US culture, as they had in the past. Fifty-six percent of the 4.1 million Asian-Americans five years old and older do not speak English fluently, nor do they use English in everyday situations. Approximately 35 percent of those are "linguistically isolated." That is, they live in homes where no one over age 14 speaks English (Fisher, 1994). Such a situation might significantly alter the role of children in household decision making.

In many Asian-American families, younger family members use English as their primary language, whereas parents or older relatives are likely to use their native tongues as primary. Thus, when they interact, conversations are likely to be a mixture of English and the native tongue. As a result, many younger Asian-Americans can understand their native language, and can respond to it in English, but they themselves cannot speak it (Ho, 1997). In addition, many Asian-Americans prefer to use their native tongues in many situations, such as reading, entertainment, and making consumer evaluations. In fact, more than half of Asian-Americans are more comfortable speaking their native language, and 24 percent primarily use their native language.

Attraction to brand names

Brands and consumer behavior

Asian-American consumers are intensely brand-loyal and cost-conscious (Cohen, 1992). They will not buy the cheapest item, but the best item for the cheapest price. Doing business with an Asian-American means establishing a relationship. Basically, Asian-Americans do business with people, not with product attributes (Ho, 1997). A recent survey of 1,600 Asian-Americans showed that this group has a strong attraction to brand names, with 72 percent reporting that brand names are a strong influence on their purchase decisions, in contrast with 34 percent of

the general population. They also like to purchase premium products (Berkowitz, 1994). Automobiles, for instance, represent status to Asian-Americans, and they are more likely to own autos in the $20,000 to $30,000 price range.

Different motivations for coming to USA

Key similarities and differences among the five Asian-American subgroups

Although Asian-Americans come from the same area of the world, their subgroups vary in the usual ways that nationalities vary from each other. Asian Americans come from countries which differ in languages, cultural values, traditions, beliefs, religions, personality characteristics, occupational skills, and so forth. In addition, many of the Asian groups had different motivations in their move to the USA, which often has affected their desire and need to assimilate. The issues investigated across the five cultures were consumer spending and price sensitivity, household purchase decisions, language use, and advertising habits and preferences.

Chinese-Americans

About 1.6 million Chinese people live in the USA; four out of ten Chinese-Americans live in California. There are concentrations in major cities: for example, most live in New York, San Francisco, and Los Angeles. They are a hard-working people, operating numerous small businesses, and owning and developing real estate. Chinese-Americans are somewhat older than the national average. However, the China-born, compared to the American-born, are less likely to have a regular income. Seven out of ten Chinese immigrants are foreign-born. Chinese immigrants were among the first Asians to enter the USA and to establish distinct cultural communities, staying mainly on the West Cost. These "Chinatowns," as they have come to be known, have served to preserve the culture, tradition and lifestyle of China.

Chinese-American society has historically emphasized family, societal interests, and collective actions, while de-emphasizing personal goals and accomplishments (Zhang and Gelb, 1996). Immigrants from several years ago and students can be characterized by "Americanized" household decision making, in which both husband and wife participate in the decision. This is also true of recent immigrants from Hong Kong and Taiwan, but newcomers from Mainland China still practice traditional decision making, with the husband deciding large purchases (Pounds, 1998). A mid-range possibility also occurs, in which the wife makes suggestions, but the husband makes the final purchase.

Prefer ethnic markets

Chinese shoppers are typically price-sensitive, and tend to prefer ethnic markets. However, since they are bargain seekers, Chinese-Americans will shop in American discount stores as well. They often use coupons from direct mail. Moreover, they rely on advertising to provide straightforward information. Belittling or disparaging other competitors' products may be considered to be unlawful or at least unacceptable (Zhou and Belk, 1993).

Language use and learning is also a complex issues. Eighty-three percent report wanting in-language advertising, yet the language issue is quite complex. For instance, recent immigrants regularly read and watch in-language media, reinforcing both reading and hearing their homeland tongues. In contrast, US-born Chinese speak the language but do not read or write it. Thus, print messages provided in Chinese may be confusing for those born in the USA, while audio ads may be effective. While the Chinese population has several distinct language groups and dozens of dialects, Cantonese is the most accepted form of Chinese in the USA.

Racial and cultural mix

Filipino-American

Approximately 1.4 million Filipino-Americans reside in the USA, primarily in California. Los Angeles, Chicago, and New York-Newark are major cities. Filipinos may be of Chinese, Spanish, or Malayan lineage, which determines physical characteristics and subsequently influences choice and purchases of cosmetics and other appearance-related items. Lineage is also thought to determine food tastes, art and decorative preference. Thus, a variety of learned preferences is found across Filipino-Americans.

The history of the Philippines shows a nation that has been dominated by other nations for hundreds of years. The Spanish, the Americans and the Japanese have ruled over the Filipinos. Other influences include the Germans and the Chinese. Thus, there is a significant racial and cultural mix in the Philippines that is not easily captured into one uniform group of cultural behaviors. There are three major ethnolinguistic groups, which are each well-represented in the USA, as well as several smaller ones.

Acculturation is a key factor in which Filipino-Americans are likely to buy. A Filipino's level of integration into the American mainstream is greatly determined by the social class that his family belonged to back in the homeland. Class distinctions in the Philippines are similar to those underlying social class in the USA. Those who lived in large cities in the Philippines are likely to be fluent in English before coming to the USA. They are also likely to have established patterns of shopping in large depart-

ment stores and be knowledgeable regarding brands (Pounds, 1998).

Like other Asian-Americans, Filipinos place a high value on education and family. However, unlike other segments, Filipinos lack a "visible and cohesive community" (Larson and Kleiner, 1992). In families with medium to high acculturation, and where the wife also works, the wife will make most purchase decisions. Large purchases are decided jointly with the husband. Children may dominate American food and toy purchases. Newcomers with lower acculturation may depend on input from relatives or friends who have been in the USA for a while.

An interesting point is that Filipino-Americans will tend to look for the "made in the USA" mark on products while shopping in their homeland (Pounds, 1998). This can be explained by the presence of factories in the Philippines that contract the manufacturing of top name brands such as Nike and Lacoste. The Phillipine-made products are cheaper than the US-made counterparts, so Filipinos tend to prefer the US-made versions as a sign of status. Upon migrating to the USA, they tend to continue this pattern and seek products made in the USA, as assurances of quality and status. Filipinos feel that promotional efforts to their group should still include in-language media, even though a majority of them read and write English. Sixty-six percent prefer in-language media advertising. Filipino-Americans are very price-sensitive, since they often have low income and low spending power in the USA. They tend to comparison shop for quality and for bargains. They frequent discount-type stores.

Varying food shopping preferences

Filipino food shopping preferences are related to their level of acculturation. Those who have a low level of acculturation, perhaps coming from rural Philippine provinces and speaking little English, tend to avoid US grocery stores in favor of oriental food and specialty stores. Those with high acculturation prefer the convenience of one-stop shopping at American supermarkets, but will visit oriental food stores for those items that they cannot find elsewhere.

Most affluent group

Asian-Indians

Over 1 million Asian-Indians are estimated to live in the USA, with concentrations on the Eastern seaboard and the West Coast. The top three states are California, New York, and New Jersey. Metro areas such as New York, Chicago, and Los Angeles are popular. Asian-Indians are the most affluent of the five groups considered in this manuscript, and can be analyzed in terms of three identifiable periods of immigration proposed by Arun Jain of SUNY-Buffalo (Edmondson, 1997). The first group, who came to the USA in the 1960s, are generally well-educated successful men, with homemaker wives and adult children. The second group came in the 1970s and are also well-educated. However, both the husband and wife are employed, and they typically have young children. The third group is generally less-educated, and typically own motels and convenience stores (Mogelonsky, 1995).

India is a country of diverse classes with many ethnic subgroups. Indian society is characterized by a distinct division between the upper and lower classes. Because labor is cheap, most households in India can afford live-in domestic help. Since they are accustomed to conveniences in the home, products that promise to be labor-saving are popular with Indian customers who migrate to the USA. Asian-Indians are typically interested in comparison shopping, seeking to attain security, financial stability, and good value. They prefer to shop in areas that are convenient.

Importance of education

Asian-Indians believe highly in education for their children, and thus invest in computers and technological items. They traditionally value money and wealth, and thus invest in stocks, bonds, CDs, and insurance. Since banking and savings are high in importance, they seek banks and investment firms which will cater specifically to them and offer the best value. They also tend to invest in businesses, paying particular heed to franchise businesses, such as gas stations and convenience stores.

Older immigrant families adhere to traditional Indian custom, in which the male head of household makes most of the purchase decisions. Newcomers to the USA, in contrast, tend to follow a more typical American style of decision making, in which both husband and wife are eligible to take part in the decision. Thus marketing campaigns that appeal to traditional norms are likely to miscommunicate with some Asian-Indian groups.

Acceptability of English in advertising

In contrast to Chinese and Filipinos, Asian Indians find English to be highly acceptable for advertising. However, they also welcome use of the Indian language in promotional messages, with 55 percent preferring in-language media. Word-of-mouth is also important in transmitting consumer information. Given these preferences, the marketer must also consider both acceptable and unacceptable thematic presentations. For instance, advertisements to Indians should avoid sales arguments, which may be interpreted as confrontational or highly impolite. Ads

should also avoid trying to motivate the consumer by using psychological appeals. Direct, clear information is best, with an emphasis on verbal messages. India is a country that does not place much emphasis on using visual information in advertising (Zandapour, 1994).

Japanese-Americans

The Japanese originally began to immigrate to the USA in the late nineteenth century due to hard economic times in Japan at that time. When Japan relaxed emigration laws in the early twentieth century and allowed women to emigrate, many Japanese families moved to the USA. As a result, a large portion of Japanese-Americans are older and better established than other Asian-Americans. Many Japanese immigrants own and operate their own businesses, from large corporations to small stores. They value land ownership and investment in real estate.

The 1990 Census states that about 850,000 Japanese Americans live in the USA, with the top states being California, Hawaii and New York. Many Japanese-Americans, especially in California, come for experience, training, or education. They do not plan to stay in the USA, but instead leave once their goals are complete. Thus, learning behaviors and norms of US cultures is not as important as it is to those who plan to stay permanently in the USA. An important characteristic of these "temporary" Japanese-Americans is that the husband usually speaks English, while the wife does not speak English. Since their stay is considered short-term, the wife often does not consider it to be necessary that she learn English. That is, the traditional assimilation model breaks down under conditions of short-term residence plus isolation from mainstream culture.

Distinct cultural characteristics

The Japanese have many distinct cultural characteristics that are thought to shape their behavior. They value conformity, as expressed in the statement *hitonami consciousness*, which roughly translates to "aligning oneself with other people." They are also reserved and extremely polite. The household decision roles are somewhat more complex. The wife typically researches products and ads, making suggestions of what to buy. However, the husband generally makes the final decision on major purchases.

Emphasis on quality

Quality is a must for the Japanese shopper. They look for signals of quality in packaging and branding, and shop at specialty stores to obtain what they want. For example, they loyally patronize Asian food stores for their cooking ingredients, gadgets, small appliances, and other items and brands from Japan. They insist on products such as noodles, dried fish and seaweed, and various types of fish and fish parts for their traditional recipes.

Like ads in their native Japan, Japanese-American consumers prefer short ads that include humor, celebrities, and indirect messages (Di Benedetto *et al.*, 1992). Important themes include the company's loyalty to the customers, with product quality being less emphasized. Product quality is taken for granted. In-language media are preferred by 42 percent, especially on Asian television and in print. Japanese consumers prefer to see young people in ads, for any product or service.

Indirectness, subtlety, and symbolism have always been important in Japanese cultures (Graham *et al.*, 1993). Printed material is considered to be impersonal and perhaps insincere. Although there is a definitive preference in US advertisements for critical, realistic impressions, this is not the case with the Japanese-American consumers. The Japanese-American consumers are likely to have developed expectations that advertisements should resemble those from their home country that are typified by illustrations and cartoon figures.

Three pillars of marketing in Japan

Marketers in the USA may also want to consider incorporating themes of ads that occur in Japan. For instance, as much as 70 percent of all Japanese print ads mention the price of the advertised item (Javalgi *et al.*, 1994). In addition, emotional rather than informational appeals are used (Lin, 1993). Customer service along with product quality and after-sales service are the three pillars of marketing and selling in Japan. It would be reasonable to assume that careful attention and detail must be paid to quality and service when targeting Japanese-American consumers.

More homogeneous group

Korean-American consumers

In contrast to several of the other Asian-American groups, Koreans are homogeneous and consider themselves to be one big family. They speak only one language and, interestingly, there are only 25 predominant surnames. The overwhelming majority of Korean immigrants, 82 percent, were foreign-born, with most having immigrated since 1965. Unlike other groups, Koreans are largely Christian. The churches serve a dual purpose of a religious center and that of a center for maintaining the Korean social and cultural bonds. Over 800,000 Korean-Americans live in the USA, according to the 1990 Census, with 44 percent living in the West, 23 percent in the

Northwest, 19 percent in the South, and 14 percent in the Midwest. They are possibly one of the most geographically-diverse of the Asian Americans groups under consideration.

Husband and wife roles in household decision making tend to vary by age. Thus, younger Koreans tend to make purchases independently, while older Korean-Americans are more traditional, with the male head of household making major purchase decisions. Children tend to influence their fathers in American food and toys. While the male tends to make most of the decisions, Korean-American couples tend to shop together.

Korean-Americans have a strong interest in quality products and in well-established brand names. They shop with the goal of getting the most for their money, using top-of-the-line products and services. Korean-Americans indicate a preference for in-language advertising. Many ignore mainstream media altogether. Ads are most popular which feature young to middle-aged males, unless the product is specifically for females. Korean-Americans appreciate participation in their communities by companies.

Easy to reach

Managerial implications and applications

Asian-Americans consumers represent a growing market, with spending power and identifiable purchasing and media habits. They are generally easy to reach, since they concentrate in major metropolitan markets. Asian-American media rates are generally less expensive than mainstream media. Newer media, such as Asian-American Web sites, attempt to address the needs of several Asian groups, while maintaining the cultural identities of each. In addition, many Asian-Americans live in extended family situations. Influence throughout the family helps to extend advertising reach. Communicating with immigrants who have settled permanently in the USA is critical since they become influencers to newly-arrived immigrants who are unaware and unsure of which brand to purchase.

Common set of variables

When attempting to counter the misconceptions listed above, there are no absolute rules of thumb that can be confidently applied to Asian-American consumers. Instead, there is a common set of variables that can affect whether it is appropriate to try to reach "the" Asian-American group as a whole, or whether subgroups or even an individual group needs to be targeted independently. The issue of language, similarly, becomes an "it depends" issue, based on the level of assimilation and acculteration of the subgroups or parts of subgroups whose needs are being addressed. The following list presents a summary of guidelines:

1. Asian-Americans have been over-stereotyped in promotional media. Numerous other common characteristics have been overlooked, such as extended household cohesiveness and interaction. Use of these themes can be beneficial in presenting accurate images of Asian-American households (Taylor and Stern, 1997).

2. Desire to assimilate and degree of cultural learning are related to the reason for migration and intended length of stay in the USA.

3. While, on the average, all Asian-American groups are similar in preferring to receive advertising in their own languages (Wiesendanger, 1993), those who are more highly-acculturated and those who are second- and third-generation often prefer English messages.

Acceptable themes in advertising

4. Acceptable themes in advertising to Asian-Americans are related to acceptable interpersonal interaction and inherent "truthworthiness" of certain types of media.

5. Shopping gender roles and shopping opinion leadership are related to length of time in the USA and to consumers' acculturation levels (Ownbey and Horridge, 1997).

6. Certain Asian-American groups are composed of various subgroups and subclasses, which determine rank and privilege in their homeland societies. While less familiar in the USA, there are carried-over shared feelings that may affect behavior.

Shared needs

7. Certain needs are shared among Asian-American groups. For instance, all groups are likely to need to contact families in their homelands. Thus, long-distance service, Internet providers, and airlines are strong contenders for the Asian-American business. Messages may require adjustments for specific subgroups.

8. Other needs are specific to any given Asian-American subgroup. Food ingredients and preparation methods may be native to a specific subgroup, although there may be some cross-over of foods with other Asian-American subgroups.

Marketing to Asian-Americans requires careful balance. There are often parts of a specific marketing process that can target Asian-Americans as a mass market, and other parts in which a specific subgroups' needs must emerge. When needs are common, creating a standardized advertising campaign can be possible. However, the decision process and household interaction may differ among subgroups. Similarly, the purpose for immigration and consequent degree of acculturation are likely to affect the language used and the media selected.

References

Baron, D. and Gall, S. (Eds.) (1996), *Asian-American Chronology*, UXL, New York, NY.

Berelson, B. and Steiner, G. A. (1967), *Human Behavior: An Inventory of Scientific Findings*. Harcourt, Brace, Jovanovich, New York, NY.

Berkowitz, H. (1994), "Concerning a market," *Newsday*, December 5, p. 4.

Braun, H. D. (1991), "Marketing to minority consumers," *Discount Merchandiser*, February, pp. 44–6.

Campanelli, M. (1995), "Asian studies," *Sales and Marketing Management*, March, Vol. 147, No. 3, Part 1, p. 51.

Cohen, J. (1992), "White consumer response to Asian models in advertising," *Journal of Consumer Marketing*, Vol. 9, Spring, pp. 17–27.

Di Benedetto, C. A., Tamate, M. and Chandran, R. (1992), "Developing creative advertising strategy for the Japanese marketplace," *Journal of Advertising Research*, January/February, Vol. 32, No. 1, pp. 39–48.

Edmondson, B. (1997), "Asian Americans in 2001," *American Demographics*, Vol. 19, No. 2, pp. 16–17.

Fisher, C. (1994). "Marketers straddle Asian-American curtain," *Advertising Age*, Vol. 65, No. 47, pp. 2, 18.

Graham, J. L., Kamis, M. A. and Oetomo, D. (1993), "Content analysis of German and Japanese advertising and print media from Indonesia, Spain, and the USA," *Journal of Advertising*, June, Vol. 22 No. 2, pp. 5–15.

Ho, B. (1997), "Communicating with the Asian-American traveler," unpublished manuscript.

Javalgi, R., Cutler, B. D. and White, S. D. (1994), "Print advertising in the Pacific Basin: an empirical investigation," *International Marketing Review*, Vol. 11, No. 6, pp. 48–64.

Larson, H. H. and Kleiner, B. H. (1992), "Understanding and effectively managing Asian employees," *Equal Opportunity International*, pp. 18–22.

Lin, C. A. (1993), "Cultural differences in message strategies: a comparison between American and Japanese television commercials," *Journal of Advertising Research*, July/August. Vol. 33 No. 4, pp. 40–8.

Marketing Review (1994), Vol. 50, pp. 6–18, 22–5.

Mogelonsky, M. (1995), "Asian-Indian Americans," *American Demographics*, Vol. 17, No. 8. pp. 32–6+.

Natividad, I. and Gall, S. B. (Eds) (1996), *Asian-American Almanac*, UXL, Detroit, MI.

Ownbey, S. F. and Horridge, P. E. (1997), "Acculturation levels and shopping orientations of Asian-American consumers," *Psychology and Marketing*, Vol. 14, No. 1, January, pp. 1–18.

Paisano, E. L. (1993). *We the Americans: Asians*, US Department of Commerce, Bureau of the Census, Washington, DC.

Penaloza, L. (1989), "Immigrant consumer acculturation," *Advances in Consumer Research*, Vol. 16, pp. 110–18.

Sturdivant, F. D. (1973), "Subculture theory: poverty, minorities and marketing," in Ward, S. and Robertson, T. S. (Eds), *Consumer Behavior: Theoretical Sources*, Prentice-Hall. Englewood Cliffs, NJ.

Taylor, C. R. and Lee, J. Y. (1994), "Not in vogue: Portrayals of Asian-Americans in US advertising," *Journal of Public Policy and Marketing*, Vol. 13, Fall, pp. 239–45.

Taylor, C. R. and Stern, B. B. (1997), "Asian-Americans: television advertising and the 'model minority' stereotype," *Journal of Advertising*, Vol. 26, No. 2, pp. 47–61.

Valencia, H. (1985), "Developing an index to measure Hispanicness," in Hirschman, E. and Holbrook, M. (Eds), *Advances in Consumer Research*, Vol. 12, Association for Consumer Research, Ann Arbor, MI, pp. 118–21.

Wallendorf, M. and Reilly, M. D. (1983), "Ethnic migration, assimilation, and consumption," *Journal of Consumer Research*, Vol. 10, December, pp. 292–302.

Weisendanger, B. (1993), "Asian-Americans: the three biggest myths," *Sales and Marketing Management*, September, pp. 86–8, 101.

Zandapour, F. (1994), "Global reach and local touch: achieving cultural fitness in television advertising," *Journal of Advertising Research*, September/October, Vol. 34, No. 5, pp. 35–63.

Zhang, Y. and Gelb, B. D. (1996), "Matching advertising appeals to culture: the influence of product use conditions," *Journal of Advertising*, Fall, Vol. 25, No. 3, pp. 29–46.

Zhou, N. and Belk, R. (1993), "China's advertising and the export marketing learning curve: the first decade," *Journal of Advertising Research*, November/December, Vol. 33, No. 6, pp. 50–66.

The author wishes to extend appreciation to Bryan Ho, Darwin Lacorte, William Mason, Celeste Pounds, Karen Parikh, and Meredith Roash for detailed literature reviewing and integration.

Head Trips

A new way to understand consumer psychology

BY DAVID J. LIPKE

Anne-Marie Wong, 31, a pediatrician, and Yanik Wagner, 38, a photographer, both live in Manhattan's Greenwich Village neighborhood, just two blocks apart. They share many similar patterns of consumer behavior—both use Colgate toothpaste, own iMacs (one graphite, one tangerine), drink Starbucks coffee, belong to health clubs, and use the Internet several hours a week. To a marketer examining their brand preferences and lifestyles, their consumer profiles would be very similar, and they would be prime targets for identical product pitches and marketing messages.

However, while Wong's and Wagner's consumer profiles are alike, they are, of course, two unique individuals. In fact, when you dig below their superficial spending patterns, it becomes readily apparent that they have widely divergent lifestyles, political and social beliefs, outlooks on life, and reasons for choosing the brands they do. Because of these differences, each responds to marketing messages in a different way. For a marketer wooing them for a particular product or service, it would be more effective to approach them as individuals, not consumer clones.

This is one of the challenges facing traditional consumer segmentation systems, which group people together by demographics, geography, and consumer behavior. "Really getting into the mind of the consumer is obviously the 'holy grail' of marketing," says J. Walker Smith, president of Yankelovich Partners Inc. And Smith believes he has come up with a unique tool for marketers in their quest to get inside the consumer mind: Yankelovich's new psychographic segmentation system, called Monitor Mindbase.

There are numerous commercial segmentation tools available to marketers today—the latest EPM Consumer Segmentation Survey lists 60—which slice and dice the American public into a multitude of classes, categories, and clusters. Segmentation has become somewhat of a cottage industry among market researchers, and the introduction of a new one could be yawn-inducing. However, Mindbase is premised on the idea of segmenting individuals by values, attitudes, and mindsets, rather than by geography, demographics, consumption patterns, and brand preferences. In essence, the program sets the ambitious goal of uncovering the underlying psychology of consumer behavior, on an individual level, in an actionable, database-compatible format. It does this by segmenting people into categories of consumers with varying degrees of materialism, ambition, orientation to family life, cynicism, openness to technology, and a host of other elements.

Marketers have used specialized segmentation techniques to find the most fruitful target audiences since Jonathan Robbin, the founder of Claritas Inc., created the PRIZM (Potential Rating Index for ZIP Markets) clustering system in 1974. Robbin, considered the father of geodemography, grouped people who had similar demographics and lifestyles into neighborhood clusters, on the theory that "birds of a feather, flock together."

A slew of similar programs have popped up to compete with PRIZM—such as CACI's Acorn and SRI's VALS—all based on the premise that people in the same zip code or neighborhood tend to buy the same products, prefer similar brands, and use the same media. VALS (Values, Attitudes, and Lifestyle Survey), like Mindbase, strives to segment consumer psychology, but does so only on a larger neighborhood basis, while Mindbase reaches the individual household level. Smith points out that, "While two families on the same block may appear similar based on demographics, their perspectives of the world around them will influence how they respond to messaging." Understanding these perspectives on an individual level can provide important insight into how and why one person will respond to a particular message while others in the same geographic segment do not.

INSIDE THE CONSUMER MIND
The Eight Major Mindbase Segments

UP AND COMERS
16% OF ADULT POPULATION

Generation X. Young, single, no children. Average incomes. Ambitious, optimistic, and novelty-seeking. Perceive themselves as intelligent, creative, attractive, and funny. Do not view themselves as neighborly or old-fashioned. Ideal targets for products and services which offer something new.

YOUNG MATERIALISTS
8% OF ADULT POPULATION

Generation X. Young, single, no children. Average incomes. More men than women. Believe money and success equal happiness. Low level of social consciousness, highly self-focused, don't enjoy socializing. Perceive themselves as adventurous and attractive, not practical, spiritual, or open to new ideas. Highly stressed and style-conscious. Enjoy shopping. Prime targets for products and services that make them feel important and successful, as well as fun and stylish.

STRESSED BY LIFE
12% OF ADULT POPULATION

Generation X. Young, mostly female, often unmarried, parents with lower incomes. Have a strong desire for novelty to help escape stress of daily life. Enjoy spending time with family and friends, watching movies, and playing games. Receptive to new technology but cynical about changes it brings. Perceive themselves as family-oriented, funny and attractive, but not practical or old-fashioned. Good targets for products and services which offer to reduce stress and escape from reality.

NEW TRADITIONALISTS
14% OF ADULT POPULATION

Boomers. Married with high incomes but low levels of materialism. Conservative, family- and community-oriented. High levels of social consciousness and low levels of cynicism. Enjoy nesting, reading, crafts, and gardening. Perceive themselves as old-fashioned, neighborly, and responsible. Receptive to new technology and comfortable with high levels of media consumption. Excellent target for products and services that help them maintain control of their well-ordered lives.

FAMILY LIMITED
14% OF ADULT POPULATION

Boomers. Married with children. High incomes. Intense focus on family life, which impedes their social and community consciousness, as well as independent activities. Do not like novelty or technology, and are disinterested in style. Cynical. Do not perceive themselves as ambitious, creative, adventurous, or attractive. Can be reached in messages with a family focus, in mediums such as family-programming and children's cartoons.

DETACHED INTROVERTS
9% OF ADULT POPULATION

Boomers. Usually male, with no children. Average incomes. Inactive, not social, do not care about style. Not socially conscious or novelty seeking. Neither community-oriented nor focused on self. Have very few interests. Do not perceive themselves as self-confident, creative, spiritual, or funny. Somewhat cynical. Are considered a less-desirable consumer group.

RENAISSANCE ELDERS
15% OF ADULT POPULATION

Older, with average incomes but financially comfortable. Active seniors for whom family and community are very important. Socially conscious and old-fashioned. Open to new technology; many outside interests. Perceive themselves as spiritual, neighborly, self-confident, and open to new ideas. Not materialistic but somewhat style-conscious. Ideal target for products and services that help them maintain their health, financial security, and family ties.

RETIRED FROM LIFE
12% OF ADULT POPULATION

Older. Not attracted to novelty and highly cynical about modern life. Care little for style or material goods. Perceive themselves as neighborly and old-fashioned, but not intelligent, creative, spiritual, or funny. They are overwhelmed by information. Enjoy gardening and game shows. Hold little appeal to marketers as a target.

Source: Yankelovich Partners, Inc.

In creating Mindbase, Yankelovich examined four years of in-depth data on American values and attitudes from its annual Monitor survey—a comprehensive study of American opinions on topics such as government, health, sex, business, and religion, which it has carried out since 1971. From this data, Yankelovich identified eight major consumer groups with shared life attitudes and motivations. These eight groups were further divided into 32 distinct sub-segments for greater differentiation and clarification. "We conduct 2,500 interviews a year for Monitor, which is one of the last door-to-door surveys in America," says Doug Haley, chief knowledge officer at Yankolovich. "Each survey lasts about 2 1/2 hours, so we have really gained some deep insights into the American psyche, and consumer mindset."

Haley believes that while databases devised on a geographic or consumer behavior model are highly valid, "there is an increasing diversity in values among people who live closely together." Fur-ther, knowing that someone is a frequent consumer of a product or service doesn't explain the story behind their purchase pattern, and understanding this motivating factor is a key benefit of the new segmentation system. Geographic models can be successful in locating prime targets, while this psychological model can provide guidance in tailoring the right message to the right audience. For this reason, Yankelovich encourages use of Mindbase in conjunction with other segmentation systems, such as PRIZM.

Three of the eight main groups created by Mindbase are predominant among Generation Xers: Up and Comers, Young Materialists, and Stressed by Life. Boomers comprise the New Traditionalist, Family Limited, and Detached Introvert segments. The Renaissance Elders and Retired From Life groups constitutes the elderly population. Mindbase distinguishes many important psychographic differences among the groups (see chart for in-depth segment descriptions).

DIFF'RENT STROKES

Consumer behavior of Mindbase segments.

INDEX VALUES   AVERAGE FOR ALL ADULTS=100

	CURRENTLY USE THE INTERNET	NO. OF OVERNIGHT TRIPS	HAVE A CAR LOAN	NO. OF ANN. STOCK TRANS.	CONTR. THIS YEAR TO 401K ACCT.
Up and Comers	126	131	89	106	78
Young Materialists	109	92	61	236	26
Stressed By Life	84	91	100	77	72
New Traditionalists	129	100	145	91	194
Family Limited	112	81	137	140	133
Detached Introverts	123	97	108	140	117
Renaissance Elders	95	121	89	70	94
Retired from Life	40	68	54	66	45

For example, Up and Comers take 31 percent more overnight trips than the average adult.
Source: Yankelovich Partners, Inc.

Understanding these mindset segments can be very helpful in crafting the creative in advertising, direct mail, and other targeted marketing material. For example, a cross-selling opportunity for a financial-services product can be improved by understanding the type of message each recipient will best respond to. "While saving for college is considered an obligation for the Family Limited segment, it's more of a pleasurable reward for having successful kids for those in the New Traditionalist segment," says Smith. "This obviously would affect how you should market an educational investment product."

One of the key attributes of Mindbase is its ability to use third-party data, from providers such as Acxiom or Experian, to glean which Mindbase segment each customer in a client database falls into. For example, one Yankelovich client who tested Mindbase earlier this year was a regional bank, which was introducing a new set of investment products. After overlaying a set of third-party data onto the bank's client list, Yankelovich used that information to categorize each client into a Mindbase segment. It found two prime targets for the mailing: New Traditionalists and Detached Introverts.

Both groups had frequent bank interactions and above-average transaction values. Taking into account their Mindbase characteristics, New Traditionalists were targeted with a message emphasizing the presence of local experts who could manage the investments of busy customers. Meanwhile, Detached Introverts received a message highlighting the ability to access balances and manage transactions via computer. The test found that using this targeted messaging resulted in a 2 to 4 times better response rate than a control sample of random bank customers with similar transaction activity, depending on the creative material used in the mailing.

According to Kirk Boothe, a principal at IBM's Business Intelligence Financial Solutions unit, "Ten percent of a bank's customers provide 120 percent of their profits." Finding this group by data mining and segmentation is critical. "In the near future, every business will be a database business," predicts Smith. "This was a trend anyway, but it has only been intensified by the Internet," where every business can be conducted on a national or global scale.

Internet businesses are marketing to consumers they have little or no first-hand knowledge of, and customer intelligence is vital to understanding their needs and desires. Consumers who are subject to an increasing number of marketing messages every day will filter out any messages that do not appeal to their basic attitudes and mindsets. Understanding not only past purchase behavior, but the values and self-perception of your target consumer, could be an essential aspect of capturing their attention and disposable dollar.

HOW WE
SELL

If shopping is the great American indoor sport,
why isn't it more fun? Why isn't it easier? Why isn't it *better?*
Paco Underhill, founder of Envirosell Inc. and author of *Why We Buy:
The Science of Shopping*, decodes the secrets of retail design
to explain the rules behind how we shop.

By Keith H. Hammonds

NEW YORK CITY'S CHELSEA NEIGHBORHOOD, WEDGED BETWEEN Greenwich Village and midtown, is a square-mile shrine to cusp-of-the-millennium mainstream retailing. Barnes & Noble, Victoria's Secret, and Restoration Hardware have all established big, boisterously appointed outposts amid turn-of-the-century office buildings. The Body Shop, J. Crew, Banana Republic, and the Gap have also arrived. ABC Carpet & Home, a rug shop-turned-home-furnishings megaboutique, has become a consumer destination unto itself.

Two floors above Chelsea's mercantilist fray, tucked into a former hotel, you will find the headquarters of Envirosell Inc., home to managing director Paco Underhill and 25 of his colleagues, who are perhaps the world's savviest students of the art and science of America's favorite indoor sport—shopping. Its offices are, to be generous, utilitarian: white walls, plain windows, and a hodgepodge of oak-laminate cubicles situated beneath bulky air-conditioning ducts. From the looks of things, this is a company of the retailing business, but clearly not *in* the retailing business.

The single distinguishing feature of Envirosell's two floors, in fact, is the collection of videotapes. There are thousands of them: Some rest on shelves that rise from floor to ceiling, some are piled into plastic tubs, and others are simply stacked on top of one another. Each is carefully labeled: "Chicago/White Hen, Gatorade/July-94"; "Costa Mesa/Pepsi Drive-Thru/11-6-98"; "Deerfield/Blockbuster/12-9-95"—city/store/data, videotape after videotape.

> **"The marketing engine that we have built with some care during the 20th century still works, but it doesn't work nearly as well as it needs to."**

"This," says Paco Underhill slyly, pointing to the massive collection of tapes, "is my retirement annuity." He's not kidding. Outside of Hollywood, this could well be the most valuable film library in the nation. The tapes are meticulous diaries of retailing sociology and, if you will, markers of cultural history. They tell us a bit about who we are, and they show us a lot about how we shop.

Underhill, 47, founded Envirosell in 1978, a few years after hearing urban anthropologist William H. Whyte Jr. speak on the subject of the mechanics of city planning. It was an epiphany for Underhill, who soon realized he could apply Whyte's tools to the retail world. Equipped with a movie camera and a notebook, he could record how many steps shoppers took past a store entrance before pausing, which direction they turned, and where their eyes came to rest. He could track how often parents reached for a certain brand of cereal, with which hand, where the box was located on the shelves at the store, and whether their children's protests changed the parents' decision.

THE PACO PRINCIPLES

IN A SHORT PERIOD OF TIME, PACO UNDERHILL'S *Why We Buy: The Science of Shopping* (Simon & Schuster, 1999) is fast becoming a business best-seller. Here, adapted from the book, are some of Underhill's key lessons on shops, shoppers, and shopping.

Bring 'em in; then keep 'em there. The amount of time shoppers spend in a store is perhaps the single-most-important factor in determining how much they will buy. The majority of advice we give to retailers involves ways of getting shoppers to shop longer.

Honor "the transition zone." On entering a store, people need to slow down and sort out the stimuli. Which means that whatever is in the zone they cross before making that transition is pretty much lost on them. If there's a display of merchandise, they're not going to take it in. If there's a sign, they'll probably be moving too fast to absorb its message. If the sales staff hits them with a hearty "Can I help you?" the answer is most likely going to be, "No, thanks."

The hand bone's connected to the wallet. The fact that most shoppers have two hands is well known. But the implications of that are often ignored. It's hard to overemphasize the importance of the hand issue to the world of shopping. A store can offer the finest, cheapest, sexiest goods, but if the shopper can't pick them up, it's all for nothing.

Mirrors versus banks. People slow down when they see reflective surfaces. And they speed up when they see banks. Bank windows are boring and so are banks. Mirrors, on the other hand, are never dull. So never open a store next to a financial institution—by the time pedestrians reach you, they'll be moving too fast for window shopping. If you can't help being next to a bank, make sure to have a mirror or two on your facade to slow shoppers down.

Take men. Please. Men always move faster than women do through a store's aisles. Men spend less time looking, too. In many settings, it's hard to get them to look at anything they hadn't intended on buying. Men also don't like asking where things are—or any questions at all, for that matter. If a man can't find the section he's looking for, he'll wheel around once or twice, then leave the store without ever asking for help.

Behold the geriatrics. By 2025, nearly one-fifth of the American people will be 65 or older. All of retailing is going to have to cater to seniors because they'll have the numbers and the dollars. But we're going to need a whole new world. For starters, the words on packages will have to be large enough so people can read them.

This is what Envirosell does—in malls, in restaurants, and at kiosks around the world. Underhill's researchers patrol stores at the behest of Samsonite, Hewlett-Packard, Denny's, Toro—and dozens more merchants, retailers, ad agencies, and financial-services institutions, not to mention the U.S. Postal Service. For each assignment, Envirosell researchers position video cameras at crucial points—at the store's entrance, say, or near the cash registers—and then they discreetly cruise the aisles, mapping the routes of shoppers and taking notes on their behavior.

After returning to the offices in Chelsea, the researchers spend hours poring over the videos in fast-forward mode, studying shoppers as they zip past displays and through checkout lines. Every so often, they spot something: an abrupt turn past a table stocked with products, perhaps; an overly long pause in an aisle; or an awkward reach for an item that's been stocked on the bottom shelf—some small gesture. At this point, they slow the tape, watch it again, and jot a note. They have captured an insight.

During more than 20 years and thousands of tapes, Underhill and his crew have turned up some interesting insights: First, shoppers almost always drift to the right; they walk to the right and look toward the right, which is why merchandisers position new products just to the right of known top sellers. Second, people don't read more than three or four words of a sign in a shop window. Third, shoppers walk past banks quickly. Fourth, mirrors remind shoppers that they are being watched. And fifth, if you put chairs in a women's clothing store, men will sit and women will shop longer.

These are not opinions; they are facts. And if you are a retailer or a consumer-products marketer, they are incredibly valuable facts. But they are also significant observations about business, work, and the act of finding—or being—a customer. That is why Underhill's new book, *Why We Buy: The Science of Shopping* (Simon & Schuster, 1999), entered its ninth printing in August. His book is a remarkable business tool, a distillation of all those notes and tapes, packaged in a way that is useful, witty, and loving.

For this, Underhill, a quiet, almost awkward man, has become a minor phenomenon. In the months since his book came out, he's been featured on nearly 20 National Public Radio segments. He has been interviewed by country-music stations, the Christian Broadcast Network, and a flagship polka station—which, as he notes, "doesn't usually do books." Pacomania reigns.

> **"Women continue to be neglected in traditional male arenas, from cars to technology to hardware."**

And, at the same time, Envirosell is booming with new clients, new assignments, and new opportunities to add to the stock of tapes that feed Underhill's ability to decode the continuing evolution of shopping behavior. Despite his newfound fame as a successful author and shopping guru, Underhill still makes it a point to spend time "in the field," keeping his eye engaged in anthropological observations. On any given day, he and his researchers are more than likely holed up in a store somewhere, shooting tape and looking for new insights. FAST COMPANY caught up with him in one of his rare moments back at his office.

"Technology is a troubling issue, because as much as it facilitates, it also confuses."

How has your book and your work contributed to people's understanding of retailing?

The point is that we either love or hate shopping. This book holds up a mirror to the shopping experience, so that people can read it and see themselves. And that's what brings interest. What we do sure ain't rocket science. I mean, it's not as if we invented some magic black box. On the other hand, there's a very distinct logic that runs through much of what we do. We can tell you, "If you do this or that in a store, here's what the consequences will be."

Why are those consequences particularly important now?

There are a couple of critical issues here. One is a basic realization in the business world, whether we're talking about retail goods or consumer products: The marketing engine that we have built with some care during the 20th century still works, but it doesn't work nearly as well as it needs to. As more people realize the degree to which it does not work, they are reaching out to different sources for information or inspiration.

Increasingly, too, in our time-pressured culture, retailers are recognizing the importance of purchase decisions that are made or that are heavily influenced at the point of sale. More and more, people today tend to park their brand predisposition at the door. As we approach the 21st century, the notion of somebody being "a Chevy man," in the way that there were loyal Chevy men in 1957, is almost passé.

So we can measure brand awareness, brand image, and purchase predisposition. But even with all of those measurements, a lot of people walk in the door of a CompUSA thinking about buying one brand, and they walk out having bought another. I go into an auto showroom to look at a Ford Mustang, and if I don't like the salesperson, I get frustrated. So I leave, and then I head to the Nissan dealer. These days, we're all quicker to bail.

And I think that we consumers are eminently more cynical than we used to be. We've been flimflammed, manipulated, and marketed to, and we're starting to see through the facade. We are more experienced. Our tempers are shorter, and our patience is thinner. As consumers, we are becoming aware of our power—the power to pick up our toys and go home, or to go somewhere else to play.

Are you saying that the old tricks simply don't work anymore?

They still work. No matter how much smarter or more experienced we have become, there's still something called "retail magic," where someone is able to put something out there in a way that makes us fall in love with it and have to have it. What is different now is that the same old tricks don't work with everybody. The older we get, the more experienced we become. And while people from generation X and generation Y are def-

initely manipulable, they are still more streetwise than you and I were when we were their age.

Also, while we live in a world in which there are global brands and identities that almost everyone recognizes, we also see some measure of heterogeneous complexity. There are a lot of subpopulations to sell to, more than there used to be. On the same sidewalk, you'll see some people who wear brand names on the outside of their clothing, others who think the label is best kept inside, and others who don't care. So stores need to find subtle ways to broaden their reach. One way to do that: Stores can adjust their music. Old Navy, for example, does a great job of playing contemporary music, "oldies," and some jazz, and through its music selection, the company makes a cross section of people feel welcome.

Which shoppers are most ignored by merchandisers?

There are a few ignored groups. First, for all the attention we give seniors, that shopping segment has not been catered to in the way they could be. The AARP may negotiate discounts, but it's not negotiating focus. Marketers are just starting to make progress in senior housing and senior-friendly furniture and athletic apparel. I still have a tough time getting a generation-X marketer to believe that going to Naples, Florida to study a large senior market may be a great head start on learning what the marketing problems are going to be in 2010. So the first group I would focus on is seniors.

Women are probably a close second. Women continue to be neglected in traditional male arenas, from cars to technology to hardware—this despite the amount of purchasing power that they wield. Ethnic groups are third on the list. Reaching out to an ethnic market is often cheap and effective because the ethnic market has fewer choices. We did an interesting case study here in New York City, where we were asked to look at the dynamics of a newsstand located at Greeley Square. The client was surprised that the newsstand sat at one of the major corners of New York's Koreatown, and yet it stocked no Korean-friendly products, except for weekly papers. There were no Korean magazines, no Korean soft drinks, and no Korean beer. No one had thought about selling green tea.

The issue here: Often, marketers have no real sense of the ground. Where is my store? If there's an ethnic community adjacent to it, maybe it makes sense to cater to them! Another way to think about the "ground issue" is to recognize who's coming onto your territory. This country has become a huge tourist destination, and yet there's little that we do as marketers to cater to that offshore purchaser. I challenge you to go look for charts converting American sizes into European sizes at the Gap or at Disney stores. If you make even a minor gesture like that, you'll immediately reap rewards.

Restoration Hardware, for example, is a wonderful store. At the same time, it frustrates me. There's no thought given to the

> ## "The Web should focus on creating something better, rather than being smart about recognizing distinct niches."

international shopper: Once it had a beautiful brass frog that I wanted for my garden. (I'm one of the rare New Yorkers who has a garden.) And I wanted to buy one for my business partner in Milan. When I asked about a European hose coupling, the store manager had no idea what I was talking about. Yet, during the Christmas season, a third of the people walking into that store come from someplace where American-size fixtures aren't used very often. Having couplings available for European hoses might have meant that a lot more of those brass frogs got sold. The store is controlled by its buying office, in Marin County, California, and I don't think they have a good sense of what's going on in urban settings.

Is there a difference between the way men and the way women shop for their families?

First, when it comes to shopping for the family, most wives are better trained at it than their husbands are. Wives have a better sense of discipline, and shopping is more of a chore for them. Wives approach shopping as a money manager, as opposed to husbands, who approach it as a moneymaker. It's easier for husbands to slip into drunken-sailor mode: "That's a good deal. It's a curious product. I want it. I'll figure out how to use it when I get it home. Salsa-flavored ketchup, just what I always wanted!" In general, kids have an easier time manipulating Dad. Mom is better at saying, "No."

Do you see the gap narrowing between how men and women behave in stores? Are we more alike than we used to be?

I think that the whole question of gender and sexuality is an issue that we're eminently more comfortable with in 1999 than we have been in the past. But it's a very curious issue—whether it's looking at the men's fashion industry and at the relationship between straight and gay men, or that Gapbody has been launched, which, as I understand, is a store that sells underwear for men and women under one roof. On the other hand, some successful merchants, like Banana Republic, have separated their stores: a Banana Republic for men and a Banana Republic for women. Certainly, almost all men in those unisex stores like the Gap or Old Navy have had the experience of looking at something and realizing, "Uh-oh, this is not meant for me."

There is that terrifying prospect of being caught on the wrong side of the store.

In the women's-apparel business, it's interesting to see the number of clearly not-petite women shopping in the petite section. Who can explain that? Gender differences are going to be around for the foreseeable future. Testosterone is here for the foreseeable future. And there are still going to be significant numbers of men who don't buy their own underwear and who instead focus on buying beer, gas, and guns. But many of us are set in the midst of a much more profound gender revolution.

Despite all of the changing attributes of shoppers, are there any new developments that have actually made it easier to operate in the current retail environment?

For most retail stores, there's an absolute predictability about who is in the store and when they will be there. You can tell who's coming in and what opportunities they present. If I'm running a bookstore in a mall, I know that senior citizens come through early in the morning; stay-at-home moms shop during the day; kids come by after school; and professionals shop after work. That information ought to make it a lot easier to design retail spaces that appeal to each group at each time. For example, why not devise a rotating display facing the mall corridor? You turn it one way from 10 AM to noon, rotate it from noon to 2 PM, then turn it again from 2 PM to 6 PM. You simply put different books on the display sides depending on who will be walking past.

There are a number of things that you can do—small ideas that are fundamentally clever, that cut through the clutter, and that work. Instead of using a lot of small, clever ideas, everyone's looking for that one perfect moonstone. Here's another example of a small work of art: There's an elevator in a hotel in New York's financial district with a mirror and a sign underneath it that says something like, "You look famished." Then it lists all of the restaurant options that can be found in the hotel. It's brilliant!

There's an mtvlogic here, involving the use of icons and words to get across a complex thought. It's a technique that applies the same principles to marketing that Reginald Marsh applied to the world of graphics with his giant-size murals—that somehow there was a way in the course of one frame to get across the image of something infinitely larger. The idea of a mirror and "You look famished" uses the power of a reflective surface. A mirror has always been a magical symbol. Someone has just twisted it wonderfully.

A lot of what you've said seems like common sense. Why don't merchandisers get it?

In part, it's because the merchandising business is in a cowboy stage. It has very little accountability built in. The point-of-purchase industry is now maybe four times larger than it was 15 years ago, and, even at that, it's desperately looking for its place at the table of marketing. I had lunch today with a senior executive at McDonald's, and I asked her, "How much do you spend testing commercials? And how much do you test your merchandising and promotions?" Although McDonald's does test some point-of-purchase merchandising, it spends far more on checking commercials.

The dollars spent on merchandising crept up without anyone keeping close track. And lots of people talk strategy, but not many of them know about tactics. We've made huge strides in the past 10 years, and yet, until recently, there wasn't a major business school in the country that specifically offered a course in merchandising.

Why hasn't technology solved all of these problems?

Technology is a troubling issue, because as much as it facilitates, it also confuses. Over the past 10 years, a lot of people have knocked on the door with technology, wanting to back it into some application. Consequently, we've spent a lot of time working with technology. We found that almost all of the interactive devices that we've studied over the past decade have failed. In some cases, we have tried to apply technological solutions to human problems. And tried to apply technological solutions to human problems. And almost universally, the designers of those solutions have had an imperfect understanding of the environments that they were studying.

Time after time, we've seen merchandising approaches that involve putting computers on the retail floor—and no one has considered that somebody on the floor has to reboot the computer on a regular basis. And it's amazing that, when ideas for introducing technology into the retail space come up, no one seems to realize that eventually any flat surface in a commercial space is going to get something spilled on it. We sell an awful lot of soft drinks in this country. Sugar water isn't good for computers—and it finds its way into almost every store.

You make it sound as if the retail environment suffers from a number of disconnects: the disconnect between buyers at headquarters and salespeople on the shop floor, and (the other way around) the disconnect between the brand manager who designs a marketing campaign and the shop-floor clerk who sets it up in the store.

We ran a study a number of years ago that looked at hair-care products for a major American health- and beauty-aides maker. We went to different stores and took pictures of shelf sets—what products were located where. We enlarged about 15 of those pictures for different stores, and we took those enlargements into our client presentation. Everybody went nuts over the photos! "That's not the right shelf set! We didn't pay for that! We're supposed to get 16 facings, and we have only 12! How did that brand get on that shelf? It shouldn't be there!"

It was amazing to think about this disconnect between our clients, sitting out in their exurban campus in New Jersey, and the stores themselves, where the objects of their attention were sold. I felt as if I was dealing with a puppet master who was 10 miles away from the stage where the puppets were performing. This is not to say that all of that planning is bogus, or that the execution isn't generally pretty good, but it's by no means perfect. As we go into the 21st century, stores are struggling to control labor costs. As that happens, and as fewer people work the floor, more stores are going to get the merchandising execution wrong. In the grocery-store trade, it's been estimated that 25% of what's shipped never makes it out to the floor. A quarter of the marketing vehicles that are sent off to your local Ralph's Supermarket get in the back door and make a one-way trip to the Dumpster. That's a frightening number.

What lessons from your store research can you translate to commerce on the Internet?

I've been asked that question innumerable times, mostly from e-commerce companies. The Net is desperately looking for answers. In one sense, we can't translate much from the physical retail world to the Web. But in another sense, there's a framework in stores that could be powerful in e-commerce. Stores have a certain predictability: I enter using a doorway, after which I follow a prescribed pathway. Merchandise is presented in a certain way that is more or less consistent from store to store. I get assistance in a certain manner. Finally, goods are exchanged for units of value using an established procedure. Everyone understands those rules; it's a basic system that we've all grown up with, and it works at Calvin Klein as well as at the local Piggy Wiggly.

The Net, on the other hand, has no prescribed doorways. People can drop in as well as drop out. There is no established system for telling me, "This is the product." And most important, where the rubber meets the road in e-commerce is that there's no universally understood way of getting to the transaction. I was talking to the research director for one of the most progressive retailers in the world. He was tearing out his hair with a Web designer trying to figure out what their online shopping cart was going to look like.

Then there are some very basic issues: There are visual acuity problems and basic communication issues. Lots of stuff is designed on a 21-inch screen but is seen on a 15-inch screen. Above all, there is a basic kindness shown toward people in most stores that hasn't as yet been translated to the Web.

Even considering all that, of course, e-commerce has real power.

E-commerce has succeeded where the traditional connection between manufacturer and retailer has failed. Books, music, movies, porn, and stocks are five categories in which the relationships between manufacturer and distributor are fundamentally flawed. I say books, because the bookstore is still trying to sell them as consumables, and the market is buying them as durables. In the world of music, manufacturers are eminently closer to the artists than they are to the consuming public. And in 1999 music is still packaged the same way that it was in 1959—only the LP format has been shrunk down to the CD. To me, that's a disconnect.

The real opportunity online is with people who are ill-served today. Why isn't somebody figuring out where the disconnects are between present-day retail and present-day consumers? Is there a search engine that finds products for large-size or tall people? There are enough of them out there. The future of the Net is going to be great, but in its present form, it's trying to capture everything rather than focusing on exactly where it needs to go.

So what does that say about what the Web should be doing?

The Web should focus on creating something better, rather than being smart about recognizing distinct niches. Or it can play an important role by forming a bond between the cyberworld and the physical world so that they support each other. I love that you can go into a Borders and order a book from its warehouse via an Internet kiosk and have the book delivered to your house. And if it's not the book you want, you can return it to the store. But the Victoria's Secret Catalogue, the Victoria's Secret store, and VictoriasSecret.com are three separate businesses. That's really dumb. When you see that kind of division, you know that the Web opportunity is simply being missed.

So your forecast is, We'll always have stores.

Yes, we'll always have stores. Part of what will come out of the Web, though, is an interesting muddying of what is physical space and what is cyberspace. What if I can walk to the market here in Union Square, go shopping for vegetables, and then drop off my order at a cybercafé? Or do the same for laundry soap or toilet paper? That lets stores shrink their footprints dramatically—to get out of unprofitable commodity categories, to present the public with a relatively small front end for a much bigger warehouse and distribution operation. Part of what we're looking at, then, is the Net's future as an integrated part of our brick-and-mortar existence. Just as I can use my store to drive traffic to the Net, I can use the Net to drive traffic to my stores.

Everyone is out there searching for magical technology solutions, and I'm sure there will be better ones than those we have now. Technology may have answers. But let's start with the basics and see whether we can get them right! I'm still amazed by how far businesses get down the e-commerce road without understanding their consumers. What will always be true is that having a good pair of eyes and spending a little time out on the floor are valuable. As much as technology may be able to capture transactions and a mechanical system may be able to generate numbers, it's hard for such technologies to capture the rhythm of real life.

When you go shopping, what grabs you? How do merchandisers reach you?

To some extent, my approach to stores has been spoiled. Everywhere I go, I'm engaged in deconstructing the store. I love doing it—don't get me wrong. But it often makes me angry. When I see something done wrong, and when the solution is so obvious, I want to grab the manager and shout, "You'll make more money if you just turn it around! Why did you do it this way? It doesn't make any sense! Don't you know that about 85% of the world is right-handed? Put that on the other wall!"

KEITH H. HAMMONDS (KHAMMONDS@FASTCOMPANY.COM) IS A SENIOR EDITOR AT *FAST COMPANY*. YOU CAN REACH PACO UNDERHILL ON THE WEB (WWW.ENVIROSELL.COM) OR BY EMAIL (INFO@ENVIROSELL.COM).

From *Fast Company*, November 1999, pp. 294-305. © 1999 by Fast Company and Keith H. Hammonds.

Defining Moments: Segmenting by Cohorts

Coming of age experiences influence values, attitudes, preferences, and buying behaviors for a lifetime.

By Charles D. Schewe, Geoffrey E. Meredith, and Stephanie M. Noble

Cohorts are highly influenced by the external events that were happening when they were "coming of age" (generally between the years 17–23). For example, those now in their late seventies and early eighties lived through the Great Depression while baby boomers witnessed the assassination of JFK, saw other political assassinations, shared the Vietnam War, and lived through the energy crisis. Such shared experiences distinguish one cohort from another.

Today, many call marketing to birth groups generational marketing. Generations differ from cohorts. Each generation is defined by its years of birth. For example, a generation is usually 20 to 25 years in length, or roughly the time it takes a person to grow up and have children. But a cohort can be as long or short as the external events that defines it. The cohort defined by World War II, for example, is only six years long.

Consider how different cohorts treat spending and saving. Today's Depression cohort, those ages 79 to 88 in 2000, began working during the Great Depression. Their conduct with respect to money is very conservative. Having experienced the worst of economic times, this age group values economic security and frugality. They still save for that "rainy day." Those, however, in the 55 to 78 age category today were influenced by the Depression, but also experienced the boom times of the Post-World War II period. This group has attitudes toward saving that are less conservative; they are more willing to spend than the older group. In sharp contrast to the "Depression-scarred" is the free-wheeling generation that grew up during the "hippie revolution." Russell (1993) calls this birth group the "free agents," since its members defied the establishment, sought individualism, and were skeptical of everything. This cohort can be characterized as "buy now, pay later" and its members will carry this value into the century ahead as they journey through middle age and on into old age.

Cohort effects are life-long effects. They provide the communality for each cohort being targeted as a separate market segment. And since these cohorts can be described by the ages of their constituents, they offer an especially efficient vehicle for direct marketing campaigns.

Six American Cohorts

In 2000, American adults can be divided into six distinct cohorts, or market segments, ranging in age from the Depression cohort (age 79–88) to what many people are calling Generation X (age 24–34). This division is based on intensive content analysis of a wide range of publications and studies scanned over a 10-year period. The roughly 4 million people who are age 89 and older are not included for two reasons. First, this group is much smaller than other cohorts. Also, much of their consumption behavior is controlled by physical need. There also are more than 72 million persons under the age of 24. This newly emerging cohort can be referred to as the "N-Gen," since the impact of the internet revolution appears to be the key defining moment shaping this group's values. Yet it is too early to know their "defining moment-driven" values, preferences, and attitudes because external forces take some time to influence values. A brief description of each of the six cohorts follows.

The Depression Cohort

This group was born between 1912 and 1921, came of age from 1930 to 1939, and is age 79–88 today. Currently this cohort contains 13,054,000 people, or 7% of the adult U.S. population.

This cohort was defined by the Great Depression. Maturing, entering the workforce, trying to build and support families during the '30s had a profound influence on this cohort in so many areas, but most strongly in finances: money and savings. To many of today's business managers, the Depression seems like ancient history, almost apocryphal, like the Great Flood. Yet to this cohort, it was all too real. To put the Depression in perspective, the S&P 400 (the broadest measure of the economy as a whole available at that time) declined 69% between 1929 and 1932 in a relentless and agonizing fall. It wasn't until 1953—24 years and a World War later—before the S&P index got back to where it had been in 1929! People starting out in this environment were scarred in ways they carry with them today. In particular, financial security still rules their thinking as reflected in the following example.

A Depression Cohort Marketing Example. One savings and loan bank on the West Coast took a cohort perspective to boost deposits from this cohort. They used an icon familiar to this age group, George Feneman (Groucho Marx's television sidekick on *You Bet Your Life*), who assured this cohort of the safety of their money. He stressed that the financial institution uses their money for mortgages. "We build houses," he says, which is just what this cohort can relate to, since preserving their homes was central to the financial concerns of this age group.

EXECUTIVE
briefing

Cohorts are groups of individuals who are born during the same time period and travel through life together. They experience similar external events during their late adolescent/ early adulthood years. These "defining moments" influence their values, preferences, attitudes, and buying behaviors in ways that remain with them over their lifetime. We can identify six known American cohorts that include those from age 88 to those coming of age in 2000. While generational cohorts are far from the final solution for marketers, they are certainly a relevant dynamic. Marketers should seriously consider targeting these age groupings, especially in their marketing communications.

The World War II Cohort

Born 1922–1927, this cohort came of age from 1940 to 1945. Its members are age 73–78 today. Currently 9,465,000 people, it represents 5% of our adult population.

World War II defined this cohort. Economically it was not a boom time (the S&P 500 gained 50% from 1940 to 1945, but it was still only half of what it had been in 1929), but unemployment was no longer a problem. This cohort was unified by a common enemy, shared experiences, and especially for the 16 million in the military, a sense of deferment and delayed gratification. In World War I, the average duration of service was less than 12 months; in World War II, the average was 33 months. Marriages, careers, and children were all put on hold until the war was over.

This sense of deferment made the World War II cohort an intensely romantic one. The yearning for loved ones left behind, and for those who left to fight is reflected in the music and literature and movies of the time (e.g., *I've Got My Love to Keep Me Warm, Homesick, That's All, 'Til Then*, and *You'd Be So Nice to Come Home To*). And, while for many the war was an unpleasant experience, for many others it was the apex of their lives. They had a defined role (frequently more important in status than any other they would ever have), a measure of freedom from their particular social norms, and an opportunity to travel, some to exotic foreign shores, others just away from the towns and cornfields of their youth. The horrors and heroism experienced by our soldiers imbedded values that stay with them still. And this influence was clearly depicted in the award-winning and highly acclaimed movies of 1998: *Saving Private Ryan* and *The Thin Red Line*.

A World War II Cohort Marketing Example. Using cohort words, symbols, and memories can bring substantial rewards for marketers. A direct marketing campaign designed for a cable television provider to increase subscriptions is just such an example. Postage stamp-sized pictures of Douglas McArthur were put on the corner of the envelope with the copy "If you remember V-J Day, we've got some new programs you're going to love." This attention-getter immediately communicated that the content is for members of the targeted cohort. When this approach was used, subscription response rates surged from 1.5% to more than 10%.

The Post-War Cohort

Members of this cohort were born from 1928 to 1945, came of age from 1946 to 1963, and are age 55 to 73 in 2000. Currently 42,484,000 people, 22.7% of the adult population are Post-Wars.

This cohort is a very long one—18 years span the youngest to the oldest members. They were the beneficiaries of a long period of economic growth and relative social tranquility. Economically the S&P 500, which had struggled until 1953 just to get back to where it had been before the Depression, then tripled over the next 10 years. There were dislocations during this time—the Korean War in the early '50s, Sputnik in 1957, the first stirrings of the civil rights movement, a brief recession in 1958—but by and large, at least on the surface, things were pretty quiet.

The tenor of the times was conservative, seeking the comfortable, the secure, and the familiar. It was a time that promoted conformity and shrank from individual expression, which is why the overt sexuality of Elvis and the rebellion of James Dean were at once popular and scandalous.

A Post-War Cohort Marketing Example. The Vermont Country Store, highly successful marketers of nostalgic products difficult to find, uses cohort images and memories to target market segments. To capture the attention of Post-War cohort customers, it peppers its catalog with pictures from the '50s and value-reflective copy along the outside of various pages such as:

"When I was young, I knew kids who were allowed in their living rooms only on special occasions—and usually under adult supervision. Now, instead of a chilly room used only to entertain on holidays, we can really relax in our living rooms." and

"In high school, buying clothes was easy. The more we dressed according to the conventions of the day, the better. If we'd known then what we know now, we could have looked every bit as good—and been a lot more comfortable. But then, that wasn't the point of being a teenager."

Boomers—I

The Baby Boom is usually defined as the 76 million people born between 1946 and 1964, since this is indeed when the annual birthrate bulged to more than 4 million per year. However there are two boomer cohorts. The first of these are the leading-edge boomers and they are 32,531,000 people strong, 17.4% of the adult population. They were born from 1946 to 1954, and came of age from 1963 to 1972. They are age 46 to 54 today.

Due to their numbers, the baby boomers as a whole have dominated marketing in America since they first appeared on the scene. When they were truly babies, they made Dr. Spock's *Infant and Child Rearing* the second best-selling book in the history of the world, after the Bible. As pre-teens, they dominated the media in shows like *Leave It to Beaver* and in merchandising with fads like Davy Crockett caps and Hula Hoops. As teens they propelled Coke, McDonald's, and Motown into corporate giants, and ensured the success of Clearasil.

The "Boomer I" cohort began coming of age in 1963, the start of a period of profound dislocations that still haunt our society today. It ended shortly after the last soldier died in Vietnam. The Kennedy presidency seemed like the natural extension of continued good times, of economic growth and domestic stability. It represented a liberated and early transfer of power from an older leader to a much younger one.

The Kennedy assassination, followed by that of Martin Luther King and Robert Kennedy, signaled an end to the status quo and galvanized a very large boomer cohort just entering its formative years. Suddenly the leadership (LBJ) was no longer 'theirs,' the war (Vietnam) was not their war, and authority and the establishment which had been the bedrock of earlier cohorts disintegrated in the melee of the 1968 Democratic National Convention in Chicago.

However, the Boomer I cohort continued to experience economic good times. Despite the social turmoil, the economy as a whole, as measured by the S&P 500, continued an upward climb. The Boomer I cohort wanted a lifestyle at least as good as they had experienced as children in the '50s, and with nearly 20 years of steady economic growth as history, they had no reason not to spend whatever they earned or could borrow to achieve it.

The Boomer I cohort still heavily values its individualism (remember, they were and are the "Me Generation,") indulgence of self, stimulation (a reflection of the drug culture they grew up with), and questioning nature. Marketing to this cohort demands attention to providing more information to back up product claims and to calm skeptical concerns. And these boomers prize holding on to their youth as the following example shows.

A Boomer I Cohort Marketing Example. The California Prune Board recommended to its plum producers that they plant many more trees, since large numbers of baby boomers were turning 50 and the 50+ age bracket (indeed, the 65+) was the heaviest consumer of prunes. However, boomers did not relate to prunes; they did not come of age with prunes as part of their consumption lives. Why, then, would they eat prunes in later life? In fact, prunes reflect cohort preferences of their parents—those same parents boomers did not want to trust ("Don't Trust Anyone Over 30").

Research into the chemical composition of prunes, however, found that they naturally stimulate the body's production of testosterone and estrogen… just the ingredients aging boomers desire to hold on to their sexual vitality and sense of youth. Clinical studies to provide advertising claim support for the estrogen and testosterone benefits were being undertaken. This approach could lead to, for example, a radio or television commercial featuring Adam and Eve in the Garden of Eden. Eve requests some fruit for sustenance, since they have a big night ahead populating the earth. She is delighted to receive a platter including one lonely prune (no apples, please). Her comment as she gulps the prune: "Well, this should get us through Asia, at least!"

Boomers II

The trailing-edge boomers were born between 1956 and 1965, came of age from 1973 to 1983, and are age 35 to 45 today. Currently 46,794,000 people are Boomer II's, 26% of the adult population.

The external events that separate the Boomer I from the Boomer II cohort were less dramatic than The Depression or World War II, but were just as real. They were composed of the stop of the Vietnam War (it never really ended—just stopped), Watergate (the final nail in the coffin of institutions and the establishment), and the Arab Oil Embargo that ended the stream of economic gains that had continued largely uninterrupted since 1945.

By 1973, something had changed for a person coming of age in America. While faith in institutions had gone, so had the idealist fervor that made the Boomer I cohort so cause-oriented. Instead, those in the Boomer II cohort exhibited a narcissistic preoccupation with themselves which manifested itself in everything from the self-help movement (*I'm OK—You're OK*, and various young and aging gurus imported from India) to self-deprecation (*Saturday Night Live, Mary Hartman, Mary Hartman*).

The change in economic fortunes had a more profound effect than is commonly realized. Throughout their childhood and as they came of age, the Boomer I cohort members experienced good times; their expectations that these good times would continue were thus reinforced, and the cohort mindset formed at that time can be seen today in a persistent resistance to begin saving for retirement. Things had been good, and they were going to stay good—somehow.

For the Boomer II cohort, the money mindset was much different. The Oil Shock of 1973 sent the economy tumbling: the S&P 500 lost 30% of its value between 1973 and 1975! At the same time, inflation began to resemble that of a banana republic. During this period, the real interest rate (Prime minus the CPI) hit a record low of -4%. In those circumstances, debt as a means of maintaining a lifestyle makes great economic sense. And a cohort with a 'debt imprint' will never lose it. Boomers II are spenders just like the Boomer Is, but for a different reason. It's not because they expect good times, but because they assume they can always get a loan, take out a second mortgage on the house, get another credit card, and never have to "pay the piper."

A Boomer II Cohort Marketing Example. A major finance company is currently aggressively promoting home equity loans with radio advertising directly oriented toward this cohort mindset. The commercial in essence states "Everyone else has a BMW, or a new set of golf clubs, and they're not any better than you are. Even if you don't think you can afford them, you can have them, now—with a home equity loan from XYZ company. And, while you're at it, why not take the Hawaiian vacation, too—you deserve it!" The copy brings on severe anxiety attacks for the World War II and Depression cohorts, but it makes perfect sense to the Boomer IIs.

Generation X

Born 1966–1976, Gen Xers came of age from 1984 to 1994. They are age 24 to 34 today. Currently 41,119,000 people, they represent 21.9% of the adult population.

Much has been written about Generation X, most of it derogatory in tone: "Slackers" (from the movie of that name); "Whiners"; "a generation of aging Bart Simpsons," "armed and possibly dangerous." That seems to be unfair. The generation of F. Scott Fitzgerald was widely characterized as "Lost," and that describes Generation X. This cohort has nothing to hang on to—not the institutions of the Post-War cohort, not the Boomer I's idealism and causes and institutions to resist, not the narcissism of the Boomer IIs. These were the children of divorce and daycare, latch-key kids of the 1980s; no wonder they exhibit so little foundation. The fact that they are searching for anchors can be seen in their seemingly contradictory "retro" behavior—the resurgence of proms, coming-out parties, and fraternities that Boomers rejected.

It can be seen in their political conservatism, which is also motivated by a "What's in it for me?" cynicism that repudiates liberal redistribution tendencies. And they feel alienated, reflected in the violence and brutal sex of the popular culture, and resigned to a world that seems to have little hope of offering them the lifestyles of their parents.

A Generation X Cohort Marketing Example. So how does a marketer reach a cohort with no defining moments? One way is with irreverent, rebellious, self-mocking, and sassy portrayals—which helps explain the popularity of South Park, the Simpsons, and the infamous Married With Children. Commercials like Maybelline's ad for Expert Eyes Shadow with Christy Turlington also exemplifies this sassiness. The ad shows the stunning model with beautifully made-up eyes illuminated by moonlight. A voice-over says: "Was it a strange celestial event… that gave her such bewitching eyes?" Then Turlington, sitting on her living room sofa, laughs and says, "Get over it."

Managerial Implications

Cohort segmentation provides a most intriguing additional method for separating consumer markets. Age has long been a segmentation variable, but this innovative approach shows it is defining moments that shape mindsets and provide the true value of age targeting. While not a key behavior driver for all product categories, cohort segmentation is particularly appropriate for food, music, apparel, automotive, financial and insurance, as well as entertainment products. Product creation and management over its life cycle is clearly ripe for cohort implementation.

Cohort analysis can help in designing communication campaigns. Determining music, movie stars, or other icons that cohorts identified with in their past is an effective selling technique. These tactics work because they rely on nostalgia marketing, that is, tapping deep, pleasurable memories of what seemed simpler, better times. They also work by calling out the target in an implicit way. "This message is for you!" Many companies have already engaged in this tactic as evidenced by the growing number of songs, logos, and actual commercial footage from the past.

Additionally, the changing nature of values across cohorts has important implications for marketers. As new cohorts enter the marketplace, organizations need to keep apprised of their changing value structures. In particular, as the age distribution in the United States changes, so will consumers' wants and needs. A cohort analysis can help track and forecast these wants and needs. In the 1980s, for example, the age segment of 50–65 years was comprised mostly of Depression and World War II cohort consumers. Today, it is made up mostly of the Post-War cohort and in 2010 it will be all Boomers. The demographic age segmentation—age 50 to 65—is the same, but the composition of that segment is constantly changing. It's a moving target.

Final Thought

Cohort segmentation works in the United States. But what about outside of the United States? Would cohorts be the same as here? Our research has found cohort values derived from defining moments indeed do exist abroad. Germany, for example, witnessed no Depression as Hitler's war effort energized the economy. In Brazil, the 1970s found a dictatorship imposing severe censorship, which created the need for personal freedoms in individuals coming of age during that time. In Jordan,

the Six-Day War in 1967 dramatically displaced Jordanians from their homeland and they now long for stability in maintaining a place to live. As these examples illustrate, cohort segmentation offers a rich opportunity here… and around the world.

Additional Reading

Meredith, Geoffrey and Charles D. Schewe (1994), "The Power of Cohorts," *American Demographics*, December, 22–31.

Rentz, Joseph O. and Fred D. Reynolds (1991), "Forecasting the Effects of an Aging Population on Product Consumption: An Age-Period-Cohort Framework," *Journal of Marketing Research*, 28, (3), 355–60.

——, ——, and Roy G. Stout (1983), "Analyzing Changing Consumption Patterns With Cohort Analysis," *Journal of Marketing Research*, 20, 12–20.

Russell, Cheryl (1993), *The Master Trend: How the Baby Boom Generation Is Remaking America*, Plenum, New York.

Schewe, Charles D. and Stephanie M. Noble (forthcoming), "Market Segmentation by Cohorts: The Value and Validity of Cohorts in America and Abroad," *Journal of Marketing Management* (Scotland).

Schuman, Howard and Jacqueline Scott (1989). "Generations and Collective Memories," *American Sociological Review*, 54, (3), 359–381.

Smith, J. Walker and Ann Clurman (1997), *Rocking the Ages*, Harper Business, New York.

Strauss, William and Neil Howe (1997), *The Fourth Turning*, Broadway Books, New York.

About the Authors

Charles D. Schewe is professor of marketing at the University of Massachusetts and a principal in Lifestage Matrix Marketing. Focusing on the marketing implications of the aging process, Schewe has advised such companies as Coca-Cola, Kellogg's, Kraft General Foods, Time-Life, Lucky Stores, Grand Metropolitan, and K-Mart. He may be reached at schewe@mktg.umass.edu.

Geoffrey E. Meredith is president of Lifestage Matrix Marketing, located in Lafayette, Calif. Formerly a senior vice president at Olgivy & Mather, Ketchum Communications, and Hal Riney and Partners, he also spent two years with Age Wave (see V1,N3 MM). He may be reached at Lifestage@aol.com.

Stephanie M. Noble is a doctoral candidate at the University of Massachusetts. She may be reached at smevans@som.umass.edu.

From *Marketing Management*, Fall 2000, Vol. 9, No. 3, pp. 48-53. © 2000 by the American Marketing Association. Reprinted by permission.

UNIT 3

Developing and Implementing Marketing Strategies

Unit Selections

Key Points to Consider

- Most ethical questions seem to arise in regard to the promotional component of the marketing mix. How fair is the general public's criticism of some forms of personal selling and advertising? Give some examples.

- What role, if any, do you think the quality of a product plays in making a business competitive in consumer markets? What role does price play? Would you rather market a higher-priced, better-quality product or one that was the lowest priced? Why?

- What do you envision will be the major problems or challenges retailers will face in the next decade? Explain.

- Given the rapidly increasing costs of personal selling, what role do you think it will play as a strategy in the marketing mix in the future? What other promotion strategies will play increased or decreased roles in the next decade?

 **Links: www.dushkin.com/online/**
These sites are annotated in the World Wide Web pages.

American Marketing Association Homepage
http://www.ama.org

Consumer Buying Behavior
http://www.courses.psu.edu/mktg/mktg220_rso3/sls_cons.htm

Product Branding, Packaging, and Pricing
http://www.fooddude.com/branding.html

Welcome to CRUSH
http://www.rtks.com

Marketing management objectives, the late Wroe Alderson once wrote, "are very simple in essence. The firm wants to expand its volume of sales, or it wants to handle the volume it has more efficiently." Although the essential objectives of marketing might be stated this simply, the development and implementation of strategies to accomplish them is considerably more complex. Many of these complexities are due to changes in the environment within which managers must operate. Strategies that fail to heed the social, political, and economic forces of society have little chance of success over the long run. The lead article in this unit provides helpful insight suggesting a framework for developing a comprehensive marketing plan.

The selections in this unit provide a wide-ranging discussion of how marketing professionals and U.S. companies interpret and employ various marketing strategies today. The readings also include specific examples from industry to illustrate their points. The articles are grouped in four sections, each dealing with one of the main strategy areas: product, price, distribution (place), and promotion. Since each selection discusses more than one of these areas, it is important that you read them broadly. For example, many of the articles covered in the distribution section discuss important aspects of personal selling and advertising.

Product Strategy. The essence of the marketing concept is to begin with what consumers want and need. After determining a need, an enterprise must respond by providing the product or service demanded. Successful marketing managers recognize the need for continuous product improvement and/or new product introduction.

The articles in this subsection focus on various facets of product strategy. The first two articles describe the importance of revitalizing old brands and establishing an effective branding campaign. "Can You Spot the Fake?" reveals that to retailers' dismay, fake luxury goods have become increasingly realistic. The last article in this subsection points out the important role package design plays in product differentiation.

Pricing Strategy. Few elements of the total strategy of the "marketing mix" demand so much managerial and social attention as pricing. There is a good deal of public misunderstanding about the ability of marketing managers to control prices, and even greater misunderstanding about how pricing policies are determined. New products present especially difficult problems in terms of both costs and pricing. The costs for developing a new product are usually very high, and if a product is truly new, it cannot be priced competitively, for it has no competitors.

"Kamikaze Pricing" scrutinizes the tremendous pricing pressures that companies face and suggests some ways to make better pricing decisions. In "Discovering Hidden Pricing Power," Donald Potter reveals the importance of using subtle and creative techniques in a highly price-competitive market.

Distribution Strategy. For many enterprises, the largest marketing costs result from closing the gap in space and time between producer and consumer. In no other area of marketing is efficiency so eagerly sought after. Physical distribution seems to be the one area where significant cost savings can be achieved. The costs of physical distribution are tied closely with

decisions made about the number, the size, and the diversity of marketing intermediaries between producer and consumer.

The three articles in this subsection scrutinize ways that retailers can create value for their customers, the dynamics of online retailing, and the challenge of retail stores bringing the Internet into the world of bricks and mortar.

Promotion Strategy. The basic objectives of promotion are to inform, persuade, or remind the consumer to buy a firm's product or pay for the firm's service. Advertising is the most obvious promotional activity. However, in total dollars spent and in cost per person reached, advertising takes second place to personal selling. Sales promotion supports either personal selling and advertising, or both. Such media as point-of-purchase displays, catalogs, and direct mail place the sales promotion specialist closer to the advertising agency than to the salesperson.

The three articles in this final unit subsection cover such topics as how to gain the biggest bang for your bucks in advertising, evaluation the effective use of Web advertising, and providing suggestions for improving the personal selling process.

THE VERY MODEL OF A
MODERN MARKETING PLAN

SUCCESSFUL COMPANIES ARE REWRITING THEIR STRATEGIES TO REFLECT CUSTOMER INPUT AND INTERNAL COORDINATION

SHELLY REESE

IT'S 1996. DO YOU KNOW WHERE YOUR MARKETING PLAN IS? In a world where competitors can observe and rapidly imitate each other's advancements in product development, pricing, packaging, and distribution, communication is more important than ever as a way of differentiating your business from those of your competitors.

The most successful companies are the ones that understand that, and are revamping their marketing plans to emphasize two points:

1. Marketing is a dialog between customer and supplier.
2. Companies have to prove they're listening to their customers by acting on their input.

WHAT IS A MARKETING PLAN?

At its most basic level, a marketing plan defines a business's niche, summarizes its objectives, and presents its strategies for attaining and monitoring those goals. It's a road map for getting from point A to point B.

But road maps need constant updating to reflect the addition of new routes. Likewise, in a decade in which technology, international relations, and the competitive landscape are constantly changing, the concept of a static marketing plan has to be reassessed.

Two of the hottest buzz words for the 1990s are "interactive" and "integrated." A successful marketing plan has to be both.

"Interactive" means your marketing plan should be a conversation between your business and your customers by acting on their input. It's your chance to tell customers about your business and to listen and act on their responses.

"Integrated" means the message in your marketing is consistently reinforced by every department within your company. Marketing is as much a function of the finance and manufacturing divisions as it is the advertising and public relations departments.

Integrated also means each time a company reaches out to its customers through an advertisement, direct mailing, or promotion, it is sending the same message and encouraging customers to learn more about the product.

WHY IS IT IMPORTANT?

The interaction between a company and its customers is a relationship. Relationships can't be reproduced. They can, however, be replaced. That's where a good marketing plan comes into play.

Think of your business as a suitor, your customers as the object of your affection, and your competitors as rivals. A marketing plan is your strategy for wooing customers. It's based on listening and reacting to what they say.

Because customers' priorities are constantly changing, a marketing plan should change with them. For years, conventional wisdom was 'prepare a five year marketing plan and review it every year.' But change happens a lot faster than it did 20 or even 10 years ago.

For that reason, Bob Dawson of The Business Group, a consulting firm in Freemont, California, recommends that his clients prepare a three year plan and review it every quarter. Frequent reviews enable companies to identify potential problems and opportunities before their competition, he explains.

ILLUSTRATION BY KELLY KENNEDY

"Preventative maintenance for your company is as important as putting oil in your car," Dawson says. "You don't wait a whole year to do it. You can't change history but you can anticipate what's going to happen."

ESSENTIAL COMPONENTS

Most marketing plans consist of three sections. The first section should identify the organization's goals. The second section should establish a method for attaining them. The third section focuses on creating a system for implementing the strategy.

Although some plans identify as many as six or eight goals, many experts suggest a company whittle its list to one or two key objectives and focus on them.

"One of the toughest things is sticking to one message," observes Mark Bilfield, account director for integrated marketing of Nissan and Infiniti cars at TBWA Chiat/Day in Los Angeles, which handles national advertising, direct marketing, public relations, and promotions for the automaker. Bilfield argues that a focused, consistent message is easier to communicate to the market place and to different disciplines within the corporation than a broad, encompassing one. Therefore, he advises, "unless there is something drastically wrong with the idea, stick with it."

SECTION I: GOALS

The goals component of your plan is the most fundamental. Consider it a kind of thinking out loud: Why are you writing this plan? What do you want to accomplish? What do you want to achieve in the next quarter? The next year? The next three years?

Like taping your New Year's resolution to the refrigerator, the goals section is a constant reminder of what you want to achieve. The key difference between a New Year's resolution and your marketing goals, however, is you can't achieve the latter alone.

To achieve your marketing goals you've got to convince your customers to behave in a certain way. If you're a soft drink manufacturer you may want them to try your company's latest wild berry flavor. If you're a new bank in town, you need to familiarize people with your name and convince them to give your institution a try. Or perhaps you're a family-owned retailer who needs to remind customers of the importance of reliability and a proven track record in the face of new competition.

The goals in each of these cases differ with the audiences. The soft drink manufacturer is asking an existing customer to try something new; the bank is trying to attract new customers; the retailer wants to retain existing customers.

Each company wants to influence its customers' behavior. The company that is most likely to succeed is the one that understands its customers the best.

There's no substitute for knowledge. You need to understand the demographic and psychographic makeup of the customers you are trying to reach, as well as the best methods for getting their attention.

Do your research. Learn as much as possible about your audience. Trade associations, trade journals and government statistics and surveys are excellent resources, but chances are you have a lot of data within your own business that you haven't tapped. Look at what you know about your customer already and find ways to bolster that information. Companies should constantly be asking clients what they want and how they would use a new product.

"If you're not asking people that use your end product, then everything you're doing is an assumption," argues Dawson.

In addition, firms should ask customers how they perceive the products and services they receive. Too often, companies have an image of themselves that they broadcast but fail to live up to. That frustrates consumers and makes them feel deceived.

Companies that claim to offer superior service often appear to renege on their promises because their definition of 'service' doesn't mesh with their customers', says Bilfield.

"Airlines and banks are prime offenders," says Bilfield. "They tout service, and when the customers go into the airport or the bank, they have to wait in long lines."

The problem often lies in the company's assumptions about what customers really want. While an airline may feel it is living up to its claim of superior service because it distributes warm towels and mints after a meal, a business traveler will probably place a higher value on its competitor's on-time record and policy for returning lost luggage.

SECTION II: THE STRATEGY

Unfortunately, after taking the time and conducting the research to determine who their audience is and what their message should be, companies often fail by zooming ahead with a plan. An attitude of, "OK, we know who we're after and we know what we want to say, so let's go!" seems to take over.

More often than not, that gung-ho way of thinking leads to disaster because companies have skipped a critical step: they haven't established and communicated an internal strategy for attaining their goals. They want to take their message to the public without pausing to get feedback from inside the company.

For a marketing plan to work, everyone within the company must understand the company's message and work cooperatively to establish a method for taking that message to the public.

For example, if you decide the goal of your plan is to promote the superior service your company offers, you'd better make sure all aspects of your business are on board. Your manufacturing process should meet the highest standards. Your financial department should develop credit and leasing programs that make it easier for customers to use

GETTING STARTED

A NINE-STEP PLAN THAT WILL MAKE THE DIFFERENCE BETWEEN WRITING A USEFUL PLAN AND A DOCUMENT THAT GATHERS DUST ON A SHELF

by Carole R. Hedden and the *Marketing Tools* editorial staff

In his 1986 book, *The Goal*, Eliyahu M. Goldratt writes that most of us forget the one true goal of our business. It's not to deliver products on time. It isn't even to manufacture the best widget in the world. The goal is to make money.

In the past, making money depended on selling a product or service. Today, that's changed as customers are, at times, willing to pay for what we stand for: better service, better support, more innovation, more partnership in developing new products.

This section of this article assumes that you believe a plan is needed, and that this plan should weave together your desires with those of your customers. We've reviewed a number of marketing plans and come up with a nine-step model. It is perhaps more than what your organization needs today, but none of the steps are unimportant.

Our model combines some of the basics of a conventional plan with some new threads that we believe will push your plan over the edge, from being satisfactory to being necessary. These include:

•Using and improving the former domain of public relations, image, as a marketing tool.
•Integrating all the business functions that touch your customers into a single, customer-focused strategic marketing plan.
•Borrowing from Total Quality theories to establish performance measures beyond the financial report to help you note customer trends.
•Making sure that the people needed to deliver your marketing objectives are part of your plan.
•"Selling" your plan to the people whose support is essential to its success.

Taking the Plan Off the Shelf

First, let's look at the model itself. Remember that one of the primary criticisms of any plan is that it becomes a binder on a shelf, never to be seen again until budget time next year. Planning should be an iterative process, feeding off itself and used to guide and measure.

Whether you're asked to create a marketing plan or write the marketing section of the strategic plan for your business, your document is going to include what the business is trying to achieve, a careful analysis of your market, the products and services you offer to that market, and how you will market and sell products or services to your customer.

1. Describe the Business

You are probably in one of two situations: either you need to write a description of your business or you can rely on an existing document found in your annual report, the strategic plan, or a capabilities brochure. The description should include, at minimum:

•Your company's purpose;
•Who you deliver products or services to; and
•What you deliver to those customers.

Too often, such descriptions omit a discussion about what you want your business to stand for—your image.

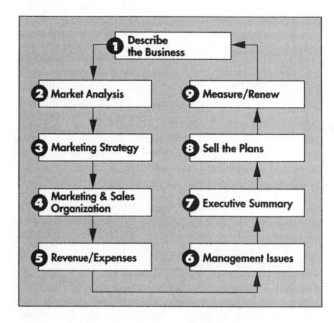

1. Describe the Business
2. Market Analysis
3. Marketing Strategy
4. Marketing & Sales Organization
5. Revenue/Expenses
6. Management Issues
7. Executive Summary
8. Sell the Plans
9. Measure/Renew

This is increasingly important as customers report they are looking for more than the product or service; they're in search of a partner. The only way to address image is to know who you want to be, who your customers think you are, and how you can bridge the gap between the two.

Part of defining your image is knowing where you are strong and where you are weak. For instance, if your current yield rate is 99.997 percent and customers rate you as the preferred supplier, then you might identify operations as a key to your company's image. Most companies tend to be their own worst critic, so start by listing all your strengths. Then identify weaknesses or the threats you face, either due to your own limitations or from the increased competency of a competitor.

The description also includes what your business delivers to its owners, be they shareholders, private owners, or employees. Usually this is stated in financial terms: revenue, return on investment or equity, economic value added, cash generated, operating margin or earnings per .share. The other measures your organization uses to monitor its performance may be of interest to outsiders, but save them for the measurement section of your plan.

The result of all this describing and listing is that you should have a fairly good idea of where you are and where you want to be, which naturally leads to objectives for the coming 6, 12, or 18 months, if not longer.

2. Analyze the Market

This is the section you probably believe you own. *Marketing Tools* challenges you to look at this as a section jointly owned by most everyone working with you. In a smaller company, the lead managers may own various pieces of this section. In a

(continued)

smaller company, the lead managers may own various pieces of this section. In a larger organization, you may need to pull in the ideas and data available from other departments, such as logistics, competitor intelligence, research and development, and the function responsible for quality control or quality assurance. All have two things in common: delivering value to customers, and beating the competition.

Together, you can thoroughly cover the following areas:

•**Your target markets**. What markets do you currently compete in? What do you know about them in terms of potential, dollars available, and your share of the market? Something frequently prepared for products is a life cycle chart; you might want to do the same for your market. Is it embryonic, developing, mature or in decline? Are there new markets to exploit?

•**Customer Knowledge**. Your colleagues in Quality, Distribution, Engineering, or other organizations can be helpful in finding what you need. *The customer's objectives.* What threats do your customers face? What goals does the customer have? Work with your customer to define these so you can become a partner instead of a variable component. *How is the customer addressing her or his markets?* Do you know as much about your customer's position as you know about your own? If not, find out. *How big is each customer, really?* You may find you're spending more time on a less important customer than on the customers who can break you. Is your customer growing or in decline? What plans does the customer have to expand or acquire growth? What innovations are in development?

What does your customer value? Price, product quality, service, innovation, delivery? The better you know what's driving your customer's purchasing decision, the better you'll be able to respond.

•**Clearly identify the alternatives your customer** has. As one customer told employees at a major supplier, "While you've been figuring out how to get by, we've been figuring out how to get by without you." Is backward integration—a situation in which the customer develops the capability in-house—possible? Is there an abundance of other suppliers? What is your business doing to avoid having your customers looking for alternatives?

•**Know your competition**. Your competitors are the obvious alternative for your customer, and thus represent your biggest threat. You can find what you need to know about your competitors through newspaper reports, public records, at trade shows, and from your customers: the size of expansions, the strengths that competitor has, its latest innovations. Do you know how your competition approaches your customers?

•**Describe the Environment**. What changes have occurred in the last 18 months? In the past year? What could change in the near future and over a longer period of time? This should include any kinds of laws or regulations that might affect you, the entry or deletion of competitors, and shifts in technology. Also, keep in mind that internal change does affect your customers. For instance, is a key leader in your business planning to retire? If so, decision making, operations or management style may change—and your customer may have obvious concerns. You can add some depth to

this section, too, by portraying several different scenarios:

•What happens if we do nothing beyond last year?
•What happens if we capitalize on our strengths?
•What might happen if our image slips?
•What happens if we do less this year than last?

3. The Marketing Strategy

The marketing strategy consists of what you offer customers and the price you charge. Start by providing a complete description of each product or service and what it provides to your customers. Life cycle, again, is an important part of this. Is your technology or product developing, mature or in decline? Depending on how your company is organized, a variety of people are responsible for this information, right down to whoever is figuring out how to package the product and how it will be delivered. Find out who needs to be included and make sure their knowledge is used.

The marketing strategy is driven by everything you've done up to this point. Strategies define the approaches you will use to market the company. For instance, if you are competing on the basis of service and support rather than price, your strategy may consist of emphasizing relationships. You will then develop tactics that support that strategy: market the company vs. the product; increase sales per client; assure customer responsiveness. Now, what action or programs will you use to make sure that happens?

Note: strategy leads. No program, regardless of how good it is, should make the

cut if it doesn't link to your business strategies and your customer.

The messages you must craft to support the strategies often are overlooked. Messages are the consistent themes you want your customer to know, to remember, to feel when he or she hears, reads, or views anything

about your company or products. The method by which you deliver your messages comes under the heading of actions or programs.

Finally, you need to determine how you'll measure your own success, beyond meeting the sales forecast. How will you know if your image takes a beating? How will you know whether the customer is satisfied, or has just given up complaining? If you don't know, you'll be caught reacting to events, instead of planning for them.

Remember, your customer's measure of your success may be quite different from what you may think. Your proposed measures must be defined by what your customer values, and they have to be quantifiable. You may be surprised at how willing the customer is to cooperate with you in completing surveys, participating in third-party interviews, or taking part in a full-scale analysis of your company as a supplier. Use caution in assuming that winning awards means you have a measurable indicator. Your measures should be stated in terms of strategies, not plaques or trophies.

4. The Marketing and Sales Organization

The most frequently overlooked element in business is something we usually rele-

(continued)

gate to the Personnel or Human Resources Office—people. They're what makes everything possible. Include them. Begin with a chart that shows the organization for both Marketing and Sales. You may wish to indicate any interdependent relationships that exist (for instance, with Quality).

Note which of the roles are critical, particularly in terms of customer contact. Just as important, include positions, capabilities, and numbers of people needed in the future. How will you gain these skills without impacting your cost per sale? Again, it's time to be creative and provide options.

5. Revenue and Expense

In this section, you're going to project the revenue your plan will produce. This is usually calculated by evaluating the value of your market(s) and determining the dollar value of your share of that market. You need to factor in any changes you believe will occur, and you'll need to identify the sources of revenue, by product or service. Use text to tell the story; use graphs to show the story.

After you've noted where the money is coming from, explain what money you need to deliver the projected return. This will include staff wages and benefits for your organization, as well as the cost for specific programs you plan to implement.

During this era of budget cuts, do yourself a favor by prioritizing these programs. For instance, if one of your key strategies is to expand to a new market via new technologies, products, or ser-

vices, you will need to allocate appropriate dollars. What is the payback on the investment in marketing, and when will revenues fully pay back the investment? Also, provide an explanation of programs that will be deleted should a cut in funding be required. Again, combine text and spreadsheets to tell and to show.

6. Management Issues

This section represents your chance to let management know what keeps you awake at night. What might or could go wrong? What are the problems your company faces in customer relations? Are there technology needs that are going unattended? Again, this can be a collaborative effort that identifies your concerns. In addition, you may want to identify long-term issues, as well as those that are of immediate significance.

To keep this section as objective as possible, list the concerns and the business strategy or strategies they affect. What are the short-term and long-term risks? For instance, it is here that you might want to go into further detail about a customer's actions that look like the beginnings of backward integration.

7. Executive Summary

Since most senior leaders want a quick-look reference, it's best to include a one-page Executive Summary that covers these points:

- Your organization's objectives
- Budget requirements
- Revenue projections
- Critical management issues

When you're publishing the final plan document, you'll want the executive summary to be Page One.

8. Sell the Plan

This is one of the steps that often is overlooked. Selling your plan is as important as writing it. Otherwise, no one owns it, except you. The idea is to turn it into a rallying point that helps your company move forward. And to do that, you need to turn as many people as possible into ambassadors for your marketing efforts.

First, set up a time to present the plan to everyone who helped you with information and data. Make sure that they feel some sense of ownership, but that they also see how their piece ties into the whole. This is one of those instances where you need to say your plan, show your plan, discuss your plan. Only after all three steps are completed will they *hear* the plan.

After you've shared the information across the organization, reserve some time on the executive calendar. Have a couple of leaders review the plan first, giving you feedback on the parts where they have particular expertise. Then, present the plan at a staff meeting.

Is It Working?

You may think your job is finished. It's not. You need to convey the key parts of this plan to coworkers throughout the business. They need to know what the business is trying to achieve. Their livelihood, not just that of the owners, is at stake. From their phone-answering technique to the way they pro-

cess an order, every step has meaning to the customer.

9. Measure/Renew

Once you've presented your plan and people understand it, you have to continuously work the plan and share information about it. The best way to help people see trends and respond appropriately is to have meaningful measures. In the language of Total Quality, these are the Key Result Indicators—the things that have importance to your customers and that are signals to your performance.

For instance, measure your ability to deliver on a customer request; the amount of time it takes to respond to a customer inquiry; your productivity per employee; cash flow; cycle time; yield rates. The idea is to identify a way to measure those things that are critical to you and to your customer.

Review those measurements. Share the information with the entire business and begin the process all over again. Seek new ideas and input to improve your performance. Go after more data and facts. And then renew your plan and share it with everyone—all over again.

It's an extensive process, but it's one that spreads the word—and spreads the ownership. It's the step that ensures that your plan will be constantly in use, and constantly at work for your business.

Carole Hedden is a writer and communication/planning consultant living in Elmira, New York.

your product. Finally, your customer relations personnel should be trained to respond to problems quickly and efficiently, and to use the contact as an opportunity to find out more about what customers want.

"I'm always amazed when I go into the shipping department of some company and say, 'What is your mission? What's the message you want to give to your end user?' and they say, 'I don't know. I just know I've got to get these shipments out on time,'" says Dawson.

Because the success of integrated marketing depends on a consistent, cohesive message, employees throughout the company need to understand the firm's marketing goals and their role in helping to fulfill them.

"It's very important to bring employees in on the process," says James Lowry, chairman of the marketing department at Ball State University. "Employees today are better than any we've had before. They want to know what's going on in the organization. They don't want to be left out."

HELP IS ON THE WAY

THREE SOFTWARE PACKAGES THAT WILL HELP YOU GET STARTED

Writing a marketing plan may be daunting, but there is a variety of software tools out there to help you get started. Found in electronics and book stores, the tools are in many ways like a Marketing 101 textbook. The difference lies in how they help.

Software tools have a distinct advantage: They actually force you to write, and that's the toughest part of any marketing plan. Sometimes called "MBA In a Box," these systems guide you through a planning process. Some even provide wording that you can copy into your own document and edit to fit your own business. Presto! A boiler plate plan! Others provide a system of interviewing and questioning that creates a custom plan for your operation. The more complex tools demand an integrated approach to planning, one that brings together the full force of your organization, not just Sales or Advertising.

1. Crush

Crush, a modestly named new product from a modestly named new company, HOT, takes a multimedia approach. (HOT stands for Hands-On Technology; Crush apparently stands for Crushing the Competition)

Just introduced a few months ago, Crush is a multimedia application for Macintosh or Windows PCs. It features the competitive analysis methods of Flegis McKenna, marketing guru to Apple, Intel and Genentech; and it features Mr. McKenna himself as your mentor, offering guidance via on-screen video. As you work through each section of a complete market analysis, McKenna provides germane comments; in addition, you can see video case studies of

marketing success stories like Intuit software.

Crush provides worksheets and guidance for analyzing your products, customers, market trends and competitors, and helps you generate an action plan. The "mentor" approach makes it a useful

Pyramid Power: Plan Write's pyramid approach asks the user to define the messages for a business as part of the tactics.

tool for self-education; as you work through the examples and develop your company's marketing plan, you build your own expertise.

2. Marketing Plan Pro

Palo Alto's Marketing Plan Pro is a basic guide, useful for smaller businesses or ones in which the company leader wears a number of different hats, including marketing. It includes the standard spreadsheet capability, as well as the ability to chart numerical data. Marketing Plan Pro uses a pyramid process.

I liked the pyramid for a simple reason: It asks you to define messages for your business as part of your tactics. Without a message, it's easy to jump around, reacting to the marketplace instead of anticipating, leaving customers wondering what really is

significant about your company or your product.

The step-by-step process is simple, and a sample plan shows how all the information works together. The customer-focus aspect of the plan seemed a little weak, demanding only sales potential and buying capacity of the customers. Targeted marketing is increasingly important, and the user may want to really expand how this section is used beyond what the software requires.

The package displays, at a glance, your strategy, the tactics you develop for each

strategy, and the action plan or programs you choose to support the strategy. That could help when you're trying to prioritize creative ideas, eliminating those that really don't deliver what the strategy demands. Within each of three columns, you can click on a word and get help. Click on the heading program: a list of sample actions is displayed. They may not be what you're looking for, but if this is your first plan, they're lifesavers.

I also really liked Marketing Plan Pro's user's manual. It not only explains how the software works with your computer, it helps with business terms and provides a guide to planning, walking you through step-by-step.

3. Plan Write

Plan Write, created by Business Resource Software, Inc., is exponentially more powerful than Marketing Plan Pro. Plan Write brings together the breadth of the business, integrating information as far flung as distribution systems and image. And this software places your marketing strategy within the broader context of a business plan, the approach that tends to prove most effective.

As with Marketing Plan Pro, Plan Write provides a sample plan. The approach is traditional, incorporating a look at the business environment, the competition, the product or service mix you are offering, the way you will tell customers about that mix, pricing, delivery, and support.

Among the sections that were particularly strong was one on customer alternatives and people planning. Under the heading of customer alternatives, you're required to

(continued)

incorporate competitive information with customer information. If you don't meet the customer's needs, where could he or she go? Most often we look only at the competition, without trying to imagine how the customer is thinking. This exercise is particularly valuable to the company who leads the market.

The people part of planning too often is dumped on the personnel guy instead of being seen as a critical component of your organization's capabilities. *Plan Write* requires that you include how marketing is being handled, and how sales will be accomplished. In addition, it pushes you to define what skills will be needed in the future and where the gaps are between today and the future. People, in this plan, are viewed as a strategic component.

Plan Write offers a fully integrated spreadsheet that can import from or export to most of the popular spreadsheet programs you may already be using. Another neat feature allows you to enter numerical data and select from among 14 different graphing styles to display your information. You just click on the style you want to view, and the data is reconfigured.

Probably the biggest danger in dealing with software packages such as *Marketing Plan Pro* and *Plan Write* is to think the software is the answer. It's merely a guide.

—*Carole Hedden*

Employees are ambassadors for your company. Every time they interact with a customer or vendor, they're marketing your company. The more knowledgeable and helpful they are, the better they reflect on your firm.

At Nordstrom, a Seattle-based retailer, sales associates are empowered to use their best judgment in all situations to make a customer happy.

"We think our sales associates are the best marketing department," said spokeswoman Amy Jones. "We think word of mouth is the best advertising you can have." As a result, although Nordstrom has stores in only 15 states, it has forged a national reputation.

If companies regard marketing as the exclusive province of the marketing department, they're destined to fail.

"Accounting and sales and other departments have to work together hand in hand," says Dawson. "If they don't, you're going to have a problem in the end."

For example, in devising an integrated marketing campaign for the Nissan 200SX, Chiat/Day marketers worked in strategic business units that included a variety of disciplines such as engineers, representatives from the parts and service department, and creative people. By taking a broad view of the business and building inter-related activities to support its goals, Chiat/Day was able to create a seamless campaign for the 200SX that weaves advertising, in-store displays, and direct marketing together seamlessly.

"When everybody understands what the mission is, it's easier," asserts Bilfield. "It's easier to go upstream in the same direction than to go in different directions."

After bringing the different disciplines within your company on board, you're ready to design the external marketing program needed to support your goals. Again, the principle of integrated marketing comes into play: The message should be focused and consistent, and each step of the process should bring the consumer one step closer to buying your product.

In the case of Chiat/Day's campaign for the Nissan 200SX, the company used the same theme, graphics, type faces, and message to broadcast a consistent statement.

Introduced about the same time as the latest Batman movie, the campaign incorporates music and graphics from the television series. Magazine ads include an 800 number

potential customers can call if they want to receive an information kit. Kits are personalized and include the name of a local Nissan dealer, a certificate for a test drive, and a voucher entitling test drivers to a free gift.

By linking each step of the process, Chiat/Day can chart the number of calls, test drives, and sales a particular ad elicits. Like a good one-two punch, the direct marketing picks up where the national advertising leaves off, leveraging the broad exposure and targeting it at the most likely buyers.

While the elaborate 200SX campaign may seem foolproof, a failure to integrate the process at any step along the way could result in a lost sale.

For example, if a potential client were to test drive the car and encounter a dealer who knew nothing about the free gift accompanying the test drive, the customer would feel justifiably annoyed. Conversely, a well-informed sales associate who can explain the gift will be mailed to the test driver in a few weeks will engender a positive response.

SECTION III EXECUTION

The final component of an integrated marketing plan is the implementation phase. This is where the budget comes in.

How much you'll need to spend depends on your goals. If a company wants to expand its market share or promote its products in a new region, it will probably have to spend more than it would to maintain its position in an existing market.

Again, you'll need to create a system for keeping your employees informed. You might consider adding an element to your company newsletter that features people from different departments talking about the marketing problems they encounter and how they overcome them. Or you might schedule a regular meeting for department heads to discuss marketing ideas so they can report back to their employees with news from around the company.

Finally, you'll need to devise a system for monitoring your marketing program. A database, similar to the one created from calls to the 200SX's 800 number, can be an invaluable tool for determining if your message is being well received.

It's important to establish time frames for achieving your goals early in the process. If you want to increase your market share, for instance, you should determine the rate at which you intend to add new customers. Failing to achieve that rate could signal a flaw in your plan or its execution, or an unrealistic goal.

"Remember, integrated marketing is a long-range way of thinking," warns Dawson. "Results are not going to be immediate."

Like any investment, marketing requires patience, perseverance, and commitment if it is to bear fruit. While not all companies are forward thinking enough to understand the manifold gains of integrated marketing, the ones that don't embrace it will ultimately pay a tremendous price.

MORE INFO

Software for writing marketing plans:

Crush, Hands-On Technology; for more information, call (800) 772-2580 ext. 14 or (415) 579-7755; e-mail info@HOT.sf.ca.us; or visit the Web site at http://www.HOT.sf.ca.us.

Marketing Plan Pro, Palo Alto Software: for more information, call (800) 229-7526 or (503) 683-6162.

Plan Write for Marketing, Business Resource Software, Inc.: for more information, call (800) 423-1228 or (512) 251-7541.

Books about marketing plans:

Twelve Simple Steps to a Winning Marketing Plan, Geraldine A. Larkin (1992, Probus Publishing Co.)*
Preparing the Marketing Plan, by David Parmerlee (1993, NTC Business Books)*
Your Marketing Plan: A Workbook for Effective Business Promotion (Second Edition), by Chris Pryor (1995, Oregon Small Business Development Center Network)*
Your Business Plan: A Workbook for Owners of Small Businesses, by Dennis J. Sargent, Maynard N. Chambers, and Chris Pryor (1995, Oregon Small Business Development Center Network)*

Recommended reading:

Managing for Results, Peter Drucker
The One to One Future: Building Relationships One Customer at a Time, by Don Peppers and Martha Rogers, Ph.D. (1993, Currency/Doubleday)*
"Real World Results," by Don Schultz (*Marketing Tools* magazine, April/May 1994)*
* Available through American Demographics; call (800) 828-1133

Shelly Reese is a freelance writer based in Cincinnati.

Michael Porter's Big Ideas

The world's most famous business-school professor is fed up with CEOs who claim that the world changes too fast for their companies to have a long-term strategy. If you want to make a difference as a leader, you've got to make time for strategy. Here's Michael Porter's clear-eyed take on why strategy matters now more than ever.

by Keith H. Hammonds

Here is how Michael E. Porter regards the business landscape:

Beginning in the mid-1980s, he more or less left the strategy world to its own devices, focusing his attention instead on the question of international competitiveness. He advised foreign governments on their economic policies and headed a U.S. presidential commission. He wrote books and papers on industry dynamics—from ceramics manufacturing in Italy to the robotics sector in Japan. He spoke everywhere. He was consumed by understanding the competitive advantage of nations.

Then, in the mid-1990s, he resurfaced. "I was reading articles about corporate strategy, too many of which began with 'Porter said… and that's wrong.'" Strategy had lost its intellectual currency. It was losing adherents. "People were being tricked and misled by other ideas," he says.

Like a domineering parent, Porter seems both miffed by the betrayal and pleased by his apparent indispensability. *I can't turn my back for five minutes.* Well, kids, the man is back. Porter seeks to return strategy to its place atop the executive pyramid.

Business strategy probably predates Michael Porter. Probably. But today, it is hard to imagine confronting the discipline without reckoning with the Harvard Business School professor, perhaps the world's best-known business academic. His first book, *Competitive Strategy: Techniques for Analyzing Industries and Competitors* (Free Press, 1980), is in its 53rd printing and has been translated into 17 languages. For years, excerpts from that and other Porter works have been required reading in "Competition and Strategy," the first-year course that every Harvard MBA student must take. Porter's strategy frameworks have suffered some ambivalence over the years in academic circles—yet they have proved wildly compelling among business leaders around the world.

This is the paradox that Porter faces. His notions on strategy are more widely disseminated than ever and are preached at business schools and in seminars around the globe. Yet the idea of strategy itself has, in fact, taken a backseat to newfangled notions about competition hatched during the Internet frenzy: Who needs a long-term strategy when everyone's goal is simply to "get big fast"?

With his research group, Porter operates from a suite of offices tucked into a corner of Harvard Business School's main classroom building. At 53, his blond hair graying, he is no longer the wunderkind who, in his early thirties, changed the way CEOs thought about their companies and industries. Yet he's no less passionate about his pursuit—and no less certain of his ability. In a series of interviews, Porter told FAST COMPANY why strategy still matters.

Business keeps moving faster—but you better make time for strategy.

It's been a bad decade for strategy. Companies have bought into an extraordinary number of flawed or simplistic ideas about competition—what I call "intellectual potholes." As a result, many have abandoned strategy almost completely. Executives won't say that, of course. They say, "We have a strategy." But typically, their "strategy" is to produce the highest-quality products at the lowest cost or to consolidate their industry. They're just trying to improve on best practices. That's not a strategy.

Strategy has suffered for three reasons. First, in the 1970s and 1980s, people tried strategy, and they had problems with it. It was difficult. It seemed an artificial exercise. Second, and at the same time, the ascendance of Japan really riveted attention on implementation. People argued that

119

strategy wasn't what was really important—you just had to produce a higher-quality product than your rival, at a lower cost, and then improve that product relentlessly.

"Strategy is about making choices, trade-offs; it's about deliberately choosing to be different."

The third reason was the emergence of the notion that in a world of change, you really shouldn't have a strategy. There was a real drumbeat that business was about change and speed and being dynamic and reinventing yourself, that things were moving so fast, you couldn't afford to pause. If you had a strategy, it was rigid and inflexible. And it was outdated by the time you produced it.

That view set up a straw man, and it was a ridiculous straw man. It reflects a deeply flawed view of competition. But that view has become very well entrenched.

The irony, of course, is that when we look at the companies that we agree are successful, we also agree that they all clearly do have strategies. Look at Dell, or Intel, or Wal-Mart. We all agree that change is faster now than it was 10 or 15 years ago. Does that mean you shouldn't have a direction? Well, probably not. For a variety of reasons, though, lots of companies got very confused about strategy and how to think about it.

Of course strategy is hard—it's about making tough choices.

There's a fundamental distinction between strategy and operational effectiveness. Strategy is about making choices, trade-offs; it's about deliberately choosing to be different. Operational effectiveness is about things that you really shouldn't have to make choices on; it's about what's good for everybody and about what every business should be doing.

Lately, leaders have tended to dwell on operational effectiveness. Again, this has been fed by the business literature: the ideas that emerged in the late 1980s and early 1990s, such as total quality, just-in-time, and reengineering. All were focused on the nitty-gritty of getting a company to be more effective. And for a while, some Japanese companies turned the nitty-gritty into an art form. They were incredibly competitive.

Japan's obsession with operational effectiveness became a huge problem, though, because only strategy can create sustainable advantage. And strategy must start with a different value proposition. A strategy delineates a territory in which a company seeks to be unique. Strategy 101 is about choices: You can't be all things to all people.

The essence of strategy is that you must set limits on what you're trying to accomplish. The company without a strategy is willing to try anything. If all you're trying to do is essentially the same thing as your rivals, then it's unlikely that you'll be very successful. It's incredibly arrogant for a company to believe that it can deliver the same sort of product that its rivals do and actually do better for very long. That's especially true today, when the flow of information and capital is incredibly fast. It's extremely dangerous to bet on the incompetence of your competitors—and that's what you're doing when you're competing on operational effectiveness.

What's worse, a focus on operational effectiveness alone tends to create a mutually destructive form of competition. If everyone's trying to get to the same place, then, almost inevitably, that causes customers to choose on price. This is a bit of a metaphor for the past five years, when we've seen widespread cratering of prices.

There have been those who argue that in this new millennium, with all of this change and new information, such a form of destructive competition is simply the way competition has to be. I believe very strongly that that is not the case. There are many opportunities for strategic differences in nearly every industry; the more dynamism there is in an economy, in fact, the greater the opportunity. And a much more positive kind of competition could emerge if managers thought about strategy in the right way.

Technology changes, strategy doesn't.

The underlying principles of strategy are enduring, regardless of technology or the pace of change. Consider the Internet. Whether you're on the Net or not, your profitability is still determined by the structure of your industry. If there are no barriers to entry, if customers have all the power, and if rivalry is based on price, then the Net doesn't matter—you won't be very profitable.

Sound strategy starts with having the right goal. And I argue that the only goal that can support a sound strategy is superior profitability. If you don't start with that goal and seek it pretty directly, you will quickly be led to actions that will undermine strategy. If your goal is anything but profitability—if it's to be big, or to grow fast, or to become a technology leader—you'll hit problems.

Finally, strategy must have continuity. It can't be constantly reinvented. Strategy is about the basic value you're trying to deliver to customers, and about which customers you're trying to serve. That positioning, at that level, is where continuity needs to be strongest. Otherwise, it's hard for your organization to grasp what the strategy is. And it's hard for customers to know what you stand for.

Strategy hasn't changed, but change has.

On the other hand, I agree that the half-life of everything has shortened. So setting strategy has become a little more complicated. In the old days, maybe 20 years ago, you could set a direction for your business, define a value proposition, then lumber along pursuing that. Today, you still need to define how you're going to be distinctive. But we know that simply making that set of choices will not protect you unless you're constantly sucking in all of the available means to improve on your ability to deliver.

So companies have to be very schizophrenic. On one hand, they have to maintain continuity of strategy. But they also have to be good at continuously improving. Southwest Airlines, for example, has focused on a strategy of serving price-minded customers who want to go from place to place on relatively short, frequently offered flights without much service. That has stayed consistent over the years. But Southwest has been extremely aggressive about assimilating every new idea possible to deliver on that strategy. Today, it does many things differently than it did 30 years ago—but it's still serving essentially the same customers who have essentially the same needs.

The error that some managers make is that they see all of the change and all of the new technology out there, and they say, "God, I've just got to get out there and implement like hell." They forget that if you don't have a direction, if you don't have something distinctive at the end of the day, it's going to be very hard to win. They don't understand that you need to balance the internal juxtaposition of change and continuity.

The thing is, continuity of strategic direction and continuous improvement in how you do things are absolutely consistent with each other. In fact, they're mutually reinforcing. The ability to change constantly and effectively is made easier by high-level continuity. If you've spent 10 years being the best at something, you're better able to assimilate new technologies. The more explicit you are about setting strategy, about wrestling with trade-offs, the better you can identify new opportunities that support your value proposition. Otherwise, sorting out what's important among a bewildering array of technologies is very difficult. Some managers think, "The world is changing, things are going faster—so I've got to move faster. Having a strategy seems to slow me down." I argue no, no, no—having a strategy actually speeds you up.

Beware the myth of inflection points.

The catch is this: Sometimes the environment or the needs of customers do shift far enough so that continuity doesn't work anymore, so that your essential positioning is no longer valid. But those moments occur very infrequently for most companies. Intel's Andy Grove talks about inflection points that force you to revisit your core strategy. The thing is, inflection points are very rare. What managers have done lately is assume that they are everywhere, that disruptive technologies are everywhere.

Discontinuous change, in other words, is not as pervasive as we think. It's not that it doesn't exist. Disruptive technologies do exist, and their threat has to be on every-

one's mind. But words like "transformation" and "revolution" are incredibly overused. We're always asking the companies we work with, "Where is that new technology that's going to change everything?" For every time that a new technology is out there, there are 10 times that one is not.

Let's look again at the Internet. In FAST COMPANY two years ago, we would have read that the Internet was an incredibly disruptive technology, that industry after industry was going to be transformed. Well, guess what? It's not an incredibly disruptive technology for all parts of the value chain. In many cases, Internet technology is actually complementary to traditional technologies. What we're seeing is that the companies winning on the Internet use the new technology to leverage their existing strategy.

Great strategists get a few (big) things right.

Change brings opportunities. On the other hand, change can be confusing. One school of thought says that it's all just too complicated, that no manager can ever solve the complex problem that represents a firmwide strategy today. So managers should use the hunt-and-peck method of finding a strategy: Try something, see if it works, then proceed to the next. It's basically just a succession of incremental experiments.

I say that method will rarely work, because the essence of strategy is choice and trade-offs and fit. What makes Southwest Airlines so successful is not a bunch of separate things, but rather the strategy that ties everything together. If you were to experiment with onboard service, then with gate service, then with ticketing mechanisms, all separately, you'd never get to Southwest's strategy.

You can see why we're in the mess that we're in. Competition is subtle, and managers are prone to simplify. What we learn from looking at actual competition is that winning companies are anything but simple. Strategy is complex. The good news is that even successful companies almost never get everything right up front. When the Vanguard Group started competing in mutual funds, there was no Internet, no index funds. But Vanguard had an idea that if it could strip costs to the bone and keep fees low—and not try to beat the market by taking on risk—it would win over time. John Bogle understood the essence of that, and he took advantage of incremental opportunities over time.

You don't have to have all the answers up front. Most successful companies get two or three or four of the pieces right at the start, and then they elucidate their strategy over time. It's the kernel of things that they saw up front that is essential. That's the antidote to complexity.

Great strategies are a cause.

The chief strategist of an organization has to be the leader—the CEO. A lot of business thinking has stressed the notion of empowerment, of pushing down and getting a lot of people involved. That's very important, but empowerment and involvement don't apply to the ultimate act of choice. To be successful, an organization must have a very strong leader who's willing to make choices and define the trade-offs. I've found that there's a striking relationship between really good strategies and really strong leaders.

That doesn't mean that leaders have to invent strategy. At some point in every organization, there has to be a fundamental act of creativity where someone divines the new activity that no one else is doing. Some leaders are really good at that, but that ability is not universal. The more critical job for a leader is to provide the discipline and the glue that keep such a unique position sustained over time.

Another way to look at it is that the leader has to be the guardian of trade-offs. In any organization, thousands of ideas pour in every day—from employees with suggestions, from customers asking for things, from suppliers trying to sell things. There's all this input, and 99% of it is inconsistent with the organization's strategy.

Great leaders are able to enforce the trade-offs: "Yes, it would be great if we could offer meals on Southwest Airlines, but if we did that, it wouldn't fit our low-cost strategy. Plus, it would make us look like United, and United is just as good as we are at serving meals." At the same time, great leaders understand that there's nothing rigid or passive about strategy—it's something that a company is continually getting better at—so they can create a sense of urgency and progress while adhering to a clear and very sustained direction.

A leader also has to make sure that everyone understands the strategy. Strategy used to be thought of as some mystical vision that only the people at the top understood. But that violated the most fundamental purpose of a strategy, which is to inform each of the many thousands of things that get done in an organization every day, and to make sure that those things are all aligned in the same basic direction.

If people in the organization don't understand how a company is supposed to be different, how it creates value compared to its rivals, then how can they possibly make all of the myriad choices they have to make? Every salesman has to know the strategy—otherwise, he won't know who to call on. Every engineer has to understand it, or she won't know what to build.

The best CEOs I know are teachers, and at the core of what they teach is strategy. They go out to employees, to suppliers, and to customers, and they repeat, "This is what we stand for, this is what we stand for." So everyone understands it. This is what leaders do. In great companies, strategy becomes a cause. That's because a strategy is about being different. So if you have a really great strategy, people are fired up: "We're not just another airline. We're bringing something new to the world."

KEITH H. HAMMONDS (KHAMMONDS@FASTCOMPANY.COM) IS A *FAST COMPANY* SENIOR EDITOR BASED IN NEW YORK. CONTACT MICHAEL PORTER BY EMAIL (MPORTER@HBS.EDU).

Can Brand Management Help You Succeed?

Branding isn't just about the perfect name—it's about how you organize and run your business.

by MARY JANE GENOVA

Just like mega-companies Pepsi, Ford, and FedEx, some small businesses have discovered that developing brand names is a great way to run a business. Branding or brand management can simplify what you do. And in the process you may be able to get better results at less cost. Remember Ben & Jerry's? Remember Snapple? By using brand management, those small businesses became household words.

But don't let the term "brand name" mislead you. Branding is much more than selecting a hot name.

Basically, branding or brand management is an approach to how you structure and run your business. And that approach is integrated. Branding is, you might say, a "pull" force that determines your overall image, all your strategies, and all your priorities for using resources. This consistency helps deliver one clear message, distinguishing you from much of the competition and preventing you from trying to be too many things to too many markets.

For example, presskits, a Massachusetts-based printing company, specializes in custom pocket folders and media packaging. Nothing else. That's because the company is run like a brand.

"What our brand is all about," explains presskits' vice president Roy Weinstein, "is the innovative designs (over 1,000 styles), high quality, fast service, conve-

nience, and fair prices we provide in our niche—pocket folders and CD packaging. That immediately differentiates us from a lot of the competition out there, all those other printing firms. Our clear brand identity also led us to promote more on the Internet. That [website] even allows our designer customers to download our templates and email their artwork files to us. That gives them a quicker turnaround and reinforces our image as state-of-the-art."

Prior to using the Internet, presskits spent the lion's share of its promotions budget attending trade shows. Now its money goes into ensuring that its website is promoted and picked up by the major search engines. Presskits, whose customers range from Nike to *New York* magazine, is growing at a pace of 30 percent annually.

PLAY IN YOUR OWN SANDBOX

Ann Shoket, creator of Manhattan-based tagmag.com, manages her online magazine as a brand. "Tagmag.com is a community of people searching for information, events, and meaning outside mainstream pop culture. The 'tag' part of our name comes from urban graffiti in which 'tag' means to leave your mark. Our young, urban readers want to leave their mark on the world and stand out from the

mainstream. And they know that we give them the tools and support to do that. That's the message we're sending," she says.

Right now, tagmag.com has no direct competitor online. It plans to extend its brand name to books, fashion, and music.

Because of its youthful target market and iconoclastic tone, tagmag.com is promoted mainly through street-level posters and the Internet. It would be "counter-brand" to promote the magazine, for instance, on network television, which has an older viewing audience, or in a mainstream medium like *Redbook*. The sandbox Shoket is playing in is clear to her, to her readers, and to venture capitalists. That simplifies every management step along the way.

In public relations, Robert Dilenschneider runs the Manhattan-based Dilenschneider Group as a premier brand name. His clients are Fortune 500 firms and high-profile celebrities. He promotes his firm through speeches, articles, books, and direct mail—always and consistently targeting successful businesspeople.

Dilenschneider says he doesn't waste energy outside the identity or parameters of his brand name. His firm already has more business than it can handle.

GET DOWN TO BASICS

How can you manage your small business as a brand? In his recent book Brand Leadership (Free Press, 2000), University of California marketing professor David Aaker says that the first step in brand management is to identify your customers and competitors, and given your unique strengths and resources, determine what products or services you can offer. The name that you then give your company will likely be a natural fit for all that, he says. (Remember that you'll keep your brand name for a long time; changing brands is very expensive.)

But even if you do this analysis after you already have a name, you can still build a strong brand identity. What's most important is how you manage your niche.

Job No. 1 in branding—analysis—can be done on a shoestring budget. The Internet is the friend of small brands. *Researching Online for Dummies* (IDG Books, 1998) and similar Internet research guides can help you find just about anything, from target-market demographics to intelligence about your competition. And you can always visit the reference desk at your local library. A third approach is to open your eyes wide. If you want to know about independent bookstores, visit plenty of them and think about what you're seeing and experiencing.

Try conducting informational interviews with others in the field you're thinking of entering. To find out if you have the right stuff, spend some time with someone already working in that business.

SEND A CLEAR MESSAGE

Your business name alone isn't the key to successful branding. For example, a family called its jewelry business "Bedford" after the street where the store was located in Stamford, Conn. The store thrived because of the unrelenting customer service the family gave. When the family relocated the business to another part of the city, they retained the name for continuity. The store is still going strong because of how the business is run—not because of its name.

Bedford Jewelers' single consistent message is that it is an ethical family business that cares about each customer, whether they're buying a $50 watch or a $10,000 ring.

In *Guerilla Marketing: Secrets for Making Big Profits from Your Small Business* (Houghton Mifflin, 1998), Jay Conrad Levinson explains how small businesses can use the Internet and other cost-effective tools for promotion. Those tools include special events, direct mail, the Yellow Pages, billboards, word of mouth, telemarketing (without being a pest), getting media coverage (without hiring a public relations firm), and using classifieds (instead of display advertising).

In promotions, creativity, not big bucks, counts the most. Dilenschneider says he finds reasons to send "snail mail" to clients instead of a fax or email. Clients are delighted that he took the time to write a letter on paper and pay for a stamp to send it.

Once a brand name is launched, there is only one way a small business keeps track of how it's doing: by profits. Larger corporations, like Amazon.com, can lose money for extended periods in hopes of building a brand name. Small businesses can't. Your brand name has to register on the bottom line within the first few years after startup.

If your business isn't moving toward profitability, then it's time to examine all the systems supporting the brand, from target markets to cost of promotions. And there's plenty of help out there.

A Checklist for Branding

- I have the discipline to manage my business in an integrated way.

- I know my customers.

- I know my competitors.

- I'm confident about what I can offer as a product or service.

- I've researched and chosen an effective business name.

- I know how to do research cheaply.

- I tailor the tone and kind of promotions I undertake to support my brand name.

- I measure results in profits.

- If the brand name is in trouble, I'll get help.

The Small Business Administration's SCORE, a group of retired executives, will pitch in for free. You can also barter with a management consultant to evaluate what you're doing.

Since the early 1930s, brand management has proven to be a disciplined, integrative approach that can produce winners. Now ask yourself: How can brand management help my business succeed?

Mary Jane Genova is president of Genova Writing Services, Bradley Beach, N.J., and a marketing communications consultant to corporate, celebrity, and non-profit clients.

MAKING **OLD** BRANDS **NEW**

A good brand doesn't have to go the way of Hai Karate men's cologne or Ajax cleaning scrub. Most mature brands pack plenty of brand equity and characteristics that can set them apart from competitors. With astute management, their appeal can shine for new generations of users.

BY BRIAN WANSINK

Burma Shave, Brylcreem, Pepsodent, Ovaltine, William's Lectric Shave, RC Cola, Barbasol, Hai Karate, Black Jack Gum. At one point, these brands were widely recognized and frequently purchased. Many have now faded or become "ghosts" of their former selves. Their numbers are legion. In 1993, Nabisco reported 29 ghost brands; Shering-Plough 17; and Smith-Kline 14, according to Stuart Elliott of the *New York Times*.

While some fading brands are dying because of shifting consumer needs, heavy competition, or waning awareness, others are suffering from marketing malpractice. Many well-trained brand managers believe that brands—like people—follow predictable, irreversible life cycles: they grow, they mature, they decline, and they die. When sales fall, they respond by cutting back on marketing activities and reallocating funds to new brands.

Without ongoing investment of time, thought, or money, a fading brand's sales will continue to drop. This strengthens the original prognosis that there's no help for an old brand, thus leading to even less attention and care. Some brands are nurtured back to health when this happens, but many die a lingering death as heavily discounted or regionalized brands.

Lately, however, the $75-to-$100-million price tag on launching a new brand is renewing corporate interest in the less costly option of revitalizing old brands. Not all brands are worthy of a new life. The challenge for brand managers is determining which brands can be revitalized and how best to do it.

THE SECOND TIME AROUND

Many companies take little time or effort to understand the life and death of ghost brands, which is why "brands that fail tell no tales." Yet many mature brands have untapped potential. At the Brand Lab at the University of Illinois, we set out to identify what makes a brand a candidate for revitalization by analyzing mature brands that were successfully relaunched, and older brands that are still well liked by consumers.

Altering the characteristics of a brand or changing its packaging are often good ways to sweep away negative attitudes and boost sales.

First, we collected extensive information on 84 brands of consumer packaged goods. This included annual dollar sales, volume sales, and distribution channels, such as grocery stores, mass merchandisers, and drugstores. Then we talked to 360 members of the Brand Revitalization Consumer Panel, a group of primarily female household decision-makers from five states. We asked them a series of subjective questions about their favorite brands among the 84, and what distinguishes them from similar products.

When we matched data from panelists' interviews with objective information on the brands, here's what we learned. In general, brands that have been revitalized were perceived as having meaningful characteristics that set them apart from other brands. They typically have a time-tested heritage or reputation, are widely distributed in grocery stores, drug stores, and mass merchandisers, and are under-advertised and under-promoted compared with other brands in their category. Revitalized

NOT JUST FOR THANKSGIVING

(percent increase in average monthly amount used for selected products after viewing "choosing" and "using" advertisements*, 1994)

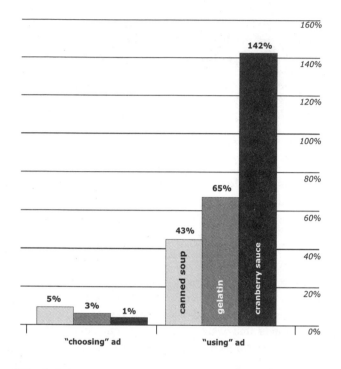

*"Choosing" ads tout common uses for products; "using" ads suggest nontraditional uses. Use was tracked for a three-month period after subjects viewed ads.

Source: experiments by the author

Cranberry sauce gets a big boost in consumption when ads suggested nontraditional uses.

brands weren't the cheapest, either. They tended to be medium- to premium-priced products.

Jeffrey Himmel, chairman and chief executive of the Himmel Group in New York, is a veteran of brand revitalization. His firm has breathed new life into Porcelana fade cream, Topol toothpaste, Doan's Pills, Gold Bond Medicated Powder, and Ovaltine. The best candidates for revitalization, he says, are high-margin products with few shelf-keeping units (SKUs). SKUs are assigned to each size and variety of consumer packaged good on the market. Crest toothpaste, for instance, once had more than 60 SKUs. Products that come in multiple variations often have difficulty communicating a focused marketing message. The best brands to revitalize are those that can be contract-manufactured through multiple sources, and can be heavily advertised on radio or television 52 weeks a year, says Himmel.

These criteria have worked well for the Himmel Group. In 1973, it purchased Topol tooth polish for $200,000. Over the next ten years, Himmel built it into a brand with sales of $23

million a year. The same strategy raised Ovaltine from its deathbed to a vital, high margin, market leader.

Once a brand is chosen for revitalization, it's on to the work of getting it back into the minds—and households—of consumers. Brand managers have two opportunities to influence customers: when they choose a brand, and when they use it.

CHOOSING OLD FAITHFUL

Consumers shun old brands for many reasons. Bay Rum might remind a 20-year-old of his feeble grandfather. Aspergum is perceived as a relic by cold sufferers, who assume that modern medicine has come up with a better treatment for sore throats. Yet the underlying reason for rejecting mature brands is unfavorable attitudes toward them. In research with our consumer panel, we often heard that older brands had lost their appeal, lost their identity, and were overshadowed by competing brands.

The best way to jump-start a mature brand is by understanding its uniqueness and equity.

Altering the characteristics of a brand or changing its packaging are often good ways to sweep away negative attitudes and boost sales. These changes aren't without risk—witness New Coke. But for some brands, a new look on the inside or outside has made a positive difference.

Aqua Velva aftershave lotion retained its trademark scent and color, and started its revitalization by developing a more convenient bottle and a snappier label. Lavoris mouthwash generated sizable sales increases because the clear "crystal fresh" version of its product appealed to young customers who had never used it before. Other successful modifications, such as some done by the Leaf Company (manufacturer of Good & Plenty, Heath bars, Zero, and Payday), involve reverting to original recipes, and extending familiar favorites into new forms, such as bite-size Heath Sensations.

Updated formulations or packaging are important, and they may result in modest sales increases. The best way to jump-start a mature brand is by understanding its uniqueness and equity, and making the most of them.

The most significant characteristics that separate one brand from another may not be the most obvious ones. Understanding the deeper meanings of brands to the people who buy them is the focus of a laddering research method developed by Charles Gengler, a marketing professor at Rutgers University–Camden. Consumers are first presented with three brands, including the mature brand being tested, and queried about their preferences.

The researcher then probes responses by asking questions that build on each answer. For instance, if one reason the respondent likes a breakfast cereal is because of its mascot, the next question is, "What is it you like about the mascot?" The respondent might say, "He's always positive and full of energy." The researcher's next question is, "Why is that important to you when eating a breakfast cereal?" to which the respondent says, "It reminds me of being young, and it makes me think the day might be off to a good start." At this point, the researcher has uncovered an underlying emotional, or higher-order, attribute of the brand being tested—it conjures up images of energy and youthful possibilities.

WHEN BIGGER
IS BETTER

(units consumed for three products, by size of package, 1996)

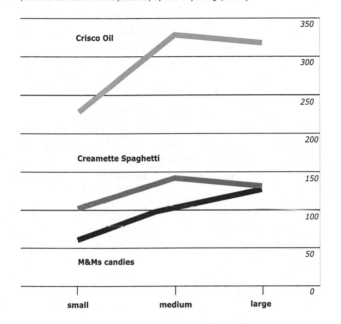

Note: Results are from an experiment conducted with members of the Consumer Brand Revitalization Panel. Units for oil and spaghetti are based on the amount used to make a meal for two; units for M&Ms are amount consumed while watching a video.

Source: experiments by the author

A medium-sized package prompts consumers to use more of the products tested.

Data from laddering interviews are analyzed to determine the likely importance of various higher-order attributes in brand choice. The results are then compared with customer prototypes to identify the highest-yield consumer segments for targeting.

One company used this technique to generate more sales of a brownie mix. Laddering interviews and analysis revealed that many consumers associate making brownies with being a good mother and with baking for special occasions. The company turned this information into a promotion with a greeting card company. Some kids' birthday cards included a coupon for brownie mix and a recipe for decorating pans of brownies with candy.

When a North American dairy council used the research technique, it learned that current adult milk drinkers tended to have warmer and happier memories of childhood than did non-

drinkers. People with fond childhood memories who weren't milk drinkers were an untapped market for the product. The council pitched milk as a comfort food, targeting adults who had the highest potential to become heavy milk drinkers.

Laddering research typically yields many higher-order points of differentiation among brands. So even though it's a rich source of information, brand managers must be careful not to communicate too much information to potential purchasers. Multiple messages delivered in various forms dilute brand equity and confuse consumers, says Kevin Lane Keller, a marketing professor at Duke University. To make the most of a brand's uniqueness, advertising, packaging, and promotions should all emphasize a single, clear, consistent message.

HEY, BUY ME!

Salient brands are the brands people buy. A salient brand is one of which consumers are aware, either by seeing it at the point-of-purchase, or by having it in mind. That top-of-mind awareness is what leads them to put a specific brand on a shopping list or to make a special trip for it.

Trade journals and retail associations consistently report many creative ideas for generating point-of-purchase awareness. The sales-boosting success of many of these ideas confirms what seem like obvious strategies. Bright packages, sale signs, catchy displays, and wide shelf-facing all increase our awareness of a brand. Yet less obvious are recent findings that end-aisle displays and suggestive selling can increase sales, even if the product is not discounted.

Arm & Hammer marketed its baking soda as a deodorizer for refrigerators, freezers, and kitchen sink drains.

A recent study I conducted with Robert Kent and Stephen Hoch demonstrated that ticklers like "Buy 12 Snicker's Bars for your freezer" not only increase awareness, but can nearly double the number of units a shopper intends to buy.

Brands have top-of-mind awareness when they have recently been used, or when recently advertised. Himmel, the brand revitalization pro, attributes his successes to raising top-of-mind awareness for a mature brand, and commanding a large share of the total advertising messages for products in its category.

By focusing on a simple, single-minded point of differentiation, his advertising campaigns use testimonials that are broadcast frequently and consistently. Brands with limited advertising budgets have effectively increased top-of-mind awareness by advertising distinctions on their labels. Trix Cereal, for instance, used a side panel to note complementary products on which Trix could be sprinkled. And Murphy's Oil Soap printed a series of uses for the product under peel-off stickers affixed to its spray bottles.

Research with the Consumer Brand Revitalization Panel shows how important suggestions like these can be. Simply encouraging purchase is not enough. The unfortunate curse that's befallen some brands is that they are "cupboard captives"—owned but not used. Sixty-three percent of the panel households in my studies possessed Tabasco sauce. But 32 percent had had their bottle so long the sauce had turned from red to brown. Similarly, 35 percent had vitamins they had not opened in the past 12 months. An unopened package of cookies lasted more than 6 months in 41 percent of households without children.

THE MORE WE HAVE, THE MORE WE USE

(average units used daily for selected stockpiled and nonstockpiled products, 1997)

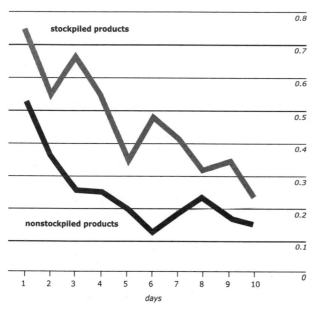

Note: Daily use is the average amount of chips, candy, juice, and granola consumed.

Source: experiments by the author and Pierre Chandon

People tend to eat more of things that are in large supply around the house.

NEW USES FOR OLD BRANDS

A brand manager who increases the number of units, such as cans of soup, that a household uses from four to five each year, realizes a 25 percent increase in sales without having to convert a single new user. This is true for both light and heavy users. One way to increase frequency of use is to suggest new uses for a brand.

Numerous old brands have revitalized their sales this way. Consider Arm & Hammer's situation in 1969. Sales were dropping because of a decline in home baking and the introduction of ready-to-bake packaged food products. Revitalization was critical. Arm & Hammer responded by marketing its baking

soda as a deodorizer for refrigerators, freezers, and kitchen sink drains. Sales skyrocketed.

The key to effectively advertising a new use for an old brand lies in making new uses appear similar to existing ones. The original use provides an "attitude halo" for the new use, and eases its adoptability.

This was demonstrated in a series of studies in which homemakers viewed a series of advertisements for canned soup, cranberry sauce, and gelatin. The "choosing" soup ad touted soup as hot and nutritious; the "using" ad described soup as a hot and nutritious option for a snack. The "using" ads increased the amount used over a three-month period for the three products tested by an average of 73 percent, or 1.2 units per month.

Perhaps the quickest way to increase usage frequency is to position a brand as a substitute for products in other categories. For instance, advertising campaigns encourage consumers to eat Philadelphia cream cheese instead of butter on bread, to eat Special K breakfast cereal instead of cookies in the afternoon, and to serve Orville Redenbacker popcorn instead of potato chips and peanuts at a party. These attempts are most successful when the substitute is seen as different—but not too different—from the original product. If the substitute brand and the original product are too different, their similarities should be advertised. If they are too similar, their differences should be advertised.

Altering package sizes can also effectively increase use frequency. As a general rule of thumb, if a brand manager is trying to decide which of two packages to introduce—say 20 ounces versus 24 ounces—the larger of the two packages should encourage greater volume consumption per use. In tests of 47 products in various categories, larger packages increased single-occasion usage by 19 percent to 152 percent, with a median increase of 32 percent.

Part of the reason usage acceleration occurs is because larger packages are simply perceived as less expensive to use than smaller packages. Nevertheless, there is a limit to how much spaghetti a household can eat on one occasion, or how much detergent it can use in a week. Once the limit or saturation point is reached, a larger package has no additional impact on use volume.

In one experiment, subjects were asked to prepare a meal for two using vegetable oil and spaghetti. The volume of oil used was greater for medium than for small bottles, but it does not increase further with large bottles. Goodies are a different story, though. When subjects munched M&Ms candy while viewing a video, the larger the package, the more they ate.

Packaging can make products seem more convenient, and convenience often makes people use more. Recent research with the Brand Revitalization Consumer Panel suggests that perceptions of convenience are primarily based on the time and effort required to use a product. If it's not possible to reduce the time required or "hassle," perceptions or convenience may be improved by careful selection of a comparison product. For instance, pizza mixes are perceived as 62 percent more convenient when advertisements compare them with scratch pizza rather than frozen pizza.

My Aftershave Belongs to Daddy

Remember the Old Spice mariner, dressed in a burly sailor cap and pea coat with a seagoing burlap sack slung over his shoulder? That's him over there playing beach volleyball. Old Spice aftershave is younger than ever, despite turning 60 this year. It has to be. Successfully selling a mature product to young men means staying contemporary. And for Old Spice, that means body splash and professional beach volleyball tournaments.

"Old Spice users are very, very loyal," says Carol Boyd of Procter & Gamble, makers of aftershave since 1990. The Old Spice fragrance remains attractive after all these years, going head-to-head in blind tests with any designer cologne you care to mention."But the image is an issue that we look at all the time," says Boyd. The same capital a mature brand accrues in name recognition has the potential to trap it in a time warp.

But both Old Spice and another mature aftershave, Aqua Velva, are successfully reaching younger men by keeping to the timeless strengths of the product, expanding the line, and updating their image. Aqua Velva has refocused on its traditional identity as a refreshing, invigorating part of the morning routine. This has been as important as sprucing up its image, says Bob Sheasby, vice president of marketing at the J. B. Williams Company, makers of Aqua Velva.

The brand got off track in the 1970s by trying to compete with the emerging designer cologne market. Television spots featuring likable football star Dick Butkiss chiding quarterbacks for wearing sissy colognes put the brand at a competitive disadvantage by abandoning its fundamental identity as a refreshing toner.

By the early 1990s, "Aqua Velva men" were mature themselves—the typical user was aged 50 or older. Yet in mall-intercept interviews and focus groups, the tried and true Ice Blue fragrance proved as popular as ever. The brand hadn't lost name recognition, either. Even after years of being overshadowed by flashier fragrances, younger men remembered the aftershave. The problem was how they remembered it.

"My dad wore it," many said. For others it was an uncle, the groovy bachelor who drove a sports car. The memories were fond, the scent appealing, but the images dated Aqua Velva as a product of an earlier, older generation. Aqua Velva needed to get groovy again.

In the meantime, a dab or five or ten of CKOne behind a young man's ears has become common on a Saturday night, says Sheasby. But cologne has primarily expanded the fragrance market, not cornered it. In fact, Aqua Velva researchers were encouraged by respondents' preferences in men's daily fragrance. Both men and women said they favor a clean, comfortable scent for every day use. The heavy, spicy, sweet, or predatory smells of Saturday night weren't preferred on a weekday.

Aqua Velva was reintroduced as the refreshing, invigorating, daily slap in the face after the morning shave. It reappeared in a trendier bottle, and the line was expanded to include other grooming products, such as deodorant and body splash. A second flavor, Ice Sport, was introduced, primarily for younger men. At about the same time that researchers for Aqua Velva were hitting shopping malls, Procter & Gamble threw a retirement party for the Old Spice mariner. His replacement sports a T-shirt and base-ball cap, and commands a sleek racing yacht. He looks more like an Ivy League grad than a rugged sailor. And he's apparently on his way—not to sea—but to the health club. He's traded the burlap sack for a gym bag. Old Spice also extended its line, introducing a successful long-lasting deodorant called High Endurance.

Boyd of Procter & Gamble points to the strong sales of High Endurance as a sign of a successful strategy combining the Old Spice fragrance, new technology, a contemporary product, and youth-oriented advertising. Old Spice claims an easy majority of total aftershave sales, 31 percent for the 12 weeks ending August 1997, according to *Drug Store News*.

The Aqua Velva man these days may be your son, not your father. The average age of Aqua Velva users is quickly falling, says Sheasby of J. B. Williams. The company's new variation on the classic blue tonic, Ice Sport, is making inroads with the 25-plus crowd, he says, while the original Ice Blue is most popular with men aged 25 to 45.

With its new packaging and advertising that communicates exhilaration, Aqua Velva has outperformed many competitors since its redesign more than a year ago, Sheasby says. Dollar sales of Ice Blue and Ice Sport combined were up 21.3 percent in the 12 weeks ending in August 1997, even as overall aftershave sales among the eight major brands declined 3.4 percent, according to *Drug Store News*. Some major brands saw sales tumble up to 28 percent during the period.

We'll have to see which aftershave brands have staying power, and which hit the skids for good. Anyone remember Hai Karate?

—*Kevin Heubusch*

MAKING THE MOST OF STOCKPILING

The more soft drinks we have at home, the more we tend to drink, right? Not always. A brand that is out of sight is out of mind. While stockpiling increases how frequently people use a brand, it does so only when the brand is salient—that is, when it is either physically visible or on the top of one's mind. Brands are also highly salient and frequently used—shortly after they are purchased. Encouraging stockpiling through promotions or multi-packs increases the frequency of use, but so does any promotion that encourages consumers to frequently purchase a product.

To get consumers to clear stockpiled items out of household inventory and purchase more, marketers must keep their brands on the minds of users. While nearly any type of advertising increases salience, the most effective ads are those that are seen or heard just prior to a usage decision.

Brand managers obviously can't predict when people will stand in front of their cupboards to pick canned vegetables for dinner. Yet there are some windows of opportunity. Coke aired its "Drive-time Drinking" radio ads to encourage commuters to drink Coke while driving home. Similarly, Campbell's Soup raised brand salience by broadcasting "Storm Spot Ads" during inclement weather. Radio's flexibility allowed the ads to be broadcast prior to lunch and to dinner.

There's even a chance to speak to the customer at her cupboard—an ad on a product's package. The audience is captive, the cost per exposure is low, and the opportunity cost of what might otherwise be on the package is often negligible.

Revitalizing old brands is like reopening old mines. Some will be barren, others may hide gold. Academic research shows us that many once-successful brands have something to offer modern consumers, whether it's a brand they once trusted or the nostalgia of years past. The rule to remember is "Never say die." Fifty years ago, Burma Shave was a proud and prosperous brand. Forty years ago, it was the Edsel-like punch line for jokes. In late 1997, Burma Shave's relaunch was announced with a miner's zeal. Maybe this will be the text of its first outdoor advertisement:

When something's a waste
It's gone in good haste

A good brand though
Should never go
Burma Shave

TAKING IT FURTHER

Data on brand choice and use, and perceptions of mature brands were collected at the Brand Lab at the University of Illinois Urbana-Champaign. Brian Wansink and Cynthia Huffman are conducting ongoing research on brand revitalization. For more information on the Brand Lab, the Brand Revitalization Consumer Panel, and other brand-related research, contact the author at 350 Commerce West, University of Illinois, Champaign, IL 61820; telephone (217) 244-0208. Relevant research reports can be downloaded from http://www.cba.uiuc.edu/~wansink/index.html.

Brian Wansink, Ph.D., is associate professor of business administration and advertising at the University of Illinois Urbana-Champaign, and director of the Brand Revitalization Consumer Panel. His Brand Lab specializes in research on use of packaged goods and revitalization of mature brands.

Can You Spot the Fake?

*We couldn't. To retailers' dismay, fake luxury goods have become increasingly realistic.
With sales soaring, **Ken Bensinger** sees if experts can be fooled by $400
'Louis Vuitton' suitcases, 'Gucci' belts and other booty.*

B Y HER OWN admission, Jan Davidson isn't the kind of person who would change a flat tire. So what was she doing peering into the trunk of a sedan in the driveway of her Boca Raton, Fla., country club? Shopping. When Ms. Davidson's head popped up from out of the trunk, she was the owner of a $400 fake Chanel bag.

"I'm not too proud," says Ms. Davidson. "The women here drive Rolls-Royces, but these days, they have no compunction about buying a copy."

Logo lovers, take heart. As the luxury economy sputters and stalls, a boom in high-end fakes is shifting into overdrive. These aren't the old, tacky knockoffs that can be spotted a mile away, but a new breed of look-alikes, born of high-tech manufacturing techniques and savvy packaging. They are both pricier and more varied than just a year or so ago—ranging from $99 "Big Bertha" golf clubs to $1,300 fake Rolexes—and thanks to new distribution channels, more available than ever. Indeed, while figures are hard to come by, retailers estimate that in the last year alone, sales of fakes have jumped 25%, to $2 billion a year.

"This has gotten a lot bigger in just the last few months," says outgoing U.S. Customs Service commissioner Raymond Kelly, who attributes some of the jump to the slowing economy. "It's amazing how much the quality has improved."

To check on the quality, we went look-alikes shopping. Scoping out New York street vendors, Chinatown stalls and the Internet, we amassed a trove of top-end fakes and showed them to a group of retail experts and seasoned shoppers. The results won't exactly thrill those who make the real thing. Four out of five of our testers—including a publicist for the fashion industry—were duped by a faux Prada duffel bag. The same number were fooled by an "Hermes" Birkin handbag with leather so nice that one panelist practically cooed. We had to wrest a fake Bulgari watch off the wrist of one tester and a Burberry scarf from the hands of another.

Of course, one panelist did say the cheap lining on a faux Louis Vuitton handbag "smelled funky," and a flimsy Gucci belt didn't fool anyone (oops, it came with plastic loops). But more often than not, our testers had no idea what was real, and what was a knockoff. One frequently asked question: Can I keep it?

250,000 Pairs of Fake Adidas

As anyone in the retail industry will testify, the business of fakes is hardly new. Copies of everything from T-shirts to car parts have flourished in the gray market for decades, even though they violate federal trademark regulations. Fakes became so popular last year that luxury-goods manufacturers and law-enforcement agencies even stepped up their efforts to crack down on vendors. (One raid in Los Angeles netted a quarter of a million pairs of faux Adidas sneakers valued at a total of $7 million.) "The knockoffs are incredible now," says Diane Merrick, the owner of a trendy boutique in Santa Monica, Calif. "You can't tell the difference."

'It's cool to say you didn't pay retail, even if it's a fake,' says one analyst.

It's these improvements that increasingly tempt a wider range of customers to dabble in this shady world. (Although it's illegal to make and sell fakes, in most places, there are no laws against buying them.) For consumers who want to own the fashion of the moment—albeit a fake, at a fraction of the cost—there is little risk. If anything, owning a fake has become a status symbol, especially in circles where thriftiness is considered cool. Last fall, the HBO sitcom "Sex and the City" went so far as to feature the show's stars buying fake Fendi handbags out of the trunk of a car for just $150 (a real one can cost as much as $5,000).

It's a Faux World

To test how convincing—or not—high-end fakes are, we put them through a tough test: Letting four trend-conscious consumers and an eagle-eyed expert examine them. (We also included a ringer: a real bottle of Chanel No. 5.) Here are their conclusions:

ITEM	PRICE OF FAKE/ REAL	WHAT FORGERS GOT RIGHT	WHAT FORGERS GOT WRONG	HOW MANY FOOLED?/OUR COMMENTS
1. Hermes bag	$375/$5,225	Gold-leaf logo above closure	Hermes doesn't line its bag in ultrasuede	**4 out of 5.** Not only does this bag sport a real-looking "Hermes-Paris" logo and practically perfect hardware, it even smelled expensive, said one panelist.
2. Fendi pants	$40/$400	Fendi-logo button	Side "L" tag on *outside* of pants!	**2 out of 5.** Our panelists didn't go for the heavily logo-ed look of these pants. "These are ugly. I know that," one of them said, "They look cheap and horrible."
3. Gucci shoes	$150/$295-$395	Heat stamp inside shoe	The heel's molded plastic instead of stacked leather	**2 out of 5.** "It's got the fashionable design of the moment," said Sarah Mason, an account manager. But she said the shoes felt like they'd been bought at a discount store.
4. Prada airplane duffel bag	$140/$420-$670	Trademark "Prada" patterned nylon lining	Odd mixture of styles from different Prada lines	**4 out of 5.** Most convincing fake. No one could put this beauty down. Two favorite touches—it came in a "Prada" plastic bag and even the tiny steel lock has a logo. "Very cool," gushed lawyer Robyn Greenberg. "Are you sure it's not real?"
5. Tommy Hilfiger children's jeans	$9/$35	Cardboard sales tag attached to pocket	Size on label is written in felt tip pen	**3 out of 5.** There were lots of faults, but our panelists weren't complaining. "Who can really tell with licensed jeans anyway?" said our fashion writer, Teri Agins.
6. Bulgari 'Rettangolo' Chronograph watch	$135/$4,300	Stainless-steel band and perfect logo.	Oops! Black dial (Bulgari only makes it in white)	**3 out of 5.** Ms. Greenberg loved the sweeping (not ticking) second hand. "This has got to be real," she said. A Tourneau saleswoman, however, declared it "quite bogus."
7. Louis Vuitton luggage	$400/$1,260	Real leather logo on inside	Shoddy trim peeled right off	**1 out of 5. Least convincing fake.** After five minutes, this high-priced fake showed signs of wear. A luggage expert gave it a thumbs down: "Without the logo, its a $50 bag."
8. Burberry scarf	$40/$59	Sewn-on label appeared to be authentic	Poorly finished edges had already begun to fray	**3 out of 5.** "If this isn't real, I'm going to be upset," said one panelist. "I gave real ones to my boyfriend's parents!" Our expert's opinion: "It looks like acrylic."
9. Christian Dior saddle bag	$200/$660	Overlogoed—brass "CD" hardware everywhere	They missed the logo that matters—the one on the inside	**3 out of 5.** This was our trendiest phony. The handbag designer, however, balked at its shape: "It's supposed to look like a saddle—this looks like a left lung."
10. Chanel No. 5 eau de toilette spray	This was the real thing, and it cost $50	Not applicable	Not applicable	**2 out of 5 thought it was fake.** Though all of our testers recognized the scent of Chanel, some thought the bottle looked wrong.

Flashing Your Gucci G's

"There's something different in the mind-set today," says Tom Julian, a trend analyst at Fallon, a Minneapolis ad agency. "It's cool to say you didn't pay retail, even if it's a fake." The trend not only dovetails with cheapskate chic, it underscores just how unimportant authenticity has become in American culture. For hipsters, flaunting a fake is its own tongue-in-cheek fashion statement. "Who cares if it's fake," says Philip Bloch, a Los Angeles fashion stylist. "Just flash your Gucci Gs, make your mark and get on with your life."

That's certainly Sandy Richmond's philosophy. A retail consultant in Los Angeles, Ms. Richmond not only owns fake Gucci and Louis Vuitton belts and a faux Louis Vuitton wallet, she recently invested $220 in the Cadillac of fakes: a brown "Hermes" handbag. "Sure I would buy a real Kelly bag if I could afford it," says Ms. Richmond. But some of these things "look better than the originals."

Indeed, our own testers were surprised at how fast fakes have moved up the fashion food chain—and especially at the dead-on detailing. Inside the fake Gucci heels, for example, there was a real-looking heat stamp. On the imitation Christian Dior saddle bag, the hardware was bona fide brass and the lining was "real jacquard," noted veteran handbag designer John Truex. Even packaging has gotten more realistic: our "Prada" duffel bag came with a tiny "Prada" steel lock and was snuggled in a plastic bag stamped with the manufacturer's logo.

What's more, fake makers today are barely a step behind the fashion curve; that means there's almost no lag time between the introduction of a new designer good and the production of its fake. That Christian Dior saddle bag, for example, was available on the street just weeks after it hit the shelves of specialty retailers last spring.

Surfing the Web, we also discovered up-to-date fakes of everything from Oakley sunglasses to Pokémon backpacks.

So how were fake makers able to move upmarket without losing their customer base? For one thing, experts say, counterfeiters realized shoppers of different incomes were willing to pay a lot more for the upgraded details. That faux Burberry scarf, in lambswool, cost $40, just $19 less than the real McCoy. We found one faux Louis Vuitton wheeling suitcase with a $400 pricetag—more than a lot of real Samsonites. And fake-manufacturers have gotten better at getting their stuff into the U.S. Just a few years ago, fakers typically imported their wares fully assembled to sell on the streets; now, to try to avoid U.S. Customs agents, counterfeiters often ship the item without the telltale logo and attach the label once the item is on American soil.

Beating the Counterfeiters

But all this fakery may have its limits. With better technology, for example, bona fide manufacturers are hoping to make their products more counterfeit-proof. Prada now includes a magnetic card in its bags that verifies the item's authenticity. Likewise, Major League Baseball makes sure all of its officially licensed products bear an official hologram sticker on the tag.

On the legal side, many firms are going after retailers who have quietly started stocking fakes. Just last month, manufacturers celebrated when a federal grand jury in Columbia, S.C., indicted the operators of Fakegifts.com for selling fake Cartier and Rolex watches and fake Montblanc pens. That's because they think that this case could make it easier to sue Internet firms that sell fake goods for trademark infringement.

Ultimately, if Valerie Lichman is any indication, knockoffs could even someday become a victim of their own success. When Ms. Lichman, a New York publicist, recently found the perfect faux J.P. Tod's handbag in an uptown store, everything about it was just right, even the color of the leather. The only problem: a $600 pricetag. "I really loved it," Ms. Lichman says, "but I just couldn't afford the fake."

Color me popular: Marketers shape up packaging

By Theresa Howard
USA TODAY

NEW YORK—It is known as the last 5 seconds of advertising, and its aim is to propel a product across the threshold from shelf to shopping cart.

It is package design, and it has become an increasingly important means of product differentiation.

Color, shape and texture offer subtle but tangible cues that don't make it across the airwaves in a commercial. Done well, they make an emotional link to a consumer at the point of purchase, that vulnerable spot where about 70% of purchase decisions are made.

"Product design is one of a few key differentiators you can have" in categories with similar products, says Ed Rice, senior executive director with brand identity and design firm Landor Associates. Maybe that's why just the design of packaging represents a business with more than $100 billion in annual billings and sales.

Some recent innovations:

•Grown-up versions of Chiclets under such brand names as Dentyne Ice or Eclipse fetch more, as much as 79 cents a pack, thanks to shiny foil pop-out packaging that highlights stronger flavors.

•A redesign of the Salon Selectives shampoo and conditioner line by Helene Curtis elevates the mass-marketed brand to salon-brand status with contemporary colors and names such as "Rain."

•Gatorade gets a tighter grip on its market with an ergonomically designed bottle that fits in your hand and mouth.

•Lipton Iced Tea makes a breakthrough with a bottle that fits into a cup holder.

•Hidden Valley Ranch turns design upside down with its "Easy Squeeze" inverted bottle.

"More and more marketers are making use of shape and color," says Jim Peters, editor of *Brand-Packaging* magazine. Why? The sheer number of products in the marketplace.

Think of those pretty colors and curves as defense mechanisms in response to selection overload.

"We are in an age where there is just a glut of stuff out there," Peters adds. "There are more choices of hand wash and shampoo out there than people can deal with on a rational basis." When making a purchase, "a consumer is in an emotional vs. a rational mode."

Beverage companies have long used packaging as a way to stand out. The spirits industry set a standard for using packaging for brand differentiation. Absolut Vodka built a global brand on the shape of a bottle.

But Coca-Cola was the pioneer in making use of a unique design with its trademark bottle.

While beverage marketers led the way, other industries have followed.

Form vs. function

Gatorade's new EDGE bottle, on sale in some markets, will be available nationally by April.

"It's all about that moment," says Mary Dillon, Gatorade's vice president of product offerings and new brand development. "Consumers take 4 seconds to make that decision, so you really need a package that speaks to them."

EDGE is an acronym for the purported benefits: Ergonomically Designed Gatorade Experience. What makes the bottle special? A resealable top and an "optimal grip, so it fits in your hand really well," Dillon says. "You can throw it on the ground, and it doesn't spill." Among the design considerations: flow rate, lip shape, bottle size.

Yogurt also is getting a new look. The squeezable yogurt category has grown into a business posting $100 million a year in sales. New Hampshire-based Stonyfield Farm seeks its share with its YoSqueeze brand targeted at active youths.

"Packaging-wise, it's great," says MaryJo Viederman, a spokeswoman for Stonyfield Farm. "One of the biggest innovations of the packaging is that it brings yogurt into a bigger part of daily lives. You can eat it in a car or serve it in a lunch-box, and it doesn't require a spoon.

"You can't just add another flavor cup and get space," she adds. "But it has been great for us."

It's all in the look

A gum in any other wrapper wouldn't taste as good. Look at Adams' Dentyne Ice and Wrigley's Eclipse gums, two leaders in the adult gum category. The look says both premium and functional. A 12-piece pack features individual pockets for each piece and a shiny foil overlay (otherwise known as a blister pack). In the four years since its introduction, Adams has moved Dentyne Ice into the top spot with older chewers.

"We have experienced tremendous growth in 2000," says Heidi Dvorkin, senior product manager. "Consumption is up by 48% in volume, and we became No. 3 in the $1.9 billion gum category overall and the No. 1 brand in the breath-freshening category."

Eyeball intrigue

Shelf space is a premium in the retail market, and marketers want as much as they can get for a strong visual effect. But gaining shelf footage means nothing if the product doesn't scream, "Buy me!"

General Foods recently revamped packaging for its International Coffees with help from design specialist The Sterling Group.

In the course of the redesign, the company considered 50 options. The one thing ruled out was retiring the tin pack. With the new look came the addition of a cappuccino line.

"We wanted to optimize the shelf presence and branding so that when customers go to the shelves, they can identify the products easily," says Doug Weekes, category business director for the Kraft unit of General Foods.

"In that aisle, there is still some decision being made at the shelf."

But new designs must be true to the brand image, he warns.

"It is extremely important to be consistent about how you treat your brand and introduce new flavors."

From *USA Today*, February 8, 2001, p. 7B. © 2001 by USA Today. Reprinted by permission.

Kamikaze Pricing

*When penetration strategies run amok, marketers
can find themselves in a dive-bomb of no return.*

by Reed K. Holden and Thomas T. Nagle

Price is the weapon of choice for many companies in the competition for sales and market share. The reasons are understandable. No other weapon in a marketer's arsenal can be deployed as quickly, or with such certain effect, as a price discount. The advantage is often short-lived, though, and managers rarely balance the long-term consequences of deploying the price weapon against the likely short-term gains.

Playing the price card often is a reaction to a competitor and assumes that it will provide significant gain for the firm. Usually, that's not the case. Firms start price wars when they have little to lose and much to gain; those who react to the initiators often have little to gain and much to lose. The anticipated gains often disappear as multiple competitors join the battle and negate the lift from the initial reductions.

Managers in highly competitive markets often view price cuts as the only possible strategy. Sometimes they're right. The problem is that they are playing with a very dangerous weapon in a war to improve near-term profitability that ends in long-term devastation. As the Chinese warrior, Sun Tzu, put it, "Those who are not thoroughly aware of the disadvantages in the use of arms cannot be thoroughly aware of the advantages."

If marketers are going to use low prices as a competitive weapon, they must be equally aware of the risks as well as the benefits (see "The Prisoner's Dilemma"). They also must learn to adjust their strategies to deploy alternatives when pricing alone is no longer effective. Failure to do so has put companies and entire industries into tail spins from which they never fully recover.

Pricing Options

Marketers traditionally have employed three pricing strategies: skim, penetration, and neutral. Skim pricing is the process of pricing a product high relative to competitors and the product's value. Neutral pricing is an attempt to eliminate price as a decision factor for customers by pricing neither high nor low relative to competitors. Penetration pricing is the decision to price low relative to the product's value and to the prices of similar competitors. It is a decision to use price as the main competitive weapon in hopes of driving the company to a position of market dominance.

EXECUTIVE BRIEFING

Penetration pricing is perhaps the most abused pricing strategy. It can be effective for fixed periods of time and in the right competitive situation, but many firms overuse this approach and end up creating a market situation where everyone is forced to lower prices continually, driving some competitors from the market and guaranteeing that no one realizes a good return on investment. Managers can prevent the fruitless slide into kamikaze pricing by implementing a value-driven pricing strategy for the most profitable customer segments.

All three strategies consider how the product is priced relative to its value for customers and that of similar competitors. When Lexus entered the luxury segment of the automobile industry, the car's price was high relative to

Exhibit 1

Experience curve effects

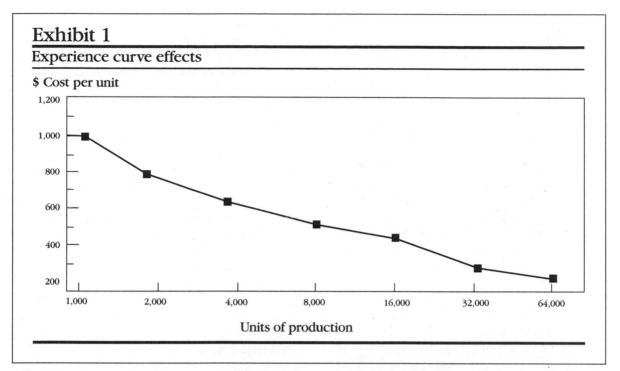

$ Cost per unit

Units of production

standard vehicles but low relative to Mercedes and BMW. The penetration strategy was defined not by the price but by the price relative to the value of the vehicle and to similar competitive products.

The main ingredient to successful penetration pricing is a large segment of customers for whom price is the primary purchase motivation.

Any of these strategies can be associated with a variety of cost structures and can result in either profits or losses. To understand when each strategy is likely to be successful, managers should evaluate their current and potential cost structure, their customers' relative price sensitivities, and their current and potential competitors. All three areas must be carefully considered before employing any pricing strategy.

Penetration Strategies Can Work

If a firm has a fixed cost structure and each sale provides a large contribution to those fixed costs, penetration pricing can boost sales and provide large increases to profits—but only if the market size grows or if competitors choose not to respond. Low prices can draw additional buyers to enter the market. The increased sales can justify production expansion or the adoption of new technologies, both of which can reduce costs. And, if firms have excess capacity, even low-priced business can provide incremental dollars toward fixed costs.

Penetration pricing can also be effective if a large experience curve will cause costs per unit to drop significantly. The experience curve proposes that, as a firm's production experience increases, per-unit costs will go down. On average, for each doubling of production, a firm can expect per-unit costs to decline by roughly 20%. Cost declines can be significant in the early stages of production (see Exhibit 1).

The manufacturer who fails to take advantage of these effects will find itself at a competitive cost disadvantage relative to others who are further along the curve. This is often the case with new technologies and innovative products, where relatively small increments in units sold yield substantial decreases in unit costs. This is also the case for many new entrants to a market who are just beginning to see experience curve cost reductions.

However, the main ingredient to successful penetration pricing is a large segment of customers for whom price is the primary purchase motivation. This can be the case in business markets where original equipment commodities are sold to the production process of a customer's business, but it rarely occurs in consumer markets where image is an important part of the use of a product.

When Omega watches—once a brand more prestigious than Rolex—was trying to improve market share in the 1970s, it adopted a penetration pricing strategy that succeeded in destroying the watch's brand image by flooding the market with lower priced products. Omega never gained sufficient share on the lower price/lower image competitors to justify destroying its brand image and high-priced position with upscale buyers. Similar outcomes were experienced by the Cadillac Cimarron and Lacoste clothing.

A better strategy would have been to introduce a totally new brand as a flanking product, as Heublein did with the Popov, Relska, and Smirnoff vodka brands and Intel did with microprocessors in 1988. After the introduction of the 386 microprocessor, Intel adopted a skim price strategy for the high value and proprietary 386 chips. It also wanted to market a circuit in the 286 market that could compete with AMD and Cirrus on a nonprice, value-added basis. The 386SX was introduced as a scaled down version of the 386, but at a price only slightly higher than the 286. The net result was to migrate price sensitive customers more quickly to the proprietary 386 market with the 386SX, while still capturing increased profit from the high value users with the 386.

In its marketing of the 486, Pentium, and Pentium Pro circuits, Intel continues this flanking strategy with dozens of varieties of each microprocessor to meet the needs of various market segments.

For penetration pricing to work, there must be competitors who are willing to let the penetration pricer get away with the strategy. If a penetration price is quickly matched by a competitor, the incremental sales that would accrue from the price-sensitive segment must now be split between two competitors. As more competitors follow, smaller incremental sales advantages and lower profits accrue to both the initiator and the followers.

Fortunately, there are two common situations which often cause competitors to let penetration pricers co-exist in markets. When the penetration-pricing firm has enough of a cost or resource advantage, competitors might conclude they would lose a price war. Retailers are beginning to recognize that some consumers who are unconcerned about price when deciding which products and brands to buy become price sensitive when deciding where to buy. They are willing to travel farther to buy the same branded products at lower prices. Category killers like Toys 'R' Us use penetration pricing strategies because they are able to manage their overhead and distribution costs much more tightly than traditional department stores. Established stores don't have the cost structure to compete on this basis, so they opt to serve the high-value segment of the market.

When the penetration-pricing firm has enough of a cost or resource advantage, competitors might conclude they would lose a price war.

The second situation conducive to penetration pricing occurs when large competitors have high-price positions and don't feel a significant number of their existing customers would be lost to the penetration pricer. This was the case when People's Express entered the airline industry with low priced fares to Europe in the 1970s. The fares were justified with reduced services such as no reservations or meal service. People's also limited the ability of the high value business traveler to take advantage of those fares by not permitting advanced reservations or ticket sales. This was a key element of their strategy: Focus only on price sensitive travelers and avoid selling tickets to the customers of their competitors.

Major airlines didn't respond to the lower prices because they didn't see People's Express taking away their high value customers. It was only when People's began pursuing the business traveler that the major airlines responded and quickly put People's out of business.

The same strategy is being repeated today by Southwest Airlines in the domestic market far more skillfully. Southwest has a cost and route structure that limits the ability of major airlines to respond. In fact, when United Airlines, a much larger competitor, did try to respond with low-cost service in selected West Coast markets, it had to abandon the effort because it couldn't match Southwest's cost structure.

Penetration or Kamikaze?

An extreme form of penetration pricing is "kamikaze" pricing, a reference to the Japanese dive bomber pilots of World War II who were willing to sacrifice their lives by crashing their explosives-laden airplanes onto enemy ships. This may have been a reasonable wartime tactic (though not a particularly attractive one) by commanders who sacrificed single warriors while inflicting many casualties on opponents. But in the business world, the relentless pursuit of more sales through lower prices usually results in lower profitability. It is often an unnecessary and fruitless exercise that damages the entire dive-bombing company—not just one individual—along with the competitor. Judicious use of the tactic is advised; in as many cases as it works, there are many more where it does not.

Kamikaze pricing occurs when the justification for penetration pricing is flawed, as when marketers incorrectly assume lower prices will increase sales. This may be true in growth markets where lower prices can expand the total market, but in mature markets a low price merely causes the same customers to switch suppliers. In the global economy, market after market is being discovered, developed, and penetrated. High growth, price sensitive markets are quickly maturing, and even though customers may want to buy a low-priced product, they don't increase their volume of purchases. Price cuts used to get them to switch fail to bring large increases in demand and end up shrinking the dollar size of the market.

A prominent example is the semiconductor business, where earlier price competition led to both higher demand and reduced costs. But in recent years, total demand tends to be less responsive to lower prices, and most suppliers are well down the experience curve. The net result is an industry where participation requires huge investments, added value is immense, but because of a penetration price

The Prisoner's Dilemma

A popular exercise in seminars and executive briefings we hold is to ask executives to participate in a prisoner's dilemma pricing game. Each team must decide whether to price its products high or low compared to those of another team in 10 rounds of competition. The objective is to earn the most money; results are determined by the decision that two competitors make in comparison with each other.

The game fairly accurately simulates a typical profit/loss scenario for price competition in mature markets. The objective is to impart several lessons in pricing competition, the first being that pricing is more like playing poker than solitaire. Success depends not just on a combination of luck and how the hand is played but also on how well competitors play their hands. In real markets, outcomes depend not only on how customers respond but, perhaps more important, on how competitors respond to changes in price.

If a competitor matches a price decrease, neither the initiator nor the follower will achieve a significant increase in sales and both are likely to have a significant decrease in profits. In developing pricing strategy, managers need to anticipate the moves of their competitors and attempt to influence those moves by selectively communicating information to influence competitive behavior.

The second lesson is that managers must adopt a very long time horizon when considering changes in price.

Once started, price wars are difficult to stop. A simple decision to drop price often becomes the first shot in a war that no competitor wins. Before initiating a price decrease, managers must consider how it will affect the competitive stability of markets.

Philip Morris discovered this when it initiated a price war in the cigarette business by cutting the prices of its top brands. Competitors followed, and the net result was a $2.3 billion drop in operating profits for Philip Morris, even as the Marlboro brand increased its market share seven points to 29%. The manufacturer of Camels experienced a $1.3 billion drop in profits.

The third lesson from the prisoner's dilemma is that careful use of a value-based marketing approach can reverse a trend toward price-based marketing. This is accomplished through signaling, a nonprice competitive tactic that involves selectively disclosing information to competitors to influence their behavior. The steel and airline industries provide prominent examples of the signaling strategy's use. They often rely on announcements that conveniently appear on the front pages of the Wall Street Journal to signal competitors of pending price moves and provide them with opportunities to follow. The strategy takes time to implement, but it provides a far better long-term competitive position for marketers who employ it.

Most managers who play the prisoner's dilemma adopt a low-price strategy. This mirrors the real world, where 63% of managers who adopt an identifiable strategy use low price, according to an ongoing research project in which we are engaged. In the game, low-price teams fail to earn any profit in a majority of cases. The strategy works in round one, but competitors quickly learn to respond and both parties end up losing any chance for profit.

Executives rationalize that, if their firm can't make money, competitors shouldn't, either. Managers quickly forget that the objective of this game—and the game of business—is profit. Price cuts in the real world can be devastating. A current example is the personal computer business, where Packard Bell sets the low price standard that many competitors follow.

Packard Bell's management is less concerned with profit than with achieving a volume of sales and market share in a growing industry. But unless the company has operational characteristics that distinguish it from competitors and permit Packard Bell to deliver a quality product at those low prices, its ability to leverage market share will be limited. Analysts estimate that Packard Bell has only made $45 million in net profit over the past 10 years and is staying afloat through loans granted by suppliers and massive cash infusions from its Japanese and European co-owners.

—*Reed Holden and Thomas Nagle*

mentality, suppliers can't pull out of the kamikaze death spiral.

There was a time when large, well-entrenched competitors took a long time to respond to new low-price competitors. That is no longer true; domestic automobiles are now the low priced brands, and even AT&T has learned to respond to the aggressive price competition of Sprint and MCI. The electronics, soft goods, rubber, and steel companies that ignored low-price competitors in the 1970s and '80s have become ruthless cost and price cutters. The days of free rides from nonresponsive market leaders are gone.

Another risk comes in using penetration pricing to increase sales in order to drive down unit costs. Unfortunately, there are generally two reasons managers run into trouble when they justify price discounts by anticipated reductions in costs. First, they view the relationship between costs and volume as linear, when it actually is exponential—the cost reduction per unit becomes smaller with larger increases in volume. Initial savings are substantial, but as sales grow, the incremental savings per unit of production all but disappear (see Exhibit 2). Costs continue to decline on a per-unit basis, but the incremental cost reduction seen from each additional unit of sale becomes insignificant. Managers need to recognize that experience curve cost savings as a percentage of incremental sales volume declines with increases in volume. It works great in early growth phases but not in the later stages.

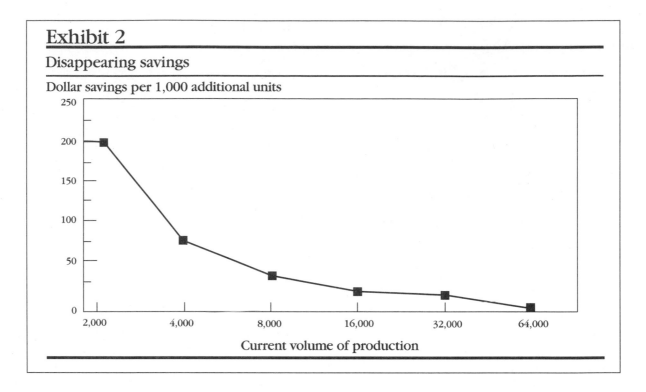

Exhibit 2

Disappearing savings

Dollar savings per 1,000 additional units

Current volume of production

Many managers believe that sales volume is king. They evaluate the success of both their sales managers and marketing managers by their ability to grow sales volume. The problem is that their competitors employ the exact same strategy. Customers learn that they can switch loyalties with little risk and start buying lower priced alternatives. Marketers find themselves stuck with a deadly mix of negligible cost benefits, inelastic demand, aggressive competition, and no sustainable competitive advantage. Any attempt to reduce price in this environment will often trigger growing losses. To make matters worse, customers who buy based on price are often more expensive to serve and yield lower total profits than do loyal customers. Thus starts the death spiral of the kamikaze pricers who find their costs going up and their profits disappearing.

Penetration pricing is overused, in large part, because managers think in terms of sports instead of military analogies. In sports, the act of playing is enough to justify the effort. The objective might be to win a particular game, but the implications of losing are minimal. The more intense the process, the better the game, and the best way to play is to play as hard as you can.

This is exactly the wrong motivation for pricing where the ultimate objective is profit. The more intense the competition, the worse it is for all who play. Aggressive price competition means that few survive the process and even fewer make reasonable returns on their investments. In pricing, the long-term implications of each battle must be considered in order to make thoughtful decisions about which battles to fight. Unfortunately, many managers find that, in winning too many pricing battles, they often lose the war for profitability.

Value Pricing

To avoid increasingly aggressive price competition, managers must first recognize the problem and then develop alternate strategies that build distinctive, nonprice competencies. Instead of competing only on price, managers can develop solutions to enhance the competitive and profit positions of their firms.

In most industries, there are far more opportunities for differentiation than managers usually consider. If customers are receiving good service and support, they are often willing to pay more to the supplier, even for commodities. A client in India produced commodity gold jewelry that was sold into the Asian market at extremely low penetration prices. Because of the client's good relationships with wholesale and retail intermediaries, we recommended a leveraging of those relationships to increase prices to a more reasonable level. Despite much anxiety, the client followed suit and major customers accepted the increases.

Opportunities to Add Value

Marketers often fail to recognize the opportunity for higher prices when they get caught up in kamikaze pricing. To avoid this, they need to understand how their customers value different product and company attributes. The objective is to identify segments of customers who have problems for which unique and cost-effective solutions can be developed. Sometimes it's as simple as a minor adjustment in packaging.

Know what customers want. Loctite Corp., a global supplier of industrial adhesives, introduced a specialty

Exhibit 3

Customer purchasing agenda

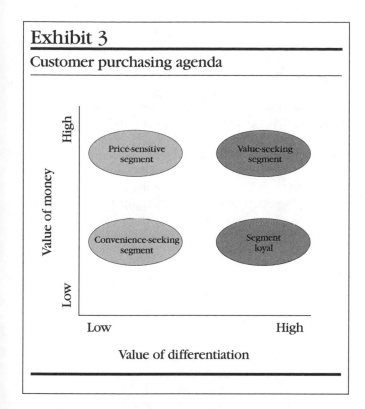

liquid adhesive in a 1-oz. bottle for use in emergency applications. Unfortunately, sales were less than spectacular. After a number of customer interviews, Loctite discovered that the liquid was difficult to apply and the bottle was difficult to carry. What customers really wanted was an easy-to-apply gel in a tube. The product was reformulated to meet these criteria and saw huge success. In the process, Loctite almost doubled the price.

> Firms that attract value customers get the loyal buyer as part of the bargain and sell to the price buyer only when it is profitable and reasonable.

Managers should identify features that they can add more cost effectively than their competitors can. IBM has been under intense price pressure in the personal computer segment. Besides introducing lower-priced flanking products (with limited success), IBM also has introduced computers with more internal memory. This feature had significant appeal because of the higher memory demands of the Windows 95 operating system. The value of this feature was greater than a price cut because IBM is arguably the most cost-effective producer of random access memory in the world. It also forced low-price competitors to incur higher relative costs to match IBM, thereby undercutting their ability to price their PCs below IBM's.

In the process of adding value to their products, firms should remember that value is achieved not only from the products themselves, but from the services associated with their use. The manufacturer of a heavy-duty truck oil broke out of commodity pricing when it began analyzing the oil from its customers' trucks to determine if there were excessively high temperatures or metal in the oil that would indicate a breakdown of the internal components of engines. The service was promoted in a mailer included with each large drum of oil. The cost of this service was minimal, and a large segment of small- and owner-operator customers placed a huge value on it. This tactic helped the firm to differentiate its product with a valued service connected to the product.

Offer complete benefits. Another way to avoid downward pricing is to offer complete product benefits, which is especially useful in the early phases of a new product's life. This tactic is not as effective when products mature and customers no longer need as much service support. However, when customers are still developing their expertise, they require complete systems to achieve the maximum benefit to their organization. This is often an expensive affair that needs to be justified by the future business and profit potential that a customer represents.

When marketers correctly assess this type of situation, they often develop a sustainable competitive advantage that makes them impervious to competitive erosion. This was the strategy that Intel employed when it introduced the 8086 microprocessor to the PC industry in the early 1980s. Although the 8086 was slightly inferior technically to Motorola's 6800, Intel adopted sophisticated customer support programs that permitted new PC manufacturers to introduce new products quickly. This and other services were backed by a strong sales and marketing program that focused on specific customer adoptions. The net result was the beginning of Intel's dominance in PC microprocessors.

Understand customer agendas. Marketers make a serious mistake when they assume that all their customers are willing to sacrifice quality to obtain low prices. A few are, but most really want to get high-quality products at the lowest possible price. The seller of a high-quality product can compete against a low-price, low-quality product by recognizing that, despite the words of the purchasing agent, pricing need not be too aggressive.

Sellers who understand why customers buy their products often find that there is a fairly uniform set of reasons underlying purchasing behavior. Price is often important, but it seldom is the sole motivation. In most business situations, there are four types of agendas with regard to the pricing of products and a buyer's desired relationship with the supplying firm (see Exhibit 3). One of the best ways for marketers to avoid the trap of excessive price competition is to develop market- and customer-level strategies that reflect those behaviors.

For example, loyal customers highly value specific things that a supplier does for them, such as technical support, quality products, and customer-oriented service agents. These customers are less concerned about the price than about the care they receive. They often have a single supplier and have no intention of qualifying another. Understanding who the loyal customers are and keeping their loyalty is critical.

The purpose of sales is not to use a lower price to close a sale, but to convince the customer that the price of a product is fair.

Conversely, price buyers care little about a long-term relationship with a supplier and want the lowest possible price for products. These commodity buyers have multiple vendors and encourage them to dive into kamikaze price wars. For consumer marketers, price shoppers who switch allegiances at the drop of a coupon provide few incremental dollars to the retailers who cater to them. For business-to-business sellers, these tend to be the buyers who scream loudest and dictate pricing and selling strategies. Unfortunately, the profits they generate rarely justify the attention they demand.

The price buyer's agenda is to get products at the lowest possible prices, so he or she uses tactics that force marketers to employ kamikaze pricing tactics even when it might not be the wisest thing to do. For the marketer, the trick is only to do business with the price buyer when it is profitable to do so and when it doesn't prompt a more profitable customer to purchase elsewhere.

Convenience buyers don't care whose product they purchase, and have little regard for price. They simply want it readily available. This often is the most profitable market segment, provided marketers can deliver their products at the locations preferred by these buyers. Unfortunately, this group exhibits little brand loyalty and provides sellers with no sustainable competitive advantage beyond their distribution systems.

Offer the best deal. Value buyers evaluate vendors on the basis of their ability to reduce costs through lower prices or more efficient operations, or to make the buyer's business more effective with superior features or services. From a customer perspective, this is the place to be; while both price and loyal buying have unique costs, value buying comes with the assumption that these customers are getting the best deal possible, given all factors of consumption. From a marketing perspective, firms that attract value customers get the loyal buyer as part of the bargain and sell to the price buyer only when it is profitable and reasonable.

Organizations that employ kamikaze pricing have a poor understanding of how their products create value for customers. This lack of understanding results in excessive reliance on price to obtain orders. Successful marketers use price as a tool to reflect the value of the product and implement systems in the organization to assure that value is delivered to customers and captured in the pricing.

The Five Cs

"Sell on quality, not on price" was once a popular marketing aphorism. Unfortunately, while product quality can reduce the seller's rework and inventory costs, it does little for customers. Selling the quality of a product is often not enough because buyers have difficulty quantifying its value and may be unwilling to pay for it. By focusing on quality, we miss the opportunity for customers to understand the true value that quality brings to the buyers of our products. Instead, resolving to "sell on value, not on price" focuses on understanding how pricing really should work. To avoid the rigors of price-based competition, marketers should adopt the five "Cs" of the value-based approach:

- Comprehend what drives customer value.
- Create value in product, service, and support.
- Communicate value in advertising.
- Convince customers of value in selling.
- Capture value in pricing strategy.

How a product provides customer value and which value-creation efforts best differentiate a product from the competition must be understood by marketers. When there is additional value that can be created, marketers need to do a better job creating it in their products, service, and support activities. Once a firm provides differentiating value to its customers, the primary responsibility of the marketer is to set up a communications system, including the salesperson, that educates the customer on the components of that value.

The purpose of sales is not to use a lower price to close a sale, but to convince the customer that the price of a product, which is based on its value in the market, is fair. Of course, most sales compensation systems do just the opposite, rewarding salespeople for closing a sale, regardless of the price. Salespeople who lack an understanding of a product's value often bend to a buyer's wishes and match a lower-value competitor's price. Product prices should reflect a fair portion of their value, and they should be fixed so salespeople will have to sell on the basis of value.

Companies that approach pricing as a process rather than an event can effectively break the spiral of kamikaze pricing.

Penetration pricing gains ground in markets against competitors, but extended use of this offensive tactic inevitably leads to kamikaze pricing and calamity in markets as competitors respond, cost savings disappear, and customers learn to ignore value. Good marketers employ such weapons selectively and only for limited periods of time to build profitable market position. They learn how to draw from a broad arsenal of offensive and defensive weapons, understanding how each will affect their overall long-term market conditions, and never losing sight of the overall objective of stable market conditions in which they can earn the most sustainable profit.

Additional Reading

Darlin, Damon (1996), "The Computer Industry's Mystery Man," *Forbes*, (April 8), 42.

Nagle, Thomas and Reed Holden (1995), *The Strategy and Tactics of Pricing*. New York: Prentice Hall.

Reichheld, Frederick F. (1996), *The Loyalty Effect*. Boston: Harvard Business School Press.

Shapiro, Eileen C. (1995), *Fad Surfing in the Boardroom*. Reading, Mass.: Addison-Wesley Publishing.

Taylor, William (1993), "Message and Muscle: An Interview with Swatch Titan Nicolas Hayek," *Harvard Business Review*, (March–April), 99–110.

Tzu, Sun (1988), *The Art of War*, translated by Thomas Cleary. Boston: Shambhala Publications.

About the Authors

Reed K. Holden is President of the Strategic Pricing Group Inc., Marlborough, Mass., where he has conducted numerous industry seminars in the United States and Asia on pricing and competitive strategy, business market research, and loyal buyer behavior. He also works with corporate clients as an educator and strategic analyst. Reed has more than 11 years of experience as a sales and marketing manager in the electrical and electronics industries. During that time, he specialized in the development and implementation of sales training and industrial marketing programs. He also was an Assistant Professor at Boston University's Graduate School of Management for nine years. He coauthored the second edition of *The Strategy and Tactics of Pricing* and "Profitable Pricing: Guidelines for Management" which was published in the third edition of the *AMA Management Handbook*.

Thomas T. Nagle is Chairman of the Strategic Pricing Group Inc., which helps firms in such diverse industries as telecommunications, pharmaceuticals, computer software, semiconductors, wholesale nursery, consumer retailing, and financial services develop pricing strategies. His seminars are offered in public programs and at major corporations in North and South America and in Europe. The second edition of Tom's book, *The Strategy and Tactics of Pricing: A Guide to Profitable Decision Making*, is used extensively as a text on the subject. He is the author of "Managing Price Competition," published in *MARKETING MANAGEMENT* (Spring 1993), and "Financial Analysis For Profit-Driven Pricing," published in *The Sloan Management Review* (1994). His articles also have appeared in the *AMA Handbook of Business Strategy*. Tom has taught at the University of Chicago and at Boston University and is currently on the executive program faculties of the University of Chicago.

Article 29

Discovering Hidden Pricing Power

Donald V. Potter

- *"Seeking Better Prices, Firms Haggle a Lot"*
- *"Price Revolt Spreading on Prescription Drugs"*
- *"Discounts Signal a National Price War"*
- *"Value Pricing Is Hot as Shrewd Consumers Seek Low-Cost Quality"*
- *"More Shoppers Bypass Big Name Brands and Steer Carts to Private Label Products"*
- *"Companies Find that Consumers Continue to Resist Price Boosts"*

Over the last few years, many companies have tried unsuccessfully to raise their prices, losing volume as customers shifted to lower-priced competitors or found a substitute for the product itself. Ultimately, many of these companies have had to lower prices again—sometimes dropping them even further than they were before the attempted price increase—in an effort to recapture lost share.

It doesn't have to be that way. Even in a mature and complex market, which is resistant to across-the-board price increases, there are still many ways to deftly raise effective prices and increase market share. Pricing policy, if wielded wisely, can still be a powerful tool.

A company's effective use of the pricing tool in a price-sensitive market requires more flexibility and market knowledge than is needed in a less hostile environment. Pricing opportunities in highly competitive markets are often hidden from the eyes of customers as well as other competitors. They have their greatest power when they remain veiled.

The path to these pricing opportunities is not hard to find. It lies in three actions management can take to use price effectively in a market that appears intolerant of increases:

- changing the structure of the price;
- building more subtlety into the pricing process; and
- exploiting pricing patterns common in other markets where price increases are difficult.

CHANGING THE PRICE STRUCTURE

The components of a price determine its structure. In a market with relatively little competition, a price structure tends to be simple, with few components and limited price variability. As a market becomes more competitive, however, the structure becomes more complex and prices far more variable (see "When Customers Take Charge of Pricing"). As this complexity develops, a firm can improve its effective price per unit by bringing more components into the pricing package. Sometimes this requires redefining the product as well.

> *Subtle and smart can win out over big and strong for a company using these "secret" techniques in a highly price-competitive market.*

Bundle Benefits

Many standard products offer options. As price competition heats up, a company may find opportunities to bundle options into a standard product in order to hold the price for the bundled product at the same level as the previous unbundled standard one. This works as long as the options cost less than the amount the price would have dropped. As the sport utility vehicle market began to take off in the early 1990s, for example, many companies jumped in with new versions. To hold its price, Chrysler responded by incorporating options, such as air conditioning and power steering, as standard equipment on its profitable and long-established Jeep Cherokee.

Another form of bundling is offering customers the right to buy or receive something else along with the product. These programs can be simple promotions or joint promotions with another brand. Marlboro cigarettes might simply offer jackets and watches adorned with the

When Customers Take Charge of Pricing

Why does a company have to deal with pricing complexity? Put simply, because customers demand it. As a market becomes more competitive, it is not the companies themselves or their competitors who determine prices, but the customers.

In a simple situation, the basic pricing structure may have only a few components. Every order has a price based on the product ordered, the customer's location, the order volume, and payment terms. The pricing process is therefore simple: The supplier commonly uses a short table to set price by product and volume ordered. Markets in which pricing is simple tend to be of two types: high-return, slow-growing, very stable markets, such as consumer goods; or very fast-growing markets, where the developing industry competitors are chronically short of capacity.

But increased industry competition brings pressures on suppliers to offer lower prices. The trigger event is usually overcapacity, which occurs when competitors bring additional products to the market and exceed the rate of growth in demand. Most competitors will then face the prospect of selling their excess capacity. Inevitably, some companies will discount their pricing sharply and drag down industry pricing. An example is the wireless communications industry of 1998. The influx of the PCS competitors into markets previously controlled by only two cellular service providers caused industry prices to plunge.

Price declines may continue while customers assume control over the prices they pay. Large customers begin getting significant discounts off list pricing. As a result, most customers begin to aggregate their purchasing volume in order to offer bigger volumes in return for lower prices. As this trend continues, even small customers will form themselves into cooperative buying groups to get lower prices in the marketplace. With time, customers bring other suppliers into their relationship in order to get price information or even pricing leverage over existing suppliers. They then begin offering all their suppliers a "last look" on the lowest of the prices offered, forcing them all to the lower price level. In the final extreme, customers may just dictate the price they plan to pay for the coming year.

During the 1980s, the auto manufacturers, rather than the steel companies, set steel prices. During the '90s, the same thing happened to the newsprint industry. The largest customers announced the prices they would pay for newsprint for the coming year and asked potential suppliers whether they would like to supply them at those prices. In an industry plagued with overcapacity, virtually all suppliers agreed to the customers' prices. Those who did not lost the largest newsprint customers.

As the competitive dynamics proceed, pricing becomes highly complex. Eventually there will be nearly as many prices as customers, and price information will confuse both customers and suppliers. A good example is the price of an airline ticket today. Walk from the front of a plane to the back and you are likely to find as many prices as seats. The reality of more complex pricing and more confusing information requires that a company develop more sophisticated pricing policies and processes.

Marlboro logo, while Lucky Stores, a large grocery chain owned by American Stores, offers a promotion with Continental Airlines in which customers can buy two discounted Continental tickets after spending $50 or more on groceries.

Rebate programs are also a form of bundling. These programs often have lower costs than the face value of the rebate either because some customers do not redeem the rebate or because the company makes the rebate contingent on some revenue-generating action of the customer. Examples of the simple rebate are common today in the auto industry, computer hardware items, and many software categories. In an example of a conditional rebate, The Sharper Image Company asked for and received rebates from its suppliers. Every time the supplier's product was displayed in the company's catalogs, the supplier paid its customer, Sharper Image, a rebate: $750 for the first time and $250 for each succeeding appearance.

Unbundle Benefits

Unbundling benefits takes the opposite tack from bundling. Here, the company removes a standard feature from the product package and makes it into an option. The company may reduce the price for the standard product, as Nissan did in the early 1990s with its 300ZX sports car. Nissan lowered the base price of the car by 4.5 percent under the pressure of falling automobile prices. At the same time, it eliminated the car's standard T-bar roof, which became an option. If the car was equipped with the T-bar roof, its price was higher than the base price.

In another form of unbundling, the company may leave the base price alone but simply charge for benefits that previously had been part of the product. As airline fares fell after deregulation, travel agencies, which based their commissions on a percentage of the ticket prices they wrote, found themselves squeezed for profits. So some began to charge for each time they booked flights with low ticket prices. In a similar case, National Car Rental System faced declining prices in the leisure auto rental market. One of its responses was to institute a cancellation fee on several of its bargain rate rental offers.

Offer Alternative Service Levels and Price Points

Sometimes making smaller changes to the product package through bundling and unbundling is not enough to arrest the price and profit decline. In these cases, the company may consider creating new price points to meet customer demands for low-priced products with a reduced level of benefits, or to offer some customers more benefits at higher levels of price and profitability.

A sharply falling price environment creates opportunities for creating new price points with lower service levels. Sometimes these new price points are simply the same products and services re-priced for use during low-demand periods. In the difficult airline business of the early 1990s, the Trump Shuttle, operating in the Northeast, cut fares by more than 50 percent for travel during off-peak hours. In other cases, the new low price point is a different product with a lower level of service. Marriott faced a difficult lodging environment in the early 1990s, and developed a number of advanced purchase product offerings with substantial savings. However, it demanded advanced payment and charged penalties for changes or cancellations of reservations. It also restricted the availability of the low-cost hotel rooms.

An alternative to offering a low price point is to offer a new premium price point with more benefits. Even tough markets will find a segment of customers willing to pay more for a better product. The tire manufacturing industry had been tough for a number of years when Goodyear designed and introduced the Aquatred, an all-season radial tire designed to provide better traction on wet roads. The company priced the tire about 10 percent higher than its previous top-of-the-line mass market tire, but the tire sold well and improved the company's profit position.

In a market where a whole fryer chicken sold for 69¢ a pound, Holly Farms offered a skinned and boned chicken breast that sold successfully at $4.59 a pound. Once selling a 16-ounce box of graham crackers for $2.39, Nabisco created some growth in this relatively lethargic market when it cut the crackers into teddy bear shapes, packaged them in single-serve bags, and charged $2.09 for just four ounces of product—a price level several times that of graham crackers.

Link Future Purchases to Current Transaction

Some markets allow a company to improve its future position by using the pricing tool. One example is to offer "buy backs" to increase the chance that the company will win both this purchase and the next to follow. A few years ago, auto makers used this technique with rental car companies. The Big Three sold their products to the rental car industry with agreements to repurchase the cars after a period of time. The arrangement enabled the rental firms to offer their customers fresh products at a known price, and raised the odds that the auto manufacturer would be in a favorable position to obtain the business when the rental firm rotated its product line.

Another variant of this technique is to offer a fixed future price to some or all customers. College tuition has been rising faster than inflation for a number of years. Feeling student and parent resistance to this trend, some schools have begun to offer fixed tuition to any current student who returns to the school.

Change Price Effectiveness Period

Some prices are effective only for a single order. Others are effective for a long period of time. A company can change this component of its pricing structure to lock in potentially volatile customer volume or to obtain a higher price over a period when it expects prices to fall.

The credit card issuing market is gradually becoming more competitive and its customers growing more price sensitive. In response, some astute credit card issuers have lengthened the period of effectiveness for their very low introductory interest rates, thereby gaining market share. Some competitors in the cellular phone industry offered low prices for extended contract lengths because they expected prices to fall throughout the contract period with the advent of competition from the new personal communications services. They bet that the average price on their long-term contracts would beat the average on short-term contracts that had to be continually renewed.

Substitute Components of the Price

Companies in challenging pricing environments may have the option to substitute components in their price structure. They may use new components that track costs more precisely or that make the price more acceptable to the customer. As market prices become more competitive, companies may shift their pricing components to more closely match pricing with their cost structure. After several years of intense competition in the air express market, margins were getting thin on some of the business. Federal Express took the lead in changing the price structure of the industry. Instead of using flat rate price components, it began charging for its package delivery services according to the distance a package travels. The result was that rates went down for short-distance packages and up somewhat for long-distance ones. Price and cost moved in parallel and margins improved. The rest of the industry followed FedEx's lead in short order.

Fleming Companies, a large wholesale grocer, faced many complaints on its maze of wholesale grocery pricing. In response, the company introduced a new pricing system, passing on all the allowances and rebates it received from its suppliers. In turn, it charged its customers for the actual net cost of the goods they purchased plus a separate charge for storage, shipping, and handling. The result was a pricing structure more closely tied to the company's cost structure.

Sometimes companies can change price components to better match what customers are trying to achieve with their purchases. A few money managers have abandoned the practice of basing all their fees on a percentage of assets managed. Some have increased the proportion of the fees they receive from the profits their customers realize on the assets managed.

The fast food industry watched as pricing on individual products fell for several years. Then McDonald's, followed by others, introduced a price-per-meal concept called an "extra value meal," offering customers a low price for what most of them wanted, a whole meal. Though the meal price was much lower than the a la carte prices, the companies realized far more volume in drinks and fries than they had seen before. Customers got a good price per meal, the industry got far more volume, and both sides benefited.

Shift Some of the Price to Suppliers

In some markets, the company has enough market power to shift some of the price decline back to its suppliers. Over the last several years, the retail grocery industry has developed and fine-tuned "slotting allowances," which are payments made by the suppliers to the retail grocery chains to win space on the grocers' shelves. These slotting allowances increase the margin on the goods sold by the retail industry and enable it to avoid some price raises for the retail shopper.

> "American Express, as a supplier to The Sharper Image, enabled the latter to cut its effective price to its customers by 15 percent, while The Sharper Image shifted some of the cost of the discount back to American Express."

Such an approach also offers the possibility of joint marketing arrangements. The Sharper Image stores appealed to an attractive set of upscale consumers, who were just the segment American Express wanted to help build usage of its charge card. So the two companies entered into a marketing promotion. A customer who made a purchase of $75 or more from The Sharper Image and charged it with an American Express card received 15 percent off the purchase. American Express, as a supplier to The Sharper Image, enabled the latter to cut its effective price to its customers by 15 percent, while The Sharper Image shifted some of the cost of the discount back to American Express.

BUILDING MORE SUBTLETY INTO THE PRICING PROCESS

As a market becomes very competitive and complex, prices on a large part of the volume sold are not set by competitors offering lower prices to gain or preserve share. In most situations, competitors have very little economic incentive to offer low prices in a highly competitive marketplace. If a competitor is already in a customer relationship, it needs a great deal of additional volume through a greater share of that relationship in order to justify the price decrease it suffers on its base business with the customer.

If the competitor offering a low price is outside the customer relationship and trying to enter, it faces two problems. First, the customer is likely to offer its incumbent suppliers a "last look"—the opportunity to match the low price being offered by the competitor outside the relationship. If any incumbent supplier matches the low price, the challenging competitor is unlikely to gain any share. In highly price-competitive markets, incumbents face strong pressure to match low prices and often do so. Second, there is some chance that this lower price can spread to the challenger's own customers, reducing the margins on those relationships.

In a highly competitive marketplace, competitors' offers of a low price do account for some price movement. But most movement seems to come as a result of customers demanding lower prices from their suppliers, who in turn grant the lower prices in order to preserve the customer relationships. Not all customers have the same incentive, savvy, and leverage in seeking advantageous prices, however.

By developing a pricing process with greater subtlety, a company can realize more revenue overall, even when prices are falling. Subtlety means a number of things. It means that any single price decline should apply to as little as possible of the firm's market volume. It means raising prices on separate ancillary benefits and services that customers do not consider when making their buying decisions. It means delaying, for a short period of time, price cuts demanded by some customers. Subtlety may also mean using discounted products more strategically to build relationships with the best customers.

Set Prices Selectively, Not Across the Board

Many companies use a broad pricing process that applies to a large segment of customers in order to contain the cost of administering the process. A product list price applicable to all customers is an example. So, too, are prices established for large customer segments, geographic regions, and customer types.

But broad pricing can be costly when the process is the pricing tool of choice in a highly competitive marketplace. Such costs are often invisible because they are opportunity costs. A broad pricing process brings the prices for all customers to the level of the customer who negotiates the lowest price. When prices are set by customers, some customers will always be below average in pricing. Others will chronically pay above-average prices. The most aggressive and demanding negotiators among the customers determine the price levels for all the customers in the broad segment. The opportunity loss occurs from those who would willingly have paid higher prices had they not been unilaterally granted a price decrease by the supplier.

In a difficult environment, a more profitable approach is to price surgically, offering different prices to ever more precisely defined customer segments. The pricing process reaches its ideal state when there is the least opportunity loss of pricing revenue. When the company reaches a separate price for each transaction with each customer, it has pushed its process to the ultimate state. Every price decline then applies only to that specific transaction.

One company facing a tough pricing market developed what it called its "cat across the carpet" program. A senior executive stated that his objective with any price cut request from a customer was to be like a cat being dragged by its tail across a carpeted floor with its claws dug deeply into the carpet. Before this program was initiated, the company had operating margins of 8 percent, and was using a pricing process that set prices applicable to wide geographic territories centered around manufacturing plants. With the "cat across the carpet" program, it instituted customer-by-customer pricing, which increased revenue per unit and operating profits by nearly a full percentage point. This profit improvement was the result of customers who were willing to purchase at somewhat higher prices than other customers in the industry.

A selective pricing approach works better in some markets than others. It works best in industries where members of distribution channels are the primary customers. In highly competitive markets with channel customers, intense price competition will often lead to customer-by-customer pricing. Selective pricing is not as effective in markets where consumers are the primary customers.

Move Prices in Smaller Increments

Another difficulty companies face in moving from a relatively easy to a more difficult pricing environment is the amount by which prices traditionally move. Industry customers have become conditioned to expect price movements, both up and down, in specific percentage or dollar increments. An example is the residential fiberglass insulation industry, where prices move in "sixes and threes" based on percentage differences from the current price. In other words, by common practice, prices in the insulation industry move up or down by at least 3 percent at a time. The size of this required price movement creates an opportunity loss for the supplier in a falling price market. When conditions require a price reduction, it may be possible to achieve the price position demanded by the customers by making relatively small moves. In fact, one industry competitor did just that.

Abandoning the traditional "sixes and threes" entirely, it moved to "net pricing," quoting the customer a specific price per unit purchased rather than a specific discount on a putative list price. As market prices fell, the company's average discount was less than the 3 percent common in the industry, yet it was still able to maintain and even grow its market share.

> *"With the 'cat across the carpet' program, it instituted customer-by-customer pricing, which increased revenue per unit and operating profits by nearly a full percentage point."*

Raise Invisible Prices

Sometimes, nothing a company does will enable it to raise prices on a standard product or reduce the rate of the price decline. It can then look for the opportunity to raise less visible prices.

Ancillary products and services usually have less visible prices. They have a price separate from that of the base product with which they are associated. The industry may have "unbundled" these services in an effort to raise effective prices in an earlier period. Customers often do not consider these ancillary services and their invisible prices when making buying decisions, or they assume they will not use them. Many hotel customers do not consider phone charges they will pay while staying in the room. Phone customers may sign on with a low-cost, long-distance carrier and not consider having to pay high charges for directory assistance. Many catalog retailer customers forget the shipping and handling charges in the price of the catalog's products. Each of these services provides opportunities for price increases to ease the pressure on competitive pricing for the base product.

A major credit card issuer found its profits squeezed by falling prices for its credit card products. Its up-front fees had disappeared for all but its high-end credit cards with rewards. Interest rates on card lending were declining. So the company analyzed its position on other fees, such as late payment fees, returned check fees, and so on. Market research indicated that customers never considered these ancillary service fees in their decision to add or retain a credit card company. So it compared its position on these fees with its competition and found itself at or below the industry average on all of them. To ease its profit pressure, the company raised all the fees to the high end of the competitive range and realized several million dollars of additional profit in the process. Customer volume continued to increase at its former rate.

Taken to extremes, raising invisible prices might get a company in trouble. Trouble happens when pricing or price administration falls badly out of line with that of competitors.

Match Price Moves to the Market

Price declines spread through a marketplace at a relatively predictable rate. The largest customers receive the decline very quickly. But for smaller customers, prices tend to fall at a slower rate. It may take up to six months for a given price decline to spread fully through a marketplace. This seems to happen because customers determine what prices they should be paying by watching their peers' advertisements or asking their peer companies what they are paying for the products. Once a customer suspects that a peer has received a lower price on purchases, it will usually demand a lower price from its supplier. In other cases, the customer simply guesses that it can extract a lower price from the supplier, and demands it. When a supplier company faces this predicament, it may find itself able to delay, for a short period of time, the demanded price decrease.

To accomplish any delay, the company will need to analyze how fast price declines typically spread across the market. Then it must determine whether the current price decline has reached the competitors or the peers of the customer who has demanded the lower price. This information enables the company to negotiate delays where appropriate. Knowing how to negotiate in this way requires an astute and well-informed sales force capable of monitoring both prices by customer type and competitors' pricing policies.

Use Discounts Strategically to Build Relationships With Desirable Clients

There is an irony in the way some firms confront markets with excess capacity and falling prices. Low prices are painful for any management group because they destroy profitability. But when confronted with falling prices, some managements use discounted products tactically rather than strategically. Tactically, they use the low prices to sell off excess volume that exists for a period. The beneficiaries of this excess, heavily discounted product are usually the firm's least attractive customers—the "sludge" (see the box below). Some or all of this volume could be used strategically to build relationships with the firm's most desirable customers.

A large producer of an international product found itself with excess capacity. The company's production process required that the manufacturing facility run at all times, so this excess capacity quickly translated into excess inventory. To get rid of some of it, the company discounted the product to its most price-sensitive customers and sold the remainder on the international market, where it had to offer even bigger discounts because of being viewed as an unreliable long-term supplier. The price-sensitive customers and the international business were the least profitable relationships for the company. Yet these customers were the principle beneficiaries of very low prices for the excess product. The company had used its volume requiring a discount tactically, and missed an opportunity to build stronger relationships with strategic customers.

So the company decided to revamp its approach. It began offering discounts to its most attractive customers in special programs designed to develop their own

---

Cutting Out Customer Sludge

Many companies have customers that are not profitable today and will not be profitable in the long term because they will never return the company's capital cost over a business cycle. We call such business "customer sludge" because it slows down the long-term performance of the company. Customer sludge often includes:

•*Churners*: These customers will change suppliers as frequently as they receive a price offer lower than the one they currently pay. They are unprofitable because they rarely stay long enough to return the investment in establishing them as customers in the first place.

•*Tough negotiators*: These customers simply negotiate harder than others. Customers who pay below-average prices tend to pay these low prices in both good and bad times. Sometimes the prices are low enough that the customers are not attractive enough to support the company's investment.

•*High-cost segments*: These customers demand unusually high levels of service. Many of them are small to medium-sized firms that the company's management information system misses with its cost allocation system.

In the short term, while the pricing in the market is very difficult, the company will usually need to continue to sell to most customers who offer low returns. These sales may not produce an attractive return on investment, but they do produce cash—more cash than the company would realize by not producing and selling to these customers.

Nevertheless, a company can lay the groundwork for getting rid of such customers by developing alternative outlets for the volume they purchase. This may be accomplished in part by offering special business-building programs to the company's most attractive customers. By offering either low price or extra benefits, these programs can then build up the good customers' business, thereby increasing the company's future sales and solidifying the customer relationships.

When "sludge" customer volume is no longer crucial, a company can raise these prices again, selling to those customers only if they are willing to pay a price that makes the sale worthwhile. As one executive put it, "If they will not pay the price we ask, they will be politely invited to buy somewhere else."

business and profitability. The product was still discounted, but the discounts were lower, and the customer loyalty that resulted was far greater than with the international and price-sensitive customers. By using the product strategically, the company increased its profitability and long-term customer retention.

Companies may resist the idea of such a flexible, complex pricing process, reasoning that the cost of operating it would erode the price advantages gained. It is true that pricing management and IT resources have real, visible costs. However, those costs are likely to be coming down as more sophisticated software and computing power become ever more available. Furthermore, the revenue benefits of a more flexible pricing policy, though a bit harder to measure than IT costs, are nevertheless real as well.

EXPLOITING PATTERNS COMMON IN DIFFICULT MARKETS

Tough markets tend to have a number of characteristics in common, among which are pricing patterns that seem to occur in many markets facing declining or low prices. These pricing patterns offer both follower and leader companies the opportunities to raise their effective prices. Followers can price against the leader in some cases or follow the leader in others. Leaders can seek out segments that tolerate higher prices.

Price Against the Leader

As market prices deteriorate from previously attractive levels, the leading firms in the industry may offer follower firms the opportunity to gain share against them. The followers can use the price tool in the face of the leaders' reluctance to cut prices and suffer the margin consequences.

Large companies, especially the top competitors in any market, are reluctant to cut prices when confronted with a declining price environment. They often believe they can sustain their higher price levels because they view their product as superior and their customers as more loyal than the average in the industry. In fact, experience tends to suggest, many of these leaders fall into the "Leader's Trap."

The "Leader's Trap" is the term for a situation in which the industry leader loses volume and suffers a decline in unit pricing at the same time. When offered very low prices, some customers will defect from the leader to the low-priced competitor, which in turn uses its resulting business and often high capacity utilization rates to improve its reputation and product quality while continuing to offer low prices. The improved reputation and product quality then attract more of the leader's customers and provide more profitability to the competitor. As the leader loses volume and market share,

it eventually must lower prices to halt share loss. It then has both lower volumes and lower prices. The prices are often the same as they might have been had the company reduced prices earlier and avoided the share loss. The leader can then find itself under more margin pressure than the average industry competitor.

The personal computer industry in the early 1990s offers a good example of the Leader's Trap. Both IBM and Compaq, the industry's unquestioned leaders, held prices high in the face of strong growth by the PC "clone" manufacturers. After losing volume, Compaq reversed its pricing stance and recaptured much of the share it had lost to the clones. IBM was much slower to reduce its prices to match those of the clones, and continued to lose both share and profitability for some time.

The tendency of industry leaders to fall into this trap offers pricing opportunities to other players in the industry. In marketplaces with deteriorating prices, these followers can continue to discount against the leader and take away share, knowing that the leader is not likely to respond until a significant part of its share has defected. Even then, at least some of this share will remain with the discounting competitor. Some customers who tend to move on low price offers in a deteriorating price market are often strategically attractive and loyal customers. They would not normally be price buyers. But they do move to the discounting competitor because they come to believe that the competitor's product is the functional equivalent of the leader's product.

Follow the Leader

The industry leader's natural tendency to demand a high price offers another opportunity for a follower company: attempt to follow the industry leader into its relationships.

Industry leaders, especially branded ones, will tend to have a higher effective price in most customer segments than will follower firms. Leaders believe they are entitled to a somewhat higher price. Many customers agree with them and willingly pay it. Many of these customers will have more than one supplier in their relationships, however. So although the leader may be the primary supplier to a customer, there may be room for a secondary or tertiary role to be filled by a follower who seeks to benefit from the leader's ability to extract higher prices.

A follower can ride the leader's coattails to better pricing as long as it does not use pricing alone as its major value thrust. That would defeat the purpose. In the average customer relationship, the primary and secondary suppliers both receive the same net prices. The same may hold true for some, though certainly not all, tertiary positions. The follower can then use its marketing efforts to secure secondary or perhaps selected tertiary positions with the leader's best customers. One follower firm employed this strategy and found that its average price realization when following the industry leader was one to two percentage points higher than in customer relationships that it or other competitors led.

Seek Out Segments That Will Tolerate Higher Prices

Industry leaders can also take advantage of pricing patterns that are common to difficult pricing environments. Specifically, they should evaluate prices for their sole-source customers and for any channel members who carry their product as a convenience for the channel's own customers.

Sole-source customers may offer an opportunity for gradual unit price realization improvements. One company analyzed two separate businesses, one of which had moderate to low price competition and the other intense competition. In the former, sole-source customers tended to pay, on average, one to two percentage points more than did customers that had multiple suppliers in their relationships. On the other hand, the intensely price-competitive market saw sole-source customers paying one to two percentage points below average. When the company researched the reasons for this disparity, it found that the pricing difference in the tough marketplace was due primarily to the sales force, which was so concerned with protecting the sole-source relationships that it offered those customers lower prices than they needed in order to remain quite competitive in the marketplace.

Another case of a segment that will tolerate higher prices are "accommodation" customers. Industry leaders may have some members of their distribution channels who buy solely to accommodate the channel's own customers. In marketing parlance, the end users are creating "pull through the channel" for the leader's products. Left to their own devices, these channel members would rely on other suppliers for all their purchases. As nonstrategic customers, they offer the company the chance to recoup some of its investment in a strong brand name through the pricing mechanism.

A well-known branded industry leader evaluated all of its channel customers that had placed it in a secondary or lower role in their relationships. Whenever the company identified customers who carried its products as an accommodation for their own customers, it evaluated the opportunity to raise its prices with them. In several cases, it raised its prices by 10 to 15 percent over those of the other incumbents in the customer relationship. The company suffered very little volume loss as a result of these price moves because the channel customers felt they had to carry its products.

Any change in pricing, even in hidden prices, requires careful judgment in implementation. The management team must weigh the benefits of higher profitability against some of the potential costs of customer ill will. The best price changes benefit both buyer and seller. Buyers pay the price they deem fair, and the sellers receive the prices that allow them to service buyers' needs.

As a company moves from a less price-sensitive to a more price-competitive marketplace, the nature of its response to pricing must change. In a less competitive market, pricing is like sumo wrestling—the biggest and most powerful competitor usually wins the match. The highly price-sensitive market, though, is much more like judo. Here, the stronger force may often lie with the opponent, and the company's response is to use both leverage and the opponent's own momentum to gain an advantage. With the hidden power of pricing, a company facing a highly price-competitive market can use knowledge and subtlety to improve its returns and share.

Donald V. Potter is the president of StrategyStreet.com.

The Old Pillars *of* New Retailing

Looking for the silver bullet that will solve your retailing woes? It doesn't exist. The best retailers lay a foundation for success by creating customer value in a handful of fundamental ways.

by Leonard L. Berry

EVERYONE WHO GLANCES AT A newspaper knows that the retailing world is brutally competitive. The demise of Montgomery Ward in the realm of bricks and mortar as well as the struggles of eToys on-line—to choose only two recent examples—make it clear that no retailer can afford to be complacent because of previous successes or rosy predictions about the future of commerce.

Despite the harsh realities of retailing, the illusion persists that magical tools, like Harry Potter's wand, can help companies overcome the problems of fickle consumers, price-slashing competitors, and mood swings in the economy. The wishful thinking holds that retailers will thrive if only they communicate better with customers through e-mail, employ hidden cameras to learn how customers make purchase decisions, and analyze scanner data to tailor special offers and manage inventory.

But the truth of the matter is, there are no quick fixes. Yes, technology can help any business operate more effectively, but many new advances are still poorly understood—and in any case, retailing can't be reduced to tools and techniques. Over the past eight years, I've analyzed dozens of retail companies to understand the underlying differences between outstanding and mediocre performers. My research includes interviews with senior and middle managers and frontline employees, observations of store operations, and extensive reviews of published and internal company materials. I've found that the best retailers create value for their customers in five interlocking ways. Doing a good job in just three or four of the ways won't cut it; competitors will rush to exploit weakness in any of the five areas. If one of the pillars of a successful retailing operation is missing, the whole edifice is weakened.

The key is focusing on the total customer experience. Whether you're running physical stores, a catalog business, an e-commerce site, or a combination of the three, you have to offer customers superior solutions to their needs, treat them with real respect, and connect with them on an emotional level. You also have to set prices fairly and make it easy for people to find what they need, pay for it, and move on. These pillars sound simple on paper, but they are difficult to implement in the real world. Taking each one in turn, we'll see how some retailers have built successful operations by attending to these commonsense ways of dealing with customers, and how others have failed to pay them the attention they require.

Pillar 1: Solve Your Customers' Problems

It has become commonplace for companies to talk about selling solutions rather than products or services. But what does this really mean for retailers? Put simply, it means that customers usually shop for a reason: they have a problem—a need—and the retailer hopes to provide the solution. It's not enough, for example, just to sell high-quality apparel—many retailers do that. Focusing on solutions means employing salespeople who know how to help customers find clothing that fits and flatters, having tailors on staff and at the ready, offering home delivery, and happily placing special orders. Every retailer hopes to meet its customers' pressing needs; some do it much better than others.

The Container Store provides its customers with superior solutions. The 22-store chain, based in Dallas, averages double-digit annual sales growth by selling something that absolutely everyone needs: storage and organization products. From boxes and trunks to hangers, trays, and shelving systems, each store carries up to 12,000 different products.

The Container Store's core strategy is the same today as it was in 1978, when the company was founded: to improve customers' lives by giving them more time and space. The company accomplishes this mission well. It starts with the selection of merchandise, which must meet criteria for visibility, accessibility, and versatility. The company's philosophy is that its products should allow people to see what they've stored and get at it easily. The merchandise must also be versatile enough to accommodate customers' particular requirements.

Store organization is another key ingredient of superior solutions at the Container Store. The merchandise is organized in sections such as kitchen, closet, laundry, office, and so on. Many products are displayed in several sections because they can solve a variety of problems. A sweater box, for example, can also store office supplies. Plastic trash cans can also be used for dog food and recyclables. Individual products are often combined and sold as a system—thus, parents in the store who want to equip their children for summer camp may find a trunk filled with a laundry bag, a toothbrush case, a first-aid pouch, leakproof bottles, a "critter catcher," and other items.

Great service is another component of the Container Store's ability to solve its customers' storage prob-

lems. The company is very careful about hiring; it patiently waits until it finds just the right person for a position. Container Store employees are well trained to demonstrate how products work and to propose solutions to complex home organizational problems. They are also treated very well, both in terms of pay and in less tangible ways. In fact, the Container Store was ranked the best place to work in the country in 1999 and 2000 by *Fortune* magazine.

A relentless focus on solutions may sound simple, but it's not. The Container Store has many imitators, but none have matched it. Many businesses have only the fuzziest concept of selling solutions. Department store chains, for example, have stumbled in recent years. They lost their one-stop shopping advantage by eliminating many merchandise categories outside of apparel and housewares. And even as they focused on apparel, they lost ground both to specialty retailers that have larger category selections and to discounters that have lower prices. Finally, they lost their customer service advantage by employing salespeople who often are little more than poorly trained order takers. As a result, these stores do a relatively poor job of solving customers' problems. That's probably why only 72% of consumers shopped in department stores in 2000 compared with 85% in 1996.

Clearly, the lesson here is that you must understand what people need and how you're going to fill that need better than your competitors. The Container Store has figured this out; many department stores and other struggling retailers must go back to the beginning and answer these basic questions.

Pillar 2: Treat Customers with R-e-s-p-e-c-t

The best retailers show their customers what Aretha Franklin sang about: respect. Again, this is absolutely basic, and most retail executives would say that of course they

treat customers with respect. But it just isn't so.

Everyone has stories to tell about disrespectful retailing. You're in an electronics store, looking for assistance to buy a DVD player or a laptop computer. You spot a couple of employees by their uniforms and badges, but they're deep in conversation. They glance in your direction but continue to ignore you. After awhile, you walk out, never to return.

Or you're in a discount store, looking for planters that have been advertised at a low price. You go to the store's garden center but cannot find the planters. This time, you succeed in flagging down an employee. You ask about the planters, but she just mumbles "I dunno" and walks away. Frustrated, you go to the customer service desk and ask the clerk where you might find the advertised planters. He suggests that you try the garden center. Once again, you head for the exit.

It's easy to go on. Stories about women trying to buy cars, as everyone knows, are enough to make your hair curl. The fact is, disrespectful retailing is pervasive. In the 2000 Yankelovich Monitor study of 2,500 consumers, 68% of those surveyed agreed with the statement that "Most of the time, the service people that I deal with for the products and services that I buy don't care much about me or my needs."

Disrespectful retailing isn't just about bored, rude, and unmotivated service workers. Cluttered, poorly organized stores, lack of signage, and confusing prices all show lack of respect for customers.

The best retailers translate the basic concept of respect into a set of practices built around people, policies, and place:

- They select, prepare, and manage their people to exhibit competence, courtesy, and energy when dealing with customers.
- They institute policies that emphasize fair treatment of customers—regardless of their age, gender, race, appearance, or size

of purchase or account. Likewise, their prices, returns policy, and advertising are transparent.

- They create a physical space, both inside and outside the store, that is carefully designed to value customers' time.

In 1971, a 30-year-old entrepreneur named Len Riggio bought a floundering Manhattan bookshop called Barnes & Noble. Today, Barnes & Noble is the nation's largest bookseller, with fiscal 1999 sales of $3.3 billion. Respect for the customer has been at the heart of the company's rise.

Riggio's biggest idea was that books appeal to most everyone, not just to intellectuals, writers, and students in cosmopolitan cities. Riggio listened to prospective customers who wanted bigger selections of books, more convenient locations, and less intimidating environments. He put superstores in all types of communities, from big cities like Atlanta and Chicago, to smaller cities like Midland, Texas, and Reno, Nevada. His respect for the customer led him to create stores with spacious and comfortable interiors, easy chairs for relaxing with a book, and Starbucks coffee bars. To this day, he considers his best decision the installation of easy-to-find public restrooms in the stores. As he said in a recent speech, "You work so hard and invest so much to get people to visit your store, why would you want them to have to leave?"

Besides the large selection of books, the stores also have an active calendar of author signings, poetry readings, children's events, and book discussion groups. Many Barnes & Noble superstores have become a social arena in which busy consumers—who normally rush in and out of other stores—linger.

Riggio sees the Internet as much more than a way to deliver books to customers; it's another opportunity to listen to them and thus show respect for them. He views the store network and Barnesandnoble.com as portals to each other. Customers can ask salespeople at Internet ser-

vice counters to search Barnesandnoble.com for out-of-stock books, for customer reviews of titles that interest them, and for information about authors, such as other books they've published. Customers in a superstore can order the books they want on-line and have them shipped either to that store or to any other address. If a return is necessary, customers can bring their on-line purchase back to the store.

The value of respect often gets little more than lip service from retailers. Some companies wait until it's too late to put words into action.

Pillar 3: **Connect with Your Customers' Emotions**

Most retailers understand in principle that they need to connect emotionally with consumers; a good many don't know how to (or don't try to) put the principle into practice. Instead, they neglect the opportunity to make emotional connections and put too much emphasis on prices. The promise of low prices may appeal to customers' sense of reason, but it does not speak to their passions.

Many U.S. furniture retailers are guilty of ignoring consumers' emotions. Although the average size of new homes in the country has grown by 25% since 1980, furniture accounts for a lower percentage of total U.S. consumer spending today (1%) than it did in 1980 (1.2%). Making consumers wait up to two months to receive their furniture contributes to these poor results. How can consumers get emotionally involved in products they know they won't see for weeks?

Poor marketing also hurts the industry. Most furniture stores focus strictly on price appeals, emphasizing cost savings rather than the emotional lift that can come from a new look in the home. "We don't talk about how easy it can be to make your home more attractive," says Jerry Epperson, an investment banker who specializes in the furni-

ture industry. "All we talk about is 'sale, sale, sale' and credit terms."

Great retailers reach beyond the model of the rational consumer and strive to establish feelings of closeness, affection, and trust. The opportunity to establish such feelings is open to any retailer, regardless of the type of business or the merchandise being sold. Everyone is emotionally connected to some retailers—from local businesses such as the wine merchant who always remembers what you like; to national companies like Harley-Davidson, which connects people through its Harley Owners Group; to catalog retailer Coldwater Creek, which ships a substitute item to customers who need to make returns before the original item is sent back.

One retailer that has connected especially well with its target market in recent years is Journeys, a Nashville, Tennessee-based chain of shoe stores located primarily in shopping malls. The chain focuses on selling footwear to young men and women between the ages of 15 and 25. Started in 1987, Journeys didn't take off until 1995 when new management took over. The chain has achieved double-digit comparable-store sales increases in five of the six years since then and is now expanding by as many as 100 new stores per year.

Journeys has penetrated the skepticism and fickleness that are characteristic of many teens. By keeping a finger on the pulse of its target market, the company consistently has the right brands available for this especially brand-conscious group of consumers. Equally important, it creates the right store atmosphere—the stores pulsate with music, video, color, and brand merchandising.

A Journeys store is both welcoming and authentic to young people; it is simultaneously energetic and laidback. Journeys' employees are typically young—the average age of a store manager is about 25—and they dress as they please. Customers frequently visit a store in groups just to hang out; salespeople exert no pressure to buy. And everyone, whether they've made a purchase or not, usually leaves with a giveaway—for instance, a key chain, a compact-disc case, a promotional T-shirt, or one of the 10 million or so stickers the stores give out over the course of a year. The stickers, which usually feature one of the brands Journeys sells, often end up on backpacks, skateboards, school lockers, or bathroom mirrors. Journeys also publishes a bimonthly magazine, *Dig*, that is available in the stores, and it runs a Web site that seeks to replicate the atmosphere of its stores. The number of site visits explodes whenever the company's commercials appear on MTV.

Journeys works in large part because it has created an atmosphere that connects emotionally with the young people it serves. Other retailers should bear in mind that it takes more than a room full of products with price tags on them to draw people in.

Pillar 4: Set the Fairest (Not the Lowest) Prices

Prices are about more than the actual dollars involved. If customers suspect that the retailer isn't playing fair, prices can also carry a psychological cost. Potential buyers will not feel comfortable making purchases if they fear that prices might be 30% lower next week, or if certain charges have only been estimated, or if they are unsure whether an advertised sale price represents a genuine markdown.

Consider some of the pricing tactics commonly used by certain home improvement retailers. One well-known company advertises products as "special buys" even though it has not lowered the regular prices. Another purposely misrepresents a competitor's prices on price-comparison signs within its stores. Still another company promotes lower-grade merchandise implying that it is top quality. One retailer puts a disclaimer in its ads that reads: "Prices in this ad may be different from the

actual price at time of purchase. We adjust our prices daily to the lumber commodity market." The disclaimer paves the way for the retailer to raise its prices regardless of the advertised price.

Excellent retailers seek to minimize or eliminate the psychological costs associated with manipulative pricing. Most of these retailers follow the principles of "everyday fair pricing" instead of "everyday low pricing." A fact of retail life is that no retailer, not even Wal-Mart, can truthfully promise customers that it will always have the lowest prices. An uncomfortable truth for many retailers is that their "lowest price anywhere" positioning is a crutch for the lack of value-adding innovation. Price is the only reason they give customers to care.

Retailers can implement a fair-pricing strategy by clearing two hurdles. First, they must make the cultural and strategic transition from thinking value equals price to realizing that value is the total customer experience. Second, they must understand the principles of fair pricing and muster the courage needed to put them into practice. Retailers who price fairly sell most goods at regular but competitive prices and hold legitimate sales promotions. They make it easy to compare their prices with those of competitors, and they avoid hidden charges. They don't raise prices to take advantage of temporary blips in demand, and they stand behind the products they sell.

Zane's Cycles in Branford, Connecticut, is one of the most successful independent bicycle retailers in the United States. Zane's has grown its one-store business at least 20% every year since it was founded in 1981, selling 4,250 bicycles in 2000 along with a full array of accessories. The company's success illustrates the appeal of fair pricing.

Zane's sells better bike brands with prices starting at $250. It stands behind what it sells with a 30-day test-drive offer (customers can return a bike within 30 days and ex-

change it for another) and a 90-day price protection guarantee (if a buyer finds the same bike in Connecticut at a lower price within 90 days, Zane's will refund the difference plus 10%). Zane's also offers free lifetime service on all new bicycles it sells; it was likely the first bicycle retailer in the United States to take this step. The promise of lifetime service includes annual tune-ups, brake and gear adjustments, wheel straightening and more.

Zane's holds only one promotional sale a year, a three-day spring weekend event featuring discounts on all products. Vendors and former employees come to work at the huge event—some even fly in to participate. Customers who purchase a bicycle at Zane's within 90 days before the sale are encouraged to return during the event for a refund based on the discounted price of their bike. The company refunded about $3,000 during the 2000 sale, but most of that money remained in the store because customers bought more gear. Zane's sold 560 bicycles during the 2000 sale—that's more than the typical one-store U.S. bicycle retailer sells in an entire year. And yet the limited duration of the sale means that Zane's sells about 85% of its bicycles at the regular price.

When Connecticut passed a bike-helmet law in 1992, Zane's sold helmets to kids at cost rather than take advantage of legislated demand. Owner Chris Zane convinced area school administrators to distribute flyers to students under 12 announcing that policy. "We sold a ton of helmets and made a lot of new friends for the store," Zane says. "Our customers trust us. They come in and say, 'I am here to get a bike. What do I need?' They have confidence in our ability to find them just the right bike at a fair price and to stand behind what we sell."

Constant sales, markdowns on over-inflated prices, and other forms of pressure pricing may boost sales in the short term. Winning customers' trust through fair pricing will pay off in the long term.

Are Your Retailing Pillars Solid—or Crumbling?

	Inferior Retailers...	Superior Retailers...
Solutions	gather products, stack them on shelves, put price tags on them, and wonder where their customers are.	consider what people really need and how they can meet that particular need better than competitors can.
Respect	are staffed by people who don't know what customers want and aren't about to interrupt their conversations to find out.	actually train and manage the salespeople they hire so that they are courteous, energetic, and helpful to customers.
Emotions	act as if their customers are Spock-like Vulcans who make purchases solely according to cold logic.	recognize that everything about a retail experience sends a message to customers that goes to the heart, not just the brain.
Pricing	focus exclusively on their supposed low prices, often because they have nothing else of value to offer customers.	focus on having fair prices instead of playing mind games with "special offers," fine print, and bogus sales.
Convenience	are open for business when it's convenient for them, close checkout lanes when it's convenient for them, deliver products when it's convenient for them, and so on.	understand that people's most precious commodity in the modern world is time and do everything they can to save as much of it as possible for their customers.

Pillar 5: Save Your Customers' Time

Many consumers are poor in at least one respect: they lack time. Retailers often contribute to the problem by wasting consumers' time and energy in myriad ways, from confusing store layouts to inefficient checkout operations to inconvenient hours of business. When shopping is inconvenient, the value of a retailer's offerings plummets.

Slow checkout is particularly annoying to busy people. Managers usually know how much money they are saving by closing a checkout lane; but they may not realize how many customers they've lost in the process. For a food shopper waiting behind six other customers in the "10 Items or Fewer" lane to buy a carton of milk, the time invested in the purchase may outweigh the value of the milk. The shopper may follow through this time but find another store next time. Studies by America's Research Group, a consumer research company based in Charleston, South Carolina, indicate that 83% of women and 91% of men have ceased shopping at a particular store because of long checkout lines.

To compete most effectively, retailers must offer convenience in four ways. They must offer convenient retail locations and operating hours and be easily available by telephone and the Internet (access convenience). They must make it easy for consumers to identify and select desired products (search convenience). They need to make it possible for people to get the products they want by maintaining a high rate of in-stock items and by delivering store, Internet, or catalog orders swiftly (possession convenience). And they need to let consumers complete or amend transactions quickly and easily (transaction convenience).

ShopKo, a discount chain based in Green Bay, Wisconsin, illustrates how shopping speed and ease can create value. ShopKo's more than 160 large discount stores operate in 19 midwestern, mountain, and northwestern states; 80% of the customer base is working women. With fiscal 1999 sales of $3.9 billion (including its small-market subsidiary, Pamida), ShopKo is much smaller than Wal-Mart, Kmart, or Target, yet it competes successfully against all three. Since 1995, following the arrival of new management a year ear-

lier, ShopKo has more than doubled sales and achieved record earnings growth.

ShopKo takes possession convenience seriously and is in-stock 98% of the time on advertised and basic merchandise. Search convenience is another strength. ShopKo stores are remarkably clean and neat. Major traffic aisles are free of passage-blocking displays. Customers near the front of the store have clear sight lines to the back. Navigational signs handing from the ceiling and on the ends of the aisles help point shoppers in the right direction. Clothing on a hanger has a size tag on the hanger neck; folded apparel has an adhesive strip indicating the size on the front of the garment. Children's garments have "simple sizing"—extra small, small, medium, and large—with posted signs educating shoppers on how to select the proper size.

ShopKo has a "one-plus-one" checkout policy of opening another checkout lane whenever two customers are waiting in any lane. Ready-to-assemble furniture is sold on a pull-tag system. The customer presents a coded tag at checkout and within three minutes the boxed merchandise is ready to be delivered to the customer's car. These ways of operating give ShopKo an edge in transaction convenience.

ShopKo is succeeding in the fiercely competitive discount sector by focusing on the total shopping experience rather than on having the lowest prices. Shopping speed and ease combined with a pleasant store atmosphere, a well-trained staff, and a carefully selected range of merchandise creates a strong mix of customer value.

While ShopKo creates real convenience for its customers, the term is often used carelessly in retailing. Consider that Internet shopping is commonly referred to as convenient. The Internet does indeed offer superior convenience for some stages of the shopping experience; it is inferior for other stages. On-line shoppers who save a trip to a physical store must wait for delivery. Christmas shoppers who receive gifts ordered on-line *after* the holiday learn a lesson about possession inconvenience. This is one reason that the most promising path for most retailers is a strategy that combines physical and virtual stores. Increasingly, the best-managed retailers will enable customers to take advantage of the most effective features of physical and virtual shopping, even for the same transaction.

Retail competition has never been more intense or more diverse than it is today. Yet the companies featured in this article, and hundreds of other excellent retailers, are thriving. They understand that neither technology nor promises of "the lowest prices anywhere" can substitute for a passionate focus on the total customer experience. These retailers enable customers to solve important problems, capitalize on the power of respectfulness, connect with customers' emotions, emphasize fair pricing, and save customers time and energy. In an age that demands instant solutions, it's not possible to combine those ingredients with Redi-Mix, crank out a concrete-block building, and hope the structure will stand. But retailers who thoughtfully and painstakingly erect these pillars will have a solid operation that is capable of earning customers' business, trust, and loyalty.

Leonard L. Berry is Distinguished Professor of Marketing and holds the M.B. Zale Chair in Retailing and Marketing Leadership at Texas A&M University in College Station, Texas. He founded Texas A&M's Center for Retailing Studies and directed it from 1982 to 2000. He is the author of Discovering the Soul of Service *(Free Press, 1999).*

Revolution Retail report

10 top stores put to the test

What makes a successful online retailer? Revolution tries out some of the online giants to figure out why they're attracting customers, and then parting them from their money

Just because Wall Street held a barbecue of internet retailers the other week doesn't mean the internet is dead as a retail medium. People are still shopping online, and will continue to do so in growing numbers. But it is becoming clear that in many sectors not all the current retailers are going to survive. They are insufficiently differentiated, and in many cases the brick and mortar world is biting back with its own online offerings.

So what makes a winning internet retailer? What is it that makes people buy things from one store and not another? It's a question that has been exercising retailers ever since retailing was just dusty market squares in mud-walled villages. And you only have to look at the number of stores that go out of business in main streets and local malls every year to know that we don't have all the answers yet, by any means. And online, things are more complicated, because the elements that make people prefer one store to another in the physical world do not necessarily have the same importance online.

Shopping is as much about the experience of buying things as it is about the products you're buying. In the brick-and-mortar world, it's everything from the layout of the store, the signposting and lighting, to the smiles on the faces of the shop assistants. Online, the essential ingredients of the shopping experience are to do with web site navigation, ease of finding what you're looking for, the clarity of reassurance that your personal and credit card details are secure, how well the business handles queries or unusual requests, and other related issues.

Internet retailers have to figure out new rules, and they're all still learning. But some are definitely doing better than others. The question is why. We decided to take 10 of the top internet retailers and try them out firsthand.

We talked to them to find out a little bit about their marketing strategy, how they're attracting customers and turning them into cash. And where possible, we bought something. But as you'll see, that was an occasion easier said than done. In the process we tried to figure out whether they're living up to the promise of their marketing, and how. And where they have a physical world presence, how comfortably does their online business sit with that? What is it that they're doing well? What can other retailers learn from them?

You may well disagree with some of our choices. This is not a league table, and choosing who to write about for reports like this is always somewhat subjective. These aren't flawless online stores (in this game nobody's perfect), but each is a giant in its space, with a powerhouse brand and serious numbers of customers. All of them are doing things that we think are interesting, so no matter what your line of business, we think they're worth your spending a bit of time with.

EBAY

Proposition

Founded by the supportive husband of a Pez dispenser collector, eBay's mission is simple: "We help people trade practically anything on Earth." And with some four million items on sale on any given day, practically everything is just what consumers will find. The company has grown profitable with its online version of the classic auction model: a commission on every single item sold on the site.

The company acquired San Francisco-based traditional auctioneer Butterfield & Butterfield in the fall of last year. The resulting auctions of high-end items have been joined by other niche plays, such as eBay Motors, a collaboration with Autotrader.com. Local auctions mean more yard-sale level merchandise is now available and further serve to erode classified advertising revenues for local newspapers. People are selling all types of household items through the site.

As perhaps the original online business-to-business trading service, the company has also sought to cash in on the investor cachet of an explicit B-to-B play. "EBay Business Exchange is a natural evolution of the eBay business model, enabling businesses to obtain new, used and refurbished business merchandise and providing businesses of varying sizes a targeted way to reach buyers of business items," says eBay chief operating officer Brian Swette.

Marketing

eBay built its user base during The Great Beanie Baby Craze. Indeed, tens of thousands of its daily auctions are still accounted for by Beanie Baby traders. The site consistently tops Media Metrix's ranking of e-commerce destinations. An online-centric approach to building its brand has concentrated on affiliate stores, where other online retailers (including Buy.com) are able to offer a co-branded version of the auction site, putting auctions of their own products to the fore.

User Experience

Buying and selling on eBay is not for the fainthearted. The site's huge number of concurrent auctions make navigation a nightmare. EBay does a good job of enabling searches and making popular categories easy to access. But registration is close to indispensable, and over 10 million have already signed up. A My eBay page is a necessity for tracking multiple auctions. And for the truly active (and addicted), eBay a-go-go is a service for wireless devices that lets traders keep track of when they are outbid, when a bid has been successful and when an item sells.
While online fraud remains at a level comparable with traditional sales channels, every user who has lied about his or her age, hair color or profession in an online chatroom will feel justified in worrying about buying on eBay. But those worries are dissipated by eBay's user-feedback feature: sellers are ranked according to the comments of previous customers, indicating whether they were satisfied or not.

Mark Dolley

AMAZON

Proposition

Amazon is still based on "our founding commitment to customer satisfaction and the delivery of an educational and inspiring shopping experience." It has, however, thrown in a dozen new categories since it started as a books-only site in 1996. With the boast of Earth's Biggest Selection to uphold, this marriage of selection and service is watched from Wall Street to Main Street.

Amazon puts its money where its mouth is. All of its 13 product areas offer a well-presented and wide array of brands, price points and personalities. For example, the look and feel of the art and collectibles site is more upscale than the book area. But the same accessible layout and graphic scheme pervades.

"We want to be less about push and more about inviting the consumer in," says marketing director Bill Curry. "We have a rich amount of information that helps consumers find what they want, rather than having someone tell them what they should buy."

What Amazon.com will tell consumers about next is anyone's guess. The company has actively added new categories and services. About the only hot e-commerce area they've stayed out of is financial services. Stay tuned.

Marketing

Amazon has built arguably the most extensive and active affiliate network of any online retailer. It is the official book retailer of Excite@Home and the official link for Yahoo!Search, as well as myriad other revenue producing alliances. Because it has expanded into so many areas, it has a huge audience target to hit. Marketing is accomplished more through specific areas than through the overall site. For example, full-page ads in regional Sunday newspaper book review sections only advertise the site's book business. The kitchen store may find its best audience in women 35 to 54 years of age, but the music audience may skew much younger. According to Curry, the site experience has to be a key marketing element to make sure the wide audience comes back to Amazon. "The nature of the business is that we want to get to anyone who is online and has a credit card," he says. "The individual areas need to appeal to each demographic group through their offerings and the way the site is navigated.

User Experience

We decided to take Amazon up on its claims by searching for a recent record release from a critically acclaimed but under-distributed artist, Neko Case. The site definitely invites more than pushes, as Curry says. After registering information (privacy policy plainly displayed), we entered "Neko Case" in the search box and got a quick page featuring the artist's most recent release, *Furnace Room Lullaby*. The page showed many different ways to learn about the artist and the release. Front and center were reviews from Amazon staff. More intelligent, complete and absent of hype were the user reviews.

When we clicked the selection into the shopping cart and hit continue to place the order, it was clear the order was "secure" and stored on Amazon's servers. Everything about the process was clearly explained, including what to expect in terms of shipping times and costs. On the final order confirmation page, big thank you messages were prominently posted at the top and the bottom. And you could even sign up for more information via email on artists like Neko Case.

John Gaffney

PRICELINE

Proposition

Priceline's value to online consumers is based on a business model protected by US Patent No. 5,794,207. Granted in 1998, it reads: "The present invention allows prospective buyers of goods and services to communicate a binding purchase offer globally to potential sellers, for sellers conveniently to search for relevant buyer purchase offers, and for sellers potentially to bind a buyer to a contract based on the buyer's purchase offer." In plain terms, it's a name-your-price model, where you can trade off naming a lower price against the correspondingly lower chance of getting what you want.

The company's initial focus was airline tickets. By signing up 34 airlines, Priceline was able to provide compelling deals on domestic and international fares and claims to have picked up some three percent of the US leisure fare market.

But even on the airline front, Priceline has found itself challenged by Microsoft's Expedia.com. Showing scant regard for Priceline's patent, Expedia.com offers an identical service, its Flight Price Matcher ("Flights At A Price You Like: Yours!").

Expansion has brought new categories of goods and services to Priceline's home page, including hotel stays, cars, mortgages and even groceries and telephone calls. "Further down the line, we'll add cruises, vacation packages and more. You can also expect priceline.com to begin its international expansion, beginning with Asia, later this year," says CEO Dan Schulman.

Despite charging a commission on every successful bid, the venture remains unprofitable.

Marketing

Priceline's advertising will forever be remembered for two things: making William Shatner very rich, and resurrecting radio as a means to promote dot-coms. The company combined Shatner's well-known voice with the bombardment of an uncluttered medium to earn almost overnight recognition.

Shatner cleverly chose to emulate savvy Silicon Valley landlords and take payment in equity, netting him an eight figure sum. With national radio now overrun by dot-com commercials, Priceline's more recent campaigns (still featuring Shatner) have concentrated on national TV. Local cable buys have been added in markets where the company offers specific services, such as its WebHouse Club grocery shopping scheme.

User Experience

Bidding on Priceline is no guarantee of satisfaction. In measuring its own success, the company looks at "reasonable" bids falling within 30 percent of the regular price for a product or service. In the first quarter of 2000, it was only able to satisfy 43.5 percent of those bids.

Even where users win on price, they lose on convenience. Online status checking, real-time online customer support and other helpful features abound. But to achieve maximum scalability with minimum investment, Priceline.com makes consumers sweat for their savings. For instance, first-time grocery buyers must compile their list, make their bids, pay up via credit card and then wait for a WebHouse Club Card to arrive in the mail before trekking to a participating store.

Mark Dolley

BUY.COM

Proposition

Buy.com was started as one of the truly visionary business models of the web. Its premise was one of buying computer hardware and software from Ingram Micro (a wholesaler that supplies many other dot-coms) and then selling those products at a loss. The company hoped to make up that loss with revenues from advertising shown to its customers as they shopped. Now though, post reality check, the company is regularly mentioned in reports of impending dot-com demise.

In fairness, the company widely diversified its offering. Books, CDs and DVDs form part of an online superstore that now numbers some 850,000-plus SKUs. But it still relies heavily on Ingram Micro as a supplier (for all its books, for example), and competition has driven margins to razor-thin levels. With a low price guarantee, Buy.com locked itself into the business of stacking product high and selling it cheap, though this is no bad thing for the consumer.

International expansion has seen Buy.com affiliates open in the UK, Australia and Canada. The company has also gone beyond the web, with a compact version of the store accessible on various wireless devices, including the Palm VII and Sprint PCS phones with the Wireless Web option. "Buy.com is increasing its presence within the wireless sector, says CEO Greg Hawkins. "We're catering to the growing number of consumers, professionals and corporations that recognize the importance of extending data access into the mobile, wireless internet environment."

Marketing

Buy.com tried it all: from billboards to banners and even Super Bowl ads. And not without success. The company has served more than two million unique customers. Unfortunately, those customers proved costly to acquire and as fickle as one might image for a store whose main claim has been cheapness.

User Experience

Buy.com's eSearch facility, combined with separate store departments for the main categories (book, computers, music etc.), make navigation relatively easy. But with such a breadth of items, Buy.com doesn't offer the depth of product descriptions users of other sites take for granted. Try buying a book, and you'll only find detailed information for the top 25 sellers. Lower down the list, you'll be lucky to find a one-line synopsis.

Shipping times, a key piece of information determining online purchases, are present throughout Buy.com. And for those who want to make extra sure, an ordertracker is available. The company boasts about its Anytime Customer Service, and a telephone call in the middle of the night was answered within two minutes.

Mark Dolley

EGGHEAD

Proposition

The name "Egghead" enjoys almost 70 percent brand recognition among online users, largely the by-product of Egghead's brick and mortar days gone by. The firm wants to parlay that advantage into a top place in the hierarchy of web retailers.

"We want to become the leading internet destination for technology products and services," says Bari Abdul, senior VP of marketing for the site. While online retailers have been aggressive in their fight for supremacy over the book and toy categories, which together represent a $25-billion-a-year industry, there still is no clear online leader in the $150-billion-a-year computer supplies market, Abdul says. Egghead may soon be able to claim that crown for itself. In 1999 it was the third-largest e-commerce site by sales volume after Amazon and Buy.com, with some $515 million in sales.

Marketing

The site's advertising promotes the idea of a "computer store inside a computer." Its print campaign has targeted the *Wall Street Journal, USA Today* and business publications such as *Inc.* and *Entrepreneur* magazine. Online ads have appeared on small-business sites and at portals such as CNET and ZDNet.

Egghead also sends out 20 million emails a month to its 3.7 million users who registered for email. These messages feature promotions such as private auctions that are listed only through email and five-percent-off deals on superstore sales.

The big sell here is variety. The site includes a retail "superstore," an auction area and a "Smart Deals" section offering surplus and overstock items at deep discounts.

"Most important is the selection," says Abdul. "At egghead.com we have up to 50,000 of the latest products on the site every day, and at the auction site we have about 10,000 more daily."

User Experience

This variety of offerings comes as the result of a deal last fall in which the auction site OnSale.com bought out Egghead and the OnSale.com leadership effectively took over management of the site.

On a recent test drive, we found variety—Egghead's chief selling point—to also be the site's main weakness. With no specific product in mind, we found it difficult to get a clear sense of what was available on the site. The superstore listed three categories of goods—computer products, software and electronics—each with a dozen or so subcategories to navigate. The auction half of the house has four categories, including (and we found this mystifying) travel and sports and fitness.

These seemingly mismatched offerings are perhaps part of a larger plan. Egghead wants to be the site of choice for small- and home-based business operators, and these categories may be aimed at that market. More logical is the site's plan to leap into the office products market this spring. "They need a place that they can go to get information and also get huge selection and good customer service. That is what the market is looking for," Abdul says.

Functionality on this sprawling site is sufficient. A search feature allows shoppers to track down products simultaneously in the retail store, in auctions and in the discount shop. If you know what you are looking for, that is helpful. In the travel section we found a large Samsonite suitcase that was going for $60, reduced from $150. It shipped the day after we ordered and arrived six business days later—a genuine bargain.

Adam Katz-Stone

TRAVELOCITY

Proposition

In March of this year Travelocity was the 30th most active site on the web, with over seven million unique visitors, according to the research group Media Metrix. The site's proud parents say they offer "a new way to plan and buy travel."

That phrase comes from Mike Stacy, senior VP of marketing, who explained that Travelocity is all about empowering consumers to research and plan their personal travel itineraries and vacation plans.

"All the airlines, all the hotels and vacation packages are surrounded by destination content information, and that presents a much different customer experience than you find in the traditional world," he says. "The consumer now is in control."

Marketing

Travelocity's TV ad campaign hawks the "control" message with emotional visuals. A grandfather arrives to see a new baby for the first time. A woman in the tropics awaits her lover.

In the online realm, Travelocity's innovative banner ads allow users to enter an origination city through an ad and immediately receive a list of the day's lowest fares to 10 or 15 destinations. The banner appears on all the major portals, at college sites and at financial sites.

With a target audience of 35- to 45-year-old homeowners whose income tops $75,000 per household, Travelocity seems to have a working formula. In 1998 the site did $285 million in gross sales. In 1999 the gross topped $1.1 billion, and in the first quarter of this year sales had already topped $500 million.

User Experience

We went to www.Travelocity.com to book a weekend room in Virginia Beach. This should have been easy, but it was not. Since we already knew where we wanted to go, we took control by going straight to "Find/Reserve a Hotel" and entered the city and state: Virginia Beach, VA.

Travelocity could not find that city, so we went to another site to track down the ZIP code for the resort town and then tried again, still without success. Eventually we queried Travelocity to search for a hotel "near a point of interest" and—lo and behold—the search engine recognized Virginia Beach as a point of interest.

Asked about the problem, a customer service representative said on the phone that the hotel booking tool gets a little funky sometimes. This is disappointing, but perhaps not surprising, since Travelocity has set its sights chiefly on the competitive arena of air travel bookings.

Stacy touted as a unique feature a "best fare finder," in which a traveler may enter a desired destination and get a report back detailing the lowest available airfares. Likewise, the "alternate airports" feature will search out less expensive fares that can be obtained by flying into nearby airports and then calculate the mileage from those airports to the traveler's destination.

Still, you'd think they could find Virginia Beach.

Adam Katz-Stone

TOYSRUS

Proposition

Despite some well-publicized stumbles last holiday season, Toysrus.com still finds itself the best-positioned toy e-commerce site going forward. As a division of the global Toys 'R' Us retail chain, Toysrus.com is able to leverage its parent company's incredible name recognition as well as its skills in managing inventories, giving it a huge advantage over pure online retailers such as eToys.

"They just have great brand awareness," notes Jupiter Communications Ken Cassar, in predicting Toysrus.com will likely lead online toy retailers this year.

Toysrus.com's weaknesses are the same ones faced by toy retailers in general—it is a seasonal and hits-driven business. The site will do as much as 70 percent of its annual revenues during the fourth quarter. That puts a lot of pressure on all aspects of Toysrus.com, from site management to fulfillment. Last year, Toysrus.com ended up alienating some consumers by failing to fulfill orders by Christmas. The site has since built two additional fulfillment centers to better meet surges in seasonal demand.

Marketing

The best thing Toysrus.com has going for its brand values. Plain and simple, Toys 'R' Us is the best known name in the lucrative US toy retail sector. "Our Q scores, measuring popularity and awareness, rank Toys 'R' Us equal with the likes of Disney and McDonalds," boasts John Barbour, CEO of Toysrus.com.

Toys 'R' Us leverages that stellar brand equity by including the site's URL in newspaper circulars and other advertisements, generating 50 million impressions during the last post-Thanksgiving shopping period. The URL is also displayed on in-store signage and shopping bags.

"All of these bricks and mortar assets allow us to spend far less on the important aspects of marketing and customer acquisition costs—which gives us a much faster track to profitability than pure online toy retailers," Barbour says.

User experience

The Toysrus.com interface is very clean looking with lots of white space to facilitate fast load times. Consumers can search for items by age group, brand, category (i.e. dolls, games) and character and theme. This search function appears on every page within the site, as does a selection of channels that include video games, Pokemon Central and collectibles. Products are displayed with age range and a small thumbnail picture, with more information available at a single click. Toysrus.com also offers "The Toy Guy," who provides brief reviews of products.

Toysrus.com offers a reasonably helpful FAQ page, as well as the ability to check on the status of an order. Customer service can be accessed through both email and 1–800 number. Both were required during initial attempts to shop, since the screen froze several times during the shipping and billing process. The site's technical support blamed the problem on later versions of the Netscape Navigator browser, adding that it was being addressed. A later attempt using Internet Explorer was completely free of problems.

David Ward

BARNES & NOBLE

Proposition

Barnes and Noble may be the internet's best example to date of using an offline brand to build an online business. Barnesandnoble.com is constructed on the brand's offline strengths, plain and simple. Barnes & Noble was the first book superstore and the first retail brand name in the book business. Since launching its online business in May 1997, it fought through the challenge of Amazon.com to become the sixth largest e-commerce site, according to Media Metrix.

Marketing

By the company's own admission, it does not do a lot in the way of unique branding for the site, or even the promise of a unique internet experience. Like its competitors in this space B&N relies heavily on affiliate marketing. In 1998 it launched a mybnlink.com program with BeFree, which essentially made every user an affiliate. For example, if you recommend a book via email to 20 of your friends and they all buy it from BarnesandNoble.com, you get 10 percent of the total revenue generated. The site relies heavily on brick and mortar power to drive online business. One recent promotion gave consumers a 10 percent discount on any online purchase in return for filling out a demographic information card in the store. B&N maintains strategic alliances with major Web portals and content sites, such as AOL, Lycos and MSN.

User Experience

More than its competitors, Barnes & Noble's approach seems to be aimed at the 35- to 54-year-old demographic. The day we shopped, users could pre-order *The Beatles Anthology* book, not due until late summer at best, but certainly an attention-getter for this age group. The featured music entry was Carly Simon's new record, when the site could easily have opted for the new Britney Spears or Pearl Jam records, released on that very day. It is definitely book-centric. Other product lines seem to get minimal attention. Links from the home page directed readers to subsets of book interests such as the Discover New Writers program and the wildly successful Oprah's Book Club. (Both are also in-store features.)

The site was unique in its grouping of books by winners of various literary awards. We clicked on the IMPAC Dublin Literary Prize and found a great description of the winner, a novel called *Wide Open* by Nicola Barker.

Upon ordering, the site seems to become more of an AOL affiliate than Barnes & Noble. Orders are handled by a co-branded AOL Quick Checkout system. New York City customers were urged to take advantage of a new home or office delivery service.

John Gaffney

CDNOW

Proposition

CDNow is trying to stress the "now" in its company's name. After making a living off its first-mover status for the past three years, the company has repositioned its brand. The site is now more in step with the broadband era of music e-commerce, content and community. In fact, its new tagline is: "Never miss a beat."

"We want to be a music destination. Buying a CD is only part of that," says senior brand marketing director Sam Liss. "We're looking to offer the user specificity. We're not looking to be the Wal-Mart of the internet. We're looking to offer an immersive experience that will make it easier for the user to find the product they're looking for and learn a lot about other product available on the way."

Marketing

CDNOW is in a state of transition financially, and that will affect its marketing plans. It has put a lot of PR muscle behind its new interview section and other broadband applications. It has also been chastised by some analysts for overpaying for some extensive portal deals. Time Warner and Sony will explore a broader strategic relationship with the company and have committed $51 million to it. CDNOW has also hired an investment banker, Allen & Company, to investigate other strategic opportunities and partnerships.

User Experience

CDNOW gets a number one with a bullet for being a fun site to surf. The company's vision of a "destination site" for music is executed with an obsessive attention to detail, presenting literally dozens of informational and commerce choices on the home page alone.

The day we shopped, the page had a broad array of artists featured (from Matchbox 20 to Jeff Buckley to Primal Scream) in the new release section. Album reviews were broken out by editor's picks, staff picks and featured reviews. Our favorite was the artist's pick, where an artist picks their top 10 records.

Looking for jazz selections, we opted for pianist Kenny Barron's picks. On the jump page his picks and an audio sample were listed together. We listened to a mid-1960s McCoy Tyner record titled *Inception*, which had a great smoky club feel.

Meanwhile, we found something else that will help CDNOW appeal to music fans: the company sells vinyl records, where available. But they're more expensive than compact discs.

The order process seemed suspiciously similar to Amazon.com's, both in the graphic interface and the actual process. One segment of the process that could stand more direct explanation is one of supreme importance: the availability of the product is not listed until you place your order. So if an item is backordered, the customer has no information, unless he or she calls the help line, as to when it will be delivered.

John Gaffney

DELL

Proposition

Founded in 1984 as a direct supplier of built-to-order computers Dell had long realized the importance of efficient fulfillment, billing and customer service even before the advent of e-commerce and the formation of Dell.com.

Thanks in part to a growing e-commerce business, Dell current ranks number two in the PC market, with a market capitalization of $130 billion and more than 35,000 employees. Dell.com now generates nearly $40 million dollars each day, a growing percentage of which is in high-end business-to-business services and infrastructure offerings.

Over the past year Dell.com intensified its efforts in the consumer space with Dell Gigabuys, which carries both PC and consumer electronics products such as digital cameras. It also launched the Dell4Me.com initiative to raise consumer awareness about the site's ability to provide everything from PCs to an ISP service. "It gives people a reason to visit the site more than once a year," comments Jupiter analyst Cassar.

Marketing

Dell.com leverages its direct mail channel to drive traffic for the web site. Catalogs sent to businesses and homes carry the URL on the cover and on inside pages. Dell.com also maintains its brand identity through print advertising in business, trade and technical publications.

Dell offers one of the most recognizable names in computing, one that many home consumers have already come in contact with at the office. "Dell projects the image of being a leader in providing customers customized solutions for their computing and internet needs," says company spokesman Bryant Hilton, adding that TV advertising is primarily the vehicle for corporate branding campaigns. Dell has also aggressively paired with companies such as America Online in promotions.

User Experience

Shopping at Dell.com is a utilitarian experience. Pages often have a cluttered look, but information is easily retrievable. The home page has multiple channels that segment users: consumers are directed to once section while government customers are sent to another. Though Dell.com primarily highlights its own products, especially in the build-to-order segment, the Gigabuys section has over 30,000 offerings, many from brands other than Dell. The site features a selection of exclusives, as well as a top-10 list chosen by customers. The most popular items were products such as laser printers, reflecting the site's business audience.

Dell.com customers can search through categories such as printers/scanners and software and accessories, or use a keyword to locate what they want. There were no attempts at cross- or up-selling, but the site does allow you to group four products together for comparison shopping. With its foundation in direct mail, Dell.com excels in fulfillment. A CD writer ordered on Sunday evening arrived on our doorstep Thursday morning via standard delivery. Repeat customers have the option of one-click checkout, and all customers have the ability to monitor the status of their order. Customer service consists of FAQs as well as an e-mail section.

David Ward

What's Ahead for... Retailing

Retail stores are bringing the Net into the world of bricks and mortar

BY WILLIAM M. BULKELEY

TWO YEARS AGO, when people talked about technology and retailing, they meant consumers abandoning stores and shopping on the Internet.

But now that online grocers, video stores, pet-food outfits and toy emporia have crashed and burned, retailers have a different take on technology. Instead of giving people the chance to stay at home and shop, businesspeople want to use high-tech strategies to get people *into* their stores—while cutting costs at the same time.

In a sense, stores are trying to combine the best aspects of Internet shopping with the strongest points of buying in a bricks-and-mortar store. In most cases, this means tailoring sales pitches to meet individual consumers' tastes and habits—while still letting them roam the aisles and touch and feel the products they're about to buy.

"We're Webifying the store," says Nat Fry, managing principal of International Business Machines Corp.'s distribution-solutions operation. Retailers want to "leverage the Internet in the store to simultaneously enrich the shopping experience and cut labor costs."

What will that mean in real life? For one thing, some stores are creating the real-world equivalent of the Web's ultra-specific targeted ads, putting up electronic price displays and shelf tags that can be updated with the touch of a button, or offering customers personal digital assistants that flash messages about promotions that are specifically geared to their buying habits.

The new technology also lets stores take advantage of Web retailers' low overhead. Wireless, computer-controlled signs mean fewer workers have to change prices by hand, for example. And some stores are even eliminating cashiers by letting customers pass their purchases over a scanner and swipe their own credit card. Not pointing and clicking, perhaps, but close.

Hand to Mouth

Retailers are normally tight-fisted when it comes to capital spending. But many of the new devices could pay for themselves by reducing labor costs, while boosting sales and making shoppers happier. That leads marketers to predict that consumers could see the new devices proliferate in many stores in the next three years.

Some of the most promising applications are gadgets that try to create a middle ground between the ease of shopping at home and going to the store.

In a pilot project, some 500 shoppers at three Safeway Inc. stores in Britain have been given a customized Palm Pilot called Easi-Order, a PDA with a modem and bar-code reader. Using data gathered from its loyalty-card program, Safeway, of Pleasanton, Calif., compiled personal shopping lists for each of the 500 participants, listing the items the shoppers purchased most frequently.

So, the shoppers can hook their PDAs up to a phone line and check off items on the digital list—and those items will be waiting for them at the store, bagged and ready to go, at whatever time they specify. Thus, customers get an easier way to shop—and the store, or so it hopes, gets happier customers who are prepared to do more business there.

If shoppers want to put more items on the shopping list, they can take the PDA down to the store and swipe the bar-code reader on the products. Safeway's system, designed by IBM, also stores lists of ingredients for favorite recipes; the user simply checks off the ones he or she wants. The system even suggests an appropriate bottle of wine.

It will also send warnings about certain products—telling a customer, for example, that the jar of mayonnaise he bought three months ago is due to expire, and offering a discount on a new jar.

In the U.S., office-superstore chain Office Depot Inc. is providing small-business customers the opportunity to buy a Palm Pilot with a bar-code scanner so they can go through the store and create a personalized catalog of items they regularly buy. Anytime they need, say, a new inkjet-printer cartridge, they can tap a shopping-cart icon on the screen. Next time they "hotsynch" the handheld with a computer (in other words, hook the two gadgets together to share data), the computer will automatically send the information via the Internet to Office Depot, and the selected items will be delivered.

It's a "highly efficient way to buy and replenish their office products," says Steve Embree, executive vice president of merchandising at Office Depot, based in Delray Beach, Fla.

Many stores are taking a different approach to arming customers with technology. Instead of giving customers PDAs, they're installing Web kiosks in stores. Take, for example, the labor-intensive task of creating a wedding registry. Cincinnati-based Federated Department Stores Inc. is buying more than 400 Web kiosks from NCR Corp. for wedding registries in its Bon Marche, Lazarus, Macy's and Rich's department stores. Customers can check the registry for anything a couple has listed, from any of the Federated stores, look at the item in the store and then order and have it delivered. The registries are stored on databases at WeddingChannel.com, a unit of closely held Wedding Channel, a Los Angeles-based online-registry and wedding-planning service.

Paper, Plastic, Proactive

While such efforts try to streamline the process of picking out products, other technology focuses on simplifying the end of the shopping expedition: the checkout line. Many big retailers are adopting technology that lets customers do their own scanning and bagging at the cash register.

Lars Nyberg, chairman of NCR, descendant of National Cash Register, says that "we have convinced some significant players to adopt self-checkout," including Kmart Corp. and a number of grocery chains. "In the coming five years, self-checkout will become a significant business," although he expects it will never account for more than half the checkout lanes in most stores.

Daniel Hopping, a manager in IBM's retail-solutions unit, says that "self-checkout is being accepted. Two days ago, I was in a store and there was a line at the self-checkout register even though nobody was in the human-operated line."

The technology, boosters say, offers big benefits to stores and shoppers. NCR, based in Dayton, Ohio, calculates that 90% of the cost of maintaining a checkout lane is the cashier. And that means stores can afford to open more lanes, the argument goes, thus cutting queues and speeding up checkout.

For some customers, though, the advantage of self-checkout isn't speed. "In retirement communities, you sometimes see big usage of self-checkout because they like to see how much

they're being charged," says Joanne Walter, NCR's vice president, future retailing. "They can slow it down."

Retailers, naturally, were worried about the potential for theft—what retailers call "shrinkage"—with self-checkout. However, NCR and other vendors have developed a number of techniques to encourage honesty.

In part, retailers rely on psychological deterrents. Self-check lanes are set up with video cameras that can be monitored by store personnel, and the lanes have video screens where shoppers can see themselves passing merchandise over the scanner. "People really don't like to see themselves stealing on video," says Ms. Walter.

Moreover, the self-checkout aisles are only waist-high, giving shoppers a sense that they can be watched easily. And there's an electronic scale beneath the shopping bags that knows what's just been scanned and how much it's supposed to weigh. So if a shopper scans a candy bar while slipping a rib roast in the shopping bag, the system beeps and asks that the item be entered again.

At the end, the video screen asks shoppers to check that there is nothing left in the carriage. "You wouldn't believe the look of guilt they get," says Ms. Walter.

In addition, self-checkout eliminates security problems many retailers have with clerks conspiring with friends to steal multiple items. For example, cashiers have been caught putting a bar-code for a cheap item on their wristwatch and scanning it over and over, while covering up the bar code on expensive items. The scale in a self-checkout prevents that, because the weight of the products in the bag wouldn't match the weight of the "product" being scanned.

Technology is also starting to change the mundane world of displaying prices. A Xerox Corp. spinoff, Gyricon Media Inc., of Palo Alto, Calif., has developed an 11-inch by 14-inch display that it is marketing as an instantly changeable sign.

Goodbye, Pricing Gun

The technology, dubbed SmartPaper, is light enough to sit atop a shelf or "gondola" stand-alone display; it is powered by double-A batteries and costs about $100. Scientists at Xerox's Palo Alto Research Center have been working for more than a decade on the device, which consists of tiny two-colored balls in a flexible sheet. The signs are controlled through a wireless radio connection from a central computer. When given an electrical charge, each ball can turn its white or black side toward the viewer, forming letters.

Federated's Macy's East division is starting to experiment with the signs in New Jersey. "If this is successful, it will replace all our paper signs," says Benjamin Diss, director of information systems for Macy's. "We see this as a large issue. We have sales where we have hundreds of thousands of signs that need to be updated."

Fedcrated nationally spends up to $250,000 a month changing signs. Worse, signs that are changed incorrectly infuriate some customers, who end up arguing with cashiers when scanned prices are different than those shown on signs.

Another pricing technology seeks to replace the shelf tags in grocery stores. NCR is selling electronic labels that receive instructions from a radio transmitter and can be changed at a manager's whim. Ms. Walter of NCR says it costs about $100,000 to place the wireless tags throughout the store; they can be updated by radio transmitters in the ceiling that send along a jolt of electric power to recharge the built-in battery each time the price is changed.

One of the first customers was a Turkish retailer "because inflation there is so high," says Ms. Walter.

Such products don't just offer the chance to save on manpower. There's also flexible pricing. Once a store is fully equipped, store managers can change every price in the store for sales that last for hours or even minutes instead of days.

For instance, items that appeal to seniors, who have flexibility in when they shop, could be discounted during slow times of the day to draw them in. Or stores could more easily offer time-dependent specials. If, say, strawberries are approaching their shelf life, a quick price cut in the evening might move them. If a rainstorm breaks out suddenly, a store manager could change the price for umbrellas; if the clouds clear and the temperature rises, a manager could create a special on bathing suits.

"If supermarkets can run their sales by the hour of the day, that could be a big thing," says Mr. Hopping of IBM.

MR. BULKELEY IS A STAFF REPORTER IN THE WALL STREET JOURNAL'S BOSTON BUREAU.

More for Less

DISPATCHES FROM THE FRONT LINES ON MARKETING AND ADVERTISING TECHNIQUES THAT DELIVER THE BIGGEST BANG FOR YOUR BUCKS.

BY SUSAN KUCHINSKAS

The backlash, the correction, the free fall, the shake-out, the day of reckoning—call it what you will, the end of the dot-coms' free ride down Wall Street was a long time coming. Analysts finally turned their focus from stock prices to the sums spent on Internet advertising and marketing.

The numbers were stunning. The flush-rate for some impetuous companies reached an unbelievable 75 percent of total cash reserves. Dot-coms sunk an incredible $1.6 billion, for instance, into high-profile TV spots, and traffic rates barely budged, even for established ecommerce sites. The average cost for Internet-only companies to acquire a customer reached $82 a pop; for those companies going after consumers through portal deals, the price of customer acquisition averaged a whopping $300. In a few short weeks, marketing budgets went from full-on to throttle-back, TV ad campaigns went from *de rigueur* to *de trop*, and investors learned a new kind of hurt.

"It used to be [a matter of] who could be out there the loudest," says Rob Martin, an Internet analyst who covers 12 technology companies including CNET and CBS Sports-Line.com for Arlington,Va.–based investment firm Friedman Billings Ramsey. "Now it's who can be out there the most effectively."

Now that the sector is in detox, Internet companies are taking a hard look at what works and what doesn't in marketing and advertising, and at what provides the biggest bang for the buck. So did we.

Email discussion lists

www.egroups.com
www.topica.com

The thrill of email marketing may be gone, but the value lives on. One emerging email venue is advertising within email discussion lists. San Francisco–based eGroups, which provides free "listservs," offers ads targeted by context or user. Another player in the space, Lassoo Interactive, is an ad agency that specializes in email and newsletter campaigns. Says Jim Lin, media planner for the Los Angeles–based shop, "We target interests, not demographics."

www.jaboom.com

Lassoo client Jaboom! is building a music database, so it tapped Lassoo for a three-month customer-acquisition campaign starting last April. The goal was to attract people to the site who would listen to and rate a wide variety of music clips. In return, users received points to spend at Amazon.com.

When Lassoo's media buyers couldn't find enough targeted newsletters, they bought email tags on Topica, a Web portal for email discussion lists. When a Topica subscriber posts a message to a list there, it goes to other list members through Topica's servers, which adds brief text messages at the end.

BANG! JabooM!'s campaign has an average acquisition cost of $4 per customer.

BUCKS An estimated $9,000 bought 300,000 impressions.

"We need a broad reach," Lin says, "and these hobby newsletters don't go out to that many people. Topica itself is a credible media company and, whereas newsletters carry five or six [ads each], email tags advertise alone." Lin says that Lassoo surpassed Jaboom!'s acquisition goals just two months into the program.

Radio

www.edmunds.com

On-air is no longer the media buyer's secret weapon. Radio spots are getting more expensive and inventory is growing scarce, according to Avi Steinlauf, vice president of marketing for Edmunds, the 34-year-old automotive information publisher. That's because radio works.

Though Edmunds has enjoyed an online presence since 1995, it launched its first ad campaign this past December.

Edmunds.com wanted to lift its monthly traffic numbers—from a very respectable one million unique users—and provide quality traffic to its commerce partners. Edmunds.com earns revenue from referral fees and transaction cuts from auto-related businesses such as online car dealer autobytel.com and parts retailer Crutchfield.

Los Angeles agency Suissa Miller produced three 30-second radio spots using the tag "People in the know informing others," according to Steinlauf. Starcom IP of San Francisco placed the spots in the top 10 wired U.S. markets, with an estimated 33 percent reach.[1] They started airing the week after Christmas and ran through February. A second series began in May. The radio campaign was backed up with a few billboards and ads that appeared in newspaper automotive sections.

BANG! The site gained 500,000 new unique visitors per month.

BUCKS The company spent $2 million on its initial round of radio spots.

Steinlauf says that while he'd expected traffic spikes from the radio spots, he was pleasantly surprised by the quality of that traffic. Edmunds.com defines quality users as those who click through to and become customers of its commerce partners. During the first radio campaign, site traffic increased 50 percent. "We assumed conversions on a percentage basis would go down," Steinlauf says. "We found that not only did traffic increase, but the quality increased as well."

Viral marketing

Everyone still wants a piece of this one. In fact, investment firm Draper Fisher Jurvetson, whose Steve Jurvetson coined the term, says it won't consider funding companies whose business plans don't contain at least a germ of the idea, which involves getting your customers to pass your marketing messages along to friends and associates.

> www.cometsystems.com

Comet Systems is a New York technology company that offers Web users and publishers a cuter Web pointer. It provides a client-side plug-in; when users who have downloaded the plug-in visit a site that has licensed the Comet Cursor technology, the cursor changes, on that site only, from the usual arrow to a tiny graphic. The sites pass along the technology to users via a link to a download URL, so in this case, the viral model is not user-to-user, but trusted-Website-to-user.

Comet claims it hasn't run a single ad in the Comet Cursor's two-year history. With 40 million users, it has repeatedly cracked the Nielsen//NetRatings weekly top 25 Web properties list beginning last April. Ben Austin, Comet's director of marketing, says the decision to go the viral route and eschew advertising was a philosophical one. "Advertising in the early stages of a company is an intensely risky endeavor," he says.

> http://cometzone.cometsystems.com

Instead, Comet has spent its time learning from its users. Its original model was B-to-B; it planned to license its technology to Web publishers such as Mattel, Comedy Central, and Warner Bros. Online, which used it to turn cursors on its site into such things as the WB logo and Bugs Bunny. "When we deployed cursor changing with our large customers," Austin says, "thousands of people began writing us, saying that they wanted dog cursors and cat cursors and Christian cursors and Japanese-flag cursors."

> www.mycometcursor.com

Comet Systems responded by creating Comet Zone, a place where smaller Web publishers could go to grab the technology for their sites free, and My Comet Cursor, a desktop cursor library for individual users. Comet Systems got extra bang from its viral marketing scheme by embedding an ad for Comet Zone into the comments field of the HTML source code of a Comet Zone-enabled Website. "It didn't affect the code," Austin explains, "but whenever a Web builder comes across a really cool Website, the first thing they do is look at the code. There they see our ad that tells them where they can go to get the cursor for their own sites."

BANG! Austin reports 40 million unique users for the Comet Cursor, and 200,000 Websites for Comet Zone.

BUCKS Zero spent on advertising. (Comet Systems spent half of its $9.5 million capital on partnerships and business development deals related to customer acquisition. So the cost to acquire each customer has been just 10 to 15 cents.)

Guerrilla marketing

Jay Conrad Levinson, who coined the term, uses it to mean marketing efforts that eschew big-budget traditional media in favor of crafty, less expensive, and often theatrical strategies.

> www.ammonmarketing.com

Amy Finn, principal of Ammo Marketing in San Francisco, prefers to call the guerrilla campaign her company created for LetsTalk.com "alternative." LetsTalk, also of San Francisco, is an online retailer of wireless phones and calling plans. It wanted to create awareness in two markets, then extend the buzz nationally. "For everything we do," says Nancy Friedman, LetsTalk.com vice president of brand marketing, "we try to take it to the max and leverage it as fully as possible. We were trying to wrap a local and strategic guerrilla marketing campaign into a national story."

Ammo created a character, Uncle Cell, and a pseudo-political campaign referred to as the Cell Phone Bill of Rights. "One of the challenges of the Internet is that it's not tactile, there's no way to touch and feel a company's products," Finn says. "We give the brand a personality and enable it to reach consumers on a more intimate level."

Ammo commissioned a national research study on mobile phone etiquette, then sent actors decked out as Uncle Cell in yellow and purple striped costumes, white wigs, and beards, to Atlanta and Washington, D.C. After making a big splash with a motorcade featuring a yellow Cadillac and yellow-and-purple motorcycles, Uncle Cell and his entourage stopped D.C. pedestrians, asking them to take the etiquette survey. They gave away coupons, phone calls, mobile phones, and accessories.

BANG! A minimum of 2 million media impressions, and 20,000 personal impressions for the first phase, and 10 million media impressions for the second phase, according to LetsTalk.

BUCKS Just $ 195,000 for production and staff for street events and for organizing author Sabath's tour.

New York–based Jupiter Communications' report on guerrilla marketing says that a strong public relations effort can take a campaign to the next level, which is exactly what LetsTalk.com planned. The second phase of the campaign sent company spokespersons on a media tour with etiquette expert Ann Marie Sabath, author of *Business Etiquette in Brief*. More than 40 radio and television stations gave her free airtime to mention LetsTalk.com.

Friedman says she evaluates guerrilla-marketing efforts by how well she can extend the public-relations dimension of a campaign. Her advice: "You have to make sure you spend enough to execute well."

Customer relationship management

CRM, the strategy of understanding and communicating with current, potential, and future customers, is here to stay. The larger and more complicated the enterprise, the more important it is to keep track of customers. It's just good business.

---

www.nissandriven.com
www.infiniti.com

According to Scott Nelson, vice president and research director for Stamford, Conn.—based research firm Gartner-Group, "Many firms have the idea that they'll buy a piece of software and install it and that will be CRM. I call that the rocket ship in the garage syndrome, a shiny piece of technology that doesn't solve any problems." Nelson says that strategy, tactics, process, and the requisite skill sets are just as important as any software.

With 1,100 Nissan and 152 Infiniti dealerships in the United States alone, Nissan North America decided that a customer database wasn't enough. "We realized it was possible to get an integrated tool set that would let us access customer information, analyze data or demographics, profile buyers, segment them, do data mining, predict response to campaigns, and generate outbound campaigns," says Ted Ross, a corporate manager for Nissan. His company is now in the second phase of a two-year project to integrate E.piphany's E.4 system, a CRM software and services platform, with all the company's marketing and customer retention systems.

E.piphany CEO Roger Siboni says that too many businesses fail to take "a holistic view of the customer relationship." They may do a great job on analysis or segmenting them, then fail to use that information effectively. They also tend to focus on a single channel, whether that's the Web, deals, or a toll-free customer service center.

BANG! Nissan calculates that each percentage point increase in customer loyalty is worth at least $14 million in annual gross profit.

BUCKS The average installation fee for E. piphany E.4 is $500,000 for software and services.

Nissan will eventually tie its call center and fulfillment departments to the dealers themselves, aiming to understand what creates "hand-raisers," what turns them into buyers, repeat customers, and what turns them off.

Outdoor

www.familywonder.com

Outdoor advertising—from taxi tops to billboards—has been a good buy for dot-coms. Spending in the category by Internet companies jumped from $13 million in 1998 to more than $100 million last year. Why? It's cheap (compared to a TV ad), and boosts brand awareness, says Simon Fleming-Wood, senior director of marketing for Family-Wonder.com, a San Francisco entertainment and ecommerce site for families.

"There's an awareness part of building a brand, and that's what the outdoor vehicles provide," Sleming-Wood says. He admits that outdoor is the most difficult ad medium to measure, but adds, "Brand-building is in great measure an art, not a science."

FamilyWonder launched a billboard campaign in San Francisco and New York that ran from the fourth quarter of 1999 through March 2000. Sausalito, Calif.–based Butler, Shine & Stern handled the creative work for the colorful billboards, which were designed to be thought-provoking but clear. One, for example, simply said, "Inspected by parent Number 52," with the site's URL. There were six billboards in San Francisco, most in shopping districts, and three in New York, one of which faced down Silicon Alley.

The billboard campaign was designed to hit key "influencers," which Sleming-wood defines as capital and commerce partners as well as end users—parents and kids.

BANG! FamilyWonder estimates it gained 567,000 daily impressions.

BUCKS It spent roughly $1 million.

While the company's objectives weren't measurable—you can't measure click-through rates from a billboard, for example—Sleming-Wood calls outdoor advertising "a perfect medium for gaining a lot of hits with a simple brand message."

Mixed Media

Many media buyers believe it's unrealistic to expect a quick TV ad to carry the entire weight of an advertiser's goals. It takes planning and money, but different vehicles in a cross-media campaign can reinforce each other and emphasize different parts of the message.

www.campsix.com

Campsix is a B-to-B Internet business incubator that launched last October, when the segment had become both glamorous and crowded. Its ad campaign had multiple goals, says Neil Cohen, co-founder and chief marketing officer. The San Francisco–based company needed to recruit its own employees, form a talent pool of executives to work at its incubated companies, and create what Cohen calls "quality deal flow." All this was to be accomplished while branding the company as serious and competent.

"The arena of incubators is crowded and confusing, with a couple big players," Cohen explains. "We're competing for deals and ideas with them and other companies."

The campaign by San Francisco boutique ad agency TackleBox included print, radio, and outdoor vehicles, plus a public relations push by San Francisco firm InterActive Public Relations that included sponsorships of conferences and events. Three print ads calling on people to submit "serious Internet business plans" appeared in vertical New Economy publications, including *Business 2.0,* the *Industry Standard,* and *Red Herring.*

Campsix ran spots on San Francisco's KFOG radio during morning and evening drive time, and also bought advertorials on the adult alternative rock station, in which members of the Campsix executive team expound for one minute on such topics as "What's wrong with dot-com advertising?" and "What is an incubator, anyway?" Total radio spending for the six-week radio campaign was $175,000. Finally, it rented a billboard across from San Francisco's new Pacific Bell Park baseball stadium.

Cohen prefers to concentrate advertising in a few venues in a short period of time. "Instead of spreading over 50 books in the space," he says, "by being in *The Standard* every week, I own that space and become a dominant brand in one book."

BANG! Campsix closed a round of funding with 32 business partners, hired 60 new employees thus far, and raised the number of business plans submitted from five per week to an average of 35 per week.

BUCKS The campaign cost less than $750,000.

Cohen knows where to find his target. In addition to speaking engagements at the usual round-up of high-tech schmoozes, Campsix sponsored business plan competitions at MIT, Harvard University, and the University of Pennsylvania's Wharton School.

"We're targeting the cream of the crop," he says, "not only students but their alumni networks."

Note

1. **Reach** reach refers to the approximate percentage of the population who read, hear, or view a particular media message.

CHOICES, CHOICES

A look at the pros and cons of various types of Web advertising

By JENNIFER REWICK

For many marketers, the big question isn't whether to advertise on the Web, but how.

Do they go with horizontal banner ads or skyscrapers? Sponsorships or e-mail?

Here is a look at the kinds of Web ads currently available, along with their pros and cons.

BASIC BANNER ADS

Banner advertisements still are the staple of Web advertising. They are to the Internet what 30-second commercials are to television. Typically, banners are rectangular strips that run horizontally across the top of a Web page. Some blink; some flash; some just sit there quietly. In the late-1990s heyday of banner ads, consumers were said to be clicking on lots of these ads. But in recent years, the novelty wore off and viewers began to shrug. Now the "click-through" rate is less than 0.5%.

Banners originally were pitched as a direct-marketing tool, because consumers can click on them and be taken to another page or Web site to buy a product or get more information.

PROS: After consumers got click-resistant, some people began hailing banners as a brand-building tool—something with the same potential as a TV commercial to stick in a shopper's mind.
CONS: Banners' graphics are relatively crude. So advertisers and publishers are trying to become more aggressive, developing eye-catching ads and experimenting with new formats, not just placing the ads at the top of the page but all over it.

SKYSCRAPERS

Banners represent a lot of the real estate on a Web page. So perhaps it isn't surprising that one of the latest offshoots is known as the "skyscraper." It's simply a tall, skinny banner ad, and it can take up even more space than the pioneering top-of-the-screen rectangles.

PROS: Like real skyscrapers with their strengthening girders and beams, advertising skyscrapers have a structure that adds to their durability—namely, their vertical shape. Because a typical personal-computer monitor is wider than it is high, a skyscraper ad can perch on either side of the screen without infringing too much on the page itself.

CONS: Text in vertical ads is harder to read. And if an ad sits too far off to the side, a viewer may never even scan it.

BULKY BOXES

Banners are moving all over the place, turning into buttons and carefully positioned squares and rectangles as advertisers try to catch the reader's eye.

On the News.com Web site of San Francisco's Cnet Networks Inc., banner ads are about the size of a CD case and sit smack in the middle of the page. Instead of being taken to another site, readers who click on the ad get more information without having to leave the page. News stories wrap right around the ad box.

PROS: "It's a lot harder to ignore," says Jim Nail, an analyst with Forrester Research Inc., a Cambridge, Massachusetts, Internet market-research firm. But he adds a caveat about the ads, which Cnet likes to refer to as "Messaging Plus" ads.

CONS: The problem with the Cnet ad, says Mr. Nail, is simply this: "The reader's eye has to track around it in order to see the content. My guess is you will probably see some backlash. There probably will be some grumbling from readers."

BUTTONS AND 'BIG IMPRESSIONS'

Not all banners are so aggressive. Walt Disney Co.'s Web sites, including ESPN.com and ABC.com, now run business-card-size banners on the upper-right-hand corner of the page. Disney calls this format "the Big Impression."

PROS: Because the Disney ads sit off to the right side, they aren't interfering with other material on the screen and can remain there for a long time.

CONS: Because the ads are off in a corner on the right side, they might get overlooked. After all, people read from left to right.

Whether banners in general are a strong tool for brand campaigns also is questionable. Measurement firms are working on ways to gauge the impact. But it's much more difficult to quantify the impression a banner ad leaves with a consumer than it is to track an action, such as whether a consumer clicked on a mortgage-loan ad or bought a bath mat.

Dynamic Logic Inc., a New York ad-measurement firm, says it analyzed the brand impact of banners by comparing the responses of consumers exposed to a banner campaign with those of consumers who used the same site but weren't exposed to the ads. In a recent study, the results showed an average increase in brand awareness of 5%, says Nick Nyhan, president of Dynamic Logic.

POP-UP ADS

Some ads don't hesitate to get in your face. So-called pop-up ads appear in a second window that pops up on the screen while a Web page is loading.

Paving the way is the growth in high-speed Internet connections. These speedy connections allow for what online-ad types call "rich media" ads, which use animation, sound and streaming video. While banner ads can include rich media and are getting livelier these days, flashy content is found more often in the pop-up ads.

PROS: These lively ads fill a bigger space than most banner ads. They're more intrusive and memorable because they pop up and have to be clicked on to be gotten rid of. And they can be more entertaining, because they often use moving images. They're used primarily as a brand-building tool by auto makers, consumer-products companies and movie studios.

Unicast Communications Corp., a closely held online-ad firm in New York, says it has developed rich-media ads with an edge: technology that allows an ad to pop up without slowing down the loading of the page behind it. So, readers are less tempted to click the ads off just to keep things moving. Unicast says these ads boast a 6% click-through rate, compared with a high of 0.5% for banners and a 1% to 3% response rate generated by traditional direct-mail marketers.

CONS: Readers can click these ads off—and they do. Many banish the box from their screens even before they see the ad.

Pop-ups can be incredibly annoying to consumers, precisely because they are so intrusive. They often slow down the loading of the site you're trying to view. And even the ads that don't increase loading time tend to irritate users because they pop up unexpectedly on the screen.

Industry analysts doubt this is the next big thing and think a lot of the appeal is based on novelty and experimentation. Not to mention that high-speed Internet access has yet to penetrate the market, which means that these ads' use is not widespread. And readers are getting in the habit of reacting to a flurry of pop-ups simply by clicking them off before the ads can even start to make their point.

E-MAIL

E-mail marketing has surged in the past year. Jupiter Media Metrix Inc., a New York Internet-research firm, expects e-mail to be a $7.3 billion (8.4 billion euros) market by 2005, up from $164 million in 1999. Because recipients have to subscribe to receive e-mail newsletters and ads on topics in which they have expressed interest, marketers are guaranteed a highly targeted audience. Response rates can run as high as 5% to 15%, says Jupiter.

PROS: While it's most effective for retaining customers (61% of marketers using e-mail say that's their primary goal), e-mail marketing has proved to be a useful and cost-efficient way to acquire new customers as well. The cost of keeping customers is only one-third as much for e-mail as for direct mail.

One Low Price
What advertisers pay for spots in various media

TRADITIONAL ADVERTISING

LOCAL TV: A 30-second television commercial on a local station in a top 10 market ranges from $4,000, generally during a movie, to $45,000 for time on one of the highest-rated shows.

NETWORK TV: A 30-second spot in prime time ranges from $80,000 to $600,000, depending on how high a show is rated and the show's genre. The average is $120,000 to $140,000.

CABLE TV: A 30-second spot in prime time runs between $5,000 and $8,000, depending on the network.

RADIO: Commercials range from $200 to $1,000 for a 60-second spot, depending on criteria such as the time of day and the program's ratings.

NEWSPAPERS: A full-page ad in the top 10 markets runs an estimated $120 per 1,000 circulation.

MAGAZINE: Ads in regional editions of national magazines cost an average of about $50 per 1,000 circulation. The average cost of an ad in a local magazine is about $120 per 1,000 circulation.

DIRECT MAIL: The most common forms of direct mail include packages of coupons in letter-sized envelopes, which cost $15 to $20 per 1,000 delivered, and single-sheet newspaper inserts like fliers, which cost between $25 and $40 per 1,000 circulation.

BILLBOARDS: To place several short-term ads for one to three months on those 14x48 signs along the freeway ranges from $5,000 to $25,000 in top 10 markets.

ONLINE ADVERTISING

BANNER ADS: Banner ads range from $5 to $50 for every 1,000 ad impressions that appear on the site, depending on how targeted the ad and the site where it appears.

RICH MEDIA: Rich-media ads that appear in pop-up windows run between $40 and $50 per 1,000 ads that appear, depending on the quality and demographic of the site's audience.

E-MAIL NEWSLETTERS: Content sponsored by an advertiser in a newsletter format ranges from $15 to $25 per 1,000 e-mail addresses targeted, depending on the cost to create and develop the e-mail. An e-mail in the form of an advertisement ranges from $100 to $300 per 1,000 e-mail addresses targeted, depending on the quality and demographic of the list of addresses.

SPONSORSHIPS: A sponsorship per 1,000 viewers ranges from $30 to $75, depending on the exclusivity of the sponsorship. The more exclusive, the higher the cost.

Sources: Initiative Media North America in Los Angeles, a division of Interpublic Group; Carat Interactive Inc.

There are no postage fees, and "creative" costs are lower. The cost to create the e-mail runs about $1,000 and might take three weeks for a campaign, compared with $20,000 and three months for a traditional direct-mail campaign, Jupiter says. The research firm adds that e-mail also gets a faster response from subscribers—typically 48 hours—compared with snail mail, which takes three weeks.

CONS: As the e-mail market surges, so will the clutter in customers' in-boxes. Industry analysts warn that marketers are likely to become victims of their own success, and that it will grow increasingly difficult for advertisers to maintain response rates.

By one reckoning, the average number of e-mail messages from marketers per person in a year is expected to rise 40-fold to 1,612 in 2005, from 40 in 1999. The challenge will be to retain high response rates and low "unsubscribe" rates.

"Everybody thinks e-mail is the Holy Grail of online marketing," says Marissa Gluck, a Jupiter analyst. "It can be very effective, it's cheap and it's fast. But consumers can only manage a couple of relationships with advertisers. They don't want to have a relationship with every brand they buy."

SPONSORSHIPS

Analysts disagree about whether the online version of the old-fashioned "Brought to you by..." TV-show model is picking up speed or running out of steam. Regardless, sponsorships are still a popular form of online advertisement, especially among veteran advertisers looking for places to promote their brand names.

The idea behind a sponsorship is that a marketer pays to link its brand to an area of content on the Web such as a page, a section of a Web site or an entire site. Financial-services provider Charles Schwab & Co. became an early advertiser on women's site iVillage.com by sponsoring its finance channel. On a recent day, a message at the top of the site's investor page read: "Brought to you from the folks at Charles Schwab."

A more recent example is Verizon Communications Inc.'s $3 million deal to sponsor the Lifestyle channel of African-American Web site BET.com. As part of the deal, Verizon negotiated to be the entire site's only telecommunications advertiser.

PROS: With sponsorships, an advertiser can own a large chunk of Web "real estate" and often can work with the publisher to custom-build that area of the site.

CONS: Just like a banner ad, an advertiser's logo may be overlooked by a viewer who is focused on the Web page and trying to read an article. Second, fairly or not, sponsored pages invite some skepticism about the objectivity of the information, as people wonder whether the sponsor has an influence. Third, sponsorships don't make use of the interactivity of the Web medium. "It's tough to measure the impact" of a sponsorship, says Forrester's Mr. Nail.

ice cubes to ESKIMOS

NOT POSSIBLE, YOU SAY? WE'VE GOT 35 PIECES OF ADVICE THAT WILL CHANGE THE WAY YOU THINK ABOUT SELLING.

BY ROBERT McGARVEY

Have you ever wished you could distill the teachings of the sales masters, so that in those nervous moments just before trying to make a big deal you could pull out a cheat sheet that summed up all the key points you or your sales team had to know? Well, guess what: Your wish has been granted.

Following, you'll find essential tips and expert advice from seven leading sales trainers: Barry Farber, Marc Diener, Brian Tracy, Tom Hopkins, Jeffrey Gitomer, John Tschohl and Kevin Davis. Normally, clients pay thousands of dollars to pick their brains—but here before you (for free, no less) you'll find the basic sales secrets necessary for success. Our complete guide covers the situations you face every day, from closing deals and getting repeat business to responding to a prospect's no and negotiating great deals. You'll also find an insightful look at the biggest mistakes you *must* avoid and the tactics and ideas you simply can't live without.

So get cracking. Before you know it, your company will be making more sales—and having more fun doing it.

Gone Fishin'

Make every sale the one that *didn't* get away.

For more than 20 years, Barry Farber has been selling and teaching others everything he knows about sales. Author of *Diamonds in the Rough* (Berkley Books), a handbook for maximizing personal achievement, Farber hosts a cable TV show, writes for *Entrepreneur* and still finds time to keep selling and teaching.

Here, Farber provides five top sales tips. He agreed, but not without a disclaimer: "There's always another place I can improve... I'm still learning," Farber says.

1. **Persist**. "Sales are made by the tenacious. You have to stay in there, even when you're getting rejected," says Farber, who adds that often, multiple sales calls are necessary to sell to a customer. Many give up too

early—and therefore miss the chance to make the sale.

2. **Qualify**. Don't rush in to give your pitch without first finding out if there's a chance this person will buy from you. Customers won't buy if they're not qualified (interested in what you're selling). How to deal? "Ask questions," says Farber. "Listen. Learn about the customer and his business."

3. **Move On**. Congratulations, you made the sale... or maybe you didn't. Either way, the successful salesperson knows when it's time to move on. You can't afford to waste time gloating over successful sales, nor can you waste time trying to sell prospect who will never buy. Farber's advice: "Learn as quickly as you can how to know when it's time to move on."

4. **Differentiate**. How are you and your product or service different? What makes you better than your competitors? "Don't try to copy others. What will shape your success is how you deliver a personal touch," says Farber, who adds: "Knowing what makes you unique lets you sell that much more effectively."

5. **Form relationships**. "Build relationships with customers, then turn those relationships into partnerships," says Farber. "Provide enough value so that your customers really appreciate doing business with you. That creates lasting sales success."

Art Of The Deal

Before waging your sales campaign, do your homework.

If you think haggling is the route to sales success, think again. According to Marc Diener, Los Angeles attorney, speaker, columnist for *Entrepreneur* and author of *Deal Power: 6 Foolproof Steps to Making Deals of Any Size* (Owl Books/Henry Holt), "Too much emphasis is put on haggling. Preparation is the real key to making better deals."

Never fear, even the inexperienced can become savvy dealmakers. Diener offers this advice:

- **Know what you want from the deal**. "People jump into deals too quickly—before they know what they want," says Diener. "Step back and ask yourself what you're really going after."
- **Get help and information**. "Dealmaking is a team sport," says Diener, who urges entrepreneurs to involve professionals, such as accountants, lawyers and bankers, whenever a deal is important. "Or do self-help research. That's become very easy to do on the Web."
- **Check out the other side**. "Are you dealing with a crook? An incompetent? You don't want their problems to become your problems," explains Diener, who insists entrepreneurs perform "due diligence" (meticulous research into the other side) before closing any deal.
- **Plan for the downside**. "Know what can go wrong," says Diener, "and seek to minimize your risks." Ask yourself: If the other side doesn't perform as agreed, what do you lose—and how could you cope? "Using tools such as insurance and performance bonds can be good policy," adds Diener.
- **Get it in writing**. Don't let the glow of the moment prompt you to close a deal on a handshake alone, stresses Diener. A written agreement "is evidence of what everybody agreed to," says Diener, "and putting it in writing forces us to flesh out our thinking."

The Five Commandments

Dare to break these laws... and you'll fail in sales.

If you had to name one of the world's top speakers on achievement, the first name to come to mind should be Brian Tracy, who has authored several books, including *Advanced Selling Strategies* (Fireside Books) and the recently released *The 100 Absolutely Unbreakable Laws of Business Success* (Berrett-Koehler Publishers). Based on his two decades of experience, he shares these five "absolutely unbreakable" laws for sales success:

1. **Thou shalt build credibility with thy customer before attempting to sell**. "The most important ingredient in a long-term sales relationship is trust," says Tracy, who adds that the more a customer trusts you, "the easier it is to sell and keep selling to the customer."
2. **Thou shalt learn the customer's real needs by asking questions and listening carefully to the answers**. "The better you understand a customer's situation and what he or she needs to improve his or her work or life, the easier it will be for you to match the benefits of your offering to the customer so the

customer accepts your recommendation," says Tracy.
3. **Thou shalt position thyself as a problem-solver, helper and teacher in the mind and heart of thy customer**. "The way the customer thinks about you when you're not there is the most important determinant of how the customer responds to you when you are present," says Tracy. When you're viewed as a problem-solver, the customer welcomes your input.
4. **Thou shalt commit thyself to excellence in selling and never stop growing in skill**. Like anything, good selling takes hard work. Tracy urges entrepreneurs to "resolve to be the best at what you do. Read in your field. Listen to audio tapes. Take sales seminars. Never stop improving."
5. **Thou shalt set goals for every area of thy life and work on them every day**. If you want to succeed in selling, says Tracy, you must "have specific, written goals" and set daily schedules to achieve those goals.

Close Calls

Tips for perfecting "the close"

An undisputed master of selling, Tom Hopkins is one of the nation's top names in sales training. He spends much of the year on the speaker's platform, but Hopkins is also a prolific author, whose titles include *Selling for Dummies*, *Sales Prospecting for Dummies*, and *Sales Closing for Dummies* (all from IDG Books Worldwide). If you want to close more sales, take these tips to heart:

- **Eliminate distractions**. "You need to be in control of potential clients' attention," says Hopkins. "Keep them focused on the matter at hand by moving to a quiet area."
- **Be enthusiastic**. "If you're not enthusiastic about the wonderful benefits of your product, why should potential clients be?" Hopkins asks.
- **Emphasize the emotional aspects of the sale**. According to Hopkins, people make decisions emotionally, then defend those decisions with logic. "So, you must be prepared with the logic, but sell with emotion," he says. "Get them thinking about how they'll feel after they own the product or service."
- **Be direct**. "You'd be amazed at how many salespeople think they didn't make the sale because the client said no, when what really happened is that the salesperson didn't ask the client to say yes," warns Hopkins. "After doing a summary of the points you've covered, hand [the prospective client] the paperwork and pen and be certain to say, for example, 'With your approval right here, John, we'll welcome you to

the family of XYZ clients and arrange delivery of your new widget.' Those words are soft and gentle, yet get the message across that it's time for a decision to be made."

- **Stop talking**. "After you ask for the business, wait for the answer," says Hopkins. "I've long taught that the first person who talks owns the product or service. Stay quiet until the client gives you an answer. They'll either make the purchase or give you an objection. Then you can talk."

The Meaning Of No

A customer says no? It's not over.

As an entrepreneur, you will hear "no" no matter how thoroughly you follow the tips on these pages. In fact, if you haven't heard some nos by now, you're not selling hard enough. But a no isn't necessarily the end of your hopes for making a deal with a prospect, says Jeffrey Gitomer, a Charlotte, North Carolina, sales trainer and co-author of *Knock Your Socks Off Selling* (AMACOM Books). He offers tactics to use in overcoming initial nos:

1. **Use humor**. "Say to the prospect, 'Thanks for telling me no. I usually have to hear four nos before I hear yes. Do you know anybody else I can call who'll say no?' " suggests Gitomer. Or: "Say 'Is that your final answer?' " says Gitomer. These tactics can help to defuse the tension triggered by a no and move conversation to the next level.

2. **Ask why five times**. "Ask why and ask why again, and keep asking until you get to the truth about why this prospect said no," says Gitomer. For instance, if the customer says, "I said no because I need a voice-actuated wireless telephone," start by asking: Why do you need voice-actuation? Ask enough questions, and the customer may find that your product or service does what he or she needs.

3. **List the things of value you offer prospects in addition** to what you're selling. "If you don't have anything to put on the list, you don't deserve this sale," says Gitomer. He explains: If you're selling long-distance telephone service for businesses, for instance, you might offer free sales training tapes to customers who sign up. To make any deal of value, "You need to offer more than just what you're selling," he says.

4. **Tell prospects you can't accept a no until they** make two phone calls. "Ask them to call two of your customers who initially said no, then decided to buy," says Gitomer. "You may not be able to overcome a prospect's resistance, but he or she might listen to your customers."

5. **Find out whom your prospects eventually buy from** and what the criteria were. Maybe you won't

get this sale, says Gitomer, but if you get the reasons you didn't, you'll be more likely to get the next deal.

Back For More

How to get customers to buy again and again

If you're not getting repeat business—the same customers never buy from you time and time again—you're working way too hard. As any smart salesperson knows, the real profits come when past customers return to make additional purchases.

To make sure your customers are *return* customers, hungry for more, try following these tips from John Tschohl, author of *Achieving Excellence Through Customer Service* (Best Sellers Publishing) and president of Minneapolis Service Quality Institute:

- **Love your customers**. "A customer knows within five seconds if you like and care about them, and they want to do business with people who do," explains Tschohl. "There's a tremendous amount of indifference in today's wealthy economy, but customers still want to be cared for."

PRICE OF NICE
Being agreeable only gets you so far.

Do nice guys finish last? A recent study seems to support that notion.

Two professors at Vanderbilt University's Owen Graduate School of Management in Nashville, Tennessee, spent a couple years studying behavior at the bargaining table. One key finding: Agreeable folks did worse in certain types of negotiations because they tend to value cooperation over protecting their self-interests. That might not be surprising, but how about this: Intelligence had absolutely no impact on the outcome of win-lose negotiations (where one side comes out ahead), say professors Bruce Barry and Raymond Friedman.

What does matter? Nerve and toughness, say the profs. Have them and, odds are, you'll come out on top.

If you're an agreeable person by nature, your best bet is to go into the negotiation strongly focused on what you want out of the deal—not on making nice with the other side—and you'll probably do okay, say the researchers.

Incidentally, in negotiations where true win-win outcomes are possible, intelligence does benefit a negotiator because he'll be more adept at sniffing out what really matters to the other side. In fact, in those kinds of negotiations, say Barry and Friedman, intelligence is a key factor in reaching a successful conclusion.

- **Call them by name**. "This is simple, but it's a magical tool," says Tschohl. "People love it when you call them by name, and they want to do business with people who know them." But just make sure to use the proper pronunciation. (His is pronounced "shoal.")
- **Focus on speed**. "People want it now; they want immediate response," says Tschohl. "If you want to keep customers, you'll set standards for response times and keep working to do it faster."
- **Keep your promises**. "Nothing turns off a customer faster than when you don't keep your promises, but nowadays few businesses do," says Tschohl. "If you say you'll handle it tomorrow, make sure it's done by then or sooner. Whatever you say you'll do, do it."
- **Make sure everybody has been trained in service**. "It's not good enough when only the salesperson knows customer service," stresses Tschohl. "Everybody on your team has to know—and practice—service basics." A consistent commitment to serving the customer is key to winning repeat business.

Slipping Sales

What *not* to do when selling

Ask Kevin Davis for a list of the five most frequent sales blunders, and his biggest problem becomes trying to narrow down the field of countless common mistakes to a select few. That's because this Danville, California, sales trainer and author of *Getting Into Your Customer's Head* (Times Business/Random House) has made a distinguished living studying such goofs… and, believe us, he's seen plenty of them.

If any of the following sound familiar, at least you can take solace in the fact that you're not alone:

1. **Thinking about the selling process, not the buying** process. Make this big mistake, and "you're too focused on your own agenda, not the customer's. You're self-absorbed," says Davis. Worse still, customers today can actually predict your next move— at least when you concentrate too much on technique and not enough on what the customer needs. Says Davis, "Today's customers are sick and tired of self-focused product-pushers. Sell slower, and your customers will buy faster."
2. **Failing to identify behind-the-scenes decision-makers**. Up to 90 percent of the buying decision occurs when the salesperson isn't even around, says Davis, who points out that many other parties often participate in making the decision to buy. Successful selling means identifying those behind-the-scenes decision-makers—and making sure features and benefits resonate with them, too.
3. **Neglecting to educate customers about the costs of doing nothing**. "For many salespeople, the number-one competitor is the customer's decision to wait," says Davis. Savvy sellers know how to show a customer the real costs associated with delaying a purchase. Waiting might seem a safe choice to them now, but successful salespeople make a habit of popping that balloon.
4. **Calling on prospects who don't value your value**. If your big selling strength is high quality, you're probably wasting time going after purchasing agents who are far more price-focused, says Davis. A key to successful selling is identifying the right potential customers who already want, need and value the product or service you have to sell.
5. **Failing to resolve a customer's fears**. What kills the deal in the eleventh hour, when you're sure you've landed a big one? What makes customers quake in their boots before they sign on the dotted line? What's the big reason why customers pull out of a deal in those last minutes? They're afraid that, somehow, their buying decision might be wrong and that they'll suffer in the eyes of their co-workers, boss, family and friends. We're all fearful that we just might be buying the next Edsel—the little product that couldn't—and the smart salesperson "identifies the sources of a customer's fears and finds ways to alleviate them," says Davis. So in every one of your potential sales, be prepared to fall back on a plan for resolving your customers' biggest fears.

Robert McGarvey is Entrepreneur's *"Web Smarts" columnist.*

UNIT 4
Global Marketing

Unit Selections

Key Points to Consider

• What economic, cultural, and political obstacles must an organization that seeks to become global in its markets consider?

• Do you believe that an adherence to the "marketing concept" is the right way to approach international markets? Why, or why not?

• What trends are taking place today that would suggest whether particular global markets will grow or decline? Which countries do you believe will see the most growth in the next decade? Why?

• In what ways can the Internet be used to extend a market outside the United States?

 **Links: www.dushkin.com/online/**
These sites are annotated in the World Wide Web pages.

CIBERWeb
  http://ciber.centers.purdue.edu
Emerging Markets Resources
  http://www.usatrade.gov/website/ccg.nsf
International Business Resources on the WWW
  http://globaledge.msu.edu/ibrd/ibrd.asp
International Trade Administration
  http://www.ita.doc.gov
World Chambers Network
  http://www.worldchambers.net
World Trade Center Association On Line
  http://iserve.wtca.org

It is certain that marketing with a global perspective will continue to be a strategic element of U.S. business well into the next decade. The United States is both the world's largest exporter and largest importer. In 1987, U.S. exports totaled just over $250 billion—about 10 percent of total world exports. During the same period, U.S. imports were nearly $450 billion—just under 10 percent of total world imports. By 1995 exports had risen to $513 billion and imports to $664 billion—roughly the same percentage of total world trade.

Whether or not they wish to be, all marketers are now part of the international marketing system. For some, the end of the era of domestic markets may have come too soon, but that era is over. Today it is necessary to recognize the strengths and weaknesses of our own marketing practices as compared to those abroad. The multinational corporations have long recognized this need, but now all marketers must acknowledge it.

International marketing differs from domestic marketing in that the parties to its transactions live in different political units. It is the "international" element of international marketing that distinguishes it from domestic marketing—not differences in managerial techniques. The growth of global business among multinational corporations has raised new questions about the role of their headquarters. It has even caused some to speculate whether marketing operations should be performed abroad rather than in the United States.

The key to applying the marketing concept is understanding the consumer. Increasing levels of consumer sophistication are evident in all of the world's most profitable markets. Managers are required to adopt new points of view in order to accommodate increasingly complex consumer wants and needs. The markets in the new millennium will show further integration on a worldwide scale. In these emerging markets, conventional textbook approaches can cause numerous problems. The new marketing perspective called for by the circumstances of the years ahead will require a long-range view that looks from the basics of exchange and their applications in new settings.

The selections presented here were chosen to provide an overview of world economic factors, competitive positioning, and increasing globalization of markets—issues to which each and every marketer must become sensitive. "Global Marketing in the New Millennium" describes some of the significant economic and technological changes that will have a dramatic affect on all marketers. The next article reflects the importance of under-

standing local and state issues before implementing a global market segmentation strategy. "The Invisible Global Market" contends that with 86% of the world containing "hidden" markets, marketers need to take action. "The Lure of Global Branding" provides some guidelines for proper global brand leadership. "The Nation as Brand" reveals the complexity of marketing a brand in many different markets. The last article scrutinizes the future of Japanese marketing.

GLOBAL MARKETING IN THE NEW MILLENNIUM

Sea changes—from the advent of the Euro to the coming battle between national sovereignty and the borderless Internet—will dramatically affect all marketers.

By John K. Ryans, Jr.

OVER THE PAST year, much attention has been drawn to the Y2K concerns. To some degree, this may be masking the sea change occurring in global markets and especially in the way global business operations will be conducted in the new millennium. Already, major changes under way in Europe, the Far East, and this hemisphere are challenging old notions of sovereignty, competitiveness, trade policy, and organizational structure. And all will dramatically effect international markets and marketers, in general. Nine key changes are juxtapositioned with the arrival of the twenty-first century, ranging from the advent of the Euro to the approaching battle between national sovereignty and the borderless Internet.

1. The Euro. When Pradeep Rau and I were preparing our book, *Marketing Strategies for the New Europe* (published by the AMA in 1990), we felt that the critical test of the European Union would be its ability to successfully develop a common currency. That currency—the Euro—happened with great fanfare in January 1999, and its introduction will be fully operational in 2002. This event provides a unique (and most appropriate) prelude to the year 2000 festivities; its full impact occurs early in the new millennium.

For marketers, the Euro means the onset of a single pricing strategy for 11 Eu-ropean countries. Prices now can be used in Europeanwide television commercials, cross-border magazines and newspapers, and catalogs. In addition, U.S.-based companies increasingly will move to a centralized European headquarters and warehouse base, as opposed to national offices. The Euro also will make it easier to transfer personnel and build truly Europeanwide sales forces.

Perhaps even more important, however, is that the Euro signals a truly unified union of European countries. Few things reflect a spirit of nationalism more than a country's currency, and by July 2002 or sooner, the Euro will be the European currency. And it will rival the dollar and the yen as the global currency of choice. The new power of the European Union increasingly will be felt in decisions ranging from the approval (or disapproval) of mergers to major cross-border policy issues and even advertising and media regulations.

2. Concentration. In the past year or two, a wave of industry concentration has occurred at a frequency and level that have been unmatched in recent times. Global powers have merged, such as Daimler-Benz and Chrysler, and B.P. and Amoco, and MCIWorldcom and Sprint, and more and more industries have become highly concentrated.

The spillover effect of these mergers and acquisitions has been enormous, as it influences such areas as suppliers, dealerships, and national and local governments. Marketers have seen widely recognized national and international brands and long-standing relationships disappear.

Much of these changes have been explained by the desire for greater production economies of scale and the need to tighten supply structures in an effort to cut costs. Obviously, from a marketer's perspective, these new global "power-houses" will have extreme leverage in their dealings with service providers (advertising agencies, media, distributors, retailers, and the like). In many instances, consumers around the globe may be destined to have fewer choices.

3. Global Oligopoly. To state it simply, we're moving into an era of global oligopoly. In industries such as pharmaceuticals, tobacco, petroleum, and aerospace, we've seen the number of principal players drop to only three to five major producers. This concentration also is occurring in service sectors such as worldwide accounting, legal, and insurance firms. At a recent international automobile show, it was not surprising to have heard discussions suggesting that the number of worldwide auto producers would be drastically down within the next five years. Such rapid concentration in so many industries not only shapes the nature of marketing competition, but it provides openings for smaller niche players as well. Not surprisingly, this battle for positions in global industries has given increased corporate attention to global supply chains.

4. Supply Chain and Logistics. In the new millennium, the major players as well as those trying to keep up with the Daimler-Benz/Chryslers and the Wal-Marts of the world are giving much greater attention to supply chain management. Not only do firms see better management of the supply chain as a way to achieve significant cost savings, but also as a vehicle for improved process efficiency. Recently, the *Financial Times (FT)* provided a global comparison of countries based on the totals spent on logistics as a percentage of GDP in 1996. With a global average of 11.7% and a U.S. average of 10.5%, it's a small wonder that firms have looked to this critical area to improve their efficiency and overall cost situation.

IF MARKETING IS TO BE A VIABLE FORCE IN THE NEW MILLENNIUM, A NEED EXISTS FOR MARKETING ASSESSMENTS TO BECOME A REGULAR PART OF A COMPANY'S ANNUAL REPORT

Moreover, foreign outsourcing has become such an integral part of company operations in many U.S. industries, that any major logistic problems could do irreparable damage to a firm's operations. To illustrate, the bulk of U.S. toy products now are being manufactured in China. Blips on the transportation scene, such as this year's container shortages, raise the specter of what might happen to a U.S. toy firm if a major portion of its holiday products miss deadline. Without doubt, supply chain management will be in the spotlight in the year 2000 and beyond.

5. Marketing's Importance. The *FT* quoted the head of KPMG's European supply chain practice as saying, "a pound spent on the supply chain can give more value than a (pound) spent on marketing. The supply chain is part of the service offering." Surely, this quote offers a challenge to marketers to better demonstrate marketing's impact on the company's P&L statement. As Irene Herremans and I wrote in *Business Horizons* in 1995, if marketing is to be a viable force in the new millennium, a need exists for marketing assessments to become a regular part of a company's annual report. In fact, such a need seems now to have reached the critical stage. What will be extremely important will be for marketers to assert their desire for accountability. Unless marketing, and particularly advertising, shows how it adds to the firm's "bottom line" through measures of brand value, customer satisfaction, and sales effectiveness, it may be destined for second-class (or lower) corporate status in the years ahead.

6. Control: The Internet. Another challenge in the new millennium is to find ways to manage the conflict between national sovereignty and the Internet. Looking at this challenge strictly from a marketing perspective, we're seeing more and more marketing through the Internet coming in direct conflict with national laws and policies, and "feeling the heat" of consumer organizations.

A recent example is the "conflict" between Disney and Danish laws prohibiting advertising directed to children. The Danish consumer ombudsman charged that Disney's Web site invited children to play games containing "hidden advertisements," *The Wall Street Journal* reported in January '99. Regardless of the validity or importance of the claim, what's at issue is the ability of a sovereign nation to regulate something as borderless as the Internet. This will be an interesting challenge to governments (and Internet marketers) in the decade ahead.

7. Cuba and New Economic Groups. During the 1990s, the U.S. Department of Commerce's International Trade Administration began to focus its attention on what it termed the "Big Emerging Markets" or BEMs. Seeing nine markets including China, India, and Brazil, as offering the greatest potential in the coming decades, it became concerned with developing U.S. export ties with these markets. And of course most of the BEMs have become prime export and direct investment targets for U.S. manufacturers and service providers.

However, the most recent "hot" market for firms in Canada, Mexico, the European Union, and Latin America appears to be Cuba. While U.S. firms have been restricted from trade with Cuba because of a trade embargo, many of their foreign competitors have been aggressively dealing with this market.

Preparing for changes in the new millennium, the White House is taking steps to thaw U.S. controls. Despite the Helms-Burton Act and the continued unwillingness of the Cuban government to settle its long-standing confiscation claims, trade with Cuba may be flourishing in the early 2000s. This is especially noteworthy for U.S. global marketers, as Cuba represents a latent consumer market similar to Eastern Europe, but with a prime location just off-shore.

Also the next decade or so is likely to see new (or rekindled) economic groups emerging and having increased importance. Steps are slowly progressing toward turning the Southern and East African economic groups into viable trading partners, and global marketers need to keep abreast of the developments. In addition, one can expect a hemispheric agreement in the future that finally will tie together the North American Free Trade Agreement (NAFTA) and "Mercosur" countries (Argentina, Paraguay, Uruguay, and Brazil, which form the "southern common market"), and most everyone in between.

8. Importing. Let's turn to importing. For decades, importing has been given a four-letter word treatment by U.S. government agencies and their counterparts in other developed countries. In fact, for many years the governments of the United States, Japan, and Western Europe have directed their efforts (and resources) to exporting and export strategies. Take, for example, the value-added tax in Europe that offers a direct financial incentive for a firm to export. But hundreds of thousands of jobs in the United States (and elsewhere) are tied directly to importing.

MANY NEW CHALLENGES AND OPPORTUNITIES ARE AWAITING GLOBAL MARKETERS IN THE EARLY 2000s.

With the industry concentration and supply chain management emphasis noted earlier, a need exists to develop new management paradigms to coordinate the global operations of the industry giants. Similarly, it will be essential to ensure that firms in the United States have mastered the art of importing. Any inefficiencies in this direction of the channel or inability to find the best foreign supplier, for example, could result in our firms not having the lowest cost supply partners, and as a result, not being competitive here and overseas. It becomes essential that they are experts at importing.

Thus, global marketers will need new management paradigms that focus on importing channels, rules, and procedures. In fact, marketing research needs to be directed to import considerations, such as developing measures to predict importer reliability.

9. Cartel Powers. This millennium will begin with commodity cartels decreasing in importance in the global economy— their lowest point in many years. One of the few remaining commodity cartels of importance is found in the international diamond industry that is dominated by De Beers.

Clearly De Beers has used its global marketing efforts to build the image (and value) of diamonds in such countries as United States and Japan and to control the industry's "single channel marketing." According to *The New York Times* in January, the firm even has plans in place to "brand" its diamonds, but may be thwarted by EU competition rules.

This cartel's success offers a challenge to other commodity cartels, such as the Organization of Petroleum Exporting Countries (OPEC), to find ways to maintain a degree of control in the 2000s. For example, OPEC is "plagued" with more country sources of crude supply and more powerful major multinational corporations (MNCs) competing in exploration, production, and marketing. Whether the OPEC "brand name" could be sold convincingly as having a higher quality is questionable, as is the cartel's ability to get its disparate members to cooperate on controlling supply in the face of the majors personal interests.

Many new challenges and opportunities are awaiting global marketers in the early 2000s. While few are directly attached to the new millennium itself, its timing happens to occur when some immediate dramatic changes and occurrences already are under way or readily

predictable. In fact, the Euro is already here, industry concentration is occurring, and Cuba trade restrictions finally are thawing. The stage is set for the millennium's start to include a plate full of issues that can reshape the global competitive environment and the way business will be conducted in the future.

Additional Reading

Batchler, Charles (1998). "Moving Up the Corporate Agenda," *Financial Times* (December 1), I.

Herremans, Irene and John K. Ryans Jr. (1995), "The Case for Better Measurement and Reporting of Marketing Performance," *Business Horizons* (September–October), 51–60.

McNeil, Donald G. Jr., (1999), "A Diamond Cartel May Be Forever," *The New York Times* (January 12), C1.

Rau, Pradeep and John K. Ryans Jr. (1990), *Marketing Strategies for the New Europe*. Chicago: American Marketing Association.

Strassel, Kimberley A. (1999), "If There's Something Rotten in Denmark, Mickey Denies All Guilt," *The Wall Street Journal* (January 12), A1.

About the Author

John K. Ryans Jr. is a Bridgestone Professor of International Marketing at Kent State University and the global marketing editor for *MM*. His international research focuses on brand evaluation/measurement, promotion management, and entry strategy. He has been published in many leading journals and is a frequent consultant to MNCs and advertising agencies such as Goodyear International, McCann-Erickson, and Xerox.

Segmenting Global Markets:
Look Before You Leap

Before implementing a global market segmentation strategy,
it's critical to understand both local and global issues.

By V. Kumar and Anish Nagpal

*"I am a citizen, not of Athens or Greece,
but of the world."*

Today we live in a global marketplace that makes So-
crates' famous words more valid than ever before. As you
read this article, you may be sitting on a chair from Paris,
wearing a shirt made in Britain, and using a computer,
without which you are handicapped, that probably was
made in Taiwan. Have you ever wondered why and how
this happens?

Global marketing refers to marketing activities of companies that emphasize four activities: (1) cost efficiencies
resulting from reduced duplication of efforts; (2) opportunities to transfer products, brands, and ideas across subsidiaries in different countries; (3) emergence of global
customers, such as global teenagers or the global elite;
and (4) better links between national marketing infrastructures, which paves the way for a global marketing infrastructure that results in better management and reduced
costs.

As the business world becomes more globalized, global
market segmentation (GMS) has emerged as an important
issue in developing, positioning, and selling products
across national boundaries. Consider the global segment
based on demographics, global teenagers. The sharing of
universal needs and desires for branded, entertaining,
trendy, and image-oriented products makes it possible to
reach the global teen segment with a unified marketing program. For example, Reebok used a global advertisement
campaign to launch its Instapump line of sneakers in the
United States, Germany, Japan, and 137 other countries
worldwide.

What Is GMS?

Global market segmentation can be defined as the process of identifying specific segments—country groups or individual consumer groups across countries—of potential
customers with homogeneous attributes who are likely to
exhibit similar buying behavior.

The study of GMS is interesting and important for three
reasons. First of all, considering the world as a market, different products are in different stages of the product life cycle at any given time. Researchers can segment the market
based on this information, but the membership of the countries in each segment is fleeting. This makes it difficult to reevaluate and update the membership of each segment.

Second, with the advent of the Internet, product information is disseminated very rapidly and in unequal propor-
tions across different countries. The dynamic nature of this
environment warrants a continuous examination of the stability of the segment membership. Third, the goal of GMS
is to break down the world market for a product or a service
into different groups of countries/consumers that differ in
their response to the firm's marketing mix program. That
way, the firm can tailor its marketing mix to each individual
segment.

Targeted segments in GMS should possess some of the
following properties:

Measurability. The segments should be easy to define and
measure. Objective country traits such as socioeconomic
variables (e.g., per capita income) can easily be gauged,
but the size of the segments based on culture or lifestyles is
much harder to measure. Thus, a larger scale survey may be
required for segmenting global markets depending upon
the basis of GMS.

EXECUTIVE SUMMARY

The primary purpose of this article is to shed more light on the more complex challenges of global market segmentation (GMS). To provide a complete understanding, we discuss some of the well-known issues in segmenting foreign markets and move on to state the various properties of global target markets. We conclude that companies can implement GMS most effectively by first gaining a full understanding of both local and global concerns.

Size. Segments should be large enough to be worth going after. Britain and Hong Kong can be grouped together in the same segment, because of previous British supremacy in Hong Kong, but their population sizes differ.

Accessibility. The segments should be easy to reach via the media. Because of its sheer size, China seems to be an attractive market. However, because of its largely rural population, it has less access to technology.

Actionability. Effective marketing programs (the four Ps) should be easy to develop. If segments do not respond differently to the firm's marketing mix, there is no need to segment the markets. Certain legal issues need to be considered before implementing an advertisement campaign. For example, many countries, such as India, do not allow direct slandering of the competitor's products.

Competitive Intensity. The segments should not be preempted by the firm's competition. In fact, in global marketing, small companies often prefer entry of less competitive markets and use this as one of the segmentation criteria when assessing international markets.

Growth Potential. A high return on investment should be attainable. Typically, marketers face a trade-off between competitive intensity and growth potential. Currently, Latin American markets have good growth potential, but the instability of local currencies causes major problems.

Companies typically employ the following six-step process for implementing GMS:
- Identify purpose (by introducing a new or existing product and choosing appropriate marketing mix programs in groups of countries)
- Select segmentation criteria (traditional vs. emerging)
- Collect relevant information
- Segment the countries/consumers according to criteria
- Reevaluate the fit of the segment after implementation of the intended program
- Update/reassign segment membership

An interesting aspect of the GMS process is the need to constantly reevaluate segment membership. The process of assigning membership to countries into a segment could be done using traditional procedures, or by evaluating the countries by using emerging techniques.

TRADITIONAL SEGMENTATION BASES

The choice of the segmentation basis is the most crucial factor in an international segmentation study. That a segmentation approach is essential in international markets is no longer questioned. Rather, the basis for segmentation becomes the focus. For example, for its Lexus brand, Toyota would segment the market based upon household income. On the other hand, if Marlboro were planning to introduce a new brand of cigarettes, it would segment the market based on population.

Individual- and country-based segmentation includes the following categories:

Demographics. This includes measurable characteristics of population such as age, gender, income, education, and occupation. A number of global demographic trends, such as changing roles of women, and higher incomes and living standards, are driving the emergence of global segments. Sony, Reebok, Nike, Swatch, and Benetton are some firms that cater to the needs of global teenagers.

Culture. This covers a broad range of factors such as religion, education, and language, which are easy to measure, and aesthetic preferences of the society that are much harder to comprehend. Hofstede's classification scheme proposes five cultural dimensions for classifying countries: Individualism vs. Collectivism, Power Distance (PD), Uncertainty Avoidance (UA), Masculinity vs. Femininity, and Strategic Orientation (long-term vs. short-term). For example, Austria, Germany, Switzerland, Italy, Great Britain, and Ireland form one cluster that is medium-high on Individualism and high on Masculinity. These cultural characteristics signify the preference for "high performance" products and a "successful achiever" theme in advertising.

Geography. This is based upon the world region, economic stage of development, nation, city, city size and population density, climate, altitude, and sometimes, even the ZIP code. It is easy to form country segments using regional blocks such as NAFTA, European Union, MERCOSUR, or Asia-Pacific. However, the value of such segments may vary depending on the need. These groupings are viable for developing trade policies, but not for marketing products/services given tremendous variation in other factors.

Environment. GMS is further complicated by different political, legal, and business environments in each country. Economic indicators such as Gross Domestic Product (GDP) may be used. However, it may not be relevant to refer to country segments based on this criterion because a country can move from one level of GDP to another, making this criterion obsolete.

Behavior-based segmentation includes three categories, which are shown in Exhibit 1.

EXHIBIT 1   Traditional segmentation basis (behavior-based)

Segmentation Basis	Brief Description	Example
Psychographics	This segment groups people in terms of their attitudes, values, and lifestyles and helps predict consumer preferences in products, services, and media.	Porsche AG divided its buyers into five distinct categories: Top Guns, Elitists, Proud Patrons, Bon Vivants, and Fantasists—each group having a particular characteristic.
Benefit	This approach focuses on the problem a product solves, regardless of location. It attempts to measure consumer value systems and perceptions of various brands in a product class.	Toothpaste consumers can be segmented into Sensory, Sociable, Worrier, and Independent segments. Sociable consumers seek bright teeth; Worriers seek healthy teeth. Aqua packaging could indicate fluoride for the Worrier segment, and white (for a white smile) for the Sociable segment.
Behavior	This examines whether or not people buy and use a product, as well as how often and how much. Consumers can be categorized in terms of usage rates (heavy, medium, and light).	ABB classifies customers according to their switchability criterion—loyal customers, those loyal to competitors, and those who can be lost to or won from the competition.

EMERGING SEGMENTATION BASES

Countries also can be segmented by means of product *diffusion patterns* and *response elasticities*. Some countries are fast adopters of the product, whereas some countries require a lag period to adopt the product. With this in mind, a firm could introduce its products in countries that are innovators (fast adopters) and later in those countries that are imitators (lag countries).

Rather than using macro-level variables to classify countries, a firm might consider segmenting markets on the basis of new-product diffusion patterns. As Exhibit 2 indicates, country segments formed on the basis of diffusion patterns may differ by product.

This type of segmentation allows the global marketer to segment countries on the basis of actual purchase patterns. Having knowledge of purchase patterns can help marketers make mode-of-entry decisions and help determine the sequence of countries in which the product should be introduced.

Consumers in lag countries can learn about the benefits of the product from the experience of adopters in the lead country, and this learning can result in a faster diffusion rate in the lag markets. Thus, countries can be grouped according to the degree of learning they exhibit for a given lead country. Lag countries that exhibit strong learning ties are potential candidates for sequential entry (using a waterfall strategy). Entry into countries that exhibit weak learning effect can be accelerated since there is not much to gain by waiting. Here, a sprinkler strategy (simultaneous entry into the relevant markets) would work well.

If a firm wants to introduce its innovation into a new country, it must be aware that the diffusion rate depends upon the kind of innovation. The diffusion pattern of a continuous innovation (one that has a majority of features in common with earlier products plus some new features that improve performance or add value) is very different from a discontinuous innovation (which is new or drastically different from earlier forms in several relevant features or attributes).

In the case of continuous innovations, such as home computers, the introduction of a successive generation will influence not only its diffusion but also the diffusion of the earlier generations. In such cases, diffusion will occur more quickly since consumers have some related knowledge. Hence, when a new generation of the product is introduced in the lead market while the lag markets are still adopting the existing (older) generation, information on the added benefits of the new generation travels faster from the lead market to potential adopters in the lag markets. The users in the lag markets will be familiar with the innovation and can easily absorb the benefits of the next generation.

Another interesting way to group countries is according to their response elasticities. Consumers across countries respond in different ways when the price of the product changes. Grocerystore scanner systems store a wealth of information that can then be used to find customer buying patterns. If the data shows the customers are price sensitive toward a particular product, couponing strategies can help target that segment, where legal.

IMPLEMENTING GMS

It is important to consider some of the conceptual and methodological issues so GMS can fulfill its high potential. Exhibit 3 gives a brief description of the four critical types of equivalencies that should be taken into account when implementing GMS.

Construct equivalence refers to whether the segmentation basis has the same meaning and is expressed similarly in different countries and cultures. Different countries under study must have the same perception or use for the product being researched. Otherwise, comparison of data becomes meaningless. If, for example, a firm is studying the bicycle market, it must realize that, in the United States, bicycles are classified under the recreational-sports industry, whereas in India and China they are considered a basic means of transportation.

EXHIBIT 2 Segments based upon diffusion patterns

Product Categories

Segment	VCRs	Cellular phones	Home computers	Microwave ovens	CD players
1	Germany, UK, France, Sweden	Denmark, Norway	Belgium, UK, Netherlands	Germany, Italy, Denmark, Austria	Belgium, Netherlands, Sweden, Austria, Finland
2	Belgium, Denmark, Spain, Austria, Finland	Finland, France	France, Italy, Sweden, Norway, Austria, Germany	Belgium, UK, Netherlands, France, Spain	Spain, Denmark, Germany
3	Italy, Portugal	Germany, UK, Italy, Switzerland	Spain, Portugal	Norway	Switzerland, Italy

Source: Kumar, V., Jaishankar Ganesh, and Raj Echambadi, "Cross-National Diffusion Research: What Do We Know and How Certain Are We?" *Journal of Product Innovation Management*, 15, 1998.

Similar activities also may have different functions in different countries. For example, for many U.S. families, grocery shopping is a chore to be accomplished as efficiently as possible. However, in India and many other countries interaction with vendors and local shopkeepers plays a very important social function.

Construct equivalence is easier to establish for the general bases, such as geographic variables. However, for bases such as values and lifestyles, construct equivalence is much harder to achieve. VALS-2 identifies eight segments based on two main dimensions: self-orientation and resources. Another VALS system was developed for Japan, presumably because the U.S.-based VALS-2 system was not appropriate for that country. Instead it identifies 10 segments based on two key dimensions: life orientation and attitudes toward social change.

Scalar equivalence means that scores from different countries should have the same meaning and interpretation. The first aspect used to determine scalar equivalence concerns the specific scale or scoring procedure used to establish the measure. The standard format of scales used in survey research differs across countries. For example, in the United States a 5- or 7-point scale is most common. However, 20-point scales are used in France.

EXHIBIT 3 Types of equivalence

Equivalence

Construct	Scalar	Measurement	Sampling
Are we studying the same phenomena in Brazil, India, and Britain?	Do the scores on consumers in the U.S., Argentina, and Japan have the same meaning?	Are the phenomena in France, Singapore and South Africa measured in the same way?	Are the samples used in Hong Kong, China, and Romania equivalent?

The second aspect concerns the response to a score obtained in a measure. Here the question arises as to whether a score obtained in one research context has the same meaning and interpretation in another context. For example, on an intention-to-purchase scale, does the proportion of likely buyers indicate a similar likelihood of purchase from one country to another, or does a position on the Likert scale have the same meaning in all cultures?

Differences in response styles often result in a lack of scalar equivalence. Some of these response styles include "extreme" responding and "social desirability" responding. Research shows Chinese respondents show a "marked degree of agreeability," while Americans show a "marked willingness to dissent." These differences can cause problems in the data-collection process, which can lead to erroneous grouping of countries.

Measurement equivalence refers to whether the measures used to operationalize the segmentation basis are comparable across countries. For example, consider the level of education. The United States uses one educational scale while in Europe the educational system is quite different, and the term "college" is not appropriate. Also, household income is difficult to compare across countries owing to differences in the tax structure and purchasing power.

Some items of a segmentation basis have measurement equivalence, but the others do not. For example, research shows that in the U.S. consumer innovativeness is expressed both in terms of purchase of new products and in social communication about new products. In France, however, the latter does not apply. Hence, only items pertaining to the person's tendency to purchase new products have measurement equivalence across the two countries. The researcher thus faces the dilemma of either using the same set of items in each country (etic scale) or adapting the set of items to each country (emic-scale). A compromise would be a combined emic-etic scale with some core items common to all countries and some country-specific items.

Sampling equivalence deals with problems in identifying and operationalizing comparable populations and selecting samples that are simultaneously representative of other populations and comparable across countries. One aspect of sampling equivalence deals with the decision-making process, which varies across countries. For example, in the United States, office supplies are often purchased by the office secretary, whereas this decision is made by a middle-level manager or CEO in some countries.

It is also important to consider whether the sample is representative of the population. In most developed countries, information on potential markets and sampling frames is easily available. However, in Japan, the most popular residential list for sample studies was made inaccessible to researchers. Developing countries do not have extensive databases and so obtaining the sampling frame to suit the needs of the research could be difficult.

Equivalence presents a dilemma in the minds of managers. On one end, it would be wise to develop scales specifically for each culture; on the other, responses collected in this manner may not mean the same thing. This issue can be resolved to some extent by using a combination of items in the scale.

THINK GLOBALLY, ACT LOCALLY

Used effectively, segmentation allows global marketers to take advantage of the benefits of standardization (such as economies of scale and consistency in positioning) while addressing the needs and expectations of a specific target group. This approach means looking at markets on a global or regional basis, thereby ignoring the political boundaries that define markets in many cases.

The greatest challenge for the global marketer is the choice of an appropriate base for segmentation. Pitfalls that handicap global marketing programs and contribute to their suboptimal performance include market-related reasons, such as insufficient research and overstandardization, as well as internal reasons, such as inflexibility in planning and implementation. If a product is launched on a broad scale without formally researching regional or local differences, it may fail.

The successful global marketers will be those who can achieve a balance between the local and the regional/global concerns. Procter and Gamble's Pampers brand suffered a major setback in the 1980s in Japan when customers favored the purchase of diapers of rival brands.

The diapers were made and sold according to a formula imposed by Cincinnati headquarters, and Japanese consumers found the company's hard-sell techniques alienating. Globalization by design requires a balance between sensitivity to local needs and global deployment of technologies and concepts.

GMS offers a solution to the standardization vs. adaptation issue because it creates the conceptual framework for offering standardized products and marketing programs in multiple countries by targeting the same consumer segments in different countries. The formulation of a global strategy by a firm may result in the choice of one particular segment across markets or multiple segments. However, in implementing the marketing mix for maximum effect, the principle "Think globally, act locally" becomes a critical rule for guiding marketing efforts.

ADDITONAL READING

Ganesh, Jaishankar, V. Kumar, and Velavan Subramaniam (1997), "Learning Effect in Multinational Diffusion of Consumer Durables: An Exploratory Investigation," *Journal of the Academy of Marketing Science*, 25 (3), 214–228.

Hofstede, Geert (1984), *Culture's Consequences: International Differences in Work-Related Values*. California: Sage Publications.

Kotabe, Masaaki, and Kristiaan Helsen (1998), *Global Marketing Management*. New York: John Wiley & Sons Inc.

Kumar, V. (2000), *International Marketing Research*. New Jersey: Prentice Hall.

V. Kumar (VK) is Marvin Hurley Professor of Business Administration, Melcher Faculty Scholar, Director of Marketing Research Studies and Director of International Business Programs at the University of Houston, Bauer College of Business, Department of Marketing. He may be reached at vkumar@uh.edu.

Anish Nagpal is a doctoral student at the University of Houston, Bauer College of Business, Department of Marketing.

From *Marketing Research,* Spring 2001, pp. 8-13. © 2001 by the American Marketing Association. Reprinted by permission.

The Invisible Global Market

With 86% of the world containing **hidden** markets, marketers need to take action.

By Vijay Mahajan, Marcos V. Pratini De Moraes, and Jerry Wind

Is it worth marketing cellular phones to tiny villages in Bangladesh? Not according to traditional approaches to marketing. The market is too small and income is too low to make the villages attractive target markets. Yet Grameen-Phone, a Dhaka-based company, has developed a strategy for marketing cell phones to the 35,000 villages in Bangladesh. It has set up women in the villages as agents who lease phone time to other villagers, one call at a time.

Is there a market for toothpaste in the rural villages of India? With more than half of villagers illiterate and only one-third living in households with televisions, this seems like a marketer's nightmare. But these villages, with about 70% of India's 900 million people, represent a market more than twice the size of the United States, so it is easy to see why Colgate-Palmolive increased its rural marketing budget in India by fivefold between 1991 and 1996.

Colgate-Palmolive has used creative strategies to introduce villagers to the concept of brushing teeth, including rolling into villages with video vans that show half-hour infomercials on the benefits of toothpaste. The company expects to draw more than half of its revenue in the nation from rural areas by 2003. It is a market that until recently was virtually invisible. And many major companies still don't see it.

Colgate and Grameen-Phone understand something that many major companies have failed to see: A large, invisible global market. Grameen Bank, "banker to the poor," has developed innovative micro-lending strategies to give small businesses (such as the rural cell phone network) access to financial services in Bangladesh. Marketers similarly need to scale down and retool their strategies to move from Madison Avenue to dusty rural village streets.

Some of the best global market opportunities may be found beyond the competitive and saturated markets of developed nations. Until now, however, many companies have dismissed these markets as too poor to matter. Even though these customers may not be buying Rolexes, BMWs, or Gucci bags, they do matter. But it will take creative marketing strategies and a shift in perspective to reach them. These strategies and perspectives are the focus of this article.

Below the Radar

Modern marketing typically focuses on developed nations (or developed segments of nations), although most of the world market lies outside these segments. Developed nations with per capita GNP of more than $10,000—what Kenichi Ohmae refers to as the "$10,000 Club"—account for only 14% of the global population. This means that companies that focus on these markets don't see roughly 86% of the world population. This is the invisible global market.

EXECUTIVE
briefing

How can marketing managers understand and connect with 86% of the world population that may not relate to products and marketing strategies used in developing countries? Even though some of the consumers in these markets are moving up the ladder to higher income segments, finding and connecting to this huge invisible global market requires understanding 10 key insights and principles for strategic success that are quite different from those used in developed countries.

We should note that this $10,000 mark is a rather crude cutoff for developed nations, based on the premise that individuals in the developed nations have enough disposable income to support a market. There are obviously high-income segments within all developing nations, as most companies recognize. (These developing nations may have islands of "developed" customers that can be larger than some whole nations. For example, with 86 million people in Mexico, if 1% of the population

190

achieves the income status of a developed nation, that segment would be twice the size of Luxembourg.) But even if a few high-income customers are on the radar screen, the majority of potential customers in developing nations are virtually ignored because of the challenges of reaching them by conventional methods. However, marketers can reach this segment by unconventional methods.

Getting on the Radar Screen

What do you need to do to see and reach these invisible markets? There are several key insights and principles for strategic success that are quite different from those used in developed markets. To find and connect to these markets, companies need to pay attention to the following 10 insights and strategies:

1. Build products to compete against "bullock carts" rather than automobiles.

In these markets, your competitors may not be who you think they are. Understanding local product needs can lead to radically rethinking products. When an Indian-Australian car manufacturer created a rural transport vehicle, it was not designed to compete with automobiles but rather to replace the "bullock cart." The new vehicle needed to be able to navigate the rough, narrow roads of rural India and haul both people and cargo. Like the bullock cart it replaces, it functions well at low speeds, with four low gears, and carries up to two tons.

You need to focus on using the market as a laboratory for new product designs rather than on conquering markets. A company that sells washers and dryers to Japan is not just penetrating a new market. It has learned about selling products to customers with small homes. This is a lesson it can then translate from the Japanese market, where homes average 900 square feet (half the size of U.S. homes), to Hong Kong, where the average apartment is just 480 square feet.

2. Create product and service revolutions that can be exported.

A product revolution such as the motorized bullock cart can often be exported to other invisible markets. Fiat deliberately chose Brazil as the laboratory for launching its new "third-world car," the Palio, to ensure it would respond to the invisible market. The vehicle was completely rethought for Brazilian consumers. In one year after its launch, Fiat sold 250,000 of the cars, double the previous record for a new car launch in Brazil. In contrast, Ford's Fiesta, imported from Europe and launched around the same time, achieved less than one-third of Fiat's sales in Brazil. Fiat exported its Brazilian revolution to Argentina, where sales of a version of the Palio took off rapidly. The company planned to take the Palio to Turkey, Morocco, South Africa, India and perhaps China. The new car was part of a deliberate strategy by Fiat to shift its focus from the crowded Western European market to target the invisible global market.

Fariborz Ghadar, founder of Intrados Group, is bringing modern stock exchanges to the invisible global market. The lessons and software that he used to set up NASDAQ-style exchanges in Romania have been used to start stock exchanges in almost two dozen nations, for a price of about $1 million. The exchanges offer these developing nations a system for clearance and settlement to issue stock certificates to buyers and cash to sellers.

Corporacion GEO, a low-income housing developer in Mexico, tripled its sales between 1993 and 1996 to $246 million by building thousands of low-cost, two-bedroom houses and apartments. These homes are modular, so a basic model can be upgraded as purchasers increase their income. Building on its Mexican successes, GEO has expanded its home business to Chile and poor southern U.S. communities.

Instead of focusing on conquering the market, you need to concentrate on learning as much as you can about the needs of customers and developing product and service offerings to meet these needs. A product and service revolution created in one invisible market often creates opportunities to "export the revolution" to others.

3. Pay attention to the informal economy.

Economist Friedrich Schneider has estimated that the shadow economy or informal economy may account for one-seventh of the output of the world's wealthiest nations and a much higher proportion of developing nations. According to these estimates, the shadow economy has been growing three times as fast as the formal economy since the 1960s. In India, only 12,000 of the nation's roughly 900 million citizens admitted to earning an income of more than $28,000 per year—and only one in 77 people filed a tax return at all. Other estimates are that India's unofficial economy is equal to its national income. If you don't see this shadow economy, you could be blindsided by competitors you don't even know exist.

The informal economy often competes directly with the formal economy, but without the constraints of regulation or taxation. When one Latin American country was opened to foreign companies in the mid-1990s, small entrepreneurial companies began rebottling domestic automobile oil in containers from the U.S. oil companies to sell them at the higher prices to take advantage of their brand names. This informal economy accounted for a large part of the oil sold in the country, angering both the foreign companies and the legitimate domestic firm.

Instead of fighting to change the market, companies can find ways to use it (obviously within legal channels). For example, most Westerners respond to intellectual-property violations by pressuring governments for rigid enforcement of anti-piracy laws. But instead of fighting the pirates, it might be a better strategy to take advantage of them. For example, what if Microsoft were to add advertising to its software programs in these countries? Then, gaining a wider distribution, legal or illegal, would benefit the firm. (Newspapers initially were originally concerned that non-purchasers would be reading friends' copies of the paper, but realized that increased readership added to the advertising revenues for the paper.)

Education also can be used to shine some light into the black market. In Brazil, where pirates account for an estimated 68% of software, Microsoft replaced its hard-line lobbying for trade sanctions with a $10 million deal to bring low-cost software to public schools to try to get Brazilians used to the idea of paying for software.

Activities of the informal economy can offer indications of unmet consumer needs. If these activities are in the informal economy (assuming they are not strictly illegal), are there ways to meet the same needs in a different way through legitimate channels? For example, the market for pirated books might be addressed through electronic publications, with much lower production costs but legal content.

4. Use global family networks.

Why did Japanese companies advertise products in India before the Indian economy was opened to outsiders that are not sold in India? Because close to 20 million Indian expatriates live in other parts of the world, the advertisements led Indian natives to contact relatives overseas who brought the products on their next visit. The borders of the world are permeable, with non-resident populations connecting different markets in diverse parts of the world.

There are more than 23 million people in the United States who are foreign born, with 7 million from Mexico. If these Mexican immigrants spend just $200 per year on purchases for relatives back home, this is more than $1 billion in what are effectively purchases for relatively poor Mexicans. (As another confirmation of this interaction between immigrants and their relatives back home, Mexican phone-access receipts from the United States are the highest in the world, followed by China and India, reflecting higher volumes of calling to these nations.) Are American companies aware of this? Are they advertising products in Mexico that might be bought by relatives in the United States and sent or taken back home?

Even if an economy is formally closed by regulation and income, as long as information is flowing, the market is never really closed. The Internet only accelerates this process. Sometimes the most direct route to a customer is not a straight line, but rather a global zigzag through developing and developed markets.

5. Understand that customers don't know how to be customers.

Domino's Pizza has taken off in one Latin American country, but for the wrong reasons. Customers see its 30-minute delivery guarantee as a challenge and they take advantage of complex and confusing addresses to slow the driver and receive a free pizza. In most of the invisible economy, there is not consumer culture. Customers in emerging markets do not behave the way marketers expect. They have never been taught to be customers, so you cannot assume they will respond in the way that customers respond in developed markets.

As another example, money-back guarantees don't always translate well in these markets. Amway in China told customers if they were not satisfied, they could bring the product (soap) back for a full refund, no questions asked—even if the bottles were empty. Some enterprising third parties began repackaging the soap and returning the empty bottles. Others just scoured empty bottles out of trash cans to seek refunds. When refunds mounted to $100,000 per day, Amway rescinded the policy, only to face angry distributors who marched into offices to complain. They felt they were entitled to the refunds. Amway offers the same guarantee worldwide—with very different results—so it was surprised by the Chinese reaction. Companies cannot assume that customers know how to be customers. Firms may need to rethink their approaches to reach these customers or spend more time to educate them.

6. Recognize low income doesn't mean low quality expectations.

Realizing that the Indian market for its luxury cars was limited, Mercedes-Benz built a factory in 1995 to produce an older model car used for taxis in Germany. Indian consumers turned away from what was perceived as an inferior product, leaving the plant hobbling along at 10% capacity.

Amway took a drubbing in South Korea when consumer and environmental groups began claiming its dish detergent did not meet Korean standards for biode-gradability. Although the soap meets international standards for degradability over an eight-day period, South Korean activists used a one-day test (claiming Korean streams were shorter). They also claimed the product was overpriced, although Amway officials commented this was a misperception because the detergent is concentrated. Regardless of the validity of the allegations, the perception of poor quality led to a precipitous loss of nearly two-thirds of its sales there in a seven-month period. Perceived quality is extremely important, even in emerging economies.

7. Use "demand pooling" to reach critical mass.

Sometimes to find a market large enough to serve, you need to gather customers together yourself. Because shoppers in a Latin American country buy their food fresh every day, there is not enough volume to support a large supermarket (i.e., few retail customers would buy a dozen oranges.) So a retailer in this country created a supermarket where the small grocers can also shop. The grocers buy larger quantities of the products (i.e., fresh fruit) and then divide them up for their customers. This is similar to the cell phones in villages in Bangladesh where the market is not wealthy enough to support individual sales, but becomes attractive when the demand is pooled.

Another alternative is reducing the package size to make it affordable to low-income customers. A building-supply retainer in a Latin-American country found that by reducing the size of its bags of cement, it could offer quality products in small packages to its customers who are building their own homes. This way, they can gradually accumulate enough cement for their homes. The company also offers innovative financing schemes for building materials for inexpensive shanties.

8. Bring your own infrastructure.

The competitive environment of the invisible economy is often quite different from traditional markets. Coca-Cola rarely has to think about electricity in the United States, but in the developing world it is a serious concern. How can the company keep sodas in machines cold when the public electric supply may shut down for hours? What happens to computer systems? Coca-Cola's challenge is to design refrigeration systems to ensure products remain cold, even through long power outages. Other companies need to use battery backup systems to keep computers running despite fluctuating power. Similarly, clean water is a problem in many developing countries, but portable water-purification systems can clean the water as it comes out of the tap.

Finally, the lack of telephone systems in rural areas is being overcome by the rapid spread of cellular telephones. New technology and innovative solutions help to overcome inhospitable business environments. Sometimes, as with the rapid spread of cellular systems in countries without extensive landline infrastructures, innovative technologies may allow the new markets to leapfrog more developed nations. Companies can wait years until governments build the reliable infrastructure to support their businesses or they can accept the environment as it is and work out solutions of their own. The motto should be, "Don't wait, innovate."

9. Rethink the entire marketing and business strategy.

As the aforementioned observations indicate, to address the very different dynamics of the invisible global markets, companies often have to do more than merely tweak their existing marketing and business strategies. For example, companies need to be aware that the change agent influencing a decision might not be the customer or even a family member. A wealthy homeowner in a developing nation may set the trends for maids and others employed in her household, a fact that is often missed if the companies focus on the end purchaser. And marketers need to rethink the unit of analysis, because sometimes "it takes a village" to make a

purchase. Where repair costs are high, companies need to think about the lifetime costs of ownership of major purchases such as automobiles rather than purchase price. If you can design a car less likely to need repairs, or build in insurance, the product may have much higher value in these markets.

10. Bridge the digital divide.

The "digital divide" may increase the gap between large companies and the invisible market. In India, for example, the penetration of PCs is only 0.5%, and this technological barrier threatens to make these markets even more invisible. Companies need to think of clever ways to offer access to the Internet infrastructure, as creative entrepreneurs are already doing through kiosks and other shared methods of access. Companies can begin by initiating programs for their own employees, as Ford is doing by offering PCs and Internet services to employees around the world. In addition, the content of Web-based marketing needs to be rethought for these markets—with an emphasis on educating consumers and reaching markets with a low penetration of credit cards. Companies that can use the Internet creatively may find that the lower costs of reaching customers actually makes these markets more accessible.

The Invisible Market Is the Future

Customers in these invisible markets stretch out like countless grains of sand on the beach. Individually, they may represent a very small opportunity. Because of their sheer number, however, this forgotten 86% of the world represents a huge opportunity. If you have been walking by this opportunity on your way to the visible 14%, it may be time to take another look at the opportunities in front of you. Companies that see these opportunities will find creative ways to gather these grains together to build castles.

This invisible market will become even more significant in the future. With population growth slowing in major developed countries relative to developing nations, more of the customers of the future will be in the invisible global market. Even though some of these consumers will be moving up the ladder to higher-income segments, a large portion of the potential global market will continue to fly below the radar. You cannot wait for these customers to appear on your radar screen. You have to go and find them. You need to move off the beaten path—both in the products you develop and the creative strategies you use—to turn these invisible markets into visible returns.

Additional Reading

Business Week (1997), "Microsoft to Pirate: Pretty Please?" (September 22), 4.
The Economist (1997), "A Car Is Born," (September 13), 68.
The Economist (1997), "Light on the Shadows," (May 3).
Foust, Dean (1997), "Fariborz Ghadar," *Business Week*, (October 27), 128.

India Abroad (2000), "Shakeout Is Predicted in the Internet Business," (February 11), 34.

Jordan, Miram (1996), "In Rural India, Video Vans Sell Toothpaste and Shampoo," *The Wall Street Journal*, (January 10), B-1, B-3.

Ohmae, Kenichi (1987), "The Triad World View," *Journal of Business Strategy* vol. 7 no. 4 (Spring), 8–19.

Pande, Tanni (1997), "Rural Vehicle Designed to Replace Bullock Cart," *India Abroad*, (September 12), 30.

Schuman, Michael (1997), "Amway Finds Itself Washed Over in a South Korean Soap Drama," *The Wall Street Journal*, (October 22), A-16.

Smith, Craig S. (1997), "In China, Some Distributors Have Really Cleaned Up with Amway," *The Wall Street Journal*, (August 4), B-1.

Smith, Geri, Elisabeth Malkin, Ian Katz, Andrea Mandel-Campbell, and John Pearson (1997), "The New Latin Corporation," *Business Week*, (October 27), 71–82.

Yunus, Muhammad and Alan Jonis (1999), *Banker to the Poor*. New York: Public Affairs.

Vijay Mahajan is the John P. Harbin Centennial Chair in Business and professor of marketing at the University of Texas, Austin. His research, teaching, and consulting are in the areas of marketing strategy, new product development, and marketing research methodologies. He has received several awards including the Parlin and the Churchill Awards for lifetime contributions to marketing and marketing research. He may be reached at vmahajan@utexas.edu.

Marcos V. Pratini De Moraes is the Minister of Agriculture, Brazil and is the former president of Brazilian Exporters Association. Moraes has received numerous decorations from the Brazilian government; these include the Grand Cross of the Rio Branco Order, the Grand Officer of the Order of Aeronautical Merit as well as the Grand Cross of the Royal St. Olaf's Order from the government of Norway. He may be reached at pratini@agricultura.gov.br.

Jerry Wind is the Lauder Professor and professor of marketing at the Wharton School. He is director of the SEI Center for Advanced Studies in Management, the first "think tank" on management education for the twenty-first century, and was founding director of the Lauder Institute of Management and International Studies. He is author or editor of more than a dozen books on marketing and related topics, including *Driving Change* (Free Press, 1998) and *Leveraging Japan* (Jossey-Bass, 2000). He may be reached at windj@wharton.upenn.edu.

From *Marketing Management,* Winter 2000, Vol. 9, No. 9 pp. 31-35. © 2000 by the American Marketing Association. Reprinted by permission.

The Lure of Global Branding

Brand builders everywhere think they want global brands.
But global brand leadership, not global brands, should be the priority.
Successful companies follow four principles to meet that goal.

by David A. Aaker and Erich Joachimsthaler

AS MORE AND MORE companies come to view the entire world as their market, brand builders look with envy upon those that appear to have created global brands—brands whose positioning, advertising strategy, personality, look, and feel are in most respects the same from one country to another. It's easy to understand why. Even though most global brands are not absolutely identical from one country to another—Visa changes its logo in some countries; Heineken means something different in the Netherlands than it does abroad—companies whose brands have become more global reap some clear benefits.

> **Consolidating all advertising into one agency and developing a global theme can cause problems that outweigh any advantages.**

Consider for a moment the economies of scale enjoyed by IBM. It costs IBM much less to create a single global advertising campaign than it would to create separate campaigns for dozens of markets. And because IBM uses only one agency for all its global advertising, it carries a lot of clout with the agency and can get the most talented people working on its behalf. A global brand also benefits from being driven by a single strategy. Visa's unvarying "worldwide acceptance" position, for example, is much easier for the company to manage than dozens of country-specific strategies.

Attracted by such high-profile examples of success, many companies are tempted to try to globalize their own brands. The problem is, that goal is often unrealistic. Consolidating all advertising into one agency and developing a global advertising theme—often the cornerstone of the effort—can cause problems that outweigh any advantages. And edicts from on high—"Henceforth, use only brand-building programs that can be applied across countries"—can prove ineffective or even destructive. Managers who stampede blindly toward creating a global brand without considering whether such a move fits well with their company or their markets risk falling over a cliff. There are several reasons for that.

First, economies of scale may prove elusive. It is sometimes cheaper and more effective for companies to create ads locally than to import ads and then adapt them for each market. Moreover, cultural differences may make it hard to pull off a global campaign: even the best agency may have trouble executing it well in all countries. Finally, the potential cost savings from "media spillover"—in which, for example, people in France view German television ads—have been exaggerated. Language barriers and cultural differences have made realizing such benefits difficult for most companies.

Second, forming a successful global brand team can prove difficult. Developing a superior brand strategy for one country is challenging enough; creating one that can be applied worldwide can be daunting (assuming one even exists). Teams face several stumbling blocks: they need to gather and understand a great deal of information; they must be extremely creative; and they need to anticipate a host of challenges in execution. Relatively few teams will be able to meet all those challenges.

Third, global brands can't just be imposed on all markets. For examples, a brand's image may not be the same throughout the world. Honda means quality and reliability in the United States, but in Japan, where quality is a given for most cars, Honda represents speed, youth, and energy. And consider market position. In Britain, where Ford is number one, the company positioned its Galaxy minivan as the luxurious "nonvan" in order to appeal not only to soccer moms but also to executives. But in Germany, where Volkswagen rules, Ford had to position the Galaxy as "the clever alternative." Similarly, Cadbury in the United Kingdom and Milka in Germany have preempted the associations that connect milk with chocolate; thus neither company could implement a global positioning strategy.

For all those reasons, taking a more nuanced approach is the better course of action. Developing global brands should not be the priority. Instead, companies should work on creating strong brands in all markets through global brand leadership.

Global brand leadership means using organizational structures, processes, and cultures to allocate brand-building resources globally, to create global synergies, and to develop a global brand strategy that coordinates and leverages country brand strategies. That is, of course, easier said than done. For example, companies tend to give the bulk of their brand-building attention to countries with large sales—at the expense of emerging markets that may represent big opportunities. But some companies have successfully engaged in global brand management. To find out how, we interviewed executives from 35 companies in the United States, Europe, and Japan that have successfully developed strong brands across countries. (About half the executives were from companies that made frequently purchased consumer products; the rest represented durables, high-tech products, and service brands.)

Four common ideas about effective brand leadership emerged from those interviews. Companies must:

- stimulate the sharing of insights and best practices across countries;
- support a common global brand-planning process;
- assign managerial responsibility for brands in order to create cross-country synergies and to fight local bias; and
- execute brilliant brand-building strategies.

Sharing Insights and Best Practices

A companywide communication system is the most basic element of global brand leadership. Managers from country to country need to be able to find out about programs that have worked or failed elsewhere; they also need a way to easily give and receive knowledge about customers—knowledge that will vary from one market to another.

Creating such a system is harder than it sounds. Busy people usually have little motivation to take the time to explain why efforts have been successful or ineffective; furthermore, they'd rather not give out information that may leave them exposed to criticism. Another problem is one that everyone in business faces today: information overload. And a feeling of "it won't work here" often pervades companies that attempt to encourage the sharing of market knowledge.

To overcome those problems, companies must nurture and support a culture in which best practices are freely communicated. In addition, people and procedures must come together to create a rich base of knowledge that is relevant and easy to access. Offering incentives is one way to get people to share what they know. American Management Systems, for example, keeps track of the employees who post insights and best practices and rewards them during annual performance reviews.

Regular meetings can be an effective way of communicating insights and best practices. Frito-Lay, for example, sponsors a "market university" roughly three times a year in which 35 or so marketing directors and general managers from around the world meet in Dallas for a week. The university gets people to think about brand leadership concepts, helps people overcome the mind-set of "I am different—global programs won't work in my market," and creates a group of people around the world who believe in and understand brands and brand strategy. During the week, country managers present case studies on packaging, advertising, and promotions that were tested in one country and then successfully applied in another. The case studies demonstrate that practices can be transferred even when a local marketing team is skeptical.

Formal meetings are useful, but true learning takes place during informal conversations and gatherings. And the personal relationships that people establish during those events are often more important than the information they share. Personal ties lead to meaningful exchanges down the road that can foster brand-building programs.

In addition to staging meetings, companies are increasingly using intranets to communicate insights and best practices. (Sharing such information by e-mail isn't as effective—there is simply too much e-mail clutter. E-mail is useful, however, for conveying breaking news about competitors or new technology.) The key is to have a team create a knowledge bank on an intranet that is valuable and accessible to those who need it. Mobil, for example, uses a set of best-practice networks to do just that. The networks connect people in the company (and sometimes from partner organizations) who are experts on, for example, new product introduction, brand architecture, and retail-site presentation. Each network has a senior management sponsor and a leader who actively solicits postings from the experts. The leader ensures that the information is formatted, organized, and posted on an easy-to-use intranet site.

Field visits are another useful way to learn about best practices. Honda sends teams to "live with best practices" and to learn how they work. In some companies, the CEO travels to different markets in order to energize the country teams and to see best practices in action.

Procter & Gamble uses worldwide strategic-planning groups of three to 20 people for each category to encourage and support global strategies. The teams have several tasks. They mine local knowledge about markets and disseminate that information globally. They gather data about effective country-specific marketing efforts and encourage testing elsewhere. They create global manufacturing sourcing strategies. And they develop policies that dictate which aspects of the brand strategy must be followed everywhere and which ones are up to country management.

Who's Responsible for the Brand?

Business Management Team

Brand Champion

Global Brand Team

Global Brand Manager

Deciding who has ultimate responsibility for global brands is the first step toward going global and ensuring buy-in among country teams. To fight local bias and exploit cross-country synergies, a company must assign managerial responsibility for its brands. Depending on the company's makeup, responsibility for global brand leadership can follow one of four possible configurations: business management team, brand champion, global brand manager, and global brand team. The first two are led by senior executives; the latter two by middle managers.

Another way that companies can communicate information about their brands is by sharing research. Ford operates very differently from country to country in Europe, but its businesses share research methods and findings. Ford UK, for example, which is very skilled at doing direct mail and research on segmentation, makes its technology and research methods available to other countries. That's especially important for businesses in small markets that are short on budget and staff.

Supporting Global Brand Planning

Two years ago, the newly appointed global brand manager of a prominent packaged-goods marketer organized a brand strategy review. He found that all the country brand managers used their own vocabularies and strategy templates and had their own strategies. The resulting mess had undoubtedly contributed to inferior marketing and weakened brands. Another packaged-goods company tried to avoid that problem by developing a global planning system. Brand managers weren't given incentives or trained

properly to use the system, however, and the result was inconsistent, half-hearted efforts at planning.

Companies that practice global brand management use a planning process that is consistent across markets and products—a brand presentation looks and sounds the same whether it's delivered in Singapore, Spain, or Sweden, and whether it's for PCs or printers. It shares the same well-defined vocabulary, strategic analysis inputs (such as competitor positions and strategies), brand strategy model, and outputs (such as brand-building programs).

There is no one accepted process model, but all models have two starting points: it must be clear which person or group is responsible for the brand and the brand strategy, and a process template must exist. The completed template should specify such aspects of a strategy as the target segment, the brand identity or vision, brand equity goals and measures, and brand-building programs that will be used within and outside the company. Although various process models can work, observations of effective programs suggest five guidelines.

First, the process should include an analysis of customers, competitors, and the brand. Analysis of customers must go beyond quantitative market research data; managers need to understand the brand associations that resonate with people. Analysis of competitors is necessary to differentiate the brand and to ensure that its communication program—which may include sponsorship, promotion, and advertising—doesn't simply copy what other companies are doing. And an audit of the brand itself involves an examination of its heritage, image, strengths, and problems, as well as the company's vision for it. The brand needs to reflect that vision to avoid making empty promises.

Second, the process should avoid a fixation on product attributes. A narrow focus on attributes leads to short-lived, easily copied advantages and to shallow customer relationships. Most strong brands go beyond functional benefits; despite what customers might say, a brand can also deliver emotional benefits and help people express themselves. A litmus test of whether a company really understands its brands is whether it incorporates the following elements into the brand strategy: brand personality (how the brand would be described if it were a person), user imagery (how the brand's typical user is perceived), intangibles that are associated with the company (its perceived innovativeness or reputation for quality, for example), and symbols associated with the brand, such as Virgin's Branson, the Coke bottle, or the Harley eagle. A simple three-word phrase or a brief list of product attributes cannot adequately represent a strong brand.

Third, the process must include programs to communicate the brand's identity (what the brand should stand for) to employees and company partners. Without clarity and enthusiasm internally about the associations the brand aspires to develop, brand building has no chance. A brand manual often plays a key role. Unilever has a detailed manual on its most global brand, Lipton Tea, that puts the answer to any question about its brand identity (What does the brand stand for? What are the timeless elements of the brand? What brand-building programs are off target?) at the fingertips of all employees. Other companies use workshops (Nestlé), newsletters (Hewlett-Packard), books (Volvo), and videos (the Limited) to communicate brand identity. To engage people in this process, Mobil asked employees to nominate recent programs or actions that best reflected the core elements of the Mobil brand—leadership, partnership, and trust. The employees with the best nominations were honored guests at a car race sponsored by the company.

Fourth, the process must include brand equity measurement and goals. Without measurement, brand building is often just talk; yet surprisingly few companies have systems that track brand equity. Pepsi is an exception. In the mid-1990s, Pepsi introduced a system based on what it calls a "marketplace P&L." The P&L measures brand equity by tracking the results of blind taste tests, the extent of a product's distribution, and the results of customer opinion surveys about the brand. In the beginning, country managers were strongly encouraged—but not required—to use the system. But the value of the marketplace P&L soon become clear, as country managers compared results at meetings and used the shared information to improve their brand-building efforts. In 1998, CEO Roger Enrico made the system mandatory—a dramatic indication of its value given Pepsi's decentralized culture and the home office's general reluctance to impose companywide rules.

Finally, the process must include a mechanism that ties global brand strategies to country brand strategies. Sony and Mobil, among others, use a top-down approach. They begin with a global brand strategy; country strategies follow from it. A country brand strategy might augment the global strategy by adding elements to modify the brand's identity. For example, if the manager of a Mobil fuel brand in Brazil wants to emphasize that the brand gives an honest gallon (because other brands of fuel in Brazil are not considered reliable in their measurements), he would add "honest measures" to the country brand identity. For example, although the term "leadership" may mean "technology leadership" in most countries, the strategist may change it to mean "market leadership" in his or her market. In the top-down approach, the country brand team has the burden of justifying any departures from the global brand strategy.

In the bottom-up approach, the global brand strategy is built from the country brand strategies. Country strategies are grouped by similarities. A grouping might, for example, be made on the basis of market maturity (underdeveloped, emerging, or developed) or competitive context (whether the brand is a leader or a challenger). While the brand strategy for these groupings will differ, a global brand strategy should also be able to identify common elements. Over time, the number of distinct strategies will usually fall as experiences and best practices are shared. As the number shrinks, the company can capture synergies. Mercedes, for example, uses one advertising agency to create a menu of five campaigns. Brand managers in different countries can then pick the most suitable campaign for their market.

Assigning Responsibility

Local managers often believe that their situation is unique—and therefore, that insights and best practices from other countries can't be applied to their markets. Their belief is based in part on justifiable confidence in their knowledge of the country, the competitive milieu, and the consumers. Any suggestion that such confidence is misplaced can feel threatening. Moreover, people are comfortable with strategies that have already proven effective. The local brand managers may fear that they will be coerced or enticed into following a strategy that doesn't measure up to their current efforts.

Most companies today have a decentralized culture and structure. They find it difficult, therefore, to persuade country teams to quickly and voluntarily accept and implement a global best practice. To ensure that local teams overcome such reluctance, an individual or group must be in charge of the global brand. Our research suggests that responsibility for global brand leadership can follow four possible configurations: business management team, brand champion, global brand manager, and global brand team. The first two are led by senior executives; the latter two by middle managers.

Business Management Team. This approach is most suitable when the company's top managers are marketing or branding people who regard brands as the key asset to their business. P&G fits that description. Each of its 11 product categories is run by a global category team. The teams consist of the four managers who have line responsibility for R&D, manufacturing, and marketing for the category within their region. Each team is chaired by an executive vice president who also has a second line job. For example, the head of health and beauty aids in Europe also chairs the hair care global category team. The teams meet five or six times a year.

Because the teams are made up of top-level line executives, there are no organizational barriers to carrying out decisions. At the country level, P&G's brand and advertising managers implement the strategy. Thus local bias cannot get in the way of the company's global brand leadership.

The 11 teams strive to create global brands without weakening brand strength locally. They define the identity and position of brands in their categories throughout the world. They encourage local markets to test and adopt brand-building programs that have been successful elsewhere. And they decide which brands will get new product advances. For example, Elastesse, the chemical compound that helps people eliminate "helmet head," was first added to the company's Pantene product line rather than one of its three sister brands.

Brand Champion. This is a senior executive, possibly CEO, who serves as the brand's primary advocate and nurturer. The approach is particularly well suited to companies whose top executives have a passion and talent for brand strategy. Companies like Sony, Gap, Beiersdorf (Nivea), and Nestlé meet that description. Nestlé has a brand champion for each of its 12 corporate strategic brands. As is true for the leaders of P&G's business management teams, each brand champion at Nestlé has a second assignment. Thus the vice president for nutrition is the brand champion for Carnation, and the vice president for instant coffee is the brand champion for Taster's Choice (known as Nescafé outside the United States). At Nestlé, brand leadership is not just talk. The additional work that the brand champion takes on has resulted in a change in the company's performance-evaluation and compensation policies.

Most global brand managers have little authority and must create a strategy without the ability to mandate.

A brand champion approves all brand-stretching decisions (to put the Carnation label on a white milk chocolate bar, for example) and monitors the presentation of the brand worldwide. He or she must be familiar with local contexts and managers, identify insights and best practices, and propagate them through sometimes forceful suggestions. In some companies, such as Sony, the brand champion owns the country brand identities and positions and takes responsibility for ensuring that the country teams implement the brand strategy. A brand champion has credibility and respect not only because of organizational power but also because of a depth of experience, knowledge, and insight. A suggestion from a brand champion gets careful consideration.

P&G plans to evolve over the next decade toward a brand champion approach. It believes that it can achieve greater cooperation and create more global brands by concentrating authority and responsibility in the hands of high-level brand champions. At the moment, P&G regards only a handful of its 83 major brands as global.

Global Brand Manager. In many companies, particularly in the high-tech and service industries, top management lacks a branding or even marketing background. The branding expertise rests just below the top line managers. Such companies are often decentralized and have a powerful regional and country line-management system. Effective global brand managers are necessary in these cases to combat local bias and spur unified efforts across countries.

Some local brand managers have sign-off authority for certain marketing programs, but most have little authority. They must attempt to create a global brand strategy without the ability to mandate. There are five keys to success in these situations:

- Companies must have believers at the top; otherwise global brand managers will be preoccupied with con-

vincing the executive suite that brands are worth supporting. If there are no believers, a brand manager can try to create them. The global brand manager for MasterCard did just that by convincing the organization to form a "miniboard" of six board members and nominating one to be its chair. That person became the brand's voice during board meetings.

- A global brand manager needs to either create a planning process or manage an existing one. To make the process effective, all country managers should use the same vocabulary, template, and planning cycle. This is the first step toward fighting local bias.

- A global brand manager should become a key part of the development, management, and operation of an internal brand communication system. By traveling to learn about customers, country managers, problems, and best practices, he or she will be able to maximize the opportunities for cooperation.

- In order to deal with savvy country brand specialists, global brand managers must have global experience, product background, energy, credibility, and people skills. Companies need a system to select, train, mentor, and reward prospects who can fill the role. At Haagen-Dazs, the global brand manager is also the brand manager for the United States, the lead market for its ice cream. The latter position gives the manager credibility because of the resources and knowledge base that come with it.

- Companies can signal the importance of the role through the title they give the manager. At IBM, global brand managers are called brand stewards, a title that reflects the goal of building and protecting brand equity. At Smirnoff, the global brand manager is given the title of president of the Pierre Smirnoff Company, suggesting how much the company values his position.

Global Brand Team. A global brand manager, acting alone, can be perceived as an outsider—just another corporate staff person contributing to overhead, creating forms, and calling meetings. Sometimes adding people to the mix—in the form of a global brand team—can solve this problem. With a team working on the issue, it becomes easier to convince country brand managers of the value of global brand management.

Global brand teams typically consist of brand representatives from different parts of the world, from different stages of brand development, and from different competitive contexts. Functional areas such as advertising, market research, sponsorship, and promotions may also be represented. The keys to success with these teams are similar to those for the global brand manager.

One problem with a global brand team (unless it is lead by a global brand manager) is that no one person ultimately owns the brand globally. Thus no one is responsible for implementing global branding decisions. In addition, team members may be diverted from their task by the pressures of their primary jobs. And the team may lack the authority and focus needed to make sure that their recommendations are actually implemented at the country level. Mobil solves that problem in part by creating "action teams" made up of people from several countries to oversee the implementation.

Some aspects of the brand's management will be firm, but others will be adaptable or discretionary.

Some companies partition the global brand manager or team across business units or segments. For example, Mobil has separate global brand teams for the passenger car lubricant business, the commercial lubricants business, and the fuel business because the brand is fundamentally different in each. A global brand council then coordinates those segments by reconciling the different identities and looking for ways to create brand synergy.

And consider how DuPont handles its Lycra brand. The 35-year-old synthetic is known worldwide for the flexibility and comfort it lends to clothing; its identity is embodied in the global tagline "Nothing moves like Lycra." The problem for Lycra is that is has a variety of applications—it can be used, for example, in swimsuits, in running shorts, and in women's fashions. Each application requires its own brand positioning. DuPont solves the problem by delegating responsibility for each application to managers in a country where that application is strongest. Thus the Brazilian brand manager for Lycra is also the global lead for swimsuit fabric because Brazil is a hotbed for swimsuit design. Similarly, the French brand manager takes the lead for Lycra used in fashion. The idea is to use the expertise that is dispersed throughout the world. The global brand manager for Lycra ensures that those in charge of different applications are together on overall strategy; he or she also pulls together their ideas in order to exploit synergies.

When local management is relatively autonomous, it may be necessary to give the global brand manager or team a significant degree of authority. Doing so can also reduce the chances that the manager or team will get smothered by organizational or competitive pressures; in addition, it can signal the company's commitment to brand building.

The team or manager may have authority over its visual representation and brand graphics, for example. In that case, the group or the individual would have to approve any departures from the specified color, typeface, and layout logo. Or a global brand team may have authority over the look and feel of a product. The IBM ThinkPad is black and rectangular; it has a red tracking ball and a multicolored IBM logo set at 35 degrees in the lower right corner. The global brand team must approve any deviations from that look. In another example, the global brand manager at Smirnoff has sign-off authority on the selection of advertising agencies and themes.

While companies are spelling out the authority of the global brand manager or team, they must also make clear what authority resides with the country team. Some aspects of the brand's management will be firm—the definition of what the brand stands for, say—but others will be adaptable or discretionary, such as the advertising presentation or the use of product promotions. The job of the person or group responsible for the brand is to make sure that everyone knows and follows the guidelines.

Delivering Brilliance

Global brand leadership, especially in these days of media clutter, requires real brilliance in brand-building efforts—simply doing a good job isn't enough. The dilemma is how to balance the need to leverage global strengths with the need to recognize local differences. Our research indicates that those who aspire to brilliant execution should do the following:

First, consider what brand-building paths to follow—advertising, sponsorship, increasing retail presence, promotions. The path you choose may turn out to be more important than the way you follow through with it. Experience shows that if the path starts with advertising, as it usually does, other sometimes more innovative and more effective brand-building approaches get the short end of the stick. Second, put pressure on the agency to have the best and most motivated people working on the brand, even if that means creating some agency-client tension. Third, develop options: the more chances at brilliance, the higher the probability that it will be reached. Fourth, measure the results.

P&G finds exceptional ideas by encouraging the country teams to develop breakthrough brand-building programs. Particularly if a brand is struggling, country brand teams are empowered to find a winning formula on their own. Once a winner is found, the organization tests it in other countries and implements it as fast as possible.

For example, when P&G obtained Pantene Pro-V in 1985, it was a brand with a small but loyal following. The company's efforts to expand the product's following in the United States and France did not increase the product's popularity. In 1990, however, brand strategists struck gold in Taiwan. They found that the image of models with shiny healthy hair resonated with Taiwan's consumers. The tagline for the ads was "Hair so healthy it shines." People recognized that they couldn't look just like the models but inside they said, "I've got to have that hair." Within six months, the brand was the leader in Taiwan. The concept and supporting advertising tested well in other markets and was subsequently rolled out in 70 countries.

Another way to stimulate brilliant brand building is to use more than one advertising agency. It's true that a single agency can coordinate a powerful, unified campaign; using only one agency, however, means putting all your creative eggs in one basket. On the other hand, using multiple agencies can lead to inconsistency and strategic anarchy.

In Europe, Audi gets the best of both approaches by following a middle course. It has five agencies from different countries compete to be the lead agency that will create the brand's campaign. The four agencies that lose out are nonetheless retained to implement the winning campaign in their countries. Because the agencies are still involved with Audi, they are available for another round of creative competition in the future. A variant on this approach would be to use several offices from the same agency. That may not lead to as much variation in creative ideas, but it still provides more options than having just one group within one agency.

Adapting global programs to the local level can often improve the effectiveness of a campaign. Take Smirnoff's "pure thrill" vodka campaign. All of its global advertising shows distorted images becoming clear when viewed through the Smirnoff bottle, but the specific scenes change from one country to another in order to appeal to consumers with different assumptions about what is thrilling. In Rio de Janeiro, the ad shows the city's statue of Christ with a soccer ball, and in Hollywood, the "w" in the hillside sign is created with the legs of two people. The IBM global slogan "Solutions for a Small Planet" became "small world" in Argentina where "planet" lacked the desired conceptual thrust.

And yet managers won't be able to tell how well they're building brands unless they develop a global brand measurement system. The system must go beyond financial measures—useful as they are—and measure brand equity in terms of customer awareness, customer loyalty, the brand's personality, and the brand associations that resonate with the public. When these measures of the brand are available, a company has the basis to create programs that will build a strong brand in all markets and to avoid programs that could destroy the brand.

All multinational companies should actively engage in global brand management. Any company that tries to get by with unconnected and directionless local brand strategies will inevitably find mediocrity as its reward. In such cases, an exceptionally talented manager will, on occasion, create a pocket of success. But that success will be isolated and random—hardly a recipe that will produce strong brands around the world.

David A. Aaker *is the E. T. Grether Professor of Marketing Strategy at the University of California at Berkeley's Haas School of Business and is a partner in Prophet Brand Strategy, a consulting firm based in San Francisco and New York.* *Erich Joachimsthaler* *is a visiting professor at the University of Virginia's Darden Graduate School of Business in Charlottesville and is the chairman of Prophet Brand Strategy.*

The Nation as Brand

Many marketers fail to exploit the national identity of their brands.

By Simon Anholt

Few things in marketing are harder to define than the personality of a brand, and seldom is this task more complex than when the brand is sold in many different markets. What is it, exactly, about the Coke brand that makes consumers around the world prefer to be associated with it than with a dozen nearly identical products in different cans?

A brand is a complex mixture of attributes: Its visible face is its packaging and visual identity, its voice is its advertising…but its actual personality is something that really exists only in the mind of the consumer.

One attribute particularly important to international brands is the influence that the brand's country of origin—or the country that people *believe* it comes from—has on the consumer's perception of the brand. The fact that Coke and Levi's and Nike and Pepsi are known to come from America is a fundamental part of their success, and the reason why their advertising messages have always stressed their sheer Americanness.

In a similar way, car brands are often strongly linked in the consumer's mind to their country of origin—it's hard to think of BMW or Mercedes except in the context of their being German; a Rover or a Jaguar is linked with Britishness (despite the fact that both brands are now under overseas ownership); and Ferrari is a brand that is Italian before it's anything else at all. Provenance is such a powerful element of a brand's equity that it's common for a company to imply a false provenance if it creates better, more natural associations than the true country of origin. For example, Brooklyn, Italy's leading brand of chewing gum, is manufactured near Milan by a company called Perfetti and, in its long history, has never been anywhere near the United States.

In fact, a brand's native country behaves exactly like the parent company of any product: At best, it can act as an umbrella of quality that reassures consumers that they're buying from a trusted source; at worst, an inappropriate or negative image can make it extremely difficult to export anything from that country unless its provenance is disguised.

Just like corporate brands, country brands evoke certain values, qualifications, and emotional triggers in consumers' minds about the likely values of any product that comes from that country. In the United Kingdom, consumers are happy to buy banking services from Sainsbury's—a grocery chain—because there is a healthy and attractive match between the values, qualifications, and emotional triggers they already associate with the Sainsbury's corporate brand, and the attributes that they demand from people who handle their money. Likewise, we're happy to buy outdoor clothing from Australia because the country that produced Crocodile Dundee is surely well qualified to protect us from weather and wild animals, and there's a good emotional match with the perceived Australian qualities of humorous, rough-and-ready, unselfconscious masculinity.

Look around, and there are many powerful parent brands that haven't yet explored the rich potential of unexpected yet compelling brand extensions: Boeing suitcases? Greyhound sunglasses? Swatch skis? NATO computers? It's a game almost as amusing to play as the converse—trying to mismatch parent brands and brand extensions as horrendously as possible: Boeing toilet paper? Greyhound air freshener? Swatch cough syrup? NATO pizza? (This is more than a game—it's an exercise I often use to help companies get their own heads around what their brand is, what it could be, and what it definitely *shouldn't* be.)

In exactly the same way, when you try to match provenance with product, there are some pairings that clearly make brand sense, others that just don't. People might well purchase Indian accountancy software or a stylish Lithuanian raincoat, and although I'm tempted to say that they probably *wouldn't* buy Peruvian modems or Dutch perfume, attitudes can and do change awfully quickly. A decade ago, who would have believed that we'd be happily consuming Japanese beer, Malaysian cars, and Danish mozzarella?

A Nation's New Reputation

These changes in purchasing habits often come about because nations can enhance their own brand values, just as manufacturers can enhance the brand equity of their commercial brands. Japan is perhaps the most striking example of a country that has succeeded in completely altering its value as a provenance brand in a short space of time. Thirty years ago, "Made in Japan" was a decidedly negative concept; most Western consumers based their perception of "brand Japan" on their experience of shoddy products flooding the marketplace. The products were cheap, certainly, but basically worthless. In many respects, the perception of Japan was much as China's is today.

Yet Japan has now become enviably synonymous with advanced technology, manufacturing quality, competitive pricing, even style and status. Japan, indeed, passes the best branding test of all: whether consumers are prepared to pay more money for functionally identical products, simply because of where they come from. In the 1950s and '60s, most Europeans and Americans would opt for Japanese products only because they were significantly *cheaper* than a Western alternative; now, in certain valuable market segments, such as consumer electronics, musical instruments, and motor vehicles, Western consumers will consistently pay *more* for products manufactured by previously unknown brands, purely because they are perceived to be Japanese. And this kind of worldwide consumer preference is of almost incalculable value to the country's economy as a whole; no wonder so many nations are working hard on their branding strategies.

Korea, too, has undergone a similar and even more rapid transformation in its brand image, thanks to the efforts of such corporations as Hyundai, Daewoo, Samsung, and LG, and perhaps the Japanese example unconsciously aided consumers in their acceptance of the brand.

Needless to say, country brands can decline as well as prosper, and the familiar, depressing marketing tenet holds as true for countries as it does for companies: It can take decades of excellent products before consumers start to equate a company with quality, but one single bad product to damage this perception (anyone remember the Yugo?).

Having said this, the most robust brands are invariably the biggest, most complex, and oldest ones, and their overall image tends to suffer relatively little as a result of occasional slip-ups. Consumers appear to need, and want to believe in, the basic validity of powerful brands, and will forgive them their mistakes more readily than they will with newer, simpler, or more superficial brands. And because a country's brand is usually highly complex and highly robust, and built up over centuries, it is relatively hard to alter or damage it except through major political, economic, or social upheaval. Like a supertanker, a country's brand image takes miles to pick up speed, but equally, it takes miles to slow down again, change direction, or stop.

Some countries, of course, are "launch brands," and don't have centuries of history, tradition, and foreign interaction upon which to build their reputations. For a country like Slovenia to enhance its image abroad is a very different matter than for Scotland or China. Slovenia needs to be *launched*—consumers around the world first must be taught where it is, what it makes, what it has to offer, and what it stands for, and this in itself represents a powerful opportunity: the chance to build a modern country brand, untainted by centuries of possibly negative associations.

A country like Scotland, on the other hand, which people around the world feel they already know, has a high profile, ready appeal, robust equities, and powerful associations. But to update or modify these qualities—and reposition Scotland as a country with commercial, economic, and technological relevance in the modern world—is correspondingly harder. In other words, this is a supertanker that has been gathering speed for centuries, so steering it is proportionally slower and harder.

Many other countries could capitalize on the success of their high-profile brands: for example, Finland and Nokia. If Finland intends to make itself into a valuable nation-brand, the country must capitalize quickly on the significance of Nokia's origin. Through a combination of high product quality, speed to market, excellent marketing (including placement in films such as *The Matrix*), and distribution, Nokia has transformed itself from a moderately successful domestic producer of rubber boots into one of the world's most successful high-tech brands. In doing this, it has also managed to create an entirely new set of associations of "brand Finland" in many consumers' minds—no longer just a quaint fairyland perched on the fringe of Europe, this is a country that can *do* technology, can *do* marketing, and can become world-beating.

And there's a good deal of that mysterious, associative consumer logic that makes this shift believable. Who knows—perhaps it's something to do with the fact that cold-climate countries are believed to be precise and efficient, and therefore good locations to design and manufacture high-tech products. If other Finnish companies—and Finland itself—don't move quickly to build on and leverage this climate of global consumer acceptance, they are missing a great opportunity. Sadly, Nokia itself seems at pains to diminish its own origins in the way it markets its products, perhaps in an effort to appear "global," which means that this valuable pro-Finnish opportunity may be going to waste.

The Upside of Stereotypes

When you look in detail at the issue of provenance, it becomes clear why certain countries behave like brands. Just like commercial brands, "country brands" are well understood by consumers around the world, have long-established identities, and can work just as effectively as an indicator of product quality, a definer of image and target market, as the manufacturer's name on the package.

I have already mentioned Coke, Levi's, Nike, and Pepsi, and the importance of their American origins to their brand values, and there's little doubt that the United States is the world's most powerful country brand. This may well be connected with the fact that Brand USA has the world's best advertising agency, Hollywood, which has been busily pumping out two-hour commercials for Brand USA for nearly a century, and which consumers around the world have enthusiastically paid to watch.

Brand USA also has a dynamic sales-promotion agency called NASA, which periodically sends a rocket into space (primarily, it often seems, to demonstrate the superiority of American technology). American brands can simply hitch themselves to this powerful national brand. . . , and a cultural and commercial trail is instantly blazed for them around the world.

Only a few other countries have clear, consistent, and universally understood brand images, and most of them are European: for example, England (heritage and class), France (quality living and chic), Italy (style and sexiness), Germany (quality and reliability), Switzerland (methodical precision and trustworthiness), Sweden (cleanliness and efficiency), Japan (miniaturization and advanced functionality).

As might be expected, all of these countries produce successful international brands, which are in turn strongly associated with the brand qualities of their provenance. In fact, it's hard to find any international brands that *don't* come from strongly branded countries: Brand-neutral countries such as Belgium, Portugal, Austria, Chile, or Canada have produced remarkably few international market leaders.

There are, however, several strongly branded countries that produce no international brands of their own. Brazil is a fine example of this phenomenon, which is surprising because the brand personality of Brazil is a strong and highly consistent one. No matter who you ask, no matter where, the same list of associations come out—samba, football, carnival, music, dancing, happiness, ecology, sex, beaches, and adventure—a list that could form the brand print of almost any successful youth product on the market today.

Of course, the average Brazilian may find these clichés depressing and even insulting, but they are undeniably an excellent platform on which to build a believable global brand. One of the more important tasks of advertising and marketing is to weave these commonplaces of provenance into something more creative, more substantial, more fair, more true.

The fact that there may be negative associations—pollution, overpopulation, poverty, drugs, crime—within Brazil's brand print isn't necessarily a problem. Strong brands tend to be rich and complex, successfully combining many different character traits within their personality. The United States' brand equity is at least half negative, but this doesn't appear to spoil it in any way. For younger consumers in particular, the suggestion of risk is irresistible—remember, these are consumers who want to challenge and to be challenged.

Many "emerging" markets in the past have exported their products around the world in the form of unprocessed or partly processed commodities, but almost none have ever managed to produce a successful international brand. The real profit margins have been enjoyed by the companies in developed nations that have finished, packaged, branded, and retailed these goods to the end user.

Such an arrangement works well to keep Third World countries firmly in the Third World, and First World countries in the First. This problem is made only more serious by the fact that the emerging markets are, by and large, able to continue exporting in quantities large enough to sustain their fragile economies only by depleting their natural resources and allowing the exploitation of their workforce.

Brands, however, unlike commodities, are made of air, and are thus infinitely sustainable, so long as the investment in marketing is maintained, which makes them the ultimate ecological export. In the long term, they can also contribute to a positive perception of the country, which in turn favors tourism and inward investment. Young Asian consumers, for example, might well be tempted to visit Brazil if that was where their favorite brands came from, just as Disney and Coke and Nike are part of the reason why they want to visit the United States now.

It's not just Brazil that could benefit from exporting brands rather than produce. Of course, few emerging countries have Brazil's natural advantages: a strong nation-brand, an increasingly vigorous economy, a government that actively encourages export, long experience in building successful domestic brands, and one of the world's most active and creative advertising industries. Even so, it doesn't take much imagination to see how certain other nations—perhaps Russia, China, India, and some African countries—could quickly develop the potential to become strong "nation brands."

Looking Beyond Brand USA

For much of this century, global brands have been the exclusive province of European and American producers. But much has changed during this time: Consumers in many parts of the world are becoming wealthier, better informed, and able to exercise more power over manufacturers than ever before. As the basic requirements of product quality and affordability are catered to and choice becomes the norm, consumers become, by degrees, more and more sensitive to brand values: how the product is presented, how it speaks to the consumer, how it addresses her needs.

As consumers begin to look for a more sophisticated combination of *import-style quality* and *domestic-style relevance* in their imported brands, we may well begin to see a consumer backlash against the insufficiently sensitive marketing techniques traditionally practiced by some foreign brand-owners. The simplicity and robustness of an approach like "buy this, it's American" won't work anymore. Sensitivity to culture could well become one of the defining characteristics of the new century's successful global brands. In the past, the brands that shouted loudest were the ones that grew fastest; in the 21st century, the ones that *listen first* could be the ones that last longest.

It may also turn out that Brazilian and other Third World brands have an innate advantage over American and European brands when it comes to making friends among consumers in the world's growth markets—the Far East, Eastern Europe, Latin America, Central Asia, and South Asia—because of their humbler provenance. Unlike the old European powers, these countries don't need to undo the damage done to their brand images by centuries of military and political colonization: They start with a clean slate, with basically benign commercial colonization. Brazil and other emerging nations enjoy the privilege of being "colleague countries," and may well find that their provenance is not merely an important characteristic of their brand personality but, rather, a fundamental preliminary to consumer acceptance.

For rich nations looking for innovative and effective ways to help developing countries become self-sufficient rather than aid-dependent, this approach is the perfect combination of capital investment and intellectual support: venture capital for building export businesses, and professional expertise for helping those businesses to build global brands.

Launching global brands requires flair, confidence, and courage as well as money (although, thanks to the way that the Internet has put global viral marketing within the reach of everybody with a brain and a computer, the level of investment in media need no longer be as colossal as it once was). It requires objectivity to an unusual degree—the ability to see yourself as others see you, and to accept that this is, at least in commercial terms, more important than the way you see yourself. It requires government support. It requires reduced trade barriers. It requires competent and internationally minded marketing people and a strong advertising resource.

It also requires a basic readiness on the part of the target consumer to believe that the country of origin possesses the necessary skills and resources to manufacture a "world-class" product. Many would claim that this factor is the biggest single obstacle standing in the way of poorer countries producing global brands. Interestingly, however, it's a barrier that appears to be diminishing, and this is partly through the experience of seeing countries like Japan and Korea develop, in an amazingly short time, from negative-equity nation brands to almost "compulsory-source" countries for certain products.

Wealth Redistribution Through Branding

But there's a more subtle reason for this change in attitudes, for which we must thank some of the world's biggest brands. For decades, companies such as Nike, IBM, Disney, Mattel, and Sony have been unwittingly promoting their supplier nations as sub-brands, simply by putting little stickers on their products saying "Made in Malaysia," "Made in Vietnam," "Made in Thailand," and so forth. This low-pressure trickle campaign has effectively communicated to hundreds of millions of consumers the simple fact that most of the world's best products are now manufactured in the Third World, thus neatly paving the way for manufacturers in those countries to start developing their own brands.

Simplistic, maybe, but undeniably attractive: Simply add the right branding expertise to a country living on sweatshop labor and break-even trading, and you have the beginning of a fast-growth manufacturing economy instead of a submerging service state.

There is much simple justice in this, and a simple formula is irresistible:

If a company in a rich country sells brands to rich consumers in the same or other rich countries, nothing really happens—money simply circulates within a more or less closed system, and there's little to criticize on moral grounds.

If a company in a rich country sells brands to poor consumers in the same or other rich countries, there is a risk of exploitation and a further widening of the wealth gap.

If a company in a rich country sells brands to consumers in a poor country, the risk of exploitation is far higher, partly because the cultural vulnerability of the consumers is greater: They haven't yet been "inoculated" against brands by repeated exposure to sophisticated marketing techniques.

But if a company in a poor country sells brands to consumers in a rich country, the overall balance begins to be redressed, and justice begins to be done.

Global brands as the ultimate distributor of wealth? It's an intriguing thought. After all, marketing did much to increase the unequal distribution of wealth during the last century, so why shouldn't marketing be used to reverse the trend—and balance things out a little better during the next?

SIMON ANHOLT is chairman and founder of World Writers, a London-based international brand strategy and advertising consultancy. He is author of *Another One Bites the Grass: Making Sense of International Advertising* (Wiley).

The Future of Japanese Marketing

Paul Herbig
Carol Howard

The Japanese have been labeled the "world's champion marketers." These authors challenge that assertion. Japan's future as a major power is dependent upon her continuing to meet increasing global competition. These authors propound that this challenge requires recognition of marketing as a separate discipline and more attention to the discipline both at home and in foreign markets. If undertaken, the researchers say that these changes will radically affect the structure and culture of the typical Japanese company.

It should not be surprising that Japanese marketing practices vary from traditional Western marketing practices because marketing is the process of satisfying wants and needs and these desires vary tremendously among cultures. In fact, it would have been surprising if differences were not seen because, in many aspects, the American culture and the Japanese culture are practically diametrical opposites. Of all the business disciplines, marketing is by far the most culturally sensitive. The critical questions most Japanese ask are not "Am I making any money?" or, "How much money am I making?" but rather, "Am I a leader in my business?" "How do I compare with my competitors?" "What must I do to survive in the 21st century?" Technological self-sufficiency, market share, and industrial rank (status) are the key phrases in Japanese business practices.

The Japanese tend to look at an emerging technology or market area from the perspective of vulnerability rather than risk or cost. Their major concern is how vulnerable the firm is if it does not enter a new technology rather than the risks or costs of entering it. The Japanese system of decision-making imposes a predisposition to enter new technologies to keep up or gain an advantage on competitors. The Japanese undertake a research project not because it will solve a particular problem, but because it may contribute to solving a number of seemingly unrelated problems. Americans, in contrast, are more narrowly focused.

> "... the success of 'Japanese' marketing in the West, particularly the United States, is derived from American marketing experts working for Japanese subsidiaries ..."

Japan and Marketing

In 1982, Philip Kotler and Liam Fahey wrote an article entitled, "The World's Champion Marketers: The Japanese."[1] At that time the Japanese had practically conquered the automobile industry, finished annexing the consumer electronics industry, was on the upward path to securing dominant share in semiconductors and several other industries, and seemed invincible. The last two decades have seen record continuous Japanese trade surpluses. Nevertheless, something happened en route to the slaughter. Japan Inc. turned out to not be as invincible as the world thought it was. Japan, too, can be a victim of strategic over-stretching.

Peter Drucker once said, "When the rest of the world was only talking about marketing, the Japanese were doing it."[2] He meant that Japan came to America to study marketing principles and philosophy and then applied the textbook principles with unparalleled success. Ezra Vogel in *Japan as Number One*[3], Philip Kotler in *The New Competition*[4], Boyd DeMente in *The Kata Factor*[5], all discuss Japan as the next economic superpower, overtaking the United States with basically Japan's marketing prowess as the major reason for its success. What most of these prophets either failed to realize, did not properly factor into their equations, or chose to ignore is that Japanese corporations when dealing in foreign markets, especially in the United States and Europe, overwhelming allow local marketers to conceive and implement local marketing programs. That is, the success of "Japanese" marketing in the West, particularly the United States, is derived from American marketing experts working for Japanese subsidiaries, in conjunction with American advertising agencies, casting their usual American marketing magic. Professor Kotler admitted that the "Japanese hire American industry specialists, consultants and executives to help them figure out how to enter a market and hire American executives to manage U.S. sales ... Japanese marketing strategy has been formulated not by the Japanese but by the Americans."[6]

Where, then, is the superior "Japanese" marketing? By extrapolation, the reason the Japanese have succeeded is precisely because they had a hands off policy and let the locals conduct marketing the way it needs to be done in each particular region or country. Perhaps it is not their marketing skills but their cultural sensitivity skills that ought to be boasted. The Japanese marketing strategy revolves around their management of product market evolution. They choose and sequence the markets they decide to enter, the products they decide to produce, and the marketing tactics they decide to adopt for the market segment. However, the most important factors in their international marketing success is their acceptance, understanding, and application of marketing principles to the markets they decide to enter.

At the time Professors Kotler and Fahey wrote their article, the world looked bleak for competition from American industry. The Japanese dominated automobiles, motorcycles, watches, cameras, optical instruments, steel, shipbuilding, pianos, zippers, radio, television, video recorders, and hand calculators. They were moving into position for the kill in other significant industries such as computers, construction equipment, chemicals, pharmaceuticals, and machine tools. In just over forty years, after beginning with a burnt-out relic of a country in 1945, Japan had achieved global market leadership in industries thought to be dominated by impregnable Western giants.

Ensuing Developments

What has happened since? The doom and gloom never actually appeared. The American auto makers rival their Japanese counterparts in quality and surpass them in affordability. Japanese engineers are once again touring American factories. Ford's factory in Georgia, which manufactures Mercury, Sable and Ford Taurus is on everyone's number one list. In a marked turnaround that would have been unthinkable even five years ago, Ford was asked by Japanese banks to manage Mazda.

The computer industry is now focused on personal computers, tele-communications, and electronic databases. The big names are not Toshiba, Hitachi or Fujitsu, but Microsoft, Intel, Compaq and Dell. In 1982, all these companies were small and inconsequential—several did not even exist. The Japanese marketplace, although still dominated by NEC, finds Dell and Compaq picking up share every year (NEC has been losing share since 1990). NEC, without an IBM compatible, has turned to Dell to help it with its marketing strategy. The software industry is dominated by American companies. Although Japan still remains dominant in semiconductors, that industry has become a commodity business with little, if any, margins, and is consistently under pressure from Korean or Taiwanese chip makers. Meanwhile, the high value added portion of the computer industry is in the microprocessor (Intel) or operating system (Microsoft) or applications programs, all dominated by American companies.

"This drive for perfection has been advantageous in their marketing of products overseas."

In the late 1980s, it was feared that Japan would dominate the next generation of television signals—the HDTV (High Density Television). Japan had a workable analog system, which in typical Japanese fashion, was an improvement of current systems. Since then, the United States elected to embrace digital signals. The quality and data throughput obtainable from digital signals puts analog systems to shame. It is like comparing the Concorde to the first Wright Brothers' plane. Japanese companies are stuck between a system they conceived and understand, but one which is already obsolete because of the leapfrog technology developed by the United States.

True, Japan still dominates in consumer electronics products such as televisions, camcorders, VCRs and radios. But the software is being developed in the United States. Hollywood is American and not even the Japanese can duplicate it. They can buy it, but can not manage or market it as

Matsushita and Sony discovered at United Artists (UA) and Columbia. The sale of UA by Matsushita indicates succinctly that even the invincible Japanese can make costly blunders. Under pressure from the lower cost manufacturers in East Asia and other developed countries, many Japanese companies have moved their production to Southeast Asia, but profit margins are negligible.

Harley-Davidson was on its death throes in 1982. But today, it is not only a thriving company, but one which cannot produce sufficient product to meet the overwhelming demand. Despite increasing capacity dedicated users wait months for their new "hogs." The machine tool industry may be down, but not out. American manufacturers learned from the Japanese and excel in productivity, quality, and state-of-the-art manufacturing, development, and research. Downsizing in the past few years has produced lean, mean, tough international competitors. The Japanese have only begun their downsizing. Caterpillar was a marked company in 1982—Komatsu had the inside track. By 1996 Caterpillar dominated the world market. It has a strong presence even in Japan. Komatsu is ever-present and still a dangerous competitor, but not immortal as it was presumed to be during the early and mid-1980s.

In the fields of chemicals and pharmaceuticals, the Japanese strategy has been to acquire small companies. The Japanese have no market dominance. It does not even have a market presence outside of Japan.

Patterns Appear

Some patterns become clear in contrasting Japanese strengths and weaknesses in different market segments within industry sectors.

- Japan exports middle-of-the-line ready-to-wear clothes and textile fabrics. It imports high-fashion items (from the West) and inexpensive garments from the LDCs.
- Japan exports massive quantities of inexpensive watches; it remains one of Switzerland's largest markets for fashion and jewelry timepieces.

- Despite having the world's second largest pharmaceutical market, Japanese firms have made a negligible impact on international markets. Japan imports several times as many pharmaceutical products as it exports.
- Japan exports massive quantities of basic number-crunching hand-held calculators. It imports advanced complex HP programmable machines.
- Japan produces and exports large quantities of standard integrated circuits and RAM memory chips. Yet it imports virtually all its microprocessors and microcomputers. The difference is that the former are hardware, whereas the latter have a majority of their value added in the software (the programs).

Add to this the interesting fact that if automobile and auto parts exports from Japan to the United States were to be excluded from the trade deficit calculations, there would be a surplus, not a deficit. Therefore it becomes obvious that Japanese strengths are thin and narrowly focused. Kotler confirms this when he said:

"The Japanese have not yet demonstrated much marketing success in markets where major cultural differences are paramount... success has been almost exclusively in product markets where the notions of function and utility are reasonably consistent across cultures... The Japanese have yet to exhibit sophisticated marketing skills and approaches in services and food products industries." [7]

American companies outperform the Japanese in pretax returns on equity and operating profits. Although IBM and Hitachi have roughly equivalent revenues, Hitachi's profit is one-fifth of IBM.

So what is Japanese marketing? Marketing as practiced in Japan is not that which is performed outside the country. As the Japanese have catapulted to become an economic power, many reasons have been given about their rapid progression—one is the claim that they are the world's premier marketers. Certainly American marketers would

argue the point. How well are the Japanese versed in the development and implementation of marketing strategy? Is there really a difference between marketing practices used in the West and those implemented in Japan? Are they the world's greatest marketers? Or, do they merely have a very vocal fan club doing superb public relations? And, is the marketing that we Americans see of Japanese companies in the United States actually representative of Japanese marketing practices in Japan? What is the future of Japanese Marketing?

Japanese Marketing Practices

Basically the Japanese view marketing in a different fashion than the West. The Japanese idea of marketing is that if a good, quality, lower priced product is produced based on consumer information, people should buy it. They rely on this belief to succeed. This, and the belief by most Americans that Japanese products are of superior quality, gives them a huge advantage over their competitors. Most Japanese companies, however, continue to overemphasize manufacturing at the expense of marketing as it is known in the West. In many cases, the Japanese do not place much importance on marketing. An obsession still exists with production. They basically have the opposite mindset vis-a-vis American companies. Both the Japanese company and the Japanese culture are well suited to manufacturing.[8] They approach projects from a manufacturing point of view—but good manufacturers are not necessarily good marketers. The marketing success of Japanese products in the United States is derived from the Japanese hiring American marketers to sell their products to Americans. Therefore, it is American marketing of Japanese products that has made Japanese goods in the United States so successful.

This lack of emphasis on marketing is also not necessarily unusual or fatal. The United States and American companies went through many of the same stages that Japan and Japanese companies are now undergoing. Many parallels exist between the United States of the 1950s and

Japan of the 2000. The Japanese consumer is similar to an American consumer during the decades of the 1920s and the 1950s. Both societies during those time periods were very much producer-oriented societies (1920s America with the Model T and the 1950s postwar pent-up demand boom). Both nations had just turned from world debtor to world creditor and had been thrown into the forefront of world power and had no idea of how to manage their newfound power. Even the "ugly Japanese," the ethnocentricity and arrogance seen by locals of Japanese businesses abroad, is analogous to the "ugly Americans" of an earlier era. Their lack of desire to turn the reigns of their businesses over to locals can be excused as lack of international experience that mirrors the American experience 40 years earlier. The really important question for Japan is will it take a severe event like depression or war to produce a consumerist society in Japan and when will it acknowledge its correct place in the world and begin paying the appropriate price of entry—a free, open market?

The differences between the Japanese and American marketing practices are summarized in the following discussion.[9]

Products—Although Japanese and Americans appear very similar in their product needs, wants, and uses, the vast cultural distance between the two cultures creates a huge gulf that must be bridged. The Japanese tend to diffuse faster and to a greater extent than Americans. Americans will be the first to try new products, but American markets develop slower than Japanese markets because of the differences between individual and collective cultures. In Japan, once a product becomes hot everyone must have it.[10]

Service—Japanese are probably a decade or more ahead of American consumers in their fetish for service and quality. American consumers will close the gap, but it is doubtful that they will ever catch up—basically for cultural reasons. In the years ahead the value Americans place on service and quality will increase, but it will never reach the pinnacle that it has in the Japanese culture because of the many choices and options that Americans have that the Japanese do not. Americans seem to be able to conduct a trade-off between price and quality, and are willing to accept lower quality goods (discount stores, etc.) for a break in the price. The Japanese consumer demands high quality and pays high prices as a result—only recently beginning to trade quality for discounts. In this respect the Americans are a generation ahead of the Japanese. The Japanese view service as a labor-intensive function that must be present to show the customer how much he is valued. The American view is to automate the function as much as possible to minimize the cost while providing maximum choice and individual flexibility for the customer.

Consumerism—The ineffective Japanese consumerist movement and the lack of concern of goods by producers are analogous to U.S consumers and producers in the 1950s. As incomes keep growing, more Japanese are exposed to living conditions abroad and the number of the shinjinrui increase—Japanese baby boomers who want affluence now and not sacrifice to acquire it later—this gap will close in the years to come. However, like its penchant for service, it is doubtful if the Japanese will ever totally catch up because of the American cultural worship of the individual and his or her rights compared to the Japanese obligations to its society and the acceptance of some limitations for the greater good of the country and the corporation.

Demographics—Demographics will adversely affect Japan early in this new century. Japan has the highest share of seniors in the world. A nation of pensioners is due by 2010. Japan's personal savings rate will be depressed by the aging of its population—old people tend not to be money savers. The greater the number of elderly, the greater the drain on savings. The Bank of Japan thinks the savings rate could fall as low as 8 percent from the current 16. It could fall so much that Japan may well return to a deficit on the current account of its balance of payments and will need to import capital. As unit labor costs rise, older workers have to be paid more, especially if

pay is tied to seniority rather than merit as has been the tradition.

Japan is rapidly on its way to becoming a nation of consumers, pleasure seekers, importers, investors and speculators. The abundant money and free financial markets risk creating a boom and bust cycle. Japanese workers are becoming more concerned about personal fulfillment and less willing to devote their entire lives to the companies who employ them. Eighty percent of workers indicated they consider personal fulfillment more important than the traditional goals of professional advancement.[11] Greater than half believed that their companies sometimes interfered too much with their private lives. Japanese workers are beginning to ask for some leeway during off-hours. Many believe that boundaries for work-related duties should be established. Nearly 85 percent said that some type of legal contract should be used to clearly define an employee's work responsibilities.

Current Status

The Japanese have more than a few feathers in their collective cap. Japanese industry recognizes that it must continually learn, hone, and develop skills and at the same time be aggressively curious about new knowledge, discoveries, and new markets. This is based on a deep appreciation that in order to ensure the survival of the group they must be quicker than the competition to adopt new knowledge or move into new markets. This attitude is reinforced by Buddhist thought that propounds the view that all facets of life and nature are in a state of constant change.

A brief consideration of the history of Japanese companies illustrates this adaptability. For example, Hitachi turned itself into a massive engineering company with a vast range of innovative high-technology products. Sharp moved rapidly in recent years from making automatic pencils to making computers. Cannon moved from cameras to computers. Toray turned an ailing textile company into the world's largest manufacturer of carbon fibers for the aerospace industry and is now moving rapidly into biotechnology. Yamaha moved from pianos to motorbikes and then to computers. During the decade of the '90s, more than 35 percent of manufacturing industries in Japan with 300 or more employees were moving to serve new markets—for small corporations (four to ten employees) the percentage was over 50 percent and the trend is increasing.

The Japanese have also developed exacting standards for product quality, durability and reliability, and at the same time demand fashions and styles that match their individual lifestyles and ages. Individualization, while maintaining high quality and reasonable cost, has become one of the keynotes in consumer marketing in Japan. The Japanese market demands not only the basics such as good finish, ease of operation, diversity, and high level of reliability and service, but it is a highly demanding market in almost all other aspects. This drive for perfection has been advantageous in their marketing of products overseas.

If nothing else, the Japanese will tend to overwhelm rather than underwhelm their customers. It was neglect of consumers and markets by established and entrenched American companies that gave the Japanese their opportunities. The initial marketing thrust was an emphasis on low prices and the selection of thin market segments—particularly the smaller sized, compact and miniaturized product segments. They were aided by large protected domestic markets capable of supporting mass production, economies of scale, low costs and very competitive prices. Japanese companies, by selecting target markets carefully, were able to improve quality while maintaining low prices and deeper penetration.

Nevertheless, as mentioned earlier, emphasizing manufacturing abilities can be a detriment in marketing, especially in the marketing of fast-moving products. The same type of slow, deliberate consensus building thought process that helps the Japanese produce quality products has a negative impact when they introduce those products into a real time competitive environment.

Japanese do not delegate much authority to their line positions. Simple decisions often take a week or more to be made. It becomes almost impossible to react quickly to changes in the marketplace. Group decision-making in Japan makes it difficult for someone to do anything that does not go by the book—thus creating an atmosphere where a lack of creativity dominates. The chain of command must be adhered to. Everything is done by a committee. No one takes responsibility for the marketing plan because of job ambiguity—although no one is praised or blamed for its outcome, either. Individuals take few risks. Like McDonalds, if you have it their way it will be great, but specifically-designed goods and services can take much longer for the Japanese to design, manufacture, process, and ship.

Japanese companies get very close to their customers. This, however, is not necessarily equated with strong marketing. Excessive dependence on customers also inhibits the development of radically new products to fulfill needs of which customers are unaware or only vaguely aware.

In addition, the Japanese have not yet demonstrated much marketing success in markets where major cultural differences are paramount; their success has been almost exclusively in product markets where the notions of function and utility are reasonably consistent across cultures, autos, electronics, steel, etc. However, where major elements of cultural differences exist, they have not been as successful (e.g., food products, cosmetics, fashion, services). Japanese companies also typically use large Japanese trading companies that are familiar with the social atmosphere, business customer, legal procedures and language of the host countries. Their scale of operation and experience allows economies of scale which helps reduce distribution costs. The trading companies often take on the role of the sales and marketing arm, allowing the firm to concentrate on economies of scale to provide a low cost, good quality product. For many Japanese companies, the sogo shosha is their marketing arm—companies merely keep the plants humming to manufacture high quality, low-priced goods.

The Future of Marketing in Japan

What will Japan's future be in the highly competitive world market? As the emerging world market continues to become more competitive, Japan will face many factors that will influence its position and stability within its markets. Japan has witnessed an economic slowdown, a collapse of its "bubble economy," and a stock market collapse during the 1990s. Its policy of lifetime employment has caused a real unemployment rate of over 10 percent—too many corporate employees are deadwood. In an era of high growth, this could be ignored. In today's era of small to no growth, a growing consumerist domestic marketplace, pressures both abroad to limit exports and internally to grow exports, those days are over for good. Japanese companies must also get lean and mean to compete internationally. This puts the Japanese company and its paternal relationship with its employees into a dramatic turning point: stay traditional and fall behind or become lean and mean and eliminate the lifetime employment paternal arrangement. If this were not enough, the domestic Japanese marketplace can no longer be a protected turf because of external pressures. Inevitably, it will be invaded by all types of gaijin companies, each aggressively pursuing a Japanese market that has eluded them for over 50 years.

> **"The future for marketing in Japan is a continuation of the past with a Western twist."**

If open competition from the West is not enough, Japan has seen the Third World countries (especially the mini-dragons of Southeast Asia) become tough and aggressive competitors. These countries are copying Japan's approach to invading new markets, and are now offering high quality products at a lower cost than the Japanese. The protectionist trend in the United States and Europe to protect local industries by import quotas and non-tariff barriers has Japan implementing more expansion moves within those countries. In 1995, Japan's building or buying of plants in the United States was up by 9 percent from 1994. It had a total of 1,568 plants in the United States that employed approximately 350,000 people with equivalent numbers in Europe.

Japans's swift response of building factories in the United States and Europe will allow it to keep goods within those markets, and provide employment to some workers that have been displaced by Japanese imports. If the protectionist trend continued, and if Japan had not responded with factories being built within those market segments, their companies could have been shut out of certain markets. Japan also must contend with the growing pressure from the United States to open its market and allow an easing of Japan's barriers for importers. With the large imbalance of trade, it was hoped the economic and trade practices that led to such large trade imbalances would be altered. With only limited progress made on the trade deficit, the Japanese face growing dissatisfaction among the United States and other countries.

Which Road to Pick?

What does the future hold for Japanese marketing? Professor Kotler indicates that the term "marketing" has at least four different definitions. The first is that marketing is the company's promotion and distribution function. The second definition is that it is the company department that handles all "marketing" activities. The third meaning is that to best serve the company, one must first serve the customers' interests. The fourth definition is that it is the continuous process of evaluating and reevaluating the marketplace.[12] The Japanese view of marketing merges the first and third meanings. (Of course, in keeping with the cultural overtones, the Japanese view of serving the customers' interest is akin to that of a parent-child with the customer the superior. To an American, serving the customer amounts to a working relationship among equals, a situation unlikely in hierarchical Japan). The archetypical American marketing company believes in the fourth meaning, the marketing process.

Marketing, as practiced in Japan (just as marketing as practiced in the United States or France), is culturally biased and optimized to its particular culture. Behaviors that consumers in the West might find unusual, illogical, ineffective, or unacceptable are commonplace elsewhere and are attune to the country's particular mores (it is just as likely other countries would find Westerner behavior just as unlikely).

The future for marketing in Japan is a continuation of the past with a Western twist. Japanese success overseas has resulted more from high product quality, pricing muscle, and economies of scale made possible by a protected market. As the latter gives way, impacts will be felt on the former. As Western companies meet Japanese product quality and attributes and pricing advantages disappear (previously conferred by low capital costs and premium prices in its domestic marketplace), Japanese companies must begin to turn away from the first meaning of marketing and toward the last meaning—the full marketing process. This will require hiring and training marketing specialists, a difficult and unusual process in a cultural environment that trains and rewards its workers to be generalists.

If Japanese companies allow local marketing specialists (who know the marketing process philosophy and use it expertly) to run the marketing operations in the local market, success will continue. But if Japanese companies have very visible "glass ceilings" for non-Japanese managers, that same success can also be fleeting as local personnel leave for other companies that do not have the same ethnocentric limitations. This dilemma will haunt the Japanese: allow more and more non-Japanese into its higher management and thus disrupt the homogeneous Japanese cultural roots of the company, or loose the more talented and capable locals upon which the company must depend for its success in foreign markets. Success overseas will eventually depend on Japanese companies becoming more process oriented and incorporating more locals into their operations. Because success is still the overriding concern among Japanese companies, the inevitable conclusion is major changes-not merely in marketing practices-in overall company practices are necessary for the typical Japanese company to survive and compete in the international markets of the twenty-first century.

Notes

1. Kotler, Philip and L. Fahey, "The World's Champion Marketers: The Japanese," *Journal of Business Strategy*, 2, 1982, Summer, 3–13.

2. Drucker, Peter F., *"Behind Japan's Success,"* *Harvard Business Review*, January/February, 1981, 83–92.

3. Vogel, Ezra F., *Japan as Number One,* 1985, New York: Harper and Row.

4. Kotler, Philip, Liam Fahey, and S. Jatusripitak, *The New Competition,* 1985, Englewood Cliffs, NJ, Prentice Hall.

5. DeMente, Boye, *The Kata Factor,* 1990, Phoenix, Phoenix Book Publishers.

6. Kotler, Philip and L. Fahey, loc. cit.

7. Kotler, Philip, Liam Fahey, and S. Jatusripitak, loc. cit.

8. Kelley, Bill, "Culture Clash: West Meets East," *Sales and Marketing Management*, July 1991,28–34.

9. Herbig, Paul A. and Pat Borgstorff, "The Japanese Consumer: Are They Really Different From the U.S.?," *Journal of International Marketing*, 2/1 1994, 11–17.

10. Herbig, Paul A. and Joseph C. Miller, "The Affect of Culture in the Adoption Process: A Comparison of Japanese and American Behavior," *Entrepreneurship, Innovation, and Change*, 3/2, June 1994,22–35.

11. Tateisi, Nobuo, "In Search of a Better Relationship Between Japanese Corporations and Employees," *Keidanren Review*, February 1994, 12–15.

12. Kotler, Philip, "Reconceptualizing Marketing," *European Management Journal*, 12/4, December 1994, 353–361.

Additional Footnotes:

1. Herbig, Paul and Robert Milam, "The Secret of Japan's Economic Su*cc*ess: Myths, Facts, and Realities," *American Business Review*, II/2, May 1994, 30–36.

2. Herbig, Paul and Robert Milam, "More Japanese Myths: What the Press Forgot to Mention," *American Business Review*, 2/1 Winter 1994, 29–39.

3. Thurow, Lester. (1992), *Head to Head*, New York: William Morrow.

4. Woronoff, Jon, Japan, *The Coming Economic Crisis*, Tokyo: Lotus Press, 1980.

PAUL HERBIG, MBA, is chair of the Department of Business and assistant professor of marketing at TriState University in Angola, IN. He operates a busy international marketing and consulting business with U.S. clients located in San Antonio, Dallas, San Francisco and Kansas City as well as in numerous overseas ports of call. His articles have been published in over 100 journals and magazines and he has written six books. Before entering academia, his work experience includes marketing management and product management positions at AT&T, Honeywell, Datapoint and Intermec.

CAROL HOWARD, Ph.D., is an assistant professor of International Business at Oklahoma City University. She teaches undergraduate and graduate courses in the World Economy and International Business, Multinational Marketing Management, Global Competitive Strategy, and Strategic Marketing Decisions. Her research interests include the effects of culture on international business operations, the management of innovation, and integration into shipping and part terminal services by global automobile manufacturers and bulk commodity firms. Her articles have appeared in several journals. Previous to her academic career, she held manager positions in marketing and manufacturing.

From *Business Forum*, Vol. 24, Nos. 1, 2, Summer/Fall 1999. © 1999 by School of Business and Economics, Calif. State University, Los Angeles. Facsimile: (323) 343-6432.

Industry/Company Guide

This guide was prepared to provide an easy index to the many industries and companies discussed in detail in the selections included in *Annual Editions: Marketing 02/03*. It should prove useful when researching specific interests.

INDUSTRIES

212

Industry/Company Guide

COMPANIES AND DIVISIONS

Glossary

This glossary of marketing terms is included to provide you with a convenient and ready reference as you encounter general terms in your study of marketing that are unfamiliar or require a review. It is not intended to be comprehensive, but taken together with the many definitions included in the articles themselves, it should prove to be quite useful.

acceptable price range
The range of prices that buyers are willing to pay for a product; prices that are above the range may be judged unfair, while prices below the range may generate concerns about quality.

adaptive selling
A salesperson's adjustment of his or her behavior between and during sales calls, to respond appropriately to issues that are important to the customer.

advertising
Marketing communication elements designed to stimulate sales through the use of mass media displays, direct individual appeals, public displays, give-aways, and the like.

advertorial
A special advertising section in magazines that includes some editorial (nonadvertising) content.

Americans with Disabilities Act (ADA)
Passed in 1990, this U.S. law prohibits discrimination against consumers with disabilities.

automatic number identification
A telephone system that identifies incoming phone numbers at the beginning of the call, without the caller's knowledge.

bait and switch
Advertising a product at an attractively low price to get customers into the store, but making the product unavailable so that the customers must trade up to a more expensive version.

bar coding
A computer-coded bar pattern that identifies a product. *See also* universal product code.

barter
The practice of exchanging goods and services without the use of money.

benefit segmentation
Organizing the market according to the attributes or benefits consumers need or desire, such as quality, service, or unique features.

brand
A name, term, sign, design, symbol, or combination used to differentiate the products of one company from those of its competition.

brand image
The quality and reliability of a product as perceived by consumers on the basis of its brand reputation or familiarity.

brand name
The element of a brand that can be vocalized.

break-even analysis
The calculation of the number of units that must be sold at a certain price to cover costs (break even); revenues earned past the break-even point contribute to profits.

bundling
Marketing two or more products in a single package at one price.

business analysis
The stage of new product development where initial marketing plans are prepared (including tentative marketing strategy and estimates of sales, costs, and profitability).

business strategic plan
A plan for how each business unit in a corporation intends to compete in the marketplace, based upon the vision, objectives, and growth strategies of the corporate strategic plan.

capital products
Expensive items that are used in business operations but do not become part of any finished product (such as office buildings, copy machines).

cash-and-carry wholesaler
A limited-function wholesaler that does not extend credit for or deliver the products it sells.

caveat emptor
A Latin term that means "let the buyer beware." A principle of law meaning that the purchase of a product is at the buyer's risk with regard to its quality, usefulness, and the like. The laws do, however, provide certain minimum protection against fraud and other schemes.

channel of distribution
See marketing channel.

Child Protection Act
U.S. law passed in 1990 to regulate advertising on children's TV programs.

Child Safety Act
Passed in 1966, this U.S. law prohibits the marketing of dangerous products to children.

Clayton Act
Anticompetitive activities are prohibited by this 1914 U.S. law.

co-branding
When two brand names appear on the same product (such as a credit card with a school's name).

comparative advertising
Advertising that compares one brand against a competitive brand on at least one product attribute.

competitive pricing strategies
Pricing strategies that are based on a organization's position in relation to its competition.

consignment
An arrangement in which a seller of goods does not take title to the goods until they are sold. The seller thus has the option of returning them to the supplier or principal if unable to execute the sale.

consolidated metropolitan statistical area (CMSA)
Based on census data, the largest designation of geographic areas. *See also* primary metropolitan statistical area.

consumer behavior
The way in which buyers, individually or collectively, react to marketplace stimuli.

Consumer Credit Protection Act
A 1968 U.S. law that requires full disclosure of the financial charges of loans.

consumer decision process
This four-step process includes recognizing a need or problem, searching for information, evaluating alternative products or brands, and purchasing a product.

Consumer Product Safety Commission (CPSC)
A U.S. government agency that protects consumers from unsafe products.

consumerism
A social movement in which consumers demand better information about the service, prices, dependability, and quality of the products they buy.

convenience products
Consumer goods that are purchased at frequent intervals with little regard for price. Such goods are relatively standard in nature and consumers tend to select the most convenient source when shopping for them.

cooperative advertising
Advertising of a product by a retailer, dealer, distributor, or the like, with part of the advertising cost paid by the product's manufacturer.

corporate strategic plan
A plan that addresses what a company is and wants to become, and then guides strategic planning at all organizational levels.

countersegmentation
A concept that combines market segments to appeal to a broad range of consumers, assuming that there will be an increasing consumer willingness to accept fewer product and service choices for lower prices.

customer loyalty concept
To focus beyond customer satisfaction toward customer retention as a way to generate sales and profit growth.

demand curve
A relationship that shows how many units a market will purchase at a given price in a given period of time.

demographic environment
The study of human population densities, distributions, and movements that relate to buying behavior.

derived demand
The demand for business-to-business products that is dependent upon a demand for other products in the market.

differentiated strategy
Using innovation and points of difference in product offerings, advanced technology, superior service, or higher quality in wide areas of market segments.

direct mail promotion
Marketing goods to consumers by mailing unsolicited promotional material to them.

direct marketing
The sale of products to carefully targeted consumers who interact with various advertising media without salesperson contact.

discount
A reduction from list price that is given to a buyer as a reward for a favorable activity to the seller.

discretionary income
The money that remains after taxes and necessities have been paid for.

disposable income
That portion of income that remains after payment of taxes to use for food, clothing, and shelter.

dual distribution
The selling of products to two or more competing distribution networks, or the selling of two brands of nearly identical products through competing distribution networks.

dumping
The act of selling a product in a foreign country at a price lower than its domestic price.

durable goods
Products that continue in service for an appreciable length of time.

economy
The income, expenditures, and resources that affect business and household costs.

electronic data interchange (EDI)
A computerized system that links two different firms to allow transmittal of documents; a quick-response inventory control system.

entry strategy
An approach used to begin marketing products internationally.

environmental scanning
Obtaining information on relevant factors and trends outside a company and interpreting their potential impact on the company's markets and marketing activities.

European Union (EU)
The world's largest consumer market, consisting of 16 European nations: Austria, Belgium, Britain, Denmark, Finland, France, Germany, Greece, Italy, Ireland, Luxembourg, the Netherlands, Norway, Portugal, Spain, and Sweden.

exclusive distribution
Marketing a product or service in only one retail outlet in a specific geographic marketplace.

exporting
Selling goods to international markets.

Fair Packaging and Labeling Act of 1966
This law requires manufacturers to state ingredients, volume, and manufacturer's name on a package.

family life cycle
The progress of a family through a number of distinct phases, each of which is associated with identifiable purchasing behaviors.

Federal Trade Commission (FTC)
The U.S. government agency that regulates business practices; established in 1914.

five C's of pricing
Five influences on pricing decisions: customers, costs, channels of distribution, competition, and compatibility.

FOB (free on board)
The point at which the seller stops paying transportation costs.

four I's of service
Four elements to services: intangibility, inconsistency, inseparability, and inventory.

four P's
See marketing mix.

franchise
The right to distribute a company's products or render services under its name, and to retain the resulting profit in exchange for a fee or percentage of sales.

freight absorption
Payment of transportation costs by the manufacturer or seller, often resulting in a uniform pricing structure.

functional groupings
Groupings in an organization in which a unit is subdivided according to different business activities, such as manufacturing, finance, and marketing.

General Agreement on Tariffs and Trade (GATT)
An international agreement that is intended to limit trade barriers and to promote world trade through reduced tariffs; represents over 80 percent of global trade.

geodemographics
A combination of geographic data and demographic characteristics; used to segment and target specific markets.

green marketing
The implementation of an ecological perspective in marketing; the promotion of a product as environmentally safe.

gross domestic product (GDP)
The total monetary value of all goods and services produced within a country during one year.

growth stage
The second stage of a product life cycle that is characterized by a rapid increase in sales and profits.

hierarchy of effects
The stages a prospective buyer goes through when purchasing a product, including awareness, interest, evaluation, trial, and adoption.

idea generation
An initial stage of the new product development process; requires creativity and innovation to generate ideas for potential new products.

implied warranties
Warranties that assign responsibility for a product's deficiencies to a manufacturer, even though the product was sold by a retailer.

imports
Purchased goods or services that are manufactured or produced in some other country.

integrated marketing communications
A strategic integration of marketing communications programs that coordinate all promotional activities—advertising, personal selling, sales promotion, and public relations.

internal reference prices
The comparison price standards that consumers remember and use to judge the fairness of prices.

introduction stage
The first product life cycle stage; when a new product is launched into the marketplace.

ISO 9000
International Standards Organization's standards for registration and certification of manufacturer's quality management and quality assurance systems.

joint venture
An arrangement in which two or more organizations market products internationally.

just-in-time (JIT) inventory control system
An inventory supply system that operates with very low inventories and fast, on-time delivery.

Lanham Trademark Act
A 1946 U.S. law that was passed to protect trademarks and brand names.

late majority
The fourth group to adopt a new product; representing about 34 percent of a market.

Glossary

lifestyle research
Research on a person's pattern of living, as displayed in activities, interests, and opinions.

limit pricing
This competitive pricing strategy involves setting prices low to discourage new competition.

limited-coverage warranty
The manufacturer's statement regarding the limits of coverage and noncoverage for any product deficiencies.

logistics management
The planning, implementing, and moving of raw materials and products from the point of origin to the point of consumption.

loss-leader pricing
The pricing of a product below its customary price in order to attract attention to it.

Magnuson-Moss Act
Passed in 1975, this U.S. law regulates warranties.

management by exception
Used by a marketing manager to identify results that deviate from plans, diagnose their cause, make appropriate new plans, and implement new actions.

manufacturers' agent
A merchant wholesaler that sells related but noncompeting product lines for a number of manufacturers; also called manufacturers' representatives.

market
The potential buyers for a company's product or service; or to sell a product or service to actual buyers. The place where goods and services are exchanged.

market penetration strategy
The goal of achieving corporate growth objectives with existing products within existing markets by persuading current customers to purchase more of the product or by capturing new customers.

marketing channel
Organizations and people that are involved in the process of making a product or service available for use by consumers or industrial users.

marketing communications planning
A seven-step process that includes marketing plan review; situation analysis; communications process analysis; budget development; program development integration and implementation of a plan; and monitoring, evaluating, and controlling the marketing communications program.

marketing concept
The idea that a company should seek to satisfy the needs of consumers while also trying to achieve the organization's goals.

marketing mix
The elements of marketing: product, brand, package, price, channels of distribution, advertising and promotion, personal selling, and the like.

marketing research
The process of identifying a marketing problem and opportunity, collecting and analyzing information systematically, and recommending actions to improve an organization's marketing activities.

marketing research process
A six-step sequence that includes problem definition, determination of research design, determination of data collection methods, development of data collection forms, sample design, and analysis and interpretation.

mission statement
A part of the strategic planning process that expresses the company's basic values and specifies the operation boundaries within marketing, business units, and other areas.

motivation research
A group of techniques developed by behavioral scientists that are used by marketing researchers to discover factors influencing marketing behavior.

nonprice competition
Competition between brands based on factors other than price, such as quality, service, or product features.

nondurable goods
Products that do not last or continue in service for any appreciable length of time.

North American Free Trade Agreement (NAFTA)
A trade agreement among the United States, Canada, and Mexico that essentially removes the vast majority of trade barriers between the countries.

North American Industry Classification System (NAICS)
A system used to classify organizations on the basis of major activity or the major good or service provided by the three NAFTA countries—Canada, Mexico, and the United States; replaced the Standard Industrial Classification (SIC) system in 1997.

observational data
Market research data obtained by watching, either mechanically or in person, how people actually behave.

odd-even pricing
Setting prices at just below an even number, such as $1.99 instead of $2.

opinion leaders
Individuals who influence consumer behavior based on their interest in or expertise with particular products.

organizational goals
The specific objectives used by a business or nonprofit unit to achieve and measure its performance.

outbound telemarketing
Using the telephone rather than personal visits to contact customers.

outsourcing
A company's decision to purchase products and services from other firms rather than using in-house employees.

parallel development
In new product development, an approach that involves the development of the product and production process simultaneously.

penetration pricing
Pricing a product low to discourage competition.

personal selling process
The six stages of sales activities that occur before and after the sale itself: prospecting, preapproach, approach, presentation, close, and follow-up.

point-of-purchase display
A sales promotion display located in high-traffic areas in retail stores.

posttesting
Tests that are conducted to determine if an advertisement has accomplished its intended purpose.

predatory pricing
The practice of selling products at low prices to drive competition from the market and then raising prices once a monopoly has been established.

prestige pricing
Maintaining high prices to create an image of product quality and appeal to buyers who associate premium prices with high quality.

pretesting
Evaluating consumer reactions to proposed advertisements through the use of focus groups and direct questions.

price elasticity of demand
An economic concept that attempts to measure the sensitivity of demand for any product to changes in its price.

price fixing
The illegal attempt by one or several companies to maintain the prices of their products above those that would result from open competition.

price promotion mix
The basic product price plus additional components such as sales prices, temporary discounts, coupons, favorable payment and credit terms.

price skimming
Setting prices high initially to appeal to consumers who are not price-sensitive and then lowering prices to appeal to the next market segments.

primary metropolitan statistical area (PMSA)
Major urban area, often located within a CMSA, that has at least one million inhabitants.

PRIZM
A potential rating index by ZIP code markets that divides every U.S. neighborhood into one of 40 distinct cluster types that reveal consumer data.

product
An idea, good, service, or any combination that is an element of exchange to satisfy a consumer.

product differentiation
The ability or tendency of manufacturers, marketers, or consumers to distinguish between seemingly similar products.

product expansion strategy
A plan to market new products to the same customer base.

product life cycle (PLC)
A product's advancement through the introduction, growth, maturity, and decline stages.

product line pricing
Setting the prices for all product line items.

product marketing plans
Business units' plans to focus on specific target markets and marketing mixes for each product, which include both strategic and execution decisions.

product mix
The composite of products offered for sale by a firm or a business unit.

promotional mix
Combining one or more of the promotional elements that a firm uses to communicate with consumers.

proprietary secondary data
The data that is provided by commercial marketing research firms to other firms.

psychographic research
Measurable characteristics of given market segments in respect to life-styles, interests, opinions, needs, values, attitudes, personality traits, and the like.

publicity
Nonpersonal presentation of a product, service, or business unit.

pull strategy
A marketing strategy whose main thrust is to strongly influence the final consumer, so that the demand for a product "pulls" it through the various channels of distribution.

push strategy
A marketing strategy whose main thrust is to provide sufficient economic incentives to members of the channels of distribution, so as to "push" the product through to the consumer.

qualitative data
The responses obtained from in-depth interviews, focus groups, and observation studies.

quality function deployment (QFD)
The data collected from structured response formats that can be easily analyzed and projected to larger populations.

quotas
In international marketing, they are restrictions placed on the amount of a product that is allowed to leave or enter a country; the total outcomes used to assess sales representatives' performance and effectiveness.

regional marketing
A form of geographical division that develops marketing plans that reflect differences in taste preferences, perceived needs, or interests in other areas.

relationship marketing
The development, maintenance, and enhancement of long-term, profitable customer relationships.

repositioning
The development of new marketing programs that will shift consumer beliefs and opinions about an existing brand.

resale price maintenance
Control by a supplier of the selling prices of his branded goods at subsequent stages of distribution, by means of contractual agreement under fair trade laws or other devices.

reservation price
The highest price a consumer will pay for a product; a form of internal reference price.

restraint of trade
In general, activities that interfere with competitive marketing. Restraint of trade usually refers to illegal activities.

retail strategy mix
Controllable variables that include location, products and services, pricing, and marketing communications.

return on investment (ROI)
A ratio of income before taxes to total operating assets associated with a product, such as inventory, plant, and equipment.

sales effectiveness evaluations
A test of advertising efficiency to determine if it resulted in increased sales.

sales forecast
An estimate of sales under controllable and uncontrollable conditions.

sales management
The planning, direction, and control of the personal selling activities of a business unit.

sales promotion
An element of the marketing communications mix that provides incentives or extra value to stimulate product interest.

samples
A small size of a product given to prospective purchasers to demonstrate a product's value or use and to encourage future purchase; some elements that are taken from the population or universe.

scanner data
Proprietary data that is derived from UPC bar codes.

scrambled merchandising
Offering several unrelated product lines within a single retail store.

selected controlled markets
Sites where market tests for a new product are conducted by an outside agency and retailers are paid to display that product; also referred to as forced distribution markets.

selective distribution
This involves selling a product in only some of the available outlets; commonly used when after-the-sale service is necessary, such as in the case of home appliances.

seller's market
A condition within any market in which the demand for an item is greater than its supply.

selling philosophy
An emphasis on an organization's selling function to the exclusion of other marketing activities.

selling strategy
A salesperson's overall plan of action, which is developed at three levels: sales territory, customer, and individual sales calls.

services
Nonphysical products that a company provides to consumers in exchange for money or something else of value.

share points
Percentage points of market share; often used as the common comparison basis to allocate marketing resources effectively.

Sherman Anti-Trust Act
Passed in 1890, this U.S. law prohibits contracts, combinations, or conspiracies in restraint of trade and actual monopolies or attempts to monopolize any part of trade or commerce.

shopping products
Consumer goods that are purchased only after comparisons are made concerning price, quality, style, suitability, and the like.

single-channel strategy
Marketing strategy using only one means to reach customers; providing one sales source for a product.

single-zone pricing
A pricing policy in which all buyers pay the same delivered product price, regardless of location; also known as uniform delivered pricing or postage stamp pricing.

slotting fees
High fees manufacturers pay to place a new product on a retailer's or wholesaler's shelf.

social responsibility
Reducing social costs, such as environmental damage, and increasing the positive impact of a marketing decision on society.

societal marketing concept
The use of marketing strategies to increase the acceptability of an idea (smoking causes cancer); cause (environmental protection); or practice (birth control) within a target market.

specialty products
Consumer goods, usually appealing only to a limited market, for which consumers will make a special purchasing effort. Such items include, for example, stereo components, fancy foods, and prestige brand clothes.

Standard Industrial Classification (SIC) system
Replaced by NAICS, this federal government numerical scheme categorized businesses.

standardized marketing
Enforcing similar product, price, distribution, and communications programs in all international markets.

stimulus-response presentation
A selling format that assumes that a customer will buy if given the appropriate stimulus by a salesperson.

strategic business unit (SBU)
A decentralized profit center of a company that operates as a separate, independent business.

Glossary

strategic marketing process
Marketing activities in which a firm allocates its marketing mix resources to reach a target market.

strategy mix
A way for retailers to differentiate themselves from others through location, product, services, pricing, and marketing mixes.

subliminal perception
When a person hears or sees messages without being aware of them.

SWOT analysis
An acronym that describes a firm's appraisal of its internal strengths and weaknesses and its external opportunities and threats.

synergy
An increased customer value that is achieved through more efficient organizational function performances.

systems-designer strategy
A selling strategy that allows knowledgeable sales reps to determine solutions to a customer's problems or to anticipate opportunities to enhance a customer's business through new or modified business systems.

target market
A defined group of consumers or organizations toward which a firm directs its marketing program.

team selling
A sales strategy that assigns accounts to specialized sales teams according to a customers' purchase-information needs.

telemarketing
An interactive direct marketing approach that uses the telephone to develop relationships with customers.

test marketing
The process of testing a prototype of a new product to gain consumer reaction and to examine its commercial viability and marketing strategy.

TIGER (Topologically Integrated Geographic Encoding and Reference)
A minutely detailed U.S. Census Bureau computerized map of the U.S. that can be combined with a company's own database to analyze customer sales.

total quality management (TQM)
Programs that emphasize long-term relationships with selected suppliers instead of short-term transactions with many suppliers.

total revenue
The total of sales, or unit price, multiplied by the quantity of the product sold.

trade allowance
An amount a manufacturer contributes to a local dealer's or retailer's advertising expenses.

trade (functional) discounts
Price reductions that are granted to wholesalers or retailers that are based on future marketing functions that they will perform for a manufacturer.

trademark
The legal identification of a company's exclusive rights to use a brand name or trade name.

truck jobber
A small merchant wholesaler who delivers limited assortments of fast-moving or perishable items within a small geographic area.

two-way stretch strategy
Adding products at both the low and high end of a product line.

undifferentiated strategy
Using a single promotional mix to market a single product for the entire market; frequently used early in the life of a product.

uniform delivered price
The same average freight amount that is charged to all customers, no matter where they are located.

universal product code (UPC)
An assigned number to identify a product, which is represented by a series of bars of varying widths for optical scanning.

usage rate
The quantity consumed or patronage during a specific period, which can vary significantly among different customer groups.

utilitarian influence
To comply with the expectations of others to achieve rewards or avoid punishments.

value added
In retail strategy decisions, a dimension of the retail positioning matrix that refers to the service level and method of operation of the retailer.

vertical marketing systems
Centrally coordinated and professionally managed marketing channels that are designed to achieve channel economies and maximum marketing impact.

vertical price fixing
Requiring that sellers not sell products below a minimum retail price; sometimes called resale price maintenance.

weighted-point system
The method of establishing screening criteria, assigning them weights, and using them to evaluate new product lines.

wholesaler
One who makes quantity purchases from manufacturers (or other wholesalers) and sells in smaller quantities to retailers (or other wholesalers).

zone pricing
A form of geographical pricing whereby a seller divides its market into broad geographic zones and then sets a uniform delivered price for each zone.

Sources for the Glossary
Marketing: Principles and Perspectives by William O. Bearden, Thomas N. Ingram, and Raymond W. LaForge (Irwin/McGraw-Hill, 1998);
Marketing by Eric N. Berkowitz (Irwin/McGraw-Hill, 1997); and the *Annual Editions* staff.

Index

Index

F

fair prices, 155, 156
fake luxury goods, 131–133
Family Limited, segment of Mindbase, 95, 96
family money-market checking account, 66
Farber, Barry, 176
fast food industry, 147
Federal Express, 146
Federal Trade Commission (FTC), 54–55
Fidelity Investments, 46
Fiesta. *See* Ford
Filipino Americans, 89, 90
film industry, 18
First Union Corp., 44, 49
Fleming Companies, 146
food shopping preferences, Filipino American consumers and, 89
Foot, David K., 83
Ford, 191
Ford, Henry, 22
form, versus function, packaging and, 134–135
Forum Corporation, 41–43
"free agents," 103
furniture retailers, 154
Furniture.com Inc., 34–36

G

Gaffney, John, 159–160, 163–164
Galbraith, John Kenneth, 20
Gap Inc. Direct, 34, 37
Gap.com, 51
Garden.com, 51
Gatorade, packaging and, 134
gender differences, in shopping, 100
Generation Jones, 81, 82, 83
Generation X, 81, 82, 95, 103, 106
generational marketing, 82, 103
generations, 72–73, 75–78, 81–83, 103
GeoCities, 53, 55
geography, segmentation and, 186
Getting into Your Customer's Head (Davis), 179
Gitomer, Jeffrey, 178
global brand management, 195–201
global brand managers, 197, 199
global brand teams, 195, 199–200
global family networks, 192
global market, competitors and, 7
global market segmentation (GMS), 185–189
goal setting, marketing plans and, 112, 113–115
Goal, The (Goldratt), 113
Golden Rule, ethical treatment of customers and, 50–52
Goldratt, Eliyahu M., 113
Grameen-Phone, 190
Gramm-Leach-Bliley Act, 54, 55
grocery industry, 19; retail, 147
growth industries, market myopia in, 18–27
growth potential, property of GMS, 186
Gucci G's, fake, 132
guerrilla marketing, 169–170
Guerrilla Marketing: Secrets for Making Big Profits from Your Small Business (Levinson), 124

H

Haagen-Dazs, 199
Hamel, Gary, 60
Harley-Davidson, 207
health, 3
Hertz, 51–52
hidden markets, 190–194
hidden prices, 144–151
high-income consumer market, 5
Himmel Group, 126
Hispanics, marketing and, 79–80
historical context, articulating of, 63
hitonami consciousness, 90
Honda, 196
Hopkins, Tom, 177–178
Howe, Neil, 82
Hurst, Mark, 36

I

IBM, 12, 14, 16, 141, 150, 195, 199, 201
Ikea North America, 44
importing, 183–184
income, as demographic factor for customer profiling, 74, 77
Indian, Asian, 85, 89–90
individual-based segmentation, 186
industry competition, of prices, 145
industry concentration, 182
industry customers, prices and, 148
Infant and Child Rearing (Spock), 105
Infeger, 14
inflection points, 121
informal economy, 191
infrastructure, 193
innovation, customers and, 60–67
innovative adopters, targeting of, 12–13
integrated management orientation, ethical treatment of customers and, 50
"integrated" marketing plans, 110
"interactive" marketing plans, 110
Intel, 14, 121, 137
interdepartmental team, 66
international brands, 202
Internet, 9, 10, 96, 183; consumer publications on, 7; customer experience and, 33–39; privacy, 53, 54, 55
Internet advertising, 168–171; pros and cons of, 172–175
Internet shopping, 165–167
investigators, 62
invidious distinctions, 64
invisible global market, 190–194
invisible prices, 148–149

J

Japan, brands in, 203; marketing and, future of, 206–211; operational effectiveness and, 120
Japanese Americans, 85, 90–91
Journeys shoe store, 154–155
Jupiter Media Metrix Inc., 174

K

"kamikaze" pricing, 136–143
Katz-Stone, Adam, 161–162
Knock Your Socks Off Selling (Gitomer), 178
knowledge, orienting values and, 63
knowledge-building programs, as key lever to enhance relationship equity, 29
Konopacki, Allen, 9, 10
Korea, brands of, 203
Korean-Americans, 85, 91

L

laddering research method, 127
Land's End, 51, 68
language differences, Asian Americans and, 86, 88, 89
Lassoo Interactive, 168
Latin America, 192
Latino community, invidious distinctions of, 65
"launch brands," 203
laws, for sales success, 177
"Leader's Trap," 150
leadership strategy, of Michael Porter, 119–122
Leading Boomers, 82
Leaf company, 126
Levinson, Jay Conrad, 124, 169
licensing, marketing technology and, 11–12, 17
lifestyle-centered retailers, 2–3
Loctite Corp., 140–141
lodging, customer service and, 47–49
logistics, 184
Louis Vuitton handbags, fake, 131
low income, 192; package size and, 193
loyalty programs, as key lever to enhance relationship equity, 29, 30, 47

loyalty-card program, 165

M

market preparation, technology and, 11–12
marketing communication, 56
marketing concept, ethical treatment of customers and, 50–52
Marketing Plan Pro, 116, 118
marketing plans, 110–118
marketing research, 60
Martin, Rob, 168
mass media, costs of, 8
mass production, 22
mature brands, revitalization of, 125–130
mature consumers, marketing and, 5
Maytag Corp., 46
McCadden, Michael, 37
McDonald's, 100–101
measurability, property of global market segmentation, 185
measurement equivalence, 188
media: advertising and, 171, 174; new, 5–6
men, and shopping, 98
Mercedes, 198
mergers, and acquisitions, product loyalty and, 8
Mexican immigrants, 192; conflicts of, in the United States, 66
Mexico, 62, 63; women in, 66
Microsoft, 11, 14, 16, 192
mirrors, and shopping, 98
Mobil, 196, 198, 200
Monitor Mindbase, 94, 95, 96
Moscowitz Jacobs Inc. (MJI), 69
Motorola, 11

N

narratives: articulative interviewers and, 62; value conflicts and, 65–66
National Cash Register (NCR), 166, 167
Nationwide Insurance, 55
natural gas, 22
NEC Technologies, 15, 207
negotiators, customers as, 149
Nelson, Scott, 170
neutral pricing, 136
new retailing, old pillars of, 152–157
New Traditionalists, segment of Mindbase, 95, 96
"niche generations," 83
Nissan Motor Corp., 112, 117, 145, 170
Nokia, 11
Nordstrom, 51, 117
notice, component of privacy policy, 57
NTT, 13
Nutrition Labeling Education Act, 7

O

occasion-centric retailers, 2–3
OEMs (original equipment manufacturers), marketing technology and, 12
Office Depot Inc., 166
oil industry, 20, 21, 23, 24–25
oligopoly, 182–183
Omega watches, 137
100 Absolutely Unbreakable Laws of Business Success, The (Tracy), 177
OPEC (Organization of Petroleum Exporting Countries), 184
operational effectiveness, fundamental distinction between strategy and, 120
organizational goals, marketing plans and, 113–115
orienting values, conflicts among, 61–63; four techniques for identifying, 62–63
original equipment manufacturers (OEMs), marketing technology and, 12
outdoor advertising, 170–171
outdoor living markets, 2–3

Test Your Knowledge Form

We encourage you to photocopy and use this page as a tool to assess how the articles in *Annual Editions* expand on the information in your textbook. By reflecting on the articles you will gain enhanced text information. You can also access this useful form on a product's book support Web site at *http://www.dushkin.com/online/*.

NAME: DATE:

_____

TITLE AND NUMBER OF ARTICLE:

_____

BRIEFLY STATE THE MAIN IDEA OF THIS ARTICLE:

_____

LIST THREE IMPORTANT FACTS THAT THE AUTHOR USES TO SUPPORT THE MAIN IDEA:

_____

WHAT INFORMATION OR IDEAS DISCUSSED IN THIS ARTICLE ARE ALSO DISCUSSED IN YOUR TEXTBOOK OR OTHER READINGS THAT YOU HAVE DONE? LIST THE TEXTBOOK CHAPTERS AND PAGE NUMBERS:

_____

LIST ANY EXAMPLES OF BIAS OR FAULTY REASONING THAT YOU FOUND IN THE ARTICLE:

_____

LIST ANY NEW TERMS/CONCEPTS THAT WERE DISCUSSED IN THE ARTICLE, AND WRITE A SHORT DEFINITION:

We Want Your Advice

ANNUAL EDITIONS revisions depend on two major opinion sources: one is our Advisory Board, listed in the front of this volume, which works with us in scanning the thousands of articles published in the public press each year; the other is you—the person a ctually using the book. Please help us and the users of the next edition by completing the prepaid article rating form on this page and returning it to us. Thank you for your help!

ANNUAL EDITIONS: Marketing 02/03

ARTICLE RATING FORM

Here is an opportunity for you to have direct input into the next revision of this volume.
We would like you to rate each of the articles listed below, using the following scale:

1. **Excellent: should definitely be retained**
2. **Above average: should probably be retained**
3. **Below average: should probably be deleted**
4. **Poor: should definitely be deleted**

Your ratings will play a vital part in the next revision.
Please mail this prepaid form to us as soon as possible.
Thanks for your help!

RATING	ARTICLE	RATING	ARTICLE
	1. Emerging and Burgeoning		36. Global Marketing in the New Millennium
	2. Future Markets		37. Segmenting Global Markets: Look Before You Leap
	3. 10 Things to Know About Customers		38. The Invisible Global Market
	4. The E-volving Salesman		39. The Lure of Global Branding
	5. Marketing High Technology: Preparation, Targeting, Positioning, Execution		40. The Nation as Brand
	6. Marketing Myopia (With Retrospective Commentary)		41. The Future of Japanese Marketing
	7. What Drives Customer Equity		
	8. The Customer Experience		
	9. A Primer on Quality Service: Quality Service Makes Happy Customers and Greater Profits		
	10. Why Service Stinks		
	11. The Ethical Treatment of Customers		
	12. Too Close for Comfort		
	13. Taking an Expanded View of Customers' Needs: Qualitative Research for Aiding Innovation		
	14. Product by Design		
	15. A Beginner's Guide to Demographics		
	16. The Next Big Market		
	17. Generational Divide		
	18. Asian-American Consumers as a Unique Market Segment: Fact or Fallacy?		
	19. Head Trips		
	20. How We Sell		
	21. Defining Moments: Segmenting by Cohorts		
	22. The Very Model of a Modern Marketing Plan		
	23. Michael Porter's Big Ideas		
	24. Can Brand Management Help You Succeed?		
	25. Making Old Brands New		
	26. Can You Spot the Fake?		
	27. Color Me Popular: Marketers Shape Up Packaging		
	28. Kamikaze Pricing		
	29. Discovering Hidden Pricing Power		
	30. The Old Pillars of New Retailing		
	31. 10 Top Stores Put to the Test		
	32. What's Ahead for . . . Retailing		
	33. More for Less		
	34. Choices, Choices		
	35. Ice Cubes to Eskimos		

(Continued on next page)

BUSINESS REPLY MAIL
FIRST-CLASS MAIL PERMIT NO. 84 GUILFORD CT

POSTAGE WILL BE PAID BY ADDRESSEE

McGraw-Hill/Dushkin
530 Old Whitfield Street
Guilford, Ct 06437-9989

NO POSTAGE
NECESSARY
IF MAILED
IN THE
UNITED STATES

ABOUT YOU

Name   Date

Are you a teacher? ☐   A student? ☐
Your school's name

Department

Address   City   State   Zip

School telephone #

YOUR COMMENTS ARE IMPORTANT TO US!

Please fill in the following information:
For which course did you use this book?

Did you use a text with this ANNUAL EDITION?   ☐ yes ☐ no
What was the title of the text?

What are your general reactions to the *Annual Editions* concept?

Have you read any pertinent articles recently that you think should be included in the next edition? Explain.

Are there any articles that you feel should be replaced in the next edition? Why?

Are there any World Wide Web sites that you feel should be included in the next edition? Please annotate.

May we contact you for editorial input?   ☐ yes ☐ no
May we quote your comments? ☐ yes ☐ no